Henry T. Bernard Jr.
331 Manzanita Dr.
Atwater, CA 95301

THROUGH A UNIVERSE DARKLY

THROUGH A UNIVERSE ·DARKLY·

A COSMIC TALE OF ANCIENT ETHERS, DARK MATTER, AND THE FATE OF THE UNIVERSE

MARCIA BARTUSIAK

HarperCollins*Publishers*

HarperCollins books may be purchased for educational, business, or sales promotional use. For information please write: Special Markets Department, HarperCollins Publishers, Inc., 10 East 53rd Street, New York, NY 10022.

FIRST EDITION

Designed by Alma Hochhauser Orenstein

Library of Congress Cataloging-in-Publication Data

Bartusiak, Marcia, 1950–
    Through a universe darkly : a cosmic tale of ancient ethers, dark matter, and the fate of the universe / Marcia Bartusiak. — 1st ed.
    p.   cm.
    Includes bibliographical references and index.
    ISBN 0-06-018310-1 (cloth)
    1. Dark matter (Astronomy). 2. Astronomy. 3. Cosmology.
    I. Title.
    QB791.3.B36   1993
    523.1'125—dc20   92-54731

93 94 95 96 97 AC/HC 10 9 8 7 6 5 4 3 2 1

For STEVE

The scientist does not study nature because it is useful; he studies it because he delights in it, and he delights in it because it is beautiful. If nature were not beautiful, it would not be worth knowing, life would not be worth living.

—JULES HENRI POINCARÉ

Contents

Prologue

Hardly do we divine the things that are on Earth, and the things that are close at hand we find with labor, but the things that are in the heavens, who ever yet traced out?

—WISDOM OF SOLOMON

Angela Da Silva received little advance warning. The young engineering physicist had only twenty-four hours to arrange a cross-country plane flight from San Francisco to Oak Ridge, Tennessee, a town noted for its nuclear research facilities, legacy of the city's wartime founding. In 1942, the U.S. government had established the small municipality, formerly an isolated forest west of the Great Smoky Mountains, to develop atom bomb materials for the Manhattan Project.

Time was of the essence. Da Silva had to pick up three particle detectors, recently fabricated by the scientific-instrumentation manufacturer ORTEC, and get them back to the Center for Particle Astrophysics, her employer in Berkeley, California, as quickly as possible. She seemed an unusual courier. With her straight, shoulder-length hair, light-brown in color, and big horn-rimmed glasses, Da Silva resembled a cerebral Alice in a scientific wonderland. And she was enmeshed in a curious adventure.

The detectors themselves, wholly composed of the purest germanium, looked like shiny oversized doorknobs. Each was cylindrical in shape, about two inches in diameter and three inches long. ORTEC personnel had spent weeks on their construction, first purifying the newly mined germanium and then slowly growing the jumbo metallic crystals from a heated melt.

Within a day of her arrival at Oak Ridge, Da Silva had the three detectors safely nestled in the trunk of her rental car, ready for a drive across the country. Flying the detectors back to California on a plane was out of the question. The Earth is continually bombarded by high-speed cosmic rays racing in from space, energetic atomic particles that can slice right through an atomic nucleus and change one atom into another. That's bad news for germanium detectors. Whenever a cosmic ray occasionally slams into an atom of germanium, it can create tritium, a radioactive form of hydrogen that interferes with the germanium's performance as a particle detector. In fact, to help cut down on this contamination in Oak Ridge while awaiting Da Silva's pickup, ORTEC temporarily stored each of its finished detectors in a local tourist attraction, a deep underground cavern far removed from cosmic-ray impacts.

With the detectors, Da Silva traveled back to California speedily. The first night of driving took her to Memphis. The next day she relentlessly pushed westward through Arkansas and Texas. Over the following two days, at a steady sixty-mile-per-hour pace, she proceeded through Arizona and into California. She didn't take the most direct route, through the Sierra Nevada mountain range, because the flux of cosmic rays sharply increases at high elevations. In order to minimize the germanium's exposure to cosmic rays while it was tucked away in the trunk of her car, Da Silva chose a more southerly itinerary. This kept her at the lowest altitude possible, ensuring that the thickest, most protective atmosphere stood between the detectors and the incoming rays. Such are the tasks of modern-day astronomers—a far cry from their past concerns with lenses and mirrors.

The germanium detectors were eventually placed hundreds of feet below the Earth, within a cavernous chamber set beneath California's Oroville Dam, a massive earthen structure located about 125 miles northeast of Berkeley. Together these crystals served as the heart of an underground telescope. The detectors passively stood watch, awaiting the arrival of an exotic particle that could slice right through the Earth, as if this planet were an insubstantial mist, and signal the presence of a heretofore unknown material spread throughout the universe.

"We have been looking for that lone signal that rises above the background levels," says Da Silva. "But, for the moment, we've been fighting that tritium noise." Hence Da Silva's transcontinental journey, with elaborate precautions taken from the start to reduce cosmic-ray contamination in the germanium as much as possible.

While contemplating the material composition of the heavens, the ancient Greek philosopher Aristotle long ago surmised that the glittering lights scattered over the celestial sphere were composed of a substance never seen on Earth. He dubbed it the "ether." Some twenty-four hundred years later, with the germanium detectors in place, scientists have been testing whether that ancient Aristotelian axiom might need to be revived. They seek a new ether.

Astronomy is regarded primarily as the science of space and time. By monitoring the rising and setting of the Sun, carefully noting the monthly waxing and waning of the Moon, and marking off an array of mythical constellations in the nighttime sky, ancient investigators began their extensive explorations of the celestial canopy poised above them. How big is the Sun? asked the first astronomers. How far is the Moon? How do those wandering stars, the planets, move about the Earth? Astronomers have always been driven by their unquenchable desire to comprehend Earth's place in the cosmos. And, in carrying out their surveys, celestial explorers have steadfastly moved the boundaries of the star-spangled roof above us farther and farther outward. For the venerable second-century geographer Ptolemy, the Sun, Moon, planets, and stars were viewed as moving within a series of nested spheres, with the Earth planted prominently and resolutely at the center. All these crystalline spheres, as Ptolemy conceived them more than eighteen hundred years ago, could fit within Earth's orbit. Today, the visible universe is known to span many billions of light-years, and the Earth is but a speck of dust in this new cosmic order.

The evolution of astronomy, writes Timothy Ferris in *Coming of Age in the Milky Way*, can be viewed as an awakening of the human species to the spatial vastness of the cosmos. Yet there is another scientific objective, a motivation often overlooked in the standard textbooks, that drives the field of astronomy just as fiercely. While astronomy has certainly flung open the doors of cosmic space, as Ferris so engagingly puts it, allowing our minds to roam freely within its depths, it should not be forgotten that astronomy is also a science of matter—for it is matter that heats up, spins madly, and darts swiftly throughout the universe, releasing the light waves that enable us to perceive the inner workings of the cosmos. The very first question asked by the world's first philosopher, Thales, was simply this: What is the universe composed of? Faced with the unknown, this ancient Greek yearned to grasp, before anything else, the essential constitution of his surroundings.

Thales's inquiry, seemingly so benign, initiated a centuries-long search that has led us to the quarks and grand unified theories of modern-day physics. Astronomy continues to be driven by this rudimentary question, which is the basis of the historic perspective stressed in *Through a Universe Darkly*. I explore how astronomers throughout the centuries have come to learn the composition of the heavens and how that knowledge currently shapes our vision of the cosmic landscape.

Many developments in this pursuit of the cosmic recipe are surprisingly recent. Only a century and a half ago, the noted French philosopher Auguste Comte grandly pronounced that "men will never encompass in their conceptions the whole of the stars." He concluded that the distances involved were insurmountable, forever preventing observers from identifying the chemical makeup of the stars. But one deceivingly simple instrument, the spectroscope, swiftly overturned Comte's conclusion within a few decades of his pronouncement. Here was a tool that could determine the chemistry of the heavens by revealing the specific wavelengths of light emitted by each element in a star. Through use of the spectroscope, astronomers were able to see that the Earth and the stars were constructed out of the exact same materials. The two formerly distinct realms were intimately united, and astronomy entered an age of enlightenment.

In subsequent years, astronomers, like Egyptologists decoding exotic hieroglyphics, discerned not only the elements in the sky but their origins as well. The lineage began some fifteen billion years ago when, in a burst of elemental cooking that took but minutes during the primordial explosion mischievously known as the Big Bang, hydrogen and helium were created. More complex materials—such as oxygen, carbon, and nitrogen, the stuff of life—had to await the birth of stars, whose fiery interiors and catastrophic deaths are hot and dense enough to construct such weightier elements.

Each and every element has had a story to tell. The radio squeals emitted by atoms of hydrogen reveal the presence of young, luminous galaxies called quasars. Other signals direct our attention to whirling neutron stars, better known as pulsars. Meanwhile, molecules of carbon monoxide, once thought impossible to assemble in space, disclose the existence of immense clouds of gas that serve as our galaxy's most prolific stellar nurseries. However, this search for the universal recipe has not always been emphasized in the annals of astronomy. The heroes of the science are more often those who have extended the cosmic horizons—observers such as Harlow Shapley, who moved our solar system from the center of the Milky Way to its outer fringes, and Edwin Hubble, who made us see that the Milky Way itself was but one of billions of other galaxies roaming the voids of space. But there are other investigators, less celebrated, who have unraveled riddles whose solutions might be regarded just as revolutionary, even awe inspiring. They are the astronomers who have offered new insights on the universe's composition and, as a consequence, gave rise to whole new avenues of astronomical investigation.

A kindly British amateur astronomer, William Huggins, helped us see that the stuff of the heavens is the same as the stuff of the Earth, thus overthrowing the Aristotelian concept of an ethereal sky. He forged the vital connection. The American astronomer E. E. Barnard, a neurotic workaholic, took hundreds of photographs of the Milky Way, pictures whose stunning quality led to a total reevaluation of the contents of interstellar space. And a young Harvard graduate student named Cecilia Payne carried out a series of painstaking calculations that led to her realization that hydrogen was the prime element in the universe. Her more conservative superiors instructed her to revise her thinking, but her suspicion was eventually confirmed, allowing physicists to pursue at last the mechanisms of stellar power.

Halfway through this century it looked as if a final tally of the universe's contents was nearing completion; except for a few details, that might have been the end of this story. Yet just as astronomers were confident that they had identified all of the universe's material constituents, a mystery arose that thrust astronomy back into a dark age: How could it be that stars in the outer reaches of our Milky Way galaxy are racing around the spiraling disk so incredibly fast and yet are not flying off into the depths of space? Something must be keeping them in. Galaxies that huddle together in clusters, too, appear to be held in place as if by invisible gravitational bonds. The evidence implies that the universe viewed by our many and varied instruments—even by the most powerful radio and X-ray telescopes—is an illusion. When astronomers today contemplate Thales's legendary query—What is the universe composed of?—they have to respond, "We simply don't know."

Astronomers are coming to suspect that there is something more out there, an unknown substance that has come to be called dark matter. And not knowing what constitutes this dark matter inhibits investigators' full understanding of how the universe constructed its vast array of objects. So much hinges on figuring out the answer to this seemingly straightforward question. The hunt is on, and Angela Da Silva's journey was but a small part of the endeavor. The luminous stars and galaxies could be mere whitecaps, whose gleaming presence diverts our eyes from a hidden ocean of matter right below. Knowledge of its composition has the potential to alter our views of the cosmos—how galaxies were born; how stars live and die; and whether our universe will end in a fiery conflagration or limp outward to icy nothingness.

These new investigations continue a quest that has lasted for nearly three millennia. To the ancient Greeks, the essence of the heavens was significantly different from any earthly substance. Today's observations, incredibly enough, suggest a return to that ancient notion. Terra firma could be a minor constituent of the cosmos. Ninety percent or more of the universe's contents could indeed be composed of a material not yet unveiled by Earthbound detectors.

It is the stuff of the universe that allows us to survey its inhabitants. The very atoms and particles of the universe write its history—element by element, chapter by chapter. At first involved with the universe's light, observers are now peering into a celestial darkness. *Through a Universe Darkly* traces the progression of this saga, from ancient times to the present day.

PART I

LIGHT

The constitution of the universe I believe
may be set in first place among all natural
things that can be known, for coming before all others in grandeur by reason of
its universal content, it must also stand
above them all in nobility as their rule and
standard.

—GALILEO GALILEI

Earth, Air, Fire, Water

Sir Toby: *Does not our life consist of the four elements?*
Sir Andrew: *Faith, so they say; but I think it rather consists of eating and drinking.*

—WILLIAM SHAKESPEARE, *TWELFTH NIGHT*

Greece is a deeply indented and rugged land that proudly juts into the vivid waters of the Mediterranean Sea. When early Hellenic settlers began to enter Greece from the north several millennia ago, they were confronted by steep mountain ridges and thickly wooded hills, which would keep the towns they established over the centuries fairly isolated. But while arable land was sparse and highly coveted by the new inhabitants, deep-water harbors were plentiful. Invigorated by such a varied terrain, the ancient Greeks came to be expert navigators as well as farmers.

Eventually driven outward by demographic pressures, the seafaring Greeks soon came in contact with more sophisticated societies. This contact expedited Greek advancement beyond the culture of the primitive tribes still traversing Europe's lush forests to the north. The many islands—peaks of ancient limestone mountains—surrounding Greece's main peninsula served as handy stepping-stones for explorers crossing the blue Aegean Sea, an arm of the Mediterranean, to Asia Minor and beyond. Upon encountering a foreign culture, the innovative Greeks would swiftly adopt and then enhance the assorted ideas that originated within each newly contacted civilization. From Phoenicia, they gained an alphabet; from Egypt, a style of sculpture; and from Babylonia, a system of mathematics. Geography was the key to Greece's manifest destiny.

As the intrepid Greek seafarers established trade routes around the Mediterranean—westward to Italy and Spain, north to the Black Sea and the Russian Crimea, south to Africa—colonies followed. Alexander of Macedonia, in his insatiable desire to conquer during his brief and glorious reign (336–323 B.C.), spread Greek culture into such remote regions as Persia, Turkestan, and India. The spoils of conquest stimulated further development along the Nile in Egypt, the Orontes in what is now Turkey, and the Euphrates in Mesopotamia. Prosperous new towns, such as Alexandria, Antioch, Smyrna, and Nicaea, became thriving centers of trade and industry. Hellenistic culture, which expanded far beyond the borders of the Balkan peninsula during several centuries, flourished until its eventual absorption into the Roman Empire two thousand years ago.

Ancient Greece was truly unique compared with the civilizations that had preceded it. The isolation of its towns encouraged the Greek townspeople to nurture independent thought, while Greek politics bequeathed certain rights and duties to each citizen. This propensity for independence made the various Greek city-states fiercely competitive, but it also made the towns less bound by stultifying traditions and myths. Their gods were well informed but prone to human frailties and hardly supra-intelligent; and their system of writing, easier and simpler than past constructs, led to widespread literacy and encouraged a coherency of Greek thought, especially regarding contemplation of the nature of the vaulted roof above.

The Egyptians and Babylonians had already begun the search for an order and repetition in the daily revolution of the sky. For ancient farmers planting their first crops in the rich deposits of the Nile and Euphrates rivers, the heavens were an enduring and comforting presence. By carefully keeping track of lunar cycles and the annual progression of the Sun against the stars, clever observers in these early kingdoms came to recognize that there was power in knowing the stars, a power that allowed them to predict when to plant and when to harvest. The patterns of the constellations helped them navigate in unknown waters. Yet many of their celestial interpretations were still constrained by divine obligations.

The unique dichotomy inherent in ancient Greek civilization—the geographic isolation of its towns coupled with the culture's cosmopolitan awareness—allowed for a completely new type of celestial examiner. In such a fertile setting arose the first philosophers, "lovers of wisdom" who depended more on logic than on religious concerns as they bravely questioned the fundamental nature of the universe. Gods and spirits, who carried out their arbitrary whims on the world stage, were either demoted or no longer required to explain varied phenomena—from the earthquakes so prevalent in the Mediterranean region to the origin of the Moon's pale light. These radical Greek thinkers hoped to discern the origins of natural events via a more reasonable and sensible route. What certain ancient Greek philosophers sought was an intellectual beauty within the cosmos: ultimate causes and ultimate forms. Spurred by such concerns, they were the first to seek, among other philosophic adventures, the essential composition of the heavens and the Earth. And after centuries of the religiosity of the Dark Ages, these primitive views of cause and effect would reemerge, eventually influencing the rise of the modern scientific tradition.

Myth and logic, it should be noted, were never completely separated in Greek philosophy. Concepts of fate, divine interventions, and a universal spirit linger in the shadows of many so-called rational Greek philosophies. While one might seek a straightforward genealogy, an uninterrupted ascent to current views on the universe's composition, that is not really possible. The atoms conceived by the Greeks did not spring from the same considerations that led twentieth-century science to embrace a similar idea. Greek atomists were spurred by philosophic necessity; modern day physicists are provoked by experimental evidence.

The manner in which the Greeks explained certain celestial and terrestrial phenomena may now seem childishly naive, but that is a judgment made with the benefit of contemporary hindsight. The early Greeks actually experienced a tremendous leap in knowledge, for they moved humanity's ideas of the cosmos from the realm of superstition, where events and objects were largely manipulated by a chorus of fickle gods, to a haven of logical thought.

THE FIRST PHILOSOPHERS

Greece's intellectual revolution burst forth in an arena that was closest to foreign cultures. Buoyed by mercantile prosperity, which allowed for a leisure class and a thriving intelligentsia, the eastern coast of the Aegean was an area particularly receptive to novel ideas. Miletus was one of some dozen cities that the Greeks established on the coast of Asia Minor (now Turkey) in the sixth century B.C. Set in a rich agricultural land known as Ionia, Miletus was a bustling Aegeatic seaport that, stimulated by ideas arriving from the East, likely introduced coinage to Greek lands. It was also home to the first person given the official designation of natural philosopher. His name was Thales.

Born around 640 B.C. during Greece's great age of expansion, Thales was a military commander and engineer who, legend has it, successfully predicted a solar eclipse that occurred in 585 B.C. during a crucial battle between the Lydians and Medes at the River Halys in Asia Minor. Thales was later proclaimed a "wise man" by the famous oracle of Delphi. It is possible that Thales acquired his astute astronomical knowledge during a visit to Egypt or from Babylonian records, but modern scholars contend that this notorious story is more likely a fable—solar eclipses were then difficult to predict, far more so than were lunar ones.

But as an entrepreneur Thales was wise indeed. Aristotle, who lived nearly three hundred years later, related the tale of Thales's predicting a great olive harvest. Confident of his forecast, the shrewd commander bid early for the use of all the olive presses in both Miletus and Chios to the north. When the bountiful harvest arrived, Thales cornered the market, leasing the presses out on his own terms. By some reports, this was all a ploy to silence his critics, who said he spent too much time on meaningless philosophy instead of making money.

Thales's critics were wrong. His dalliance with philosophy was far from insignificant—he made his boldest move not in economics but in scholarly concerns. Although he left no writings, preferring to expound his ideas orally, Thales is known as the first person to seek an ultimate substance, a matter from which all others are derived and that can never be destroyed. Here was the first question posed by the world's first philosopher: Behind the infinite variety of life, is there a common, immutable thread?

Thales concluded that the primal substance must be water. Perhaps he was influenced during his reported travels to Egypt, where the Nile waters play a central role in Egyptian cosmologies. One ancient Egyptian creation myth spoke of the world arising out of a vast, primeval abyss of waters, a limitless deep personified by the god Nu. Similar doctrines were held in Babylonia. Water, of course, was a dominant feature of Thales's own environment by the Mediterranean Sea. Water gushed from the Earth to form rivers and streams; it fell from the sky as rain. Thales's supposition, written down by later authors, was not unreasonable. He believed that the Earth rested on water, whose evaporation produced the air and whose violent agitation (not the wrath of the god Poseidon) caused earthquakes. Aristotle speculated that Thales might also have noticed that where there is life there is moisture; seeds, for example, germinate in dampness. Whatever his reasons, Thales began to ask, in his own fashion, what the universe was made of. More important, his insistence on a single unifying principle departed greatly from earlier, god-laden creation schemes.

Thales began the long-standing quest, today carried on by cosmologists, to explain the origins of the world in the simplest terms possible. Thales spoke of water, whereas a modern-day physicist invokes tiny motes, such as quarks and leptons, as the wellspring of all matter. Yet both are essentially asking how these primal substances first appeared and how they transformed themselves into the plethora of forms all around us. The embryonic stirrings of creative philosophy did not shirk from its toughest question, one still not fully answered: What is the essential composition of the universe?

Thales died at the age of seventy-eight, but the search for a unique cosmic recipe persisted. A fellow Ionian named Anaximander, who also lived in Miletus, extended and broadened the original speculation of his friend Thales. The first person to draw a map of the inhabited world (he viewed the Earth as a drum-shaped body floating in space), Anaximander was quite enamored of his role as a sage and reputedly wore splendid raiment to proclaim his high intellectual status.

According to physicist and science historian David Park, Anaximander's cosmology "filled the universe with what he called *to apeiron,* the Boundless, . . . which seems to imply that it fills all space." The Milesian may have been influenced by Persian cosmology, which spoke of a similar essence. Although not directly perceived, the Boundless is everlasting and inexhaustible, the substratum that gives rise to all substances as well as motions and energy. All were products generated out of this infinite reservoir. Our world and countless other worlds originated out of the Boundless and would eventually be reabsorbed back into it.

While ancient astronomers were establishing hierarchical structures in space—first came the Earth, then successively the Moon, Sun, planets, and celestial sphere—Anaximander laid the foundations for a seeming hierarchy of substances. He surmised that heavy items—for example, boulders—sought out the lowest levels of the Earth when they emerged from the Boundless. Awhirl in a vortex of motion, the weightiest materials tended to concentrate in the center. Lighter materials—such as water—remained on the upper terrestrial surface. The most ephemeral substances—air and fire—rose above the ground and later constituted the heavenly bodies. Here was the germ of the pre-Newtonian notion of gravity (later developed more fully by Aristotle) that objects fall to the Earth because they seek their "natural place." Anaximander also forged an early hierarchical theory of evolution, higher forms developing out of lower forerunners—he imagined that human beings originated in the sea and shed their fishlike scales as they adapted to dry land, and that animals emanated from inanimate matter by the action of sunlight on water.

Other philosophers were uncomfortable with Anaximander's concept of the "Boundless" because it was so ill defined. Anaximines, a younger contemporary of Anaximander and also a resident of Miletus, reasoned that air must be the seminal substance. Air was the very breath of life, invisible yet tangible. This crude theory, clever for its day, even explained the "physics" of air's many transformations, postulating that the myriad manifestations of air were generated by either its own condensation or its rarefaction. The Earth, still imagined as a flat disk, was merely air made dense; and fire, which formed the Sun, Moon, and planets, was air's blazing vaporization. Made just a bit thicker, the air became a bustling wind or a diaphanous cloud. This scheme enabled Anaximines to explain nature's multiplicity without recourse to the supernatural.

Such philosophic ponderings, centered in the stimulating environment of Ionia, went on for decades. Heraclitus, a haughty and cynical man who lived during the fifth century B.C. in the town of Ephesus, thirty miles north of Miletus, chose fire as the prime substance. This was not too surprising since his philosophy portrayed a world in continuing flux—and fire, by its very transitory properties, reflected this change (and probably Heraclitus's mercurial personality as well). "This ordered universe which is the same for all," he wrote, "was not created by any one of the gods or of mankind, but was ever and is and shall be ever-living Fire, kindled in measure and quenched in measure." With this vision, Heraclitus (also known as "the Obscure" because his statements are often hard to interpret) developed an imaginative cosmology. The Sun, Moon, and planets became exhalations collected in basins, which ignited when these vapor-filled, celestial ponds rose from the sea. Likewise, the basins were extinguished when they set in the west. And the Moon was dimmer because its fire simply moved through thicker air.

While these musings might appear outlandish, they were humanity's early attempts to discern, in a rational rather than a mystical manner, the definitive nature of the world and heavens. Full application of the scientific method, the belief that theories must be tested by experiment and observation to find acceptance, was centuries away, awaiting the entrance of such scientific luminaries as Galileo and Newton. The ancient philosophers assumed that logic alone allowed them to arrive at universal truths. Yet the mystery pursued by today's particle physicists—with the aid of miles-long atom smashers, bubble chambers, and stories-high detectors—remains largely unchanged from the question first posed by those curious Greeks more than twenty-six centuries ago: Is there an ultimate substance, a primal form of matter? Modern investigators must trace to the ancient Greeks their unshaking faith in an unalterable element.

HADES, HERA, ZEUS, AND NESTIS VERSUS THE ATOM

Twenty-five hundred years ago the Greeks' cerebral pursuit of a primal medium was made more difficult by nature's multifarious designs—things are hot or cold, wet or dry, in motion or at rest. The variety of life is overwhelming. Clearly, evoking one basic substance—such as the air of Anaximines or the fire of Heraclitus—was unsatisfactory. Empedocles, born around 500 B.C. on the southern coast of Sicily, another colonial center of innovative thought, recognized this shortcoming and concluded that there must be at least four indestructible elements, which were described by Aristotle in his *Metaphysics* as "heat substance, dry dust, colorless gas, and clear liquid." Empedocles named these elements after gods: Hades, Hera, Zeus, and the water-nymph Nestis. But over time they came to be known respectively as simply fire, earth, air, and water. This basic theory, the interplay of four basic substances, dominated European thinking into the age of Shakespeare. Medieval medical men, for example, spoke of balancing the four *humours*—blood, air, yellow bile, and black bile—to maintain good health.

A missionary who composed and sang verses during his travels, Empedocles was also known as a great healer. (Faithful followers claimed he brought dead people back to life.) He might be considered a forerunner to Galileo in that, unlike most other philosophers of the time, he carried out rudimentary experiments to test some of his philosophic conjectures. For instance, he proved that air had substance by plunging a clepsydra (a water clock) into water and observing that the air trapped inside the clock held the liquid back at its bottom. He even considered that light rays might have a finite speed and perceptively recognized that the heart is the center of the blood-vessel system.

According to the figurings of Empedocles, the wide diversity of matter emerged when the four basic elements either united or dissolved. Today we say that a so-called strong force keeps protons and neutrons, the building blocks of an atomic nucleus, bound within the atom, enabling a diverse series of elements to be constructed. For Empedocles, the opposing forces of love and strife (being primitive and more poetic renditions of "attraction" and "repulsion") allowed for his basic forms of matter to combine or disperse. (It should be stressed that Empedocles's fundamental materials were not literally earth, air, fire, and water. Rather, each name represented the essential properties of a primal substance. Fire, for instance, exemplified invisibility. Just as twentieth-century physicists attach certain words—such as *entropy* and *lines of force*—to unseen entities or effects, Empedocles was using language to describe specific processes.)

How Empedocles died is shrouded in myth. One version says he jumped into Mount Etna, an active volcano on the east coast of Sicily, so that people would think he had been taken up to heaven and made a god. In any case, over time most philosophers settled on his four-ingredient scheme, the grand unified theory of its era. However, there was one notable exception. Leucippus, who reputedly lived near Miletus in the mid-fifth century B.C., decided that everything in nature was constructed out of infinitesimally small particles. He called them atoms, since each could not be broken down further (the root *atomos* means "indivisible"). Here was a proposal that attacked the question of change and diversity from a quite different and inventive avenue than did Empedocles. All atoms, immutable and eternal, were too small to be seen directly by the human eye. But diversity could be explained by the way in which these tiny motes—all made of the same substance but differentiated by their size and shape—aggregated and swarmed.

Leucippus's embryonic atomic theory may have been inspired by some famous conundrums, known as Zeno's paradoxes, that taxed the ingenuity of the best Greek minds. Leucippus was a student of the Eleatic school of philosophy, which included Zeno of Elea, a man obsessed with the pitfalls of divisibility. Walk toward a wall and you will never reach it, goes one rendition of Zeno's puzzle. First take a step to cut the distance between you and the wall by half, then take another step to cut the remaining distance in half once again. Continue following these instructions. Since there's always a half step to go, you can never reach the wall! Plato was so perplexed by Zeno's dizzying view of infinity that he dismissed it as logical acrobatics.

The Scottish mathematician James Gregory finally proved in the 1600s that certain infinite series of fractions can add up to a finite sum (allowing you to reach the wall), but Leucippus preferred to think that physical division was simply not the same as mathematical division. From this he concluded that the splitting of space or matter cannot go on indefinitely. The concept of atoms was a means of besting Zeno at his paradoxical game.

Anticipating science's recognition, many centuries later, that physical processes in nature follow well-defined rules (from Newton's $F = ma$ to Einstein's $E = mc^2$), Leucippus stated that "nothing happens at random; everything happens out of reason and by necessity." That single sentence is all that survives of Leucippus's writings. It was his pupil Democritus, born in the Greek colony of Thrace, who handed down his teacher's ideas for posterity. Passionate in his pursuit of knowledge—he wrote on physics, logic, mathematics, astronomy, music, medicine, botany, zoology, and military science—Democritus once said, "I would give the crown of the king of Persia for a scientific discovery." By some questionable accounts he lived more than one hundred years, ample time to achieve his wish. Democritus's wry commentaries on life led to his being nicknamed "the Laughing Philosopher." "One must either be good," he once counseled, "or imitate a good man."

Atomism was conceived as a philosophic exercise, but its subsequent proponents pointed out that evidence of atoms could be found in everyday experience. Historian Park writes that these proponents believed that "the wind is not seen but its force results from innumerable impacts of its atoms. Scent is carried by messengers too small to see. A horn lantern gives light while protecting its flame from wind and rain because the small atoms of light pass through the horn window while the larger atoms of wind and rain do not. If wet clothes dry in the wind it must be because the water in them has blown away as particles." Democritus even envisioned dreams and phantoms comprising the airiest of the atomic species. Color was the result of an atom's texture: "White is made up of smooth atoms, for what is not rough . . . is wholly bright," the Laughing Philosopher is reported to have taught. "Black is made up of atoms of the opposite kind, jagged. . . . Hence their pores are dark and not straight and are not easily penetrated by light."

The theory of atomism as expounded by Leucippus and Democritus, however, turned out to be an imaginative construct founded on quicksand. The physics of the day couldn't accommodate some of the inevitable consequences of discrete particles. The idea of atoms had to acknowledge the existence of empty space or vacuum; change occurred when atoms rushed in to fill these voids. All those immutable atoms were constantly running about, colliding and careening, within a sea of emptiness. Aristotle, as well as other Greek philosophers, abhorred this notion of nothingness. For them, the world was a continuum, occupied by matter at each and every point. Given Aristotle's (incorrect) understanding of motion, one of his many arguments against atomism possessed a strange and compelling logic. He reasoned that if the velocity of an object regularly increases as the resistance to that motion decreases, then when the resistance plummeted to zero (as would happen in a vacuum) the object's velocity would be infinite. This was impossible, he declared emphatically. Thus, the vacuum, or "non-Being" as the Greeks called it, could not exist. Rejected by the influential Aristotle, atomism was not fully revived for some two thousand years.

By the banks of the Cephissus River in Athens, where he established his famous Academy in 387 B.C., the aristocratic philosopher Plato taught a more abstract, geometric vision of matter. He chose to represent the four basic elements as certain types of objects, now known as Platonic solids. Fire was a four-sided tetrahedron, whose sharp triangular sides could slice the connections between other atoms; earth was a six-sided cube, stable and steady; air was an eight-sided octahedron; and water was a twenty-sided icosahedron. A fifth Platonic solid, the twelve-sided dodecahedron composed of regular pentagons, denoted the universe at large.

Unlike atoms, Plato's elementary bodies could be broken up into a series of triangles and rearranged, thus providing the means to transform the elements (e.g., air into fire or water into air). When mathematicians proved that the Platonic solids were the only regular solids possible (that is, all lines and angles in the faces of these solids are equal), Plato's influence on the subject carried into the Middle Ages. (His Academy remained in operation for more than nine hundred years, until A.D. 529.) Plato had turned abstract mathematical form into substance. A dim echo of Plato's approach resonates today when quantum-mechanical wave equations are used to describe our currently preferred bits of ultimate matter; instead of geometric solids, we have ephemeral wave packets.

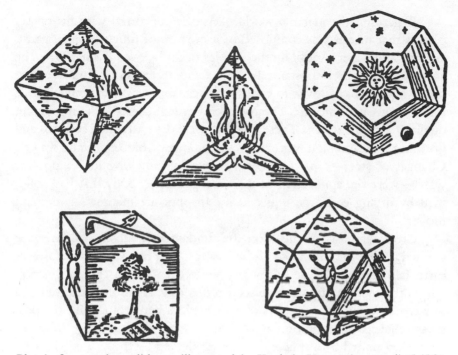

Plato's five regular solids, as illustrated in Kepler's *Harmonice mundi* (1619). *Courtesy of Owen Gingerich*

ETHEREAL SPLENDOR

Aristotle—student of Plato, tutor of Alexander the Great, and the Greek philosopher whose ideas exerted the greatest influence on Western thought—established an agenda of scientific inquiries that would endure until the Renaissance. Born in northern Greece in 384 B.C. into a well-connected medical family, Aristotle arrived at Plato's Academy at the age of seventeen and stayed for some twenty years, until he saw his dream of succeeding Plato as the Academy's director pass him by. A bit of a dandy, with his elaborate robes and fashionable haircuts, he went on to found his own school in Athens, the Lyceum. Exhibiting an amazing appetite for firsthand explanation and examination, this polymathic philosopher classified animal species, constructed a system of logic, observed the courtship of birds, dissected sea life, described the growth of chick embryos, and established some basic laws of motions, in and around a wealth of other accomplishments. No wonder Plato drolly dubbed Aristotle what might be loosely translated as "the Brain."

Regarding the material world, Aristotle concurred with his prede-
cessors that matter was composed of a mixture of four elements: earth,
air, fire, and water. Adopting the physics of his beloved teacher Plato, he
also agreed that each substance had the ability to transform, but he added
his own philosophic twist to explain this capability: Water could change
into air, or earth into fire, because each element shared certain inherent
qualities with the others. These qualities were dry (exhibited by earth and
fire), hot (fire and air), wet (water and air), and cold (earth and water).
Changes of state—a piece of ice, for example, melting into a pool of
water—were the application of these properties. A body that had solid-
ified by drying could be liquefied by an opposite material, something
moist.

Given his basic premises on the fundamental substances, Aristotle
devised a fairly logical model of the cosmos: Fire tends to move upward;
earth falls; air rises. Each element appeared to seek a certain position
within the cosmos, its natural place. In this way, Aristotle conceived of a
universe constructed as a series of concentric spheres, much like the pro-
gressive layers of an onion. In the center there was earth, the abode of
man, surrounded by a sphere of water, followed by the air, and at last a
fiery domain, each realm situated successively outward.

How did the heavens fit into this logical scheme? Aristotle reserved
a special niche for the stars and planets, the wandering stars. "We may
infer with confidence," he declared, "that there is something beyond the
bodies that are about us on this earth, different and separate from them;
and that the superior glory of its nature is proportionate to its distance
from this world of ours." In other words, Aristotle decided that the
heavens and all its contents were made of a material quite different from

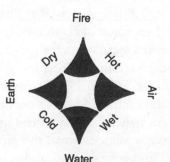

The four Aristotelian elements and their associated qualities.
Illustration by John Hamwey

anything found in the earthly domain, where mere terrestrial substances dwelled. And its essence became purer and purer as one moved farther and farther from our home planet. The Moon was obviously the least perfect object in this realm, as seen by its blotched appearance. The sphere of the fixed, immovable stars was the most perfect form composed of this fifth and pure element, the quintessence.

Aristotle named this heavenly substance ether, borrowing a word already used by the Greek poet Homer and others in describing the fiery upper atmosphere. The Greek root, *aithein,* means "to burn" or "to ignite." Here was the image of stars and planets basking in fire yet never snuffing out.

The idea of the heavens being different from terra firma was certainly not new. In fact, it could have been dangerous to assume otherwise: A century earlier, in 467 B.C., word had reached Athens that a tremendous meteorite had fallen near the shore of the Dardanelles, at Aegos Potamoi. The Ionian scholar Anaxagoras decided that the stone fell from the Sun, which led him to suspect that the entire solar disk was a ball of glowing rock. This forged a direct connection between the Earth and the Sun. Moreover, he surmised that all the stars were stony lumps of material torn from the Earth and rendered luminous by their friction against the rapidly revolving, fiery ether. The imaginative Anaxagoras was put on public trial and exiled from Athens on charges of impiety. The religious beliefs of more conservative Greeks asserted that the Sun and Moon were part of the realm of gods; celestial orbs could hardly be composed of ordinary matter.

Anaxagoras's banishment was probably more due to his friendship with Pericles, the great Athenian leader, whose political enemies wanted to embarrass him, than to his so-called impiety. But Anaxagoras didn't help his cause by also suggesting that the Moon, instead of being self-luminous, actually reflected the light of the Sun. Anaxagoras ended his days teaching at Lampsacus in what is now northwestern Turkey. There he contemplated a Milky Way composed of myriad stars, an idea shared by his contemporary Democritus and quite advanced for its day. He assumed the cloudlike swath was a strip of sky caught in the Earth's shadow, which allowed more stars to be seen where the Sun's light was blocked off. Anaxagoras was soon forgotten, though, and a century later Aristotle's ideas would reign supreme.

Like some celestial gossamer, Aristotle's ether filled all of space beyond the Moon, all the way out to the celestial sphere where each and

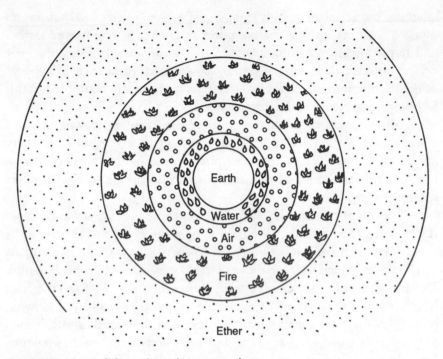

Aristotle's view of the universe's construction.
Based on a drawing by Robin Brickman in The How and the Why *by David Park,*
Princeton University Press, 1988

every star on its surface was fastened into position. This seemed indisputable—after countless generations had gazed at the nighttime sky with their own, unaided eyes, no one had yet detected a stellar object (other than the Moon, Sun, and planets) shift its position on the star-studded ceiling that daily rotated about the Earth. The Aristotelian system sharply separated the heavens, a region of unalterable order and circular motion, from the space below the sphere of the Moon, where the more mundane elements resided in relentless turmoil. Faced with explaining the unknown and untouchable, Aristotle turned the heavens into a special, hallow province. It would remain that way for nearly two thousand years.

The Rise and Fall of the Great Ether

It is the theory that decides what we can observe.

—ALBERT EINSTEIN

It was a small but telling gesture. Near the start of the second century B.C., the Greek island of Chios established a cult of Roma, the personification of the growing power of Rome. Townspeople flocked to the celebratory festival, complete with sacrifices, competitions, and a dedication depicting the legendary she-wolf suckling Rome's mythic founders, Romulus and Remus. Greece was entering a new stage in its history, the beginning of its demise.

More than two thousand years ago the Roman Empire began to establish its dominance over the Mediterranean region and, in the process, greedily absorbed many of the tenets of Greek philosophy. The empire's more practical-minded citizens, however, never really advanced those ancient philosophic investigations. The Greek mind, once so curious, adventuresome, and brave, became shackled under its new masters. "The Roman's character was a lazy one . . . ," historian Lawrence Durrell has noted, "his temperament less that of poet than of grammarian, jurist, lawgiver, moralist." Later, with the eventual fall of the Caesars, the knowledge and methods of inquiry so meticulously acquired by the imaginative Greeks were simply swept aside in the tide of reform. As the crumbling empire converted to Christianity, salvation and religious mysteries became the more preferable (and acceptable) pursuits of the educated classes.

According to the third-century bishop Lactantius Firmianus, any attempt to describe the universe's properties was a futile exercise: "For to investigate or wish to know the causes of natural things . . . of what magnitude the heaven itself is, of what material it is composed," the learned bishop wrote, "is as though we should wish to discuss what we may suppose to be the character of a city in some very remote country . . . of which we have heard nothing more than the name." The momentous mission begun by Thales gradually became inconsequential. "The virtues of the heathen were but splendid vices," another Dark Age commentator curtly noted.

A symbolic death knell was sounded with the destruction of Egypt's resplendent Library of Alexandria, with its hundreds of thousands of papyrus rolls, many of them preserving Greek learning. Cyril, Alexandria's patriarch, instigated the sacking in A.D. 415 because he believed pagan texts promoted heresy. While fanatical mobs burned the priceless treasures, others brutally murdered Hypatia, a noted woman mathematician and avowed pagan associated with the museum. The first tentative steps toward a rational assessment of the heavens and earth—their size, motions, and material essence—were stopped in the name of spiritual salvation, at least for a while.

The Islamic faith, rooted in the Near East, was very dependent on a lunar calendar to keep track of its many feasts, holidays, and religious rituals. Fueled by this need, astronomical knowledge slowly made its way back to civilization. In 820 one of science's most famous cosmological treatises was translated by learned Moslems and given the title *Al Majisti* (Arabic for "the greatest"), which was later modified to the *Almagest*. In this classic work, Claudius Ptolemaeus of Alexandria, an accomplished geographer and astronomer of the second century A.D., immortalized the long-standing Greek view that the Moon, Sun, planets, and stars were fastened to a series of crystalline concentric spheres, with a motionless Earth poised prominently in the center. For Ptolemy (the Anglicized name by which he is generally known), the sky was an intricate maze of wheels within wheels that soundlessly revolved around God's foremost creation—humanity. The estimated width of Ptolemy's universe, with the stellar sphere serving as the outer boundary, was no larger than Earth's orbit.

Other Greek texts, saved from the hands of destructive zealots, were unearthed and interpreted within a flourishing Islamic culture that extended from Spain and Morocco to India and the mid-Asian steppes. It is through this route that medieval scholars came to resurrect the many riches of Greek thought. This Arabic influence is commemorated in the numerous Arab names attached to prominent stars in the nighttime sky, such as Aldebaran ("the Follower"), Algol ("the Ghoul"), and Altair ("the Flier"). The astronomical terms *azimuth, zenith,* and *nadir* are also retained directly from the Arabic. Aristotle's celestial *ether,* as well, was recast. To the Arabs, the fifth essence, found above the Moon, was the Alacir, devoid of lightness and heaviness and not perceptible to the human senses.

There were a few obstacles to overcome in reintroducing medieval scholars to the ancient Greeks. In 1215 doctors in Paris were forbidden to lecture on Aristotle's findings on medicine, since they emanated from a non-Christian (and thus were obviously the work of the devil). A Parisian council decreed that neither Aristotle's books nor commentaries on them could be read publicly or privately. But these fears slowly dissipated. By 1254, at the University of Paris, a certain number of hours were prescribed for teaching Aristotle's physical treatises. And the four fundamental elements, so popular in Greek philosophy, made their reappearance in medieval tracts. One manuscript, published as a dialogue between a teacher and pupil, related that "Earth, air, water, and fire do not move of themselves but each tends toward its nature and its being." Aristotle's influence had returned with a vengeance.

Indeed, as soon as church scholars, particularly Thomas Aquinas in the thirteenth century, found a way to forge a synthesis between the doctrines of Christian faith and Aristotle's philosophy, medieval attitudes toward Greek thinking swung like a pendulum to the opposite extreme. The Greeks, argued Aquinas, had done nothing more than reveal God's creation. So successful was Aquinas in championing the Greeks' philosophic accomplishments that Aristotle's misleading and untested views on cosmology and physics became unquestioned orthodoxy. This inflexibility generated grave repercussions when Aristotle's faulty notions were later challenged by such scientific lights as Galileo. Medieval scholars solemnly accepted Aristotle's assurance that the Earth couldn't be turning. Otherwise, everything on the planet would be torn asunder in the motion—clouds would get ripped out of the sky, and objects dropped toward a spinning Earth would obviously miss their mark because the Earth would have rotated around at great speed during the fall. (Aristotle had never mastered the concept of inertia, the tendency for objects to resist any change in their movement.)

Medieval alchemists rooted their attempts at transforming the elements, particularly the generation of gold from baser materials, in Aristotle's theories. Since every form of matter was supposedly a specific mixture of the four prime elements, it wasn't unreasonable to assume that worthless lead could be changed into precious gold, the king of all metals; it only required finding the proper proportions of the elemental constituents. If a lowly cow could turn grass into steak, a human could certainly master the transformation of a metal. Failure arose, it was believed, only because the correct "recipe" had never been found. Jabir ibn Hayian, the great alchemist attached to the court at Baghdad at the height of its influence in the late eighth and early ninth centuries, cleverly assumed that sulfur and mercury were the key elements in the supreme metamorphosis. Sulfur embodied the Aristotelian qualities of hot and dry, while mercury was indubitably cold and wet. Together, these two elements covered all the Aristotelian qualities of matter. One had only to select the right proportions to arrive at the ultimate "cold and dry" substance, which was, of course, gold. Because Aristotle's assessment of the nature of matter was held so strongly, many tried their hand at these schemes, which in hindsight were deemed worthless. Along the way, however, they did manage to discover substances with far more value, such as phosphorus and mineral acids, which had considerable applications for developing nations.

From the fall of the Roman Empire until the fifteenth century, science was the province of scholars rather than creative investigators. Natural philosophers did not conduct experiments or observe the foibles of nature firsthand. Instead they searched for their ideas and conclusions in a classical past. But a new era was close at hand. Progress toward establishing the modern scientific tradition came on two fronts. Radical thinkers began to sense that natural law might be revealed through specific, well-designed tests instead of pure logic. At the same time, creative artisans, free to invent in a burgeoning economy, devised new and more precise instruments, such as astrolabes and mechanical clocks, which allowed avant-garde researchers to quantify the world around them.

The English scholar Roger Bacon, an early champion of experimental science, was the harbinger of things to come. In the thirteenth century he wrote:

Without experience, nothing can be sufficiently known. For there are two modes of acquiring knowledge, namely, by reasoning and experience. Reasoning draws a conclusion and makes us grant the conclusion, but does not make the conclusion certain, nor does it remove doubt so that the mind may rest on the intuition of truth, unless the mind discovers it by the path of experience.

Bacon's was a lone voice. He appealed to Pope Clement IV, an admirer, to allow experiments to be conducted as part of the educational curriculum. But upon the death of this papal champion, Bacon's books were condemned.

It is ironic that Bacon may have played a small part in the exploration of the New World, an adventure that helped thrust off the chains of medieval notions of science and force investigators to seek experimental verification of their theories. Bacon had mistakenly concluded, from his reading of classical manuscripts, that the waters separating the eastern coast of Asia and the western coast of Europe were not very expansive. This "fact" found its way, two hundred years later, into a text that may have influenced Christopher Columbus to attempt his historic voyage in 1492.

By the time of Columbus, church calendars were running amok. Holy days, first set in the time of Rome's Caesars, were relentlessly moving from their assigned dates. Over centuries' time, without up-to-date astronomical tables to tell churchmen when to add extra days to the year, the vernal equinox, the signal of spring's return, gradually came to fall on March 11 instead of March 21.

Accurate assessments of the sky were needed more than ever, and not just as spiritual necessities. The increasing number of voyages to the Americas, Africa, and beyond depended on real maps of the Earth and the heavens. Seeing new constellations come into view as they journeyed into southern waters, the early explorers beheld the effects of a spherical Earth firsthand. Governments began to foster astronomy in the interest of expanding commerce; precise astronomical data were crucial for continuing the extensive oceanic explorations of the sixteenth and seventeenth centuries. And as these adventuresome seafarers freely roamed the globe, other kinds of explorers sought liberation in new religious systems, new forms of politics, and new ways of looking at old cosmic models.

THE COPERNICAN AND NEWTONIAN REVOLUTIONS

In 1543 the Polish churchman Mikolai Kopernik, or Nicolaus Copernicus (there are many versions), shook the foundations of the Aristotelian system, so cherished by classical scholars, with his publication of *De revolutionibus orbium coelestium* ("On the Revolutions of the Celestial Spheres"). Nearly thirty years in the making, this book removed Earth from the center of the universe and placed the Sun at the cosmic hub. Copernicus dared to assert that the Earth, for so long singled out as God's pivotal handiwork, was consigned to orbiting the Sun with all the other planets. With his courageous and elegant solution, Copernicus thrust Earth into motion.

Until Copernicus had made his assertions, astronomers were guided solely by Ptolemy's vision of the universe's structure, that unwieldy compilation of spheres centered on an immovable Earth. (If Ptolemy's scheme really describes how God had built the universe, a medieval monarch is reputed to have drolly commented, then God might have had some better advice.) But as the sky was studied with more and more accuracy during the Renaissance, Ptolemy's model (already some fourteen hundred years old) was headed for extinction.

At the time of Copernicus, Ptolemy's system, by then incorporating a few adjustments introduced by Islamic astronomers, was still fairly useful, given the primitive state of observations at the time. However, if such a model were going to satisfy the growing need among exploring nations to specify the movements of the Sun and planets more precisely, Ptolemy's creaky spheres would have eventually required endless fine-tuning. Yet it was not accuracy that Copernicus was primarily seeking with his Sun-centered cosmos, stresses Copernican scholar Owen Gingerich of Harvard University, but rather a system "pleasing to the mind." Copernicus's "radical cosmology came forth not from new observations," stresses Gingerich, "but from insight. It was, like Einstein's revolution four centuries later, motivated by the passionate search for commensurabilities and an aesthetic structure of the universe."

Heliocentric, or Sun-centered, universes had certainly been imagined before. The Greek Aristarchus of Samos contemplated one in the third century B.C., some eighteen hundred years before Copernicus. But these models were either lost or largely ignored until Copernicus's effort. Such a sweeping revamp of the universe's structure was not accepted, of course,

Polish churchman Nicolaus Copernicus (1473–1543).
Mary Lea Shane Archives of Lick Observatory

without a fight from church authorities. Witness Galileo's famous trial and house arrest for his claim that the truth of physical reality can be sought in nature; he saw such truth in Copernicus's grand design. Such ecclesiastical stubbornness was essentially the last gasp in medieval approaches to knowledge, approaches that fancifully imagined *why* the world should look a certain way, based on reasoning rigged to fit some sacred Greek philosophic tenet, without closely examining *how* the world actually operates.

Other chinks appeared in the Aristotelian armor. Tycho Brahe, the last and greatest naked-eye astronomer, delivered the blows. A brash and arrogant man, Tycho lost a piece of his nose at the age of twenty in a foolhardy duel with a fellow student over which of them was the better mathematician. He wore a metal nose for the rest of his life. During an early evening walk in the autumn of 1572, six years after his tempestuous quarrel, this Danish nobleman spotted what he called a *"nova stella"* in the direction of the constellation Cassiopeia. This "new star" eventually grew brighter than Venus and then faded away over the next year and a half.

Schooled in Aristotelian ways, with its abiding faith in an unalterable sky, Tycho was understandably astonished. "I was led into such perplexity by the unbelievability of the thing," he later recalled, "that I began to doubt the faith of my own eyes."

Tycho attempted to see whether this apparition shifted its position against the stellar sky, which would have indicated it was relatively nearby. His expertise was unassailable. Using his naked eye and the most advanced sighting devices of his day, he had been making measurements that were on average five times more precise than those of Ptolemy. (His observations helped spur calendar reform.) Tycho saw that the new star wasn't budging, and he concluded that the strange object resided beyond the Moon. Aristotle's image of an immutable firmament was beginning to unravel. (We now know that Tycho's *nova stella* was an exploding supernova, the death throes of an old star.)

In 1577 a comet appeared. According to Aristotle's way of thinking,

Danish astronomer Tycho Brahe (1546–1601).
Mary Lea Shane Archives of Lick Observatory

comets were nothing more than an atmospheric phenomenon: The celestial sphere, brimming with ether, daily rotated around a motionless Earth. There was bound to be turbulence and friction in the boundary between the outer sphere of fire and the ether farther out. Comets and meteors were just the resulting heat of this incessant grinding. Again, Tycho searched for a parallax, an apparent displacement in the comet's daily position when viewed from widely separated locations. This could have enabled him to judge the height of the boundary layer. But after comparing records sent to him from all around Europe, which served as the base of his celestial triangulation, he found no shift. The fiery visitor apparently dwelled in the ethereal domain far from Earth. Against Aristotle's expressed wish, the heavens were changing and evolving. And, as if to emphasize this point, the heavens unleashed another supernova in 1604, only thirty-two years after the previous one.

This new astronomical outlook was advanced in 1609 when Johannes Kepler, Tycho's German assistant and scientific heir, published in his *Astronomia Nova* that planets do not orbit in circles but in ellipses, what might be viewed as squashed circles. Astronomical measurements at last were accurate enough to discern this subtle difference, though barely.

A man of few social graces, slovenly and awkward, Kepler once applied his skills in mathematics, in which he was something of a wizard, to casting horoscopes for an assortment of European princes. Yet this peculiar man was described by the philosopher Immanuel Kant more than a century later as "the most acute thinker ever born."

The importance of Kepler's discovery cannot be overemphasized. After Tycho's death in 1601, Kepler spent nearly a decade trudging through hundreds of pages of bone-grinding calculations in an attempt to describe the true orbit of Mars, based on the decades of meticulous observations recorded by Tycho. Success came only when Kepler renounced his allegiance to circular motion and opened his eyes to the elliptical solution. In some ways, Kepler's revelation was as wrenching a jolt as Copernicus's alteration of the solar system. Some theologians and philosophers were surely dismayed to see the circle, long considered the perfect geometrical form, cast aside for an ellipse. But the scientific value of this discovery was immense. Kepler's ellipse, the path a planet traces in its journey about the Sun, became the foundation upon which Newton would later forge his triumphant law of gravitation.

Like some tectonic force that could not be constrained, the reverberations of Copernicus's and Kepler's findings swept throughout Eu-

Johannes Kepler (1571–1630),
first to accurately describe a planet's orbit.
Mary Lea Shane Archives of Lick Observatory

rope. Aristotle had asserted that the Sun was perfect, an unblemished orb of fire. During the Middle Ages, despite reports that dark splotches occasionally appeared on the face of the Sun, this ancient conception of a flawless solar globe held firm. Medieval theologians preferred their heavenly objects to be untarnished. But this celestial illusion, too, was demolished around 1611 when Galileo Galilei, a savvy professor of mathematics at the University of Padua in Italy, as well as observers in Holland, Germany, and England, pointed a newfangled instrument called a telescope at the Sun and confirmed that the solar surface was definitely spotted.

Possessing a showman's fondness for fame and fortune, Galileo had earlier acquainted Venetian officials with the military and economic advantages of spotting ships from afar through the novel "optical tubes" and secured himself a tenured university appointment. He proceeded to train his own telescope on the nighttime sky, revealing a universe filled with more richness and complexity than Aristotle ever dared to imagine.

Galileo Galilei (1564–1642).
Photograph courtesy of Yerkes Observatory

Galileo discovered a lunar landscape filled with mountains, craters, and vast dark regions that resembled seas—"just like the Earth's surface, with huge prominences, deep valleys, and chasms," he wrote in *Sidereus Nuncius* ("The Starry Messenger"), a sixty-page illustrated pamphlet that was a bestseller in its day. Celestial investigators latched onto these terrestrial comparisons with great delight. Sunspots, it was ventured, could be high rocks in a fiery sea, with the shadowy penumbras akin to shores of sand around the darker rocks. Jupiter's clouds, with their promise of water, opened up the possibility of extraterrestrial life. "It is hardly possible," wrote the seventeenth-century Dutch physicist Christiaan Huygens, "that an adherent of Copernicus should not at times imagine . . . that, like our globe, the other planets are also not devoid of vegetation and ornament, nor, perhaps of inhabitants."

Galileo spotted the moons of Jupiter, which resembled a mini solar system with its attendant satellites, and watched Venus go through crescent and gibbous phases, like the Moon, as it orbited the Sun, proof of the Copernican theory. And when he trained his instrument, a small concave lens behind a convex one, on the foggy glow of the Milky Way, he confirmed that it was composed of individual stars. "So numerous as to be almost beyond belief," he reported in his breathless prose.

Galileo's more Earthbound experiments generated heavenly repercussions as well. Aristotle's laws of physics stated essentially that if a body is in motion it must always be pushed or pulled by something; a force has to be applied at all times to keep the object going, otherwise it will just come to a halt. Only the planets, in their eternal revolutions, were the exception to this rule—their ethereal composition made them special. But Galileo came to suspect that Aristotle's mechanics were wrong.

By directing some balls to roll down one incline and up another, Galileo saw that each ball nearly reached the height from which it started. By imagining that all interferences, like friction, were reduced to zero—and the second incline made flatter and flatter—he came to perceive that the balls would roll on and on for great distances. Here was the first glimmer in the realization that ordinary, everyday stuff—not just some special concoction—could circle the Sun for all eternity once it was set in motion.

What Galileo began to infer from his experiments Isaac Newton clearly demonstrated once and for all in 1687. Generally viewed by history as the voice of detached reason, Newton was an avid student of alchemy as well as of biblical prophecy. The British economist John Maynard Keynes, a Newton aficionado, said that the deepest instincts of his idol were "occult, esoteric, semantic—with profound shrinking from the world, a paralyzing fear of exposing his thoughts. . . ." At times remote, terribly absentminded, and rude, Newton invented the calculus when he was still a college undergraduate, but he refused to publish it for twenty-seven years for fear of the public attention it would bring. "As a man he was a failure," Aldous Huxley wrote, "as a monster he was superb."

Newton's scientific masterpiece, *Philosophiae Naturalis Principia Mathematica* ("Mathematical Principles of Natural Philosophy"), popularly known as the *Principia,* might never have been written except for the dogged prodding, patient diplomacy, and financial backing of Edmond Halley (of comet fame). As if with one monumental stroke of the pen,

Isaac Newton (1642–1727).
Photograph courtesy of Yerkes Observatory

Newton established in his massive tome that motions everywhere, in the heavens and on the Earth, are described by the same set of physical laws. An object in motion will remain in motion unless altered by an outside force, just as Galileo began to suspect. And two objects exert a gravitational force on one another that is in direct proportion to their masses and in inverse proportion to the square of their distance. What draws an apple to the ground—an event that Newton presumably witnessed as a young man at his mother's farm and got him thinking about gravity—also keeps the Moon in orbit about the Earth.

As a result of Newton's genius, the cosmos and terra firma were blissfully wedded. Any specialness of the heavens was banished from physics. The grandeur of Newton's achievement resides in the powerful mathematics he brought to bear on the universe; for the first time in history, both terrestrial and celestial phenomena followed an identical, unchanging set of mathematical laws. Many began to think of the cosmos as ticking on like a gigantic watchspring.

A footnote to this triumph: With Newton's universal law of gravitation as his guide, Halley pored over historic records to match the highly elliptical path of a comet he had observed in 1682 with comet sightings of the past. After great toil, Halley confidently predicted that the celestial visitor of 1682 would return to Earth's vicinity in 1758. And when, on Christmas Day of the appointed year, a gentleman farmer in Saxony spotted the distant streak, Europe went wild. Newton's laws were beautifully confirmed and comets were shown to be mere planetoids in constant, if eccentric, orbit around the Sun. (Halley, alas, was not among those present to witness the return. He had died in 1742, after taking a last swig of his beloved brandy.)

REBIRTH OF THE ATOM

Along with his investigations into gravity, optics, and mathematics, Newton also took up the cause of atomism. His notorious experiments in alchemy, seemingly so out of character, were actually based in his firm belief in the ability of clusters of atoms to mutate. Robert Boyle, fourteenth child of Ireland's Earl of Cork, had earlier advanced this idea in 1661 with the publication of *The Sceptical Chymist,* the seminal work that helped transform alchemy into the modern field of chemistry.

According to Boyle's view, a specific aggregate of "corpuscles" corresponded to a particular substance, and these clusters could disperse ("ferment") and recombine into new forms. Such thoughts encouraged Newton in his alchemic pursuits. "If Gold could once be brought to ferment and putrefie, it might be turn'd into any other Body whatsoever," wrote Newton in "On the Nature of Acids." Earth, air, fire, and water were increasingly put aside for a more fundamental view of matter: Nature housed an array of substances, perhaps some not yet discovered, and each was composed of a special kind of particle or groups of particles.

Theologians had initially been receptive to the idea of atomism. Around A.D. 600 Isidore of Seville, a Spanish historian, encyclopedist, and bishop, wrote freely about the concept. As he explained in his encyclopedia:

You can divide a body like a stone into parts, and the parts into grains like sand, and again the sand into finest dust, continuing, if you could, until you come to some little particle that you cannot divide or cut. This is an atom of the body.

Isidore even described atoms flitting "continually through the emptiness of space." But churchmen eventually came to perceive that a world composed of atoms could arise by chance combination, making God's intervention superfluous. The soul became no different from the body. Frightened by such a loathsome prospect, the Church (not surprisingly) soon equated atomism with heresy. (A new and controversial interpretation of Galileo's trial by the Inquisition suggests that a belief in atomism may have been the noted scientist's gravest offense to papal authorities.)

Yet despite atomism's unsavory reputation, the idea that matter might consist of indivisible particles survived through the Middle Ages. A lucid poem on the subject, *De rerum natura* ("On the Nature of Things"), written by the Roman poet Lucretius in the first century B.C., was uncovered in Germany in the fifteenth century, dispatched to Italy, and reproduced many times over the ensuing years. Each copy sowed the seeds of atomism's rebirth.

In an essay that eerily resembles modern descriptions of the universe's birth, a French priest born in 1592, Pierre Gassendi, spoke of God creating atoms at genesis with

> their own weights, sizes and shapes in all their inconceivable variety, and likewise the impetus appropriate to each for motion, effort, and change, as for being loosened, rising up, leaping forward, striking, repelling, bouncing back, seizing, enfolding, holding and retaining. . . .

It was Gassendi's insights, inspired by Lucretius's poem, that encouraged many investigators, such as Newton, to reevaluate the notion of indivisible particles.

By 1738 Daniel Bernoulli, a Swiss mathematician, had adopted the idea of atomism to explain how gases behaved in a closed container. He assumed that gases were composed of a vast number of tiny particles, all flying about at great speed. In this way Bernoulli could describe mathematically what Robert Boyle had already observed in his laboratory: Squeeze a volume of air by half, and you double its pressure, since twice as many particles are slamming into the sides of the container.

But no one was convinced. Scientists were still highly skeptical. They found it difficult to fathom an image of invisible particles flitting about. Atomism in the 1700s still required a gigantic leap of faith, a belief in something that was essentially unseeable. Classical physicists were used to dealing with the substantial, objects that could be directly observed, held in the hand, or weighed in the laboratory.

Yet the rapid advances then taking place in chemistry called for fresh ways of thinking. The old Greek "elements" themselves were revealed to be far from elemental. In 1784 water was found to be composed of two gases, hydrogen and oxygen. Earlier, air had been separated into oxygen and nitrogen (then known as "azote," from the Greek words meaning "no life"). Chemists were applying their newfound skills to breaking down various compounds in the hope of figuring out which substances were truly indestructible. Mercury and sulfur were already known. To these were added iron, tin, lead, silver, and gold (putting the alchemists' ancient quest to rest at last). Along the way, entirely new elements were uncovered, such as manganese, chlorine, and magnesium.

In 1789 the great French chemist Antoine Lavoisier categorized some thirty substances as true elements. Today it is known that ninety-two elements are commonly found in nature, either on Earth or in space.[1] The lightest is hydrogen, and the most massive is uranium. Additional elements, more than a dozen substances heavier than uranium, have been made artificially. Some of these transuranics are produced in nuclear reactors or with particle accelerators; others were first isolated in the debris of atomic bomb explosions. With the last of the naturally occurring elements named after the planet Uranus, it's not surprising that elements 93 and 94 were named neptunium and plutonium, respectively. Many other transuranics were discovered at the Lawrence Berkeley Laboratory in Berkeley, California—thus, element 95 is designated americium, element 97 is called berkelium, element 98 is californium, and element 103, lawrencium, is named after the laboratory's founder, Ernest Lawrence. Other transuranic names honor famous scientists, such as curium (element 96), einsteinium (99), fermium (100), mendelevium (101), and nobelium (102). A transuranic's lifetime can be as short as minutes or seconds, but some can exist for millions of years. (One form of americium lasts for hundreds of years and is used in many smoke alarms.)

Some two hundred years ago the Englishman John Dalton, the son of a Cumberland hand-loom weaver, exerted the greatest influence in reviving the theory of atomism. A quiet and reserved Quaker teacher, Dalton had become fascinated with meteorology as a youth and compiled about a quarter of a million observations up until his death in 1844 at the

---

[1] Some would quibble over the remark that ninety-two elements occur naturally. Minute traces of element 94, plutonium, are present in uranium and thorium ores.

THE CHEMICAL ELEMENTS

Number of Protons	Name	Symbol	When Discovered	Derivation of Name
1	Hydrogen	H	1766	Greek *hydor*, "water"; *gen*, "forming"
2	Helium	He	1868	Greek *helios*, "sun"; first seen on Sun
3	Lithium	Li	1817	Greek *lithos*, "stony"
4	Beryllium	Be	1798	Greek *beryllos*, gem "beryl"
5	Boron	B	1808	Aryan *borak*, "white"
6	Carbon	C	Ancient	Latin *carbo*, "charcoal"
7	Nitrogen	N	1772	Latin, forming *niter*, compound of nitrogen
8	Oxygen	O	1774	Greek *oxyx*, "sharp"; *gen*, "forming"; since oxygen combines with hydrogen and nonmetals to form acids
9	Fluorine	F	1771	Latin *fluere*, "to flow"
10	Neon	Ne	1898	Greek *neos*, "new"
11	Sodium	Na	1807	English *soda*, compound of sodium; symbol from Latin *natrium*
12	Magnesium	Mg	1808	Latin *Magnesia*, district in Asia Minor
13	Aluminum	Al	1825	Latin *alumen*, a substance having astringent taste
14	Silicon	Si	1823	Latin *silex*, "flint"
15	Phosphorus	P	1669	Greek *phosphoros*, "light-bringer"
16	Sulfur	S	Ancient	Sanskrit *solvere*
17	Chlorine	Cl	1774	Greek *chloros*, "greenish-yellow"
18	Argon	Ar	1894	Greek *argos*, "idle"; "inert"
19	Potassium	K	1807	For potash, potassium compound; symbol from Latin *kalium*

Based on information from *The Elements*, P. A. Cox; *The Universal Almanac 1990*, John W. Wright, ed.; and the *CRC Handbook of Chemistry and Physics*.

THE CHEMICAL ELEMENTS (*cont.*)

Number of Protons	Name	Symbol	When Discovered	Derivation of Name
20	Calcium	Ca	1808	Latin *calx,* "lime"
21	Scandium	Sc	1879	For Scandinavia
22	Titanium	Ti	1791	For classical Titans
23	Vanadium	V	1801	For Scandinavian goddess Vanadis, Norse goddess of love
24	Chromium	Cr	1797	Greek *chroma,* "color"; many of its compounds are colored
25	Manganese	Mn	1774	Latin *magnes,* "magnet"; once confused with magnetic iron ores
26	Iron	Fe	Ancient	Anglo-Saxon *iren;* symbol from Latin *ferrum*
27	Cobalt	Co	1735	Greek *kobolis,* "goblin"
28	Nickel	Ni	1751	German *Nickel,* "goblin"
29	Copper	Cu	Ancient	Latin *cuprum;* island of Cyprus
30	Zinc	Zn	Ancient	German *zink*
31	Gallium	Ga	1875	Latin *Gallia,* "France"
32	Germanium	Ge	1886	For Germany
33	Arsenic	As	1649	Greek *arsenikos,* "bold"
34	Selenium	Se	1817	Greek *selene,* "Moon"
35	Bromine	Br	1826	Greek *bromos,* "stench," because of its odor
36	Krypton	Kr	1898	Greek *kryptos,* "hidden"
37	Rubidium	Rb	1861	Latin *rubidus,* "red," for red lines in its spectrum
38	Strontium	Sr	1793	For Strontian, Scottish town where element discovered
39	Yttrium	Y	1794	For Ytterby, Swedish village
40	Zirconium	Zr	1789	Arabic *zargun,* "gold color"

THE CHEMICAL ELEMENTS (cont.)

41	Niobium	Nb	1801	Latin *Niobe*, daughter of Tantalus
42	Molyb-denum	Mo	1778	Greek *molybdaina*, "galena" (lead ore)
43	Technetium	Tc	1937	Greek *technetos*, "artificial"
44	Ruthenium	Ru	1844	For Ruthenia in Urals
45	Rhodium	Rh	1803	Greek *rhodios*, "roselike"; its salts are red
46	Palladium	Pd	1803	For asteroid Pallas (named for Greek goddess) discovered in 1801
47	Silver	Ag	Ancient	Anglo-Saxon *seolfor*; symbol is from Latin *argentum*
48	Cadmium	Cd	1817	Greek *cadmia*, "earthy"
49	Indium	In	1863	Latin *indicum*, "indigo"
50	Tin	Sn	Ancient	Anglo-Saxon *tin*; symbol from Latin *stannum*
51	Antimony	Sb	Ancient	Greek *antimonos*, "opposed to solitude"; symbol from Greek *stibi*
52	Tellurium	Te	1782	Latin *tellus*, "the earth"
53	Iodine	I	1811	Greek *iodes*, "violet"
54	Xenon	Xe	1898	Greek *xenon*, "stranger"
55	Cesium	Cs	1860	Latin *caesius*, "bluish gray"
56	Barium	Ba	1774	Greek *barys*, "heavy"
57	Lanthanum	La	1839	Greek *lanthanein*, "concealed"
58	Cerium	Ce	1803	For asteroid Ceres (named after Roman goddess of agriculture)
59	Praseody-mium	Pr	1885	Greek *prasios*, "green"; *didymos*, "twin" (with neodymium)
60	Neodymium	Nd	1885	Greek *neos*, "new"; *didymos*, "twin" (with praseodymium)

THE CHEMICAL ELEMENTS (*cont.*)

Number of Protons	Name	Symbol	When Discovered	Derivation of Name
61	Promethium	Pm	1946	For Greek god Prometheus
62	Samarium	Sm	1879	For mineral samarskite, after Vasilii Erafovich Samarski-Bykhovets of Russian corps of mining engineers
63	Europium	Eu	1896	For Europe
64	Gadolinium	Gd	1880	After Johan Gadolin, Finnish chemist
65	Terbium	Tb	1843	For Ytterby, Swedish village
66	Dysprosium	Dy	1886	Greek *dysprositos*, "hard to get at"
67	Holmium	Ho	1879	From *Holmia*, Latinized form of *Stockholm*
68	Erbium	Er	1843	For Ytterby, Swedish village
69	Thulium	Tm	1879	For *Thule*, northernmost region of world, ancient name for Scandinavia
70	Ytterbium	Yb	1878	For Ytterby, Swedish village
71	Lutetium	Lu	1907	Latin *Lutetia*, ancient name for Paris
72	Hafnium	Hf	1923	From *Hafnia*, ancient name of Copenhagen
73	Tantalum	Ta	1802	For mythical king Tantalus, condemned to thirst; because of insolubility
74	Tungsten	W	1783	Swedish *tung sten*, "heavy stone"; symbol from German *Wolfram*
75	Rhenium	Re	1925	Latin *Rhenus*, "Rhine"
76	Osmium	Os	1803	Greek *osme*, "smell"

THE CHEMICAL ELEMENTS (*cont.*)

77	Iridium	Ir	1803	Greek *iris,* "rainbow," for changing color of its salts
78	Platinum	Pt	1735	Spanish *platina,* "small silver"
79	Gold	Au	Ancient	Anglo-Saxon *gold;* symbol from Latin *aurum,* "shining down"
80	Mercury	Hg	Ancient	For Roman god Mercurius; symbol from Latin *hydragyrum*
81	Thallium	Tl	1861	Greek *thallos,* a young, green twig; for bright green line in spectrum
82	Lead	Pb	Ancient	Anglo-Saxon *lead;* symbol from Latin *plumbum*
83	Bismuth	Bi	1753	German *bismut,* modification of *weisse masse,* "white mass"
84	Polonium	Po	1898	Named by Marie Curie for her native Poland
85	Astatine	At	1940	Greek *astatos,* "unstable"
86	Radon	Rn	1900	*Radium* plus *on*
87	Francium	Fr	1939	For France
88	Radium	Ra	1898	Latin *radius,* "ray"
89	Actinium	Ac	1899	Greek *aktis,* "ray"
90	Thorium	Th	1828	For Norse god Thor
91	Protactinium	Pa	1917	Greek *protos,* "first," plus *actinium,* the name of an element; decays into actinum by alpha decay
92	Uranium	U	1789	For planet Uranus, named after Greek god of heaven
93	Neptunium	Np	1940	For planet Neptune, named after Roman god of water
94	Plutonium	Pu	1940	For planet Pluto, named after the Greek god of the underworld

THE CHEMICAL ELEMENTS (*cont.*)

Number of Protons	Name	Symbol	When Discovered	Derivation of Name
95	Americium	Am	1944	For America
96	Curium	Cm	1944	For Marie and Pierre Curie
97	Berkelium	Bk	1949	First made in Berkeley, California
98	Californium	Cf	1950	For California, where first made
99	Einsteinium	Es	1952	For Albert Einstein
100	Fermium	Fm	1953	For Enrico Fermi, Italian physicist
101	Mendelevium	Md	1955	For Russian chemist Dmitri Mendeleyev
102	Nobelium	No	1958	For Alfred Nobel
103	Lawrencium	Lr	1961	For American physicist Ernest Lawrence
104	Rutherfordium	Rf	1969	For New Zealand physicist Ernest Rutherford (United States)
	(Kurchatovium)	Ku		For Soviet physicist Igor Kurchatov (USSR)
105	Hahnium	Ha	1970	For German physicist Otto Hahn (United States claim)
106	Element 106		1974	Claimed by Russia and United States
107	Nielsbohrium	Ns	1981	For Danish physicist Niels Bohr; identified in Germany
108	Hassium	Hs	1984	After Latin name for German state of Hesse; created in Hesse, Germany, by bombarding lead with iron ions
109	Meitnerium	Mt	1982	For Austrian-Swedish physicist Lise Meitner; created in Germany by bombarding bismuth with iron ions

age of seventy-seven. From these extensive weather studies, Dalton came to suspect that water vapor and other gases in the air do not chemically combine but instead intermingle as independent entities. He surmised that, in order for this to happen, each gas had to be composed of its own kind of particle. He reintroduced the term *atom,* recalling Democritus's theory of twenty-two centuries earlier. But these modern-day atoms were decidedly different from the older variety. Whereas the ancient atoms had varying shapes and textures, Dalton's atoms differed only in their mass. Each element was distinguished by the specific weight of its individual atoms.

Dalton published this idea in 1808 as a *New System of Chemical Philosophy.* Chemical reactions do not destroy or create matter, he explained, but merely separate and reunite these various elementary units of matter in set proportions. Exactly one atom of oxygen joins with two atoms of hydrogen, for example, to form a molecule of water. "We might

Hydrogen	1	Strontian	46
Azote	5	Barytes	68
Carbon	54	Iron	50
Oxygen	7	Zinc	56
Phosphorus	9	Copper	56
Sulphur	13	Lead	90
Magnesia	20	Silver	190
Lime	24	Gold	190
Soda	28	Platina	190

The symbols used by John Dalton for various elements, along with their atomic weights.
Adapted from Dalton's list of elements

as well attempt to introduce a new planet into the solar system, or to annihilate one already in existence, as to create or destroy a particle of hydrogen," wrote Dalton. After centuries of ridicule, atomism was an idea whose time had arrived. Leucippus and Democritus had relied on logic alone to support their idea, and they failed. Dalton's model was greeted with far more enthusiasm, at least by some. By the start of the nineteenth century, the existence of atoms could at last explain many of the processes that chemists, the alchemists' scientific successors, were uncovering in their laboratories. The English chemist William Prout, for instance, noted as early as 1815 that many of the elements had atomic weights that were remarkably close to integer multiples of the atomic weight of hydrogen, the lightest element. Thus, researchers began to think of hydrogen as an atomic building block, an early premonition of twentieth-century physics.

That atoms are real was beautifully confirmed in a series of elegant and painstaking experiments performed by the French physicist Jean Perrin in 1908, for which he received a Nobel Prize eighteen years later. Perrin carefully measured how minuscule particles of gamboge, a bright yellow vegetable latex, settled in a small cell of water as the uniform grains, which took months to prepare, were pulled downward by the force of gravity. Peering through a microscope at the cell, he carefully counted how many particles were hampered in their passage and by how much. The delays these particles experienced were the same as those predicted for particles being jostled by the innumerable impacts of water molecules. Einstein had earlier worked out the theoretical principle. Conceiving of matter as discrete particles was no longer a metaphysical convenience but a physical reality capable of experimental verification.

Today, pictures of individual atoms are routinely taken with scanning tunneling microscopes. Researchers have even manipulated thirty-five individual atoms of xenon, an inert gas, across a nickel surface and spelled out the name of their corporate employer, IBM (surely the smallest advertisement ever created in the world, this entire "billboard" measured a whopping six hundred billionths of an inch across). On a more practical level, this capability opens up the possibility of assembling a superminiature electrical circuit, atom by atom. Atoms, once thought by certain scientists to be no more real than Ptolemy's crystalline spheres, are now as palpable as paint and poster board.

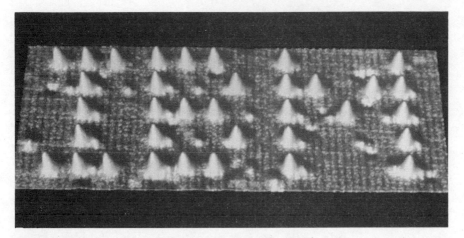

Individual xenon atoms spell out researchers' corporate employer.
IBM Research

THE FIFTH ESSENCE

The concept of atoms decisively annihilated the ancient elements of earth, air, fire, and water. But what of the fifth essence? As the world and the nature of its contents were redefined over the seventeenth, eighteenth, and nineteenth centuries, Aristotle's heavenly ether, strangely enough, never completely disappeared, although it was certainly refashioned to suit the needs of the age of reason. Kepler had earlier rejected the ethereal spheres, leaving the planets with no means of maintaining their motion. A believer in physical causes, Kepler instead thought the Sun might be putting out magnetic fingers of force that alternately attracted and repulsed the planets to keep them moving. It seemed like a reasonable idea, given the lodestone's mysterious ability to attract iron from afar. But Kepler's contemporaries concluded that his magnetic scheme smacked of magic, and so the ether reemerged.

For René Descartes (the French philosopher best known for declaring "*Cogito, ergo sum*"—"I think, therefore I am"), the ether provided a useful apparatus for carrying out planetary motion, although by a different mechanism than Aristotle's notorious spheres. In 1644 Descartes described every star as surrounded by a vortex of ether, in which the planets were carried around like leaves trapped within a swirling whirlpool. Like Aristotle, Descartes couldn't help but presume that nature abhors a vacuum.

Isaac Newton shattered Descartes's fanciful vortex theory with his law of gravitation, which allowed planetary movements to be described by exact mathematical computations. Kepler's elliptical orbits were a natural outcome of this universal law, powerful evidence of its validity. Newton argued in his *Principia* that Descartes's "hypothesis of vortices is utterly irreconcilable with astronomical phenomena and rather serves to perplex than explain the heavenly motions." A nation of explorers and merchants, England preferred accuracy over fantasy, experiment over speculation.

France and other countries on the European continent clung to Descartes's ethereal swirls a while longer. As late as the 1720s the French writer Voltaire, in his "Letters from London on the English," astutely recorded this subtle battle between the Cartesians and the Newtonians:

A Frenchman coming to London finds matters considerably changed, in philosophy as in everything else. He left the world filled, he finds it here empty. In Paris you see the universe consisting of vortices of subtle matter; in London nothing is seen of this. With us it is the pressure of the moon that cause the tides of the sea; with the English it is the sea that gravitates toward the moon. . . .

Yet even Newton could not leave his interstellar spaces entirely empty. His notion of gravity implied that imperceptible ribbons of attraction somehow emanated over distances, both short and long, to keep moon to planet, boulder to Earth. This feat appeared more resonant with the occult than with science. Apples fell to the ground and planets revolved around the Sun because a force called gravity was attracting these masses to one another. But why should this be so? What was the mechanism behind gravity? No one knew. Newton himself recognized this flaw as a gaping wound in his *Principia*. His theory could not explain the precise nature of gravity.

There were critics of Newton's theory who found this situation both unsatisfying and barren; lack of a cause was tantamount to bad science. " 'Tis also a supernatural thing, that bodies should attract one another at a distance, without any intermediate means," wrote Newton's nemesis, Gottfried Leibniz, the German mathematician who had also accused Newton of stealing the calculus from him. In a letter to the theologian Richard Bentley, Newton conceded that "gravity must be caused by an

Agent acting constantly according to certain Laws; but whether this Agent be material or immaterial, I have left to the Consideration of my Readers."

Newton himself contemplated a number of candidates, but he sometimes favored a heavenly ether, suffused through all of space, as the agent of gravitational transmission. He imagined that this medium might be thin and diffuse, "perhaps of an unctuous or Gummy, tenacious & springy nature. . . ." In his *Opticks* Newton considered that the ether might get thicker and thicker as one moved farther and farther from a celestial body. In this way, when an object got ever nearer to a star or planet, it would be forced inward (that is, attracted) because of the large amounts of ether pushing from beyond. But then, how could the planets move so readily through this dense ethereal sea? Even Newton was stumped.

The ether of the seventeenth century proved to be multipurpose; it turned up in descriptions of light as well as of gravity. Huygens pictured light as waves moving through the ether, roughly akin to sound waves traveling through the air. Experiments carried out a century later by the Englishman Thomas Young verified that light did have wavelike qualities and that different wavelengths produced different colors. An ether was vital in propagating this light because it served as the medium in which to transmit light's waves from point A to point B or from star C to planet D. No reputable physicist would have even dared to imagine that two objects could transmit light betwixt one another with nothing in between.

Young surmised that the vibrations of the ether occurred sidewise to the line of motion, like the undulations of a snake slithering across the desert or a rope manipulated from side to side. But this meant that the ether had to be fairly stiff. Young wondered, just as Newton had earlier, how the Earth, planets, and stars could possibly move through this stuff without resistance. The problem provided theoretical physicists with a cottage industry for more than a century. Scientific journals were filled with attempts to explain how the ether could be both rigid and insubstantial. The exact composition of the heavens—or at least the space between the stars—was proving quite elusive.

Elusive or not, the ether was still an indispensable material—an idea hard to give up even when alternatives were offered. While serving as an apprentice bookbinder in his youth, the Englishman Michael Faraday became fascinated with electricity as he read an article in a volume of the

Encyclopaedia Britannica that he was binding. Born into poverty, with no formal mathematical training, this self-taught scientist started talking about "fields of force" to help him visualize the invisible goings-on in the empty space around a magnet or electric wire.

Much of modern physics, from relativity to quantum electrodynamics, is now based on Faraday's abstract idea. "The field is the only reality," said Albert Einstein, who displayed a portrait of Faraday in his study in recognition of the debt. Such fields are wonderfully displayed in the way iron filings align themselves when you sprinkle them around a magnet. The highly intuitive Faraday went on to propose that light waves might be vibrations in these lines of force. "[This view] endeavours to dismiss the ether but not the vibrations," he said. No one else, though, was yet ready to relinquish the ether. Faraday's new physical arena, the field, was generally assumed at that time to be a sort of tension or motion in the ether.

Faraday, assuredly one of the greatest experimentalists of physics (he conducted thousands of experiments over his lifetime), discovered how to convert magnetic energy into electric current, which led to his invention of the electric generator. It was the first step toward the electrification of the modern world. The distinguished Scotsman James Clerk Maxwell was just one in the legion of people, both scientists and nonprofessionals alike, captivated by these findings, and he kept abreast through correspondence and meetings with Faraday. A handsome man with a delicate constitution, Maxwell became a professor of natural philosophy at the age of twenty-four. Around 1865, ten years later, he took some time off to write his monumental *Treatise on Electricity and Magnetism,* a triumph of nineteenth-century physics. With Faraday's findings as his guide, Maxwell mathematically united electricity and magnetism, two forces that on the surface seem so disparate. His derivations, a set of four partial differential equations so elegantly succinct that they show up on physics students' T-shirts, show how a changing electric field produces a magnetic field and conversely how a variable magnetic field generates an electric current. The two forces are merely two sides of the same coin, each unable to exist in isolation.

Yet Maxwell, too, needed an ether to work out this revolutionary theory of electromagnetism. He divided his ether into an array of tiny cells that turned like little gears to produce the sorts of electrical and magnetic effects observed by Faraday. The result was quite intriguing. The final equations developed from this strange mechanical model were not dependent on the ether at all. The ether was like a sculptor's mold: required at first by Maxwell to cast the theory but expendable as soon as he had completed his magnificent edifice.

There was more stunning news. Maxwell's equations revealed that an oscillating electric current, charges moving rapidly back and forth, would generate waves of electromagnetic energy coursing through space at the very same speed as that of light, around 186,000 miles per second. Such a match had to be more than coincidence. "The magnetic and luminiferous media are identical," concluded Maxwell, proving what Faraday had vaguely imagined. Light was simply a propagating wave of electric and magnetic energy, an undulation that moved outward in all directions from its source like a ripple on a pond. Scientists no longer needed to think of electrical and magnetic effects as stresses and strains in some universal ether. The ether became irrelevant. And visible light waves, each measuring about 1/50,000 of an inch from peak to peak, were just a small selection of the wide range of waves possible. There could also be waves of electromagnetic energy both shorter and longer than visible light waves. The German physicist Heinrich Hertz proved this very fact in 1888, nine years after Maxwell died of cancer at the age of forty-eight.

In a laboratory humming with spark generators and oscillators, Hertz created the first radio waves. Each wave had a length of thirty inches, and (just as Maxwell had predicted) they sped across Hertz's lab at the speed of light. Hertz did not believe his "electric" waves would ever amount to anything. But a young Italian inventor named Guglielmo Marconi, reading of Hertz's work, began to imagine communicating with "Hertzian waves," as they were then called. Marconi's first wireless message was sent in 1894, the year of Hertz's death. The signal traversed a mere thirty feet. By 1901 Marconi was able to transmit the Morse code for the letter S (dot-dot-dot) across the Atlantic Ocean, from England to Newfoundland. The ensuing years would bring radar, lasers, X-ray machines, and microwave ovens.

Despite Maxwell's triumph, almost everyone continued to embrace the old ether (even Maxwell did so at times), but this was not too surprising. First with Aristotle, and subsequently with such scientific giants as Newton, the ether was deemed a fundamental substance, making it as wrenching to give up as an Earth-centered universe. The ether was still the stage upon which Maxwell's equations acted up a storm. It seemed like common sense: Sound waves move through air, and ocean waves travel through water; if there is a wave, *something* must be waving. The very same year that Hertz was tweaking his dials, William Thomson (later raised to the peerage as Lord Kelvin) described the Sun as a mere piece of matter "bounded all round by cold ether . . . which fills all space as far as the remotest star, and has the property of transmitting radiant heat (or light) without itself becoming heated." He likened the ether to a mold of transparent jelly.

Many physicists set their cap on cornering this baffling substance. The ether was the standard frame of reference for the universe, the medium at rest in which all things moved, from comets to starlight. The trick was figuring out how to catch it. Astronomers could easily see that Earth's passage around the Sun was not hindered by the ether, so it had to be very, very thin. And this ether didn't scatter light from the stars, making it somehow different from the atoms of the air, which scattered sunlight to make the sky blue. Thomas Young had already commented that the ether must pass though telescope walls "as freely perhaps as the wind passes through a grove of trees." Nevertheless, everyone took it for granted that the Earth moved through this stationary medium, and that was the key. Investigators came to believe they could detect an "ether wind" as Earth sailed at some 67,000 miles per hour in its annual voyage around the Sun.

Albert A. Michelson, a U.S. naval officer, tried to detect this ethereal breeze in 1881 while assigned to Berlin for postgraduate work in physics. He used a special instrument of his own design, known as the Michelson interferometer, but found not one hint of a draft. He tried again in 1887 as a civilian professor at the Case School of Applied Science in Cleveland, Ohio. There he teamed up with Edward Morley, a chemist at neighboring Western Reserve University. Using a vastly improved interferometer, the two investigators sent one beam of light "into the wind" in the direction of Earth's orbital motion and directed another beam at right angles to this path. As Michelson once explained to his young daughter Dorothy, "Two beams of light race against each other, like two swimmers, one struggling upstream and back, while the other, covering the same distance, just crosses and returns." The light beam fighting the ethereal "current" was expected to move a tiny bit slower.

Michelson and Morley's elaborate equipment, set up in a basement laboratory, was mounted on a massive sandstone slab that floated on a pool of mercury to cut down on vibrations. But even with such precautions, the scientists detected no difference whatsoever in the measured velocity of the two light beams, no matter which way the beams were

Physicist Albert A. Michelson (1852–1931), whose sensitive instruments failed to detect an ether.
Photograph courtesy of Yerkes Observatory

pointed. In 1907 Michelson became the first American to win a Nobel Prize in the sciences. He was honored for the development of his exquisitely sensitive optical instruments, many of them inspired by his futile search for the ether. Others looked and failed as well.

The inability of the Michelson-Morley experiment to detect the ether was one of the most notable "failures" in nineteenth-century science. From this failure, however, arose a revolution. The absence of the ether led to a completely different vision of space, time, and matter. By 1905 Albert Einstein, then working as a clerk in the Swiss patent office, came to recognize that the speed of light is the same for all observers, whether they are on Earth, on a moving rocket, or in a far-off galaxy. No one can catch a light beam, or even make it appear to move slower, no matter how fast they are running. And with the velocity of light in the universe fixed, strange consequences can arise. When separate observers witness the same phenomenon from their individual cosmic vantage points, they might disagree on their measurements of length, time, and mass. It all becomes "relative."

Earthbound observers, for example, who could magically watch a spacecraft tear off at near light speeds, would notice that the rocket had shrunk a bit, that the spacecraft's on-board clocks ran slower, and that the astronauts increased their mass. For those inside the speeding craft, however, all lengths, times, and masses would appear unchanged. If the space voyagers measured the speed of light as they rocketed outward at a steady velocity, the light's speed would still come out to be 186,282 miles per second, the same as on the Earth that was left behind. Einstein realized that there is no absolute framework of space, no preferred position or motion. He proved, once and for all, that an ether was undetectable and hence unessential.

Einstein accomplished all this with his "Special Theory of Relativity," which describes objects moving at constant velocities. By 1915 he developed his "General Theory of Relativity" to deal with bodies in accelerated motion, such as planets revolving around a star or rocks falling off a cliff. With general relativity, this century's most illustrious physicist at last solved the mystery that so perplexed Newton: the very origin of gravity. It was a bold, new, geometric vision of the gravitational force. Some might say it introduced a new type of ether altogether.

Space, Einstein taught, may be thought of not as an enormous empty expanse but as a sort of boundless rubber sheet. Such a sheet can be manipulated in a number of ways. It can be stretched or squeezed; it can be straightened or bent; it can even be indented in spots. Massive stars, like our Sun, sit in this flexible mat, creating deep depressions. Planets then circle the Sun, not because they are held by invisible tendrils of force, as Newton had us think, but because they are simply caught, like cosmic marbles, in the natural hollow carved out by the star. Each follows the curvature of space-time imparted by the Sun's huge mass. As long as a heavenly body continues to exist, the indentation it creates in this pliable space-time mat is part of the permanent landscape of the cosmos. What we think of as gravity—the tendency of two objects to be drawn toward each other—is simply the resulting motions within these innumerable space-time dents, both large and small.

"We may say that according to the general theory of relativity space is endowed with physical qualities," explained Einstein in 1920. "In this

Albert Einstein (1879–1955).
Photograph courtesy of the Mount Wilson and Las Campanas Observatories

sense, therefore, there exists an ether." Space itself becomes a sort of ether, supple and yielding in the presence of mass. But the ether of Aristotle and of Newton and of Maxwell was certainly gone forever. The composition of the heavens was changing and, in many ways, looking more and more familiar. During twenty-four hundred years of inquiry, first by logic and then by hands-on experimentation, earth, air, fire, and water came to be supplanted by an array of basic elements, which the nineteenth-century Russian chemist Dmitri Ivanovich Mendeleyev arranged in neat, periodic order according to the elements' atomic weights and properties. Additional elements, with surprising radioactive properties, would turn up in the twentieth century and reveal further levels of complexity within the atom itself.

And as the old ethereal realm slowly disappeared, there was an associated change in the assessment of the composition of the stars, knowledge that many thought would be forever concealed from them. Light waves emanating from celestial bodies turned out to be messengers bearing news of the chemical and physical properties of that starry realm. What Newton revealed in mathematical splendor, other scientists began to demonstrate experimentally. Astronomers learned how to bring the heavens directly into their observatories and, in doing so, verified that the stars and the Earth were intimately related.

Touching the Heavens

On February 12, 1841, the gold medal of the Royal Astronomical Society of London was awarded to Friedrich Wilhelm Bessel for his discovery of the annual parallax of 61 Cygni, a star barely visible to the naked eye (it is actually a double star; a small telescope can pick out two dwarf stars with a fine orange tint). In presenting the prestigious award, the noted British astronomer John Herschel proclaimed Bessel's feat "the greatest and most glorious triumph which practical astronomy has ever witnessed."

What Bessel had detected, with a precision never before attained, was the ever-so-slight change in 61 Cygni's apparent position on the sky as the star system was viewed first from one end of Earth's orbit and then, six months later, observed from the opposite end. In this way, 61 Cygni's position against the more distant stellar background appeared to shift over the year much the way a picture on a nearby wall seems to move when observed first with one eye and then the other. Herschel's exuberance was understandable: Stationed in the nighttime sky like some far-off surveyor's stake, 61 Cygni at last allowed astronomers to measure the exact distance to a star. Using the width of Earth's orbit as a baseline, Bessel calculated the distance by knowing 61 Cygni's parallax and applying a bit of trigonometry. Almost simultaneously, other astronomers announced the distances to the stars Vega and Alpha Centauri.

Bessel had been a clerk in a mercantile firm in Bremen, Germany, when he started studying books on navigation and astronomical calculations to expand his opportunities in the seafaring trade. Inspired by a paper on Halley's comet, he successfully computed the comet's orbit and decided to switch fields altogether. He soon obtained a post as an assistant at a private observatory. His skills were so phenomenal that by 1810 King Friedrich Wilhelm III of Prussia appointed Bessel, at the age of twenty-six, to direct the newly constructed Königsberg Observatory.

It was at Königsberg that Bessel's careful measurements indicated a distance from Earth to 61 Cygni that came within several percentage points of the modern value of eleven light-years (the distance light travels in eleven years, about sixty-six trillion miles). "I congratulate you and myself," said Herschel at the awarding of the gold medal, "that we have lived to see the great and hitherto impassable barrier to our excursions into the sidereal universe; that barrier against which we have chafed so long and so vainly, . . . almost simultaneously overleaped at three different points"—at 61 Cygni, at Vega, and at Alpha Centauri. Celestial observers had finally acquired a virtual tape measure for their cosmic explorations, at least for the closest stars in which a parallax was detectable.

During the late 1700s and early 1800s, as the Industrial Revolution began to impose its immense social changes on Europe and America, handcrafted implements were supplanted by instruments commercially manufactured with superb precision. Astronomers like Bessel, who specialized in measuring the positions and magnitudes of stars, reaped the benefits. After Bessel's discovery of 61 Cygni's annual shift, the art of parallax measurements flourished and offered new clues as to the nature of the heavens. Rigel, a bright, bluish-white star in the constellation Orion, was seen to have a similar magnitude as that of Alpha Centauri, a member of the star system closest to our Sun. Yet Rigel's smaller parallax, its narrower shift on the sky over a year's time, indicated that the star in

Orion was far more distant than was Alpha Centauri. From an observatory at the tip of Africa, the Scottish astronomer Thomas Henderson had already determined that Alpha Centauri was some four light-years from Earth, a result published just months after Bessel's 61 Cygni announcement. And Rigel, astronomers reckoned, was at least 540 light-years away. Therefore, Rigel had to be tens of thousands of times more luminous than Alpha Centauri to appear as bright as the famous southern star. Through findings like these, astronomers came to learn that some stars are many times more radiant than others.

After the publication of the *Principia,* astronomy had also become a science of patient computations, in many ways a world according to Newton. Calculating the exact orbits of celestial bodies, particularly the planets and comets in our solar system, challenged the most brilliant mathematicians of the era. These scientists entered rows upon rows of figures into their notebooks as they applied Newton's laws of gravitation to planetary movements. Indeed, discrepancies in the motions of the planet Uranus, situated about two billion miles from the Sun, led to the prediction that another massive body was circling the Sun far beyond Uranus's orbit, then the solar system's outer boundary. It was to be the first planet whose discovery was based on calculations made on a piece of paper. An assistant at the Berlin Observatory, Johann Galle, with the help of an eager graduate student named Heinrich d'Arrest, spotted this new planetary member on September 23, 1846, with a nine-inch refracting telescope and in the very region of the sky anticipated by the theoreticians. There was vehement debate concerning the new planet's name. Galle suggested the name Janus, Urbain Le Verrier, the proud French theoretician who had calculated the position, wanted to name it after himself; comets are named after their discoverers, he reasoned, why not name planets after their founders? By international agreement, astronomers settled on the name Neptune, Le Verrier's second choice. Three billion miles distant, Neptune moves so slowly that, since its discovery, it will not have completed one revolution around the Sun until 2011.

The detection of Neptune was undoubtedly a triumph for astronomy. But at the time of this celebrated event there were obvious limitations to the celestial vistas that could be further revealed through a telescope alone. A British astronomer named William Huggins summed up astronomy's knowledge of the stars in the first half of the nineteenth century quite succinctly: "That they shine; that they are immensely distant; that the motions of some of them show them to be composed of matter endowed with a power of mutual attraction." Observers could know nothing more.

It was quite apparent that astronomers, unlike biologists carrying out their dissections or chemists mixing their compounds, could not get intimately acquainted with their celestial quarry. What they lacked was an ability to figure out such things as the temperature or composition of the stars in view, which left them powerless to formulate any type of reasonable theory about the universe. Astronomers believed that it was even possible for conditions to be so vastly different in other regions of space that the alien surroundings would give rise to substances bearing little resemblance to earthly chemicals. This situation prompted Auguste Comte, the French philosopher of positivism, which stressed that true science must be based on experience, to conclude that humanity will forever be barred from discerning the chemical makeup of celestial bodies: "Never, by any means, will we be able to study their chemical composition, their mineralogic structure," he wrote with firm assurance in his *Cours de philosophie positive*. "I persist in the opinion that every notion of the true mean temperature of the stars will necessarily always be concealed from us."

Comte's bold assertion that "men will never encompass in their conceptions the whole of the stars" has earned a reputation as one of the most infamous misstatements in the history of science, and for good reason. Comte was inflicted with a bad case of scientific myopia. (To be fair, so were many others in his day.) What he did not anticipate at the time of his writing, around 1835, was the development of new techniques and equipment that would sweep away his ill-timed and oft-quoted conclusion in less than three decades—and quite dramatically. With the introduction of the spectroscope, an instrument that separates light into its component wavelengths, a vastly different arena for celestial observations opened up.

At first referred to as the "new astronomy," this innovative avenue of investigation came to be called "astrophysics." Studies of the positions, magnitudes, and motions of astronomical bodies, which had been the major concern of astronomy since its inception millennia ago, were redirected to analyses of stellar compositions, laying the groundwork for the astronomical breakthroughs of the twentieth century. Within decades, ideas on the composition of the heavens, which previous researchers had deemed as nothing more than speculation, were radically revised. In a monumental review of nineteenth-century astronomy published in 1886, historian Agnes Clerke declared that astrophysics was "one of the most amazing features in the swift progress of knowledge our age has witnessed." When the poet Robert Frost asked the stars in the late 1940s to "use language we can comprehend. / Tell us what elements you blend," the spectroscope already had been serving as the translator for nearly a century.

With a spectroscope, astronomers could at last "touch" the heavens and directly assess the physical characteristics of their celestial subjects. In the process, they encountered temperatures, velocities, and pressures in the stellar sky that were inaccessible on Earth, providing scientists with a cosmic workshop whose capabilities far transcended those of Earthbound laboratories. Today, astrophysics encompasses a wide range of endeavors, including the application of the laws of physics to extrapolate what we cannot see, such as the first moments of the universe's birth, the eerie environment around a black hole, or the origin of a far-off quasar's brilliant outpourings. The effects that modern-day astrophysicists attempt to explain are among the most complex in science. Nevertheless, the field's first embryonic stirrings a few centuries ago occurred very simply and very humbly—with a prism and a bit of sunlight.

"THE CELEBRATED PHAENOMENA OF COLOURS"

In 1666, at the age of twenty-three, Isaac Newton, sitting in a darkened room, let a small stream of sunlight enter through a hole in his window shutter and pass through a triangular prism of glass. On the wall behind him, Newton beheld a rainbow of overlapping colors, an enchanting effect that has been observed with pieces of glass since antiquity. With a band of red anchoring one end, the striped array ran through orange, yellow, green, and blue, until it reached a violet band on the other end. Through a series of simple experiments, the young Newton proved "the celebrated Phaenomena of colours," as he called it. He clearly demonstrated that white light was a mixture of many hues. He saw that each individual color was bent, or refracted, by the glass to a different degree, allowing the white light to be separated into its varied components. Red was bent the least; blue and violet the most strongly. In his report (which was the first major scientific discovery to be announced in a journal rather than a book), Newton dubbed the multicolored display a *spectrum,* which is Latin for "apparition" or "specter." It took nearly two hundred years, however, before this knowledge was seriously applied to astronomical problems. William Herschel did examine the spectrum of a star in the 1790s, but his fellow astronomers were still slavishly devoted to charting the motions and positions of their celestial subjects. Spectra were a mild curiosity.

The next substantial step beyond Newton was taken in 1802 when William Wollaston, an English experimentalist with interests ranging from metallurgy to magnetism, sent sunlight through both a narrow slit and a prism in the hope of completely separating the colors from one another. What he saw with this instrument, the first crude spectroscope, were several black lines in the spectrum of the Sun, features that Newton somehow missed. Wollaston, after assuming that these dark gaps simply marked off the natural boundaries of light's various colors, seems to have dropped the subject. By doing so, he missed the opportunity to contribute to the most significant advance in the astronomical sciences since the invention of the telescope.

By 1814 the Bavarian Joseph Fraunhofer, a master optician based in Munich, cleverly combined a slit, a prism, and a small telescope to discern hundreds of dark lines in the Sun's spectrum, as if a series of black threads had been sewn across a rainbow. Today these dark streaks in the solar spectrum bear his name. More than twenty thousand Fraunhofer lines have now been detected.

How Fraunhofer arrived at his scientific station in life is a story reminiscent of a novel by Charles Dickens. The eleventh child of a poverty-stricken glazier, Fraunhofer was orphaned as a young boy and eventually apprenticed to a tyrannical looking-glass manufacturer, who overworked and underfed the frail lad. It took a tragic accident to deliver him from these dire straits. The slum tenement in which Fraunhofer lived and worked collapsed one July day in 1801, killing everyone inside except for the fourteen-year-old apprentice. A high government official, hearing of the disaster, took an interest in the young survivor and provided Fraunhofer with a large sum of money, eighteen ducats, which allowed the gifted teenager to pursue his interest in optics on his own.

Within five years, Fraunhofer joined the staff of a Munich instrument company, quickly surpassing his mentors as a lens crafter. By the age of twenty-four, he was made a full partner in the optics firm. It was Fraunhofer who initiated construction of the Königsberg heliometer, the exquisite instrument that allowed Bessel to measure the parallax of 61 Cygni. Many of the top astronomers of the day employed Fraunhofer's services. In an odd twist of fate, Fraunhofer's famous spectral studies came about as he was trying to get *rid* of the rainbow effect in lenses, their tendency to produce fringes of color in an image. Working to perfect the construction of achromatic lenses, Fraunhofer began investigating prisms and, while still in his twenties, conducted his historic experiment.

"In the window-shutter of a darkened room I made a narrow opening," Fraunhofer reported, "and through this I allowed sunlight to fall on a prism of flint-glass . . . so placed in front of the objective of the theodolite-telescope that the angle of incidence of the light was equal to the angle at which the beam emerged." Through the telescopic eyepiece, he saw countless lines, both strong and weak, in the solar spectrum generated by the prism; some of the lines were almost perfectly black.

After long investigation, Fraunhofer convinced himself (but not others) that the dark streaks were inherent in the sunlight itself and not just some optical illusion or atmospheric effect. Using his apparatus at night he even noticed that the Moon and planets, such as Venus and Mars, displayed the same fixed lines in their spectra as the Sun, proving once and for all that planetary bodies shine by reflected sunlight. But other stars, such as Castor, Capella, and Betelgeuse, exhibited their own unique spectral "fingerprints." The bright star Sirius, for example, had a prominent black line in the green band of its spectrum and two strong dark stripes in the blue, features not dominant in the Sun's spectrum. Yet the Sun and stars did have other lines in common.

What was the reason for these mysterious black slashes in the solar and stellar spectra? Fraunhofer could only guess. Sickly from his early years of deprivation, he died of tuberculosis at the age of thirty-nine. On his tombstone are carved the words *Approximavit sidera*, "He approached the stars"—it was left up to others to greet them expressly. Another forty years would pass before the true nature of the dark lines could be revealed, leading to the birth of astrophysics.

Fraunhofer lines were celestial ciphers that stubbornly lingered for nearly half a century awaiting interpretation. Answers arrived from the creative experiments being conducted in chemistry laboratories. As early as the 1750s, far before Fraunhofer's tests, chemists had already noticed that hot flames contaminated with metals or salts produced a special kind of spectrum composed of discrete lines of color, resembling a gaping picket fence with colorful posts. Whereas the solar spectrum was a continuous rainbow riddled with dark lines, these laboratory spectra were the exact opposite: thin bright lines of colorful emissions set against a dark background. Even Fraunhofer recognized that two particularly bright lines of yellow-orange, generated in the brilliant glow of a lamplight, coincided with the positions of two of his dark solar lines. Was there a connection?

Some researchers came to suspect a link with sodium, since a spectroscope focused on a laboratory flame dosed with the element always revealed the double yellow lines. But this idea stood on shaky ground, since many other substances displayed the telltale yellow streaks when heated and spectrally analyzed. Chemists were misled because they didn't yet realize that sodium was a widespread contaminant in chemistry labs, a ubiquitous presence in the air and water. Still, there was a growing suspicion that chemical substances, heated to incandescence, emitted their own distinctive set of spectral lines. Work on this problem proceeded in a number of countries—Great Britain and France, for example—and the spectral code was finally deciphered in Germany around 1859. This date marks the debut of astrophysics. Like the unearthing of the Rosetta stone sixty years earlier, which allowed Egyptologists to translate the hieroglyphics, the investigations of physicist Gustav Kirchhoff and chemist Robert Bunsen at last revealed the true meaning behind the bright and dark spectral features. Kirchhoff, a professor of physics at the University of Heidelberg, and Bunsen, creator of the famous laboratory Bunsen burner, provided the long-awaited key that unlocked the secrets of the stars.

A lifelong bachelor, Bunsen was devoted to his chemical researches, even after losing the use of his right eye in a laboratory explosion and nearly poisoning himself while working with compounds containing arsenic. In his forties he became interested in identifying substances by the specific light they emitted during chemical reactions or when burning. Kirchhoff, Bunsen's friend and colleague at Heidelberg, suggested he use a prism and slit to distinguish the colorful emissions with more assurance. Thirteen years younger than Bunsen, Kirchhoff had already established a reputation in the physics community by demonstrating that electrical impulses move at the same speed as light. Kirchhoff's generous advice led to a fruitful collaboration.

With the clear hot flame of Bunsen's improved burner, free of the deceptive contaminations that plagued earlier researchers, it soon became apparent that each chemical element did indeed produce a characteristic pattern of colored lines when heated and viewed through a spectroscope. Bunsen and Kirchhoff even came across spectra unrecorded in any laboratory, which led to their discovery of two silvery-white and highly reactive metals, the elements cesium (from the Latin for "bluish grey," the color of its most prominent lines when burned) and rubidium (from the Latin for "red," its distinctive spectral color).

A bit of serendipity may have turned Bunsen and Kirchhoff's attention to the stars. Using their spectroscope one evening to peer at a distant fire in the port city of Mannheim, visible across the Rhine plain from their laboratory window, the two researchers discerned the spectral signatures of barium and strontium in the roaring blaze. They were amazed at the ease with which they learned such intimate details about the fire from ten miles away. Some time later, while strolling through the wooded hills near Heidelberg with his young collaborator, Bunsen wondered if they could analyze the Sun's light in a comparable fashion. Other scientists of the time, such as George Stokes in Great Britain and Jean Foucault in France, had expressed similar suspicions. "But," Bunsen exclaimed, "people would think we were mad to dream of such a thing." For Kirchhoff, it was not madness but inspiration. In the voids of space, light knows no distance. Its electromagnetic vibrations can be well studied whether the light originates from a distance of one foot or a billion light-years.

"At the moment I am occupied by an investigation with Kirchhoff which does not allow us to sleep," Bunsen excitedly reported to a fellow chemist by November 1859. "Kirchhoff has made a totally unexpected discovery, inasmuch as he has found out the cause for the dark lines in the solar spectrum. . . . Hence the path is opened for the determination of the chemical composition of the Sun and the fixed stars with the same certainty that we can detect chloride . . . by our ordinary reagents."

Kirchhoff walked down that path with big, confident strides. Through a series of elegant experiments in his Heidelberg laboratory, he offered astronomers the resources with which to bring the Sun and stars directly into their observatories for examination. Within each stellar light wave could be found a star's history, composition, and temperature. Kirchhoff discovered that Fraunhofer's dark lines are generated as each element in the Sun's cooler outer atmosphere absorbs certain wavelengths from the Sun's inner hot glow. In some sense the cool layers rob the sunshine of selected light waves before it starts on its journey outward. The bright lines observed in laboratory flames are simply the reverse of this process—the elements emitting those very same wavelengths of light as they fiercely burn. The exact mechanism behind these absorptions and emissions had to await the twentieth century and the development of atomic theory, but that didn't prevent Kirchhoff from identifying a number of elements in the Sun. He did this by matching the pattern of *bright* lines emitted by an element heated in a laboratory with the *dark* lines observed in the solar spectrum.

The Sun was an immediate and popular source of study, as its great brightness made spectroscopic analysis relatively easy (although Kirchhoff still strained his eyes trying to locate and draw the many fine lines in the solar spectrum). By 1861 Kirchhoff had distinguished such familiar elements as sodium, iron, calcium, magnesium, chromium, barium, copper, zinc, and nickel in the Sun's atmosphere. The elements of Earth were clearly identical to the substances shining in the heavens. Aristotle's philosophic preference for an ethereal cosmos, separate and apart from earthly materials, was surely repudiated once and for all. The heavens and terra firma were united in a familial embrace through their shared kinship in the elements.

Almost immediately, long-held astronomical theories had to be changed in light of Kirchhoff's findings. As late as the 1850s, some wondered whether the Sun might be habitable—a dark, cool land beneath luminous clouds. The Scottish physicist David Brewster, inventor of the kaleidoscope, asked his readers in *More Worlds than One,* a popular work on life in the universe, to "approach the question of the habitability of the Sun, with the certain knowledge that the Sun is not a red-hot globe, but that its nucleus is a solid opaque mass receiving very little light and heat from its luminous atmosphere." But Kirchhoff's spectra would come to demonstrate that the Sun is a fiery, incandescent ball throughout.

Kirchhoff's discoveries generated great excitement in the astronomical community—at least in certain circles. Like children captivated by a newfound toy, the most venturesome astronomers began to utilize the spectroscope regularly. At the Florence Observatory in Italy, Giovanni Donati, the era's premier comet hunter (he discovered six), obtained the first spectrum of a comet as one heated up in its passage around the Sun. The three luminous bands that he spied—yellow, green, and blue—provided proof that comets were burning brightly as they neared the Sun and not simply reflecting sunlight, as most astronomers had believed.

Two years earlier, Donati had initiated the first extensive investigation of stellar spectra, observing and publishing the spectra of fifteen stars in 1862. In Rome, Father Angelo Secchi, hearing of this news, promptly attached a spectroscope, luckily on hand from a visiting French astronomer, to his telescope. "[I want] to see if the composition of the stars is as varied as the stars are innumerable," announced Secchi at the start of his enterprise. He was already an early pioneer in astronomical photography, having taken daguerrotypes of the Sun during a solar eclipse in 1851, as well as photographing every nook and cranny of the Moon. Secchi first applied the term *canali* (Italian for "channels" or "grooves") to dark, linear markings he observed on Mars in 1859; when the term was later adopted by Mars observer Giovanni Schiaparelli, it fueled the misconception that water-filled canals, engineered by intelligent beings, might be crisscrossing the red planet.

Secchi was born in 1818 in the northern Italian town of Reggio. Trained for the priesthood, he also excelled in physics and mathematics. When his religious order, the Jesuits, was banished from Rome during anticlerical upheavals in 1848, Secchi continued his scientific pursuits, first in England and then in the United States. After studying and teaching astronomy at Georgetown University in Washington, D.C., the Jesuit priest was called back to Italy to become director of the Roman College Observatory, which he completely refitted for the "new astronomy." This was quite a bold decision at the time; many purists believed that spectroscopes diverted astronomy from its true purpose. "Someone has even said that at the College we do not cultivate astronomical science at all, but physics instead," noted Secchi on this prejudice. It is ironic that the Vatican, the institution that some 250 years earlier had persecuted Galileo, the father of telescopic astronomy, liberally financed Secchi in his trailblazing endeavors. While the Collegio Romano was in papal hands there was no lack of funds for the observatory.

Secchi's gamble paid off handsomely. Practitioners of the new astronomy would lead observers into rich and fertile territories. The novel art of spectroscopy eventually allowed astronomers to discern the evolution of stars, to reveal the source of stellar power, and to unmask a vast and wondrous universe populated by billions of galaxies speeding away from one another at tremendous velocities, some of the farthest galaxies burning with the brilliance of trillions of stars.

But I've gotten ahead of my story. All these cosmos-shaking discoveries would, of course, emerge much later. In spectroscopy, as in many new fields of science, classification was the first order of business, a means of wrenching order out of chaos. The long and tedious job of identifying and differentiating various species within the plant and animal kingdom, carried out over the centuries by legions of biologists, ultimately had allowed Charles Darwin, himself a tenacious collector of plants and animals, to recognize the intricate workings of biological evolution. Similarly, just a few years after the 1859 publication of Darwin's *Origin of Species,* Secchi took some of the first tentative steps toward classifying the stars, an approach that would eventually allow astronomers to develop their own evolutionary picture of stellar bodies. While stars were vast in number, "their spectra," wrote the learned priest, "can be reduced to a few well-defined and distinct forms which, for the sake of brevity, we shall call *types*."

Patiently examining many hundreds of stars over several years, Secchi had noticed by 1868 that certain spectral patterns repeated over and over, four types in all. At one point he wondered whether these separate categories might represent differences in temperature. There were the brilliant blue stars and white stars, such as Sirius, the Dog Star, with four strong dark lines indicative of hydrogen gas. Another group included predominantly yellow stars, similar to the Sun, with spectra distinguished by very fine and numerous lines. A third type of spectrum emanated from the brilliant orange and reddish stars, such as Betelgeuse and Antares. The fourth and last spectral category comprised very faint, deep-red stars. (They were so faint that Secchi had to look at five hundred stars before spotting his first one.) In his lifetime, Secchi classified some four thousand stars. Here were astronomy's first clues about the way in which stars are born, age, and slowly die. Astronomers began to ask whether there was an evolutionary connection between the bright white stars and the dim red ones. One early (and mistaken) guess was that the hot blue-white stars, newly formed out of a gaseous nebula and in the heyday of their youth, moved on to a middle-aged yellow and lastly a cool, dark crimson in the twilight of their lives. But much more work had to be done before the true story of these stellar families could emerge.

With great prescience, Secchi advised his fellow astronomers to abandon their capital cities, "where the atmosphere, besides its denseness, is cluttered up with a thousand dirty things and absorbing vapors." Thus would begin astronomy's exodus to the isolated mountaintop, which forms our vision of the typical astronomical workplace. By the 1880s, the use of photography greatly advanced the power of spectroscopy, enabling astronomers to gather light far better than the human eye and to make precise measurements off photographic plates at their leisure, after exposures were complete. The combination of spectroscopy and photography changed the face of astronomy and led to the spectacular visions of the coming decades, when the true nature of the Milky Way and its place in the universe would be established.

THE MAN FROM UPPER TULSE HILL

Spectroscopy was a technique particularly favored by amateur astronomers, such as William Huggins, who lacked the formal mathematical training of a classical astronomer. Born in 1824, the only surviving child of a London textile dealer and linen draper, Huggins was a precocious boy. At the age of six, he built an electrical device and proceeded to give himself a jolt as soon as he turned it on. "I've had a shock, I've had a shock!" he shouted ecstatically as he ran through the house.

Huggins's frail health, brought on by an attack of smallpox at the age of fourteen, led to his being educated largely at home by private tutors. But he still managed to fabricate a number of apparatuses and carry out experiments in chemistry, optics, physics, and photography. Science became his passion. He was skillful in the use of a microscope, having received one as a gift from his parents, and at eighteen he paid the princely sum of fifteen pounds sterling for his first telescope, although the smoky air of London made observing difficult.

His father weakened by illness, Huggins was forced to abandon his dream of attending Cambridge University, and at eighteen he took over the family business. But all his spare time was devoted to his scientific hobbies. By the age of thirty he finally sold the mercery firm in order to pursue astronomy full-time. Not wealthy but comfortable enough to sustain a simple, independent life-style, Huggins had no professional credentials in astronomy other than membership in the Royal Astronomical Society. Freed from his business obligations, he moved with his parents to a small, two-story brick home in Upper Tulse Hill, now a part of greater London but then a more rural locale situated south of the city. The southwest winds prevalent in that area kept the sky relatively clear of city smogs. His first observatory was rather crude. The telescope, mounted on a wooden stand with wheels, was kept in the rear garden and covered with a mackintosh when not in use. Its aperture was five inches wide, a respectable size at the time. In 1856 Huggins attached a raised dome, twelve feet in diameter, to his home and installed an eight-inch refractor, whose objective lens was constructed by the American Alvan Clark, a portrait painter who earned additional fame as a skilled lens maker.

Within a few years the experiments of Kirchhoff and Bunsen began to arouse much interest in intellectual circles, and Huggins was eager to apply the results, especially after attending a soiree held by the Pharmaceutical Society in London where a number of spectroscopes were on display. "A feeling as of inspiration seized me," recalled Huggins. "I felt as if I had it now in my power to lift a veil that had never before been lifted: as if a key had been put into my hands which would unlock a door which had been regarded as forever closed to man." Dissatisfied with the routine nature of classical astronomy, with its stress on ultraprecise measurements of stellar magnitudes and motions, Huggins compared Kirchhoff's interpretation of the Fraunhofer lines to "coming upon a spring of water in a dry and thirsty land. Here at last presented itself the very order of work for which in an indefinite way I was looking—namely to extend his novel methods of research upon the Sun to the other heavenly bodies." He would drink greedily.

At the Pharmaceutical Society gathering, Huggins cornered W. Allen

William Huggins (1824–1910), pioneering spectroscopist.
Mary Lea Shane Archives of Lick Observatory

Miller, professor of chemistry at King's College in London. A trained laboratory spectroscopist, Miller had noted, even before Kirchhoff's investigations, that various metals emitted specific colors when heated by electric currents. On an impulse, Huggins invited Miller to help him design an apparatus to discern the composition of the stars.

The technical problems were immense. Huggins was quite aware that the light arriving at a telescope from a bright star, like Vega, is less than a billionth of the radiation received from the Sun. Put through a prism, this starlight diminishes in brightness even more. Huggins went so far as to fill a hollow prism with a very dense bisulphide of carbon solution, in order to spread out the spectrum and better see the spectral lines. Unfortunately the prism sometimes leaked, creating a terrible stench in his observatory. "To this day," Huggins commented in his old age, "the pungent odor reminds me of star spectra!"

Then there was the ever-shimmering atmosphere, which played havoc with those spending long nights peering intently at faint stellar spectra. "This source of difficulty presses very heavily upon observers," Huggins reported in one of his earliest papers. "On any but the finest nights the numerous and closely approximated fine lines of the stellar spectra are seen so fitfully that no observations of value can be made."

With Miller's assistance and consultation, Huggins built an elaborate contraption that allowed him to generate the spectrum of a chemical element right there in his observatory and simultaneously juxtapose it over the stellar spectrum he was seeing through his telescope. Various metals were heated by the spark of a large induction coil, powered by batteries that had to be set outside one of the windows because of the noxious fumes they gave off. Huggins's observatory took on the appearance of a commercial laboratory. Shelves with Bunsen burners, vacuum tubes, and bottles of chemicals lined its walls. Huggins later added photographic equipment, making his workplace even more jam-packed.

The 1860s were banner years for spectroscopy, which was fast becoming a global pursuit. Huggins in Great Britain, Secchi in Italy, Lewis Rutherfurd in the United States, and Hermann Vogel in Germany were all making spectral observations. Through this work astronomers came to recognize that the Sun, stars, and Earth shared the same elemental building blocks. Secchi and Vogel surveyed as many stars as possible, grouping them into classes. Huggins, on the other hand, spent more time closely examining selected stars. With this strategy he accomplished just what he had set out to do: He demonstrated, with great care and inspired ingenuity, that the elements Kirchhoff found in the Sun also dwelled in the distant stars. "The chemistry of the solar system was shown to prevail wherever a star twinkles," concluded Huggins. By comparing the celestial spectra with his terrestrial standards, this self-taught astronomer discovered such elements as hydrogen, iron, sodium, calcium, and magnesium in the stars. Miller bowed out of the collaboration in 1864 because of an increased work load at King's College, but Huggins continued on his own, applying his keen insight and newfound skills to other celestial problems, such as the true nature of the nebulae.

A host of celebrated observers had long been puzzled by nebulae. In the 1780s William Herschel, a German musician-turned-observer who became the private astronomer to England's King George III, uncovered more than two thousand of these mysterious objects in his searches. With his devoted sister and helpmate, Caroline, by his side, Herschel scanned the heavens with his homemade twenty-foot-long telescope and dictated brief descriptions of the nebulae he spotted. Some appeared round; others were cigar-shaped, disklike, or amorphous blobs. By the time Huggins had taken up astronomy, nearly a century later, between five thousand and six thousand of these objects had been cataloged. Looking through the lens of the standard nineteenth-century telescope, astronomers described a typical nebula as a feebly shining, cloudlike patch or spot (larger and more powerful telescopes were beginning to discern stars in some of the patches). Are they "dense swarms of suns melted into one mass by their enormous distance?" posed Huggins. Or were they "chaotic masses of the primordial material of the universe?" he went on to ask. The evidence was terribly inconclusive. Each interpretation had its supporters.

Huggins was sure that a spectroscope could shed some light on the mystery, although he described the task as seeming almost hopeless, given a nebula's pale illumination. He tried anyway. On the evening of August 29, 1864, Huggins aimed his telescope at a roundish nebula located in the Draco constellation. He felt "excited suspense, mingled with a degree of awe" as he put his eye to the spectroscope. Huggins wasn't really sure what he would find, but the spectrum he beheld was still a surprise. "A single bright line only!" he reported.

At first I suspected some displacement of the prism, and that I was looking at a reflection of the illuminated slit. . . . This thought was scarcely more than momentary; then the true interpretation flashed upon me. . . . The riddle of the nebulae was solved. The answer which had come to us in the light itself, read: Not an aggregation of stars, but a luminous gas.

Instead of the typical spectrum of a star—a continuous band of color broken at intervals by dark lines—he saw distinct bands of bluish-green, three in all eventually, signifying that the light source was a simple, glowing gas, which he figured was composed of hydrogen and nitrogen. He obtained similar results when looking at the Dumbbell Nebula and the Great Nebula situated in the Sword of Orion. Here was "a fiery mist," said Huggins, "out of which the heavens had been slowly fashioned."

The riddle of the nebulae was only partially solved, however. Huggins went on to examine some sixty nebulae. One-third were clearly composed of gas. Today we know that some of these clouds, called planetary nebulae, are the billowing sheets of luminous gas gradually shed off dying stars. Huggins's target in Draco was a planetary nebula. Other gaseous nebulae mark the location of stellar nurseries where huge collections of dust and gas condense over tens of millions of years to give birth to hot, new stars in a range of sizes—some as small as a twelfth the mass of our Sun, others up to sixty times more massive.

But the remaining nebulae examined by Huggins did display starlike spectra. The spectroscope, therefore, offered the means to distinguish between clusters of stars and clouds of gas, when a telescope alone was not sufficient to denote the difference. Some of these nebulae would turn out to be separate, far-off galaxies, objects not yet recognized in Huggins's day. For nineteenth-century astronomers, our home galaxy, the Milky Way, still defined the boundaries of the visible universe.

"By each discovery the vision of the world has become more glorious, the wonder of it more amazing," said Huggins of his endeavors. Astronomy's eyesight was extended once again, as observers eagerly examined the chemical footprints scattered throughout the cosmos. Within a few short years of Kirchhoff's analysis of the intriguing dark lines lurking within sunlight, spectroscopy provided the means to translate a host of celestial codes, once thought unbreakable by science's ingenuity.

Huggins scrutinized everything possible with his spectroscope, much the way Galileo, two and a half centuries earlier, had mined all the celestial riches available through his telescope. Huggins analyzed several comets, whose journeys past the Earth were visible from Tulse Hill. In 1866 the sudden appearance of a nova, now known to be an explosion on the surface of a star, captured his spectroscopic attention, too. Along the way, classical astronomers began to concede that there might be some practical uses for those curious spectroscopes after all, such as monitoring a star's motion in the "line of sight" (that is, either toward or away from the Earth).

In the 1840s the Austrian physicist Christian Doppler had surmised that the frequency of a wave, such as the tone of a sound wave or the color of a light wave, would be altered whenever the source of the wave moved. We've all heard the pitch of a siren rise to a higher tone as an ambulance races toward us. This is the very effect that Doppler spoke of: The sound waves emitted by the screeching siren crowd together as they approach us, shortening their length and likewise raising the pitch detected by our ears. Conversely, as the ambulance pulls away, the sound waves stretch out, producing a lower pitch. In an analogous fashion, a light wave's length is shortened (gets "bluer") when the source of the light approaches, and it is lengthened (gets "redder") when the source moves away. More specifically, astronomers expected to see the bright and dark lines in celestial spectra shift their well-noted laboratory positions toward the blue or red ends. Blueshifts and redshifts are the speedometers of the universe. Guided by Doppler's principle, Huggins valiantly tried to confirm that a star's motion, as well as its composition, could be read from its spectral bands.

As soon as he installed a more powerful spectroscope in his observatory, Huggins closely examined the spectrum of Sirius, the brightest star in the northern sky. After many torturous nights of observation, he announced that the star's dark lines did appear to be shifted by an ever-so-tiny amount. He believed the lines were displaced toward the red end of the spectrum, indicating that the brilliant white star was racing away from the solar system. Actually, Sirius is approaching the Earth at a velocity of about 18,000 miles per hour. Since Huggins worked by eye alone, always fighting that shimmering sky, his pioneering velocity measurements were notoriously undependable. Yet he did correctly establish that the bright stars Arcturus, Vega, and Deneb are speeding toward us, while Betelgeuse, Rigel, and Castor retreat. The introduction of photography later made these measurements much more reliable. Tracking spectral shifts eventually allowed astronomers, several decades later, to behold an entire universe expanding, with the galaxies flying away from one another like sesame seeds in an expanding loaf of cosmic bread. From such a vision, and with Einstein's theory of general relativity in hand, would evolve the popular theory of the universe originating from a big bang.

In 1875 Huggins, fifty-one years a bachelor, married Margaret Murray of Dublin, a match, according to Margaret, that rivaled "the romantic marriage of the Browning order, quite as ideally happy for thirty-five years." Huggins would wryly note that he had "secured an able and enthusiastic assistant." Margaret was twenty-five years old on the day of her wedding, less than half Huggins's age.

A picture of Huggins as an elderly man expertly captures his shy and gentle personality. A thatch of white hair sweeps back off a high forehead. Small, close-set eyes, a bulbous nose, and full beard lend an air of Santa Claus to his appearance. He sits by his telescope, one hand placed lovingly upon the instrument. Margaret displays a similar demeanor in a photographic portrait taken in her senior years. Her thick white hair, which wouldn't stay in place, was cut short at a time when women did not dare cut their tresses. In the photo she smiles a Mona Lisa smile, and thoughtful, light-colored eyes look directly into the camera lens. She was described by friends as loving, "with the most wonderful warmth, tenderness, and faithfulness; but there was no sentimentality in her and no weakness."

Daughter of a barrister, Margaret had pursued astronomy as a hobby since childhood and had even built her own spectroscope. Having no children, she worked with her husband in a very productive partnership, shared only by their dog, Kepler.[1] She was particularly helpful in photographing spectra, a venture Huggins pursued more rigorously right after his marriage. "Our exposures on each star had to be very long. I have, I think, worked on one for about three hours," Margaret wrote on their collaboration. Continuing to describe her methods, she noted:

> I can go and stand well at good heights on ladders and twist well. (Astronomers need universal joints and vertebrae of india rubber.) In our star work, having got my star into good position, I look at it, say, for three seconds, then close my eyes, say, for six or seven seconds, then

---

[1] Kepler was a pet noted for, I might add, his astute mathematical abilities. With a piece of cake in his hand as enticement, Huggins would often ask the dog to solve various arithmetic problems, such as the square root of 16, or $(6 + 12 - 3) \div 5$, to which the dog would bark out his solutions. Suspiciously, these calculations always seemed to result in the answer 3 or 4.

look again for three seconds. By looking at flashes in this way I rapidly judge as to whether the star has been kept where it should be by certain means, and if not, rapidly adjust.

Mrs. Huggins was also adept at fixing electrodes, pounding chemicals, and cleaning off the observatory steam engine. "I am a capital scientific housemaid," she boasted. If the weather was bad, Huggins would take delight in passing the time at Tulse Hill playing his violin, a Stradivarius, accompanied by his wife on the piano. As the data concerning the elements shared by the Earth and stars piled up, astronomers couldn't help but begin to speculate on the implications of a cosmos that displayed a universal composition. "It is remarkable that the elements most widely diffused through the host of stars are some of those most closely connected with the living organisms of our globe, including hydrogen, sodium, magnesium, and iron," noted Huggins. "May it not be that, at least, the brighter stars are like our sun, the upholding and energizing centres of systems of worlds, adapted to be the abode of living beings?" This wasn't the first time that scientists wondered about life on other worlds, but now they could do more than weave theoretical fantasies.

Huggins also detected a bevy of unknown lines in his celestial spectra, which he boldly suggested might indicate the presence of matter not yet "unearthed from its hiding place in terrestrial rocks by the cunning of the chemist." Sixty-five elements were known in Huggins's day. "It would be assumption," he declared, "to suppose that the 65 so-called elements constitute in its entirety the primary material of the universe. Doubtless in the spectra of the stars the chemist is introduced to many new elements—would that it were possible for him to recognize and to isolate them!" Certain mysterious lines showed up frequently, located in the green band of the visible spectrum. These are the same emissions that give certain nebulae, such as that of Orion, a ghostly greenish glow. A new element, appropriately dubbed "nebulium," was postulated as the source of this pale green light.

The Hugginses, though, never learned that nebulium was not a new element. Huggins died in 1910 at the age of eighty-six, the recipient of every honor that his country could possibly bestow; Margaret, his wife and longtime collaborator, died five years later. Not until 1927 did laboratory scientists learn that the green-tinged radiation, first spied by Huggins through his spectroscope, is emitted by oxygen atoms that are highly charged electrically.

One time—and one time only—an element was encountered in the heavens before its detection on Earth. The discoverer was Joseph Norman Lockyer. A clerk in the English civil service, Lockyer edited army regulations for the War Office. But, just like Huggins, he spent all his leisure hours on astronomical pursuits. While Huggins looked to the stars, Lockyer, also influenced and inspired by Kirchhoff and Bunsen's discoveries, became fascinated with the Sun. His work as an amateur in studying sunspots and solar prominences, huge streamers of flaming gas that stretch far above the Sun's surface, was so renowned that he eventually moved into scientific work full-time. Elected to England's Royal Society in 1869 at the age of thirty-three, he founded the prestigious scientific journal *Nature* that same year and would serve as its editor until his death in 1920. In 1885 he was appointed director of a new solar observatory established at what is now Imperial College in London.

Early in his amateur career, while using a spectroscope to analyze the

J. Norman Lockyer (1836–1920), discovered helium in Sun.
Mary Lea Shane Archives of Lick Observatory

brilliant prominences shooting off the Sun, Lockyer came across a bright orange-yellow emission radiating from the solar flames. Other observers in 1868, most notably the French astronomer Pierre Janssen, also glimpsed this spectral line during a solar eclipse. At first mistaken for the signature of sodium, this prominent yellow line did not match the spectrum of any known substance. Lockyer, a flamboyant man unafraid to grandly speculate, decided the emission was generated by a gas unknown on Earth. He called it helium, after *helios*, the Greek word for "sun." But this idea faced great resistance. Even Lockyer's collaborator, chemist Edward Frankland, opposed the explanation. In the new science of spectroscopy, claims of spotting new substances (there was also talk of "coronium" and "geocoronium") were made all too easily. For a quarter of a century, helium remained a mere hypothetical gas.

Lockyer was vindicated in 1895. Having already discovered the element argon, Scottish chemist William Ramsay was in search of similar inert gases to add to the periodic table. In the course of his experiments he extracted an unknown gas from the mineral cleveite, a variety of uranium ore. Heated in a tube, Ramsay's mystery gas gave off the very same yellow rays observed in the solar prominences. At a dinner in his honor, Ramsay was toasted for "having run helium to Earth." And for his insight, Lockyer was rewarded with a knighthood. Where Huggins's nebulium eventually vanished as a separate element, Lockyer's helium steadfastly remained—in fact, astronomers would later learn that this newfound element is one of the most prominent materials in the universe.

The early spectroscopists were finding such a vast array of spectral features, a jumbled mix of thin and broad lines, that the stellar spectra came to resemble the universal bar codes now found on many commercial products. Iron alone can generate hundreds of lines. Such intricacy lent support to the idea, then contemplated by some scientists, that atoms were far more complex than originally visualized. It was thought that atoms, rather than being simple, indivisible objects, might possess some kind of internal structure, which was revealing itself in the elaborate spectral patterns. This thinking was quite radical for its day, considering that many still thought of atoms as no more than convenient bookkeeping devices to help explain chemical properties and reactions.

In the early 1880s, Lockyer, seeing that the spectrum of an element changed somewhat when the substance was strongly heated by an electric arc, imagined the element's atoms breaking down into smaller constituents at high temperatures. He thought that the atoms of the various elements differed only in the way the atomic "bits and pieces" were grouped. He was vaguely anticipating the later realization, fully reached in the twentieth century, that each atom consists of a tiny core of protons and neutrons surrounded by a cloud of electrons, tiny particles that can be ejected from the atom at extremely high temperatures. Lockyer was one of the first to recognize that the science of the very big—light waves emanating from the universe at large—offered clues on the nature of the very small, the ultimate structure of matter. A couple of decades had to pass, though, before laboratory evidence at last convinced scientists that subatomic particles were bona fide entities. Lockyer's speculation was a premature volley in the atomic revolution to come.

Lockyer and Huggins, although quite different in temperament and often at loggerheads professionally, were splendid examples of the typical pioneering astrophysicist of the late nineteenth century, at least in Great Britain and the United States. Often self-educated in astronomy, they were the researchers willing to dirty their hands handling packs of chemicals, photographic plates, and leaky batteries. Their hard work yielded sizable returns. The early spectroscopists could proudly boast of several notable discoveries: the existence of gaseous clouds in space, the detection of stellar motions in the line of sight, and proof that the Earth, Sun, and stars shared the very same chemical ingredients. Despite these early successes, though, traditionalists continued to treat the field of astrophysics like some poor relation. These conservative critics were not being entirely unfair. In truth, the spectroscopic data was accumulating far faster than scientists could interpret it; atomic physics, the backbone of true spectroscopic understanding, was years away. Stellar astronomers in the nineteenth century still thought it best to place their emphasis on positions and motions, on parallaxes and magnitudes.

"God forbid that astronomy should be carried away by a fascination with novelty and diverge from [its] essential basis, which has been sanctified for centuries, and even millennia," the Russian astronomer Otto Wilhelm von Struve stridently pronounced in 1886. Struve needn't have worried. In the last decades of the nineteenth century, only 5 percent of the research articles published in astronomy involved astrophysics. Even Huggins at one point sounded almost apologetic for choosing a field that could not help humanity in some practical way. "The new astronomy," he said, "unlike the old astronomy to which we are indebted for skill in the navigation of the seas, the calculation of the tides, and the daily regulation of time, can lay no claim to afford us material help in the routine of daily life."

CRACKING THE SPECTRAL CODE

Within decades, despite the misgivings of the old guard, the balance of astronomical research did shift to astrophysics. German observatories, especially, took the lead in advancing spectroscopic techniques. The movement toward astrophysics also took particular hold in the United States. Here was a scientific enterprise well suited to a relatively new nation, an up-and-coming country whose astronomers were ardently trying to match the sterling reputations of the long-established European observatories. Astrophysics was a means of catching up—mining the frontier and possibly acquiring unexpected bounties. The *Astrophysical Journal,* which would become the most influential publication devoted to astrophysics, was established during the 1890s in America. At about the same time, private donations led to the creation of three major U.S. observatories committed to astrophysics: in 1876 the Lick Observatory on Mount Hamilton near San Jose, California; in 1897 the Yerkes Observatory in Wisconsin, just north of Chicago; and in 1904 Mount Wilson in southern California, an observatory later described as "the center of gravity of the astronomical world." In fact, both Mount Wilson, from which distant galaxies and an expanding universe would be discovered, and Yerkes were among the first astronomical observatories to have physical laboratories attached to their complexes for establishing spectral-line standards that could be used in analyzing celestial spectra. Such work helped unmask Huggins's notorious nebulium as a bogus element.

In the closing decades of the nineteenth century it was deemed irrefutable that the light waves coursing through the heavens offered important information on the composition of the stars. The early spectroscopists, particularly Huggins, plainly demonstrated that the spectral lines represented chemical elements very familiar to Earth's inhabitants. What lay ahead was the formidable task of classifying the varied spectra, a labor that would at last allow astronomers to make sense of the wide variety of stars. How, exactly, did stars differ in composition, temperature, size, and mass? astronomers began asking. Why did they display such different brightnesses?

Secchi offered a workable start with his system of stellar types, and other astronomers jumped in with their own schemes. By the turn of the century, twenty-three methods for classifying stars had been devised. To bring some order out of this chaos, astronomers worldwide tentatively agreed in 1913 to adopt a system that had originated at the Harvard College Observatory in Cambridge, Massachusetts—recognition of America's growing influence in astronomy and the important role that astrophysics could play in unraveling stellar secrets. At least one factor greatly contributed to the selection of Harvard's system: Astronomers there had initiated a survey of the heavens like no other study before it. They were not just examining the spectra of a few dozen or a few hundred stars; they were strip-mining the celestial sky. They eventually generated a mammoth catalogue, nine volumes in all, that incorporated the spectra of hundreds of thousands of stars in the northern and southern skies.

This impressive effort began as a memorial to an innovative spectroscopist. Henry Draper, a wealthy New York doctor who had built his own private observatory near the Hudson River, took the first successful photograph of the spectrum of a star, the prominent summertime Vega, in 1872. Draper's early death a decade later at the age of forty-five cut short these pioneering efforts. His widow, Mary Anna Draper, anxious for her husband's work to continue, established the Henry Draper Memorial at Harvard to support a program in stellar spectroscopy. Physicist Edward C. Pickering, director of the Harvard College Observatory from 1877 to 1919 and an eminent spectroscopist in his own right, had recognized the value of astrophysics early on. He introduced it at Harvard even though, like Secchi in Italy, he had to fight the snide remarks and critical attacks that he was pursuing dubious physics rather than high-quality astronomy.

With Draper's funding in hand, Pickering resolved to photograph and classify the spectra of all the bright northern stars. Vogel in Germany had already published a spectral catalogue listing some four thousand stars, but it represented nearly twenty years of work. Pickering was after faster results. To accomplish this, he adapted a method of spectroscopy originally used by Fraunhofer and Secchi. Pickering placed a thin, specially ground prism in front of the telescope's objective lens. In this way every star in the telescope's sight could be photographed directly as a spectral smear, the identifying lines readily accessible for examination. The English astronomer R. L. Waterfield remarked that it was just like America, in its fascination with mass production, to step "in with a method for photographing stellar spectra wholesale."

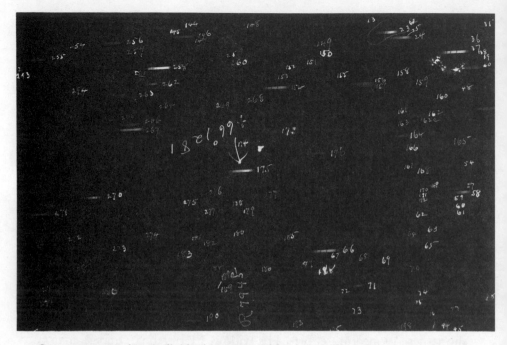

Stars appear as tiny, individual spectra in this typical plate of the Draper survey. *Harvard College Observatory*

Each night's collection of photographs was carried to a darkroom, where they were developed, copied, and enlarged on glass. Each pane of glass—about the size of a standard business letter, eight inches by ten inches—contained the spectra of all the hundreds of stars in the telescope's view. Anyone examining a plate, which is actually a photographic negative, sees what looks like a vast collection of dark, tiny tire tracks, each less than half an inch long, across a field of white. Each tire track is a separate stellar spectrum. Eventually a special building, made entirely of brick for protection against fire, was erected on the Harvard observatory grounds to house this extraordinary collection of photographic plates.

A genius at managing large projects, Pickering specifically hired women to classify—swiftly, accurately, and cheaply—the myriad spectra generated during the course of the survey. Since male scientists at this time generally assumed that their female colleagues were better at tedious detail work than at creative thinking, women educated in astronomy were not allowed to do much else in their chosen profession. No wonder, then, that these workers were dubbed "Pickering's harem." Native Scotswoman Williamina Fleming, Pickering's former housekeeper, headed the corps of

Williamina Fleming (standing) directs her "computers" while Harvard Observatory director Edward Pickering looks on. Antonia Maury is seated in the rear on the left.
Harvard College Observatory

women. Like assembly line workers in an information factory, these dedicated "computers," as they were called, worked with incredible patience and unflagging industry as they numbered each star on a given plate, determined the star's exact position on the sky, and assigned it a spectral class. Much as Secchi had done, the women tagged each star based on the overall appearance of its spectrum. By 1890, 10,351 stars were classified.[2]

That same year, Harvard established an observatory in the mountains of Peru, and the Draper spectral catalogue was extended and revised to include stars from the southern hemisphere. "The revelations of these early photographs of stellar spectra were truly remarkable," said computer Annie Jump Cannon. "It was almost as if the distant stars had really

[2] While Pickering did offer women a unique employment opportunity, he was very much aware of the financial advantage in hiring inexpensive labor. In his observatory's 1898 annual report, he specifically mentioned that the women he hired were "capable of doing as much good routine work as astronomers who would receive much larger salaries. Three or four times as many assistants can thus be employed and the work done correspondingly increased for a given expenditure." A computer's pay ranged from 25 cents to 35 cents per hour for a six-day work week that averaged seven hours a day.

acquired speech, and were able to tell of their constitution and physical condition." Indeed, the perceptive computers occasionally spotted the signs of explosions on stars.

Cannon signed onto the Draper project in 1896. The daughter of a Quaker-educated woman and a Delaware shipbuilder, she had studied physics and astronomy at both Wellesley College and Radcliffe in Massachusetts. As a child, Cannon, along with her mother, observed the skies from a makeshift observatory in the attic of their home. She was a cheerful woman who sported both a hearty laugh and fashionable apparel. Her skill at classifying stars was legendary. It was said that she could separate the rogue from the good elephant, or the grizzly from the brown bear, at a glance of the photographic plate. It was Cannon who ultimately established the stellar classification scheme that is still used today throughout the world.

The Draper classification had started out as a simple lettering system, with stars labeled as A, B, C, and so forth, up to the letter Q. It largely extended Secchi's original four types into more detailed classes. But over the years stellar groups were added, combined, deleted, and shuffled around. After much jockeying, Cannon settled on the stellar sequence O, B, A, F, G, K, and M, which organized the stars by color. Additional

Annie Jump Cannon (1863–1941) peruses one of her plates.
Harvard College Observatory

categories—the relatively rare red R, N, and S stars—were added in later years. (Several generations of astronomy students have since remembered this lineup by the [decidedly unliberated] refrain, "Oh, Be A Fine Girl, Kiss Me. Right Now, Smack.")[3]

Some early spectroscopists had initially wondered if the various spectral types might be the result of differing mixes of stellar matter in space. Some stars seemed to harbor more iron, for instance; others, more helium. But the work at Harvard tended to support the growing notion that the various spectra reflected distinct physical differences, rather than chemical differences, between the stars. The Draper classification, as it evolved over the years, was found to closely correspond to a star's surface temperature, as Secchi first ventured. The sequence commenced with the blue-white and intensely hot O stars and worked its way down the temperature scale, through yellow and orange, to the cool and dim reddish M stars.

Cannon had no hand in this interpretation. The consummate classifier and observer, whose keen eye could categorize the data crossing her desk in a flash, she never attempted (or desired) to postulate a theory that could account for her identifications. She figured her data should stand on their own, no matter what theory came along. Another computer, Antonia Maury, the niece of Henry Draper and a stern individualist, held the opposite opinion. She was Cannon's complete opposite in both dress and demeanor as well. Unconcerned with her appearance, she would sometimes show up at the office in mismatched stockings. A recent graduate of Vassar College, where she studied chemistry and mathematics, Maury had a passion for learning and was determined to understand the myriad spectra placed before her.

During a nine-year, on-again/off-again attachment to Pickering's grand venture, Maury dug ever deeper into the spectral data. In the course of an assignment to study 681 bright northern stars in more detail, she noticed that the spectra of two stars could be perfectly identical, except that the widths of the lines differed. One might have broad lines; the other, very sharp, narrow features. She suggested that this disparity

---

[3] Harvard professor Owen Gingerich has run a yearly contest in his introductory astronomy course to come up with new versions of the refrain. Among the past entries: Oh Bring Another Fully Grown Kangaroo, My Recipe Needs Some; Oh Brutal And Fearsome Gorilla, Kill My Roommate Next Saturday; Organs Blaring And Fugues Galore, Kepler's Music Reads Nature's Score; and Out Beyond Andromeda, Fiery Gases Kindle Many Red New Stars.

could be due to a star's evolution, and she developed her own elaborate classification scheme, complete with twenty-two groups and three subdivisions, to incorporate this new information. It was Maury who first arranged her stars by descending temperature, and Cannon followed suit.

Other spectroscopists did not just disagree with Maury's complex approach, they bitterly opposed it. They considered her rather sophisticated system to be superfluous. "If one believed that every barely perceptible difference in a stellar spectrum justifies setting up a new spectral class, then one would do better to put every star into a class of its own," complained one astronomer.

Pickering officially ignored Maury's work. For one, Cannon's classification scheme was far simpler and more efficient; moreover, Pickering feared Maury had stretched her evidence a bit. But a personality clash may also have contributed to his antipathy. The Harvard Observatory director preferred Cannon, amiable and lightning-fast in her work, to the aloof and ponderously methodical Maury, who chafed under Pickering's strict routine and eventually left Harvard for a while to teach.

Within a decade, however, Maury received a measure of support from overseas. Ejnar Hertzsprung, then a little-known Danish chemist and astronomer, was sparked by Maury's insights and was determined to find out the meaning behind the differing spectral-line widths she noticed. Carrying out during the early 1900s a detailed analysis of stellar data, Hertzsprung came to see that the red stars could be divided into two distinctly separate groups: the very luminous red stars, which displayed Maury's dark, narrow lines, and the very dim red stars, whose line widths were broader. There didn't seem to be any middle ground. Maury's classification scheme served as a marvelous filter for distinguishing these intrinsically bright and faint red stars.

As his researches continued over the years, Hertzsprung would begin to recognize a direct connection, superbly elegant, between a star's absolute brightness (the luminosity you would observe if you were essentially right near the star) and its color. Put simply, the bluer the star, the more luminous it was. He found that the blue-white stars, the O stars, were the most brilliant of all. The other stellar types smoothly diminished in brightness as you proceeded down Cannon's spectral lineup: O B A F G K M. Stars got progressively dimmer going from the O and B stars to the A, F, G, and K stars. At the very end of this sequence, as if depleted by the effort, were the faint red M stars. When Hertzsprung arranged the stellar types on a graph, most stars fell somewhere along this uninterrupted path, from

Danish astronomer Ejnar Hertzsprung (1873–1967).
*Photograph courtesy of Dorritt Hoffleit, Yale University
Observatory*

bright to dim. There was only one spoiler: The red stars of great luminosity, a rarer species, stood alone and isolated in a corner of the chart.

Even before he had discovered this intriguing relationship, Hertzsprung had published his initial findings on bright and faint red stars in a minor German journal for scientific photography. Needless to say, his analysis languished in obscurity. He did try to spread the news by letter. Hertzsprung wrote Pickering, more than once, hoping to convince him that Maury's work was a linchpin in his discovery. To neglect Maury's new subdivisions, Hertzsprung pleaded in one 1908 missive, "is nearly the same thing as if the zoologist, who has detected the deciding differences between a whale and a fish, would continue in classifying them together." The Harvard director, still skeptical that Maury could have detected any fine details in her spectra, did not budge.

Pickering unknowingly advanced Hertzsprung's cause nonetheless. Henry Norris Russell, who in a few years would be appointed director of the prestigious Princeton University Observatory, was then involved in an intricate observing program to determine the parallax of stars, and he needed pictures of specific stellar spectra taken. Pickering generously offered Harvard's services. Upon receiving the data in 1909, and unaware of Hertzsprung's work at first, Russell quickly recognized the same two categories of red stars, the bright and the faint, that Hertzsprung had classified. The Princeton investigator distinguished the whale from the fish. In correspondence with Pickering, Russell began to call these two types of red stars the "giants" and the "dwarfs," respectively. And, like his Danish counterpart, he too came to behold that marvelous link between a star's brightness and its spectral type.

Each man's realization, made independently on both sides of the Atlantic, is now visually expressed in the famous Hertzsprung-Russell (H-R) diagram prominently displayed in every introductory astronomy textbook. This famous graph remains the cornerstone of all astronomical research related to the evolution of stars. Science historian David DeVor-

Astronomer Henry Norris Russell (1877–1957) seated at a Princeton measuring machine for spectrograms.
Photograph courtesy of Yerkes Observatory

kin of the Smithsonian Institution has said that one cannot effectively discuss how stars "are born, live, and die, how they are distributed in space and how our Sun fits amongst them . . . without using this [diagram]."

Knowledge of the celestial elements enabled astronomers not only to touch the stars but to perceive the varied stages of the stars' lives. The stars were no longer fixed objects, steadily burning without alteration. With the Hertzsprung-Russell diagram in front of them, astronomers could more easily imagine the stars as ever-changing over cosmic time scales—from infancy, through middle age, to a cold and final death. Darwin's *Origin of Species,* which proposed a system of dynamic evolution that led to the myriad species found on Earth, loomed large as a paradigm for the other sciences. With thoughts of evolution in the air, Russell began to talk more rigorously of a certain stellar life cycle, extending an earlier idea of Lockyer's: A big reddish star condenses out of a diffuse gaseous nebula, grows more luminous as it contracts and heats up to a blue-white brilliance, and then eventually extinguishes itself after a gradual shrinking and cooling   from yellow, to orange, and back to red once again—at the conclusion of its life. This scenario made a lot of sense in an era when astronomers believed that a star derived its energy from gravitational contraction alone.

Russell had decided that the two distinct types of red stars, so apparent on his graph, were simply from different stellar epochs: the giants at the earliest stage of a star's life, the dwarfs at its oldest stage. This interpretation is now vastly outdated. Subsequent discoveries in the twentieth century—the most important being the knowledge that a star is powered by the fusing of elements within its fiery core—would lead to a far different model of a star's development. An average star like our Sun, a small, yellow G star in the suburbs of a spiraling galaxy, begins its life within the dark womb of a dust-filled cloud. This protostar, a swirling mass of gas, contracts and contracts until nuclear fusion ignites in its blazing center. When its hydrogen fuel runs out several billion years later, the yellow star balloons into a luminous red giant. Then slowly—ever so slowly—its red gaseous envelope is whisked into space, unveiling a tiny hot core, what is called a white dwarf star, that eventually cools and dims over the eons. This is the typical story of a typical star.

There are other plot lines as well. A star does not evolve over its lifetime through each spectral type, as Russell once thought; rather, each star experiences its own distinct history, based on its mass at birth. Smaller

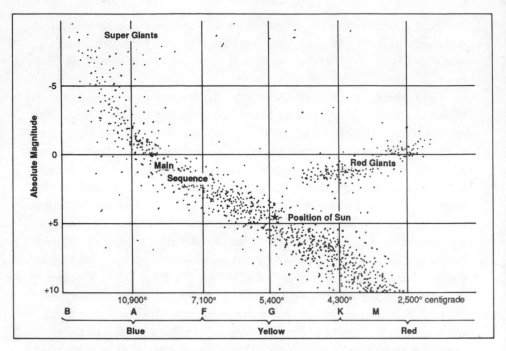

The Hertzsprung-Russell diagram, which shows how stars smoothly diminish in brightness as you proceed from the hot blue stars to the cool red stars. Red giant stars occupy a special corner of the chart.
Illustration by John Hamwey

stars, such as tiny red dwarf stars, will never reach the red-giant stage but just dully burn away like red-hot ovens. Stars that are born with appreciably more mass than our Sun, such as the white-hot O and B stars, will burn swiftly and eventually blow up, leaving behind a city-sized neutron star or even a black hole, a gravitational pit from which no light or matter can escape. Of course, such revelations came to astronomers much later; the term *black hole* wasn't even coined until 1968. Yet the first tentative steps toward understanding this grand metamorphosis, the distinct and striking stages in a star's life, were taken at the turn of the century. The elements in the stars themselves were telling the tale in the spectral messages they were telegraphing throughout the cosmos.

Russell was headed in the right direction. He was thinking evolution, and Russell's growing influence (in his senior years he would be known as the dean of American astronomy) drove others to look more closely into the problem.

*   *   *

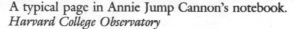

A typical page in Annie Jump Cannon's notebook.
Harvard College Observatory

In 1911 a new Draper catalogue was commissioned to survey the stars that are up to fifty times fainter than the eye can see. Between October 1911 and September 1915, Cannon classified more than a quarter of a million stars from her corner office on the top floor of the "Brick" building. This astounding achievement was described by one historian as the "most ambitious program in spectroscopic data gathering yet undertaken." Studying each plate with meticulous care under a magnifying glass, Cannon could distinguish a star's spectral lines, mentally choose its alphabetical category, and call out the identification to a waiting assistant— all at the rate of three stars per minute. With each plate displaying a couple hundred stars, she could have finished off a plate in about half an hour, if need be. Over those four years, she handled 709 plates of the northern sky photographed from Cambridge and 1,409 plates taken of the southern sky.

The processed data eventually appeared as *The Henry Draper Catalogue,* which was published in nine volumes from 1918 to 1924. Pickering was determined to see it through completion but only lived long enough to see three volumes in print. Cannon oversaw the publication of the remaining six volumes and continued classifying stars almost until her death in 1941. Throughout her forty-five years of devoted service, Cannon categorized nearly 400,000 spectra.

To this day, 201 aged, canvas-covered ledgers, stored in an inconspicuous gray metal cabinet at the Harvard-Smithsonian Center for Astrophysics, retain the original Draper (or should we say Cannon) data. On the spine of each book are written the letters A J C, for Annie Jump Cannon. At the dawn of the twentieth century, these notebooks comprised a virtual treasure chest of astronomical riches, but one in dire need of a key—the knowledge of an atom's structure and the way in which an atom radiates. Once that knowledge was obtained, the field of astrophysics bloomed and grew exponentially. And, as a consequence, astronomers were greatly surprised to find out which element formed the bulk of the universe.

4

The Prime Element

Knowing that Nature never did betray
The heart that loved her . . .

—WILLIAM WORDSWORTH,
LINES COMPOSED A FEW MILES ABOVE TINTERN ABBEY

alking along the red-tiled floors of the venerable Robinson building at the California Institute of Technology in Pasadena, walls adorned with lunar maps and massive art-deco etchings of observatory domes and telescopic instruments, a visitor at last locates Jesse Greenstein's office at the end of the wide hallway on the second floor. A few days remain before Greenstein's eightieth birthday, and he huddles over a computer monitor in the darkened room. A stocky man, distinguished-looking in a white shirt, blue blazer with gold buttons, and gray pants, his thinning gray hair combed straight back, the veteran astronomer swiftly punches a series of commands onto the keyboard with two fingers. "I control my computer terror," he says with a smile.

At the final press of a button, hundreds of white points splash across the black screen in a matter of seconds. "This type of work keeps you busy," he muses, "but it's so mechanical, so hypnotic, that there's no time for thinking. I now have to do my thinking late at night when I'm away from this machine." In the precomputer era, following an astronomical tradition, Greenstein often hired women at minimum wage to handle similar types of computing by hand. To the bemusement of Greenstein, who openly admits to a bit of male chauvinism, several of these women went on to become respected astronomers in their own right.

For the moment, Greenstein contemplates a very unusual stellar spectrum displayed on the computer screen. He reads off the wavelengths of each spectral feature with ease, the result of decades of practice. "Look," he says, motioning his visitor to come closer, "here's a helium line, but this one is surely a molecule, which implies that this object is a cool star, maybe an early M star."

Picking up a graph from the top of a craggy paper mountain on his desk, Greenstein presents another type of spectrum. This time the plot displays a series of graceful arches, as if deep gorges were cut at regular intervals into a high plateau. This spectrum of hydrogen lines, known to atomic physicists as the Balmer series, appears to dance rhythmically across the page. "Yes, it is music," notes Greenstein, quickly stepping over to a blackboard and effortlessly writing down the equation for the Balmer series from memory. "This equation produces numbers that are harmoniously related, like notes of a chord."

Raised in a prosperous Jewish household in New York City, Greenstein was his family's first "urban dropout," as he likes to put it. He surprised his relatives by choosing science over the business world. But his grandfather, a Russian émigré who physically resembled Theodore Roosevelt and rose to prominence as a wealthy furniture manufacturer, had a high regard for learning. Greenstein fondly recalls the incredible library his grandfather amassed on the first floor of a Brooklyn brownstone; young Jesse spent many hours sitting in the bay window of this house reading books on the wonders of chemistry and the splendors of the heavens. At the age of eight, he received a small, brass-mounted telescope from the grandfather he adored. Later, crystal radio sets, spectroscopes, and prisms occupied his summer days at the family's New Jersey seacoast retreat.

When starting out at Harvard in the 1920s, Greenstein first thought of science as a hobby, not a career; he toyed with the idea of being a literary critic. But by the time Greenstein was a junior undergraduate at the age of eighteen in 1927, he was regularly walking up Garden Street in Cambridge, Massachusetts, to the Harvard College Observatory. He had sensed that something new and radically different was occurring in astronomy at that time. Great debates were taking place over the nature of a star's interior, the source of stellar power, and the existence of other galaxies besides the Milky Way. He was witnessing no less than the triumph of astrophysics.

For Greenstein, that revolution was personified in Harvard astron-

Cecilia Payne-Gaposchkin (1900–1979).
Photograph courtesy of Yerkes Observatory

omer Cecilia Payne (later Payne-Gaposchkin). He remembers an extraordinary woman whose dignified bearing and imposing stature (five-foot-ten) matched her intense personality. She was a scientist so engrossed in her work that she was said to have developed personal friendships with individual stars, readily describing their peculiar spectra.[1] She even succumbed to bursts of jealousy if she felt a colleague had trespassed on her celestial territory. Truly a Renaissance woman, she also maintained a passionate devotion to English and American literature. In a personal recollection of her mother's vast repertoire, Payne-Gaposchkin's daughter, Katherine Haramundanis, made sure to include "world traveler . . . an inspired cook, a marvelous seamstress, an inventive knitter and a voracious reader," as well as chain smoker, pun addict, avid card player, proficient linguist, and accomplished musician.

Payne-Gaposchkin has been described as the most eminent woman astronomer of all time. Her Ph.D. in astronomy was the first ever granted

[1] Payne-Gaposchkin, a subtle wit, once recommended to Greenstein that he study an eccentric young variable star whose name aptly described its odd behavior—RU Lupi.

to a student at the Harvard Observatory (the university's physics department having refused to accept a woman candidate). She was only nine years older than Greenstein, but at the time of their first meeting she had already made a substantial mark in her field as one of the first scientists to apply the sweeping and novel laws of atomic and quantum physics to astronomical bodies. Young Greenstein, oddly enough, had been advised by a Harvard professor to forego the college's course in quantum mechanics, certain that the controversial subject would be dead in two or three years, a short-lived fad. Fortunately for astronomy, Payne had harbored no such qualms. In the course of her painstaking thesis calculations, which drew heavily on the new physics, she had uncovered the very first hint that the simplest element, hydrogen, was the most abundant substance in the universe. The reverberations that have resounded from this single, plain fact still echo long and hard through the corridors of astronomy. Here is the abundant fuel for a star's persistent burning; here is the gaseous tracer that enables radio astronomers to reveal a dark, long-hidden universe; here is the remnant debris from the first few minutes of the universe's creation. Payne-Gaposchkin's discovery did no less than change the entire face of the material cosmos.

THE NEW WORLD ORDER

"At the age of five Cecilia saw a meteor, and thereupon decided to be an Astronomer." So wrote Betty Grierson Leaf, a close friend of Cecilia's when both attended Cambridge University. Actually, other childhood pursuits diverted young Cecilia's attention for a while.

Cecilia Helena Payne was born in Wendover, England, in 1900. Her father, a barrister, died when she was four. Her mother, an accomplished musician, carefully guided her daughter's education. Descended from a family of scholars and historians, Payne eagerly unearthed books on botany, chemistry, and physics and essays by Thomas Huxley in the extensive library at her family home. "I knew, as I had always known," wrote Payne-Gaposchkin in her autobiography, *The dyer's hand,* "that I wanted to be a scientist . . . [but] was seized with panic at the thought that everything might be found out before I was old enough to begin!" This resolve to pursue science was not an easy choice for a young girl in the Edwardian Age. As a preteen, Payne attended a church school in London, where the female principal told her that she would be prostituting her gifts by embarking on such a career. Only one other profession tempted

Payne: She once confided that if she had not gone into science, she would have become an English stage actress because of an early love of the theater. Her education was classically oriented. She could speak French and German by the age of twelve; Latin, algebra, music, and poetry were all part of her curriculum.

But science bewitched Payne. Despite her principal's admonitions concerning science, she continued to sneak up to the top floor of the school where a room was set aside for science instruction. She wrote:

> The chemicals were ranged in bottles round the walls. I used to steal up there by myself . . . and sit conducting a little worship service of my own, adoring the chemical elements. Here were the warp and woof of the world, a world that was later to expand into a Universe.

When Cecilia was a teenager, a move to a new and more modern school enabled her to immerse herself in scientific studies.

In the autumn of 1919, shortly after the end of World War I, Cecilia Payne entered Cambridge University's Newnham College with unbridled exuberance, caught up in the postwar fervor. By the time Payne arrived at college, the physics community was reeling from the startling new discoveries thrust upon it. Seemingly endless streams of additional findings were continuing to arrive, and the very foundations of physics were being shaken. Toward the end of the nineteenth century, the universe had been moving along quite nicely, akin to a well-oiled clock. The success of Newton, whose equations made the motions of orbiting planets and falling apples so predictable, led to a smug assurance that every other object in the cosmos, both big and small, would follow rules just as orderly. It was generally believed that all physical phenomena could ultimately be explained mechanically. But nature, to everyone's surprise, was not following the desired script. Things quickly went awry as soon as scientists tried to apply the mechanistic laws of classical physics to the workings of an atom, an entity a billion times smaller than a billiard ball.

One of the first tremors in this upheaval—a catalyst, really—occurred in Germany in November 1895. While experimenting with a cathode-ray tube (the device that still serves as the picture tube of the modern television set), a competent but unassuming physics professor at the Royal University of Würzburg, Wilhelm Röntgen, chanced to discover X rays. A lifelong tinkerer and eagle-eyed scientist, Röntgen had covered up his discharge tube with cardboard in the course of an experiment and noticed that a nearby screen of fluorescent material glowed brightly, somehow energized by rays emanating from the covered tube.[2] Here was radiation that passed through paper, thin layers of metal, and human flesh with extraordinary ease, a power almost immediately applied to medical diagnosis. Röntgen took X-ray photographs of objects in closed boxes, the chamber of a shotgun, and the bones in his wife's hand. No doubt it was this last capability that made Röntgen's discovery the first modern scientific breakthrough to spark banner headlines in newspapers around the world. Some anxious people even began taking baths fully clothed, convinced that scientists were lurking about their homes peering at them with these mystery rays.

What Röntgen had revealed (it was later learned) was the very energetic end of the electromagnetic spectrum, and he received the first Nobel Prize in physics for this discovery. Seven years earlier Heinrich Hertz had generated radio waves, which can measure many feet or even miles from peak to peak. An X-ray wave, radio's extremely short and penetrating relative, measures less than a millionth of an inch across. While X rays by themselves didn't overturn any laws of physics—Maxwell's equations of electromagnetism could well account for them—the repercussions from Röntgen's experiments certainly did.

X rays became the rage of the physics world. When word of the new sensation reached Paris, Antoine-Henri Becquerel, scion of a French family distinguished in science for three generations, immediately began to look for signs of the newfound X rays in luminescent crystals, substances he was quite familiar with because of his father's earlier researches on them. But instead of X rays, Becquerel discovered a novel form of radiation altogether. An innocent-looking piece of potassium uranyl sulfate, which Becquerel had stored on top of an unexposed photographic plate in a closed drawer, fogged the plate even though the plate was heavily wrapped in black paper. Surprised by this unexpected turn of events, Becquerel examined other luminescent materials but found that only those containing uranium could fog a photographic plate in the dark. The

---

[2] Cathode-ray tubes, also known as Crookes tubes after the English physicist William Crookes, had been used in laboratories for more than thirty years before Röntgen's discovery. The device consists of two metal plates, between which a high voltage difference exists, all enclosed in a glass tube under extreme vacuum. This allows streams of electrons, a current, to pass from one plate to the other. Other scientists had earlier complained of their photographic plates fogging up when stored near a tube but failed to follow up on this observation.

uranium was spewing penetrating rays continuously, without the need for an external power source like a cathode-ray tube. The forty-three-year-old Frenchman, only three months after Röntgen's surprise, had stumbled upon a process that seemed to defy all the laws of physics: Without any outside provocation whatsoever, matter was somehow spontaneously disintegrating. Marie Curie would later invent the word *radioactivity* to describe this surprising phenomenon and, with her husband, Pierre, would isolate entirely new radioactive compounds, such as polonium and radium.

Like a set of tumbling dominoes, discovery followed discovery. By the following year, 1897, J. J. Thomson, director of Cambridge's Cavendish Laboratory, demonstrated conclusively that electricity was not a special fluidlike substance, as some had argued, but rather a stream of discrete, negatively charged "corpuscles" that were present in all matter. This was an idea that had long been championed by English investigators, who already had a name for these tiny motes: electrons. Atoms were not the smallest building blocks in the universe after all. Thomson had introduced physicists to a form of matter more finely subdivided than an atom and weighing almost nothing—each particle had a mass around eighteen hundred times lighter than that of the lightest atom. Some of Becquerel's mysterious radioactive "rays" were, in fact, found to be electrons.

There were a few holdouts, scientists who continued to resist the notion of what we today call the subatomic realm. They figured that this model of an atom, with its ever more deeply nested levels of structure, was good for computations but hardly an image of physical reality. Yet the evidence for these lilliputian entities only grew with time. Scientists soon came to recognize that the negative charge of each electron in an atom was balanced and attracted by the positive charge of a more massive particle called the proton, making the overall atom electrically neutral. By 1911 a creative and boisterous New Zealander named Ernest Rutherford, Thomson's former research student, beautifully demonstrated that these protons, which constitute much of an atom's mass, are clustered in a tight ball at an atom's center.

Rutherford's laboratory assistants had shot some positively charged particles at a thin gold foil and were surprised to behold a few of the particles ricocheting back. "It was almost as incredible," mused Rutherford, "as if you fired a fifteen-inch shell at a piece of tissue paper and it came back and hit you." Rutherford figured this could not happen unless most of the mass in any one gold atom was concentrated in a tiny knot that spanned $\frac{1}{100,000}$ the diameter of the atom as a whole. Positively charged, this compact nucleus would strongly repel any other positively charged particles that got too close. By 1932 James Chadwick, Rutherford's right-hand man, revealed that a second particle, the chargeless neutron, also resided in the atomic nucleus.

As these subatomic players were being identified, the periodic table of the elements began to make a lot more sense. It was simply an orderly progression—the addition of one more proton and one more electron—up the ladder of matter. Hydrogen, the simplest element, starts off with one proton and one electron. The next element, helium, has two protons and two electrons, and so on up the line of cosmic matter. Only the neutron, a particle as heavy as the proton but with no electric charge whatsoever, fails to follow this pattern. The number of neutrons in any given element can actually vary. A helium atom, for example, might have either one neutron or two in its nucleus. The six protons packed into a carbon atom's nucleus might be joined by six, seven, or even eight neutrons. These different versions of an element, although chemically similar, are called isotopes, and some isotopes are more abundant than others. All in all, nature can handle making about ninety-two elements on its own, up through uranium. After that, it has difficulty squeezing many more protons and neutrons into a nucleus. This is why many of the higher elements—and all those artificially created beyond element 92—are radioactive; they must spew out the excess nuclear particles to achieve some stability, turning into atoms of another element in the process.

These findings ultimately led to the popular conception of the atom as a solar system in miniature (a notion still used today despite its obsolescence). In place of the Sun, one imagines a compact kernel of protons and neutrons. Circling around this central hub, rather like planets in assorted orbits, are the tiny electrons. The protons and electrons are held together by the electromagnetic attraction of their opposite charges. However, physicists now realize that an atom's structure is more like a fuzzy cloud, with the atomic particles behaving with less predictability than such ordinary objects as rocks or moons. In the strange world of the microcosm, an electron can be considered as either a particle or a wave. With an electron frenetically buzzing and darting about the atomic nucleus like an angry bee, its position and velocity cannot be pinpointed as precisely as a planet lumbering around the Sun. Yet the solar system model, with its image of electrons whirling around an atomic nucleus in concentric orbits, does help in talking about how an atom radiates.

For several decades astronomers had been identifying elements in the heavens by their spectral emissions, but the actual origin of that light was a complete mystery. "We could hardly hope to understand the behavior of matter in the distant stars, when the mechanism of the light given out by a candle flame was still quite unknown to us," Caltech astronomer Walter Adams once pointed out. By 1913, however, the mechanism was at last revealed. Danish physicist Niels Bohr conceived the ingenious solution. Inspired by the nuclear model of the atom established by Rutherford, Bohr deduced that an atomic spectrum, so successfully exploited in astronomy, is generated as the electrons in an atom of a given element jump from one orbit to another, emitting or absorbing bursts of light (that is, photons) along the way.

Jostled by a nearby atom or a passing photon, an electron that is quietly orbiting at one level might absorb the energy from that neighborly bump and jump to a higher atomic orbit, which puts it in an excited, more energetic state. In this way, the electron robs the system of a specific energy—the exact energy needed to move from that lower orbit to the higher one. When many electrons collectively absorb that same energy in the atmosphere of a star, the result is a gap, or dark line, at that wavelength in the spectrum. When the electron drops back down from an excited state, it radiates a photon of light at a wavelength equal to the energy difference between the higher and lower orbits. Each element has its own distinctive pattern of spectral absorptions and emissions because each material has unique tiers of orbits between which its electrons can jump to and fro.

With his theory in hand, Bohr calculated the specific wavelengths of light that hydrogen was expected to either absorb or radiate. His figures matched the observed spectrum of hydrogen almost perfectly. Upon hearing this news, Einstein was said to have commented, "Then this is one of the greatest discoveries ever made."

The excitement and hubbub surrounding the "new physics" eventually filtered into astronomical circles. Arthur Eddington, then the foremost astronomer at Cambridge, was particularly intrigued. Payne-Gaposchkin would call Eddington the greatest intellect she ever had the privilege to meet. As well a man of considerable charm and wit, Eddington held the honored Plumian Chair of astronomy at Cambridge from 1913 until his death in 1944. While he heartily embraced the scientific advances of modern physics, he liked to think of them as new words set to old music, so that what "has gone before is not destroyed but refo-

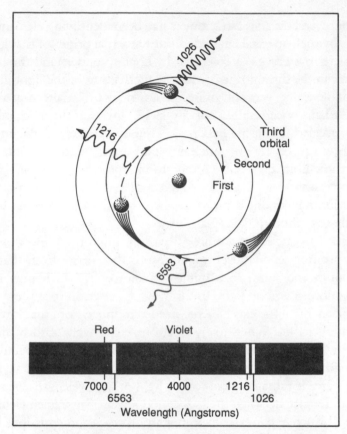

A hydrogen atom can emit different frequencies of light depending on the way in which its electron moves from a high orbit to a lower, less energetic orbit.
Reproduced by permission of Prentice-Hall from Universe: An Evolutionary Approach to Astronomy *(1988) by Eric Chaisson*

cussed." A photographic portrait, prominently displayed at Cambridge University's Institute of Astronomy, shows him with hand poised on his brow, as if in deep thought. Sparse white hair sets off a high forehead. His vest, tie, and gray suit seem more like the vestments of a banker, perhaps appropriate attire for a man who was concerned with a star's debits and credits.

Eddington, the son of a Quaker schoolmaster, rose in the ranks of astronomy by applying his sharp mathematical skills to a wide range of astronomical problems. Casting his keen theoretical eye on a star's internal structure, he came to realize that the tremendous force of gravity pulling inward, trying to squeeze a star's great gaseous envelope tighter and tighter, is countered by the monstrous pressure of the hot gases and electrons that are bouncing around inside the star pushing outward. As a result, a star neither wafts away nor shrinks into oblivion. The two opposing forces—gravity and pressure—keep the star in an exquisite celestial balance. Nonetheless, the stupendous pressures compel the stellar interior to reach temperatures of millions of degrees, a finding that would prove of great importance when others tried to determine the source of stellar energy.

In the hands of Eddington, a masterful writer, a star's inner recesses turned into a wild and magical landscape. In *The Internal Constitution of the Stars,* a seminal work published in 1926, he suggested:

> Try to picture the tumult! Dishevelled atoms tear along at 50 miles a second with only a few tatters left of their elaborate cloaks of electrons

Arthur Eddington (1882–1944).
Photograph courtesy of the Astronomical Society of the Pacific

torn from them in the scrimmage. The lost electrons are speeding a hundred times faster to find new resting places. Look out! There is nearly a collision as an electron approaches an atomic nucleus; but putting on speed it sweeps round it in a sharp curve. . . . As we watch the scene we ask ourselves, can this be the stately drama of stellar evolution? It is more like the jolly crockery-smashing turn of a music hall.

Those "dishevelled atoms," bereft of some of their outer electrons, become positively charged, a state known as ionized. In 1920 in Calcutta, an obscure twenty-seven-year-old Indian physicist named Meghnad Saha, who applied his expertise in thermodynamics and the Bohr atom to astronomy, recognized that these ionized atoms could serve as powerful diagnosticians of a star's condition. In the early days of spectroscopy, some astronomers had wondered whether the intensity of a spectral line said something about that star's major ingredients. If carbon lines stood out in a particular star, then that star was assumed to be largely composed of carbon. Likewise, stars with strong helium lines supposedly abounded in helium. But Saha, turning to the Sun as the typical star, argued that there is no good reason why "certain elements should be favored to the exclusion of others. On the contrary, it seems natural to infer that the sun is composed of the same elements as the earth, and contains all the 92 elements known to the chemists on earth. . . ." Saha was certainly not the first to espouse a universal composition, that the Sun, Earth, and stars shared the same blend of elements, but there was an outstanding problem in that assumption: Why was there still such a variety of stellar spectra, from the O stars to the M stars?

Saha argued that an element will either vividly stand out in a stellar spectrum or remain hidden from view, depending on a star's particular temperature and pressure. By knowing how hard or how easy it was to ionize an element, it became possible to predict whether that element would be seen in the spectrum of a star of a particular atmospheric temperature. Saha's theory provided, for the first time, a real physical basis for the striking distinctions between the various spectral classes. He was able to justify what earlier workers could only surmise: that Annie Cannon's stellar sequence—O, B, A, F, G, K, M—was indeed arranged by temperature. The intensely hot O stars have surface temperatures of tens of thousands of degrees, verified by the fact that most of their atoms are ionized. The cooler M stars, whose surface temperatures are a "mere" three thousand degrees, have atoms much less disturbed—even simple molecules can form there. (Not all great ideas are readily noticed. The *Astrophysical Journal* rejected Saha's first paper on this subject, "Ionization in the Solar Chromosphere." It was finally published in the *Philosophical Magazine* and went on to inspire a whole generation of theoretical astrophysicists. Some historians mark the beginning of modern astrophysics with the publication of Saha's ionization theory.)

"I SHOULD LIKE TO BE AN ASTRONOMER"

Many of the ideas in the new physics and astronomy were swirling around Payne (or about to) when she matriculated at Newnham College. She initially leaned toward a career in botany, a childhood love that had thrived under the kind attentions of a beloved science teacher in her youth. She was further inspired by a maternal aunt who worked in a biology laboratory at Cambridge. But she still made sure to add physics and chemistry to her course of study. The presence of Ernest Rutherford, the renowned modern physicist then conducting some of his most creative experiments at Cambridge's Cavendish Laboratory, was "irresistible," said Payne, ". . . he was always on the horizon, a towering blond giant with a booming voice." She was introduced to the Bohr atom by Bohr himself, whose lectures during a stay at Cambridge were "rendered almost incomprehensible by his accent," Payne recalled. "There were endless references to what I recorded as 'soup groups,' only later emended to 'sub-groups.' "

According to Payne, the science to which she would dedicate her life's work was decided in the course of a night. In 1915 Einstein had introduced his general theory of relativity, which, among other things, suggested that space-time was as pliable as a rubber mat, capable of being warped and stretched by the massive objects residing in it. Einstein predicted that, to prove this point, beams of starlight that happen to graze the Sun would get bent by a slight but detectable amount owing to the dimpling of space around the Sun—twice the bending postulated from previous theories. After World War I, British astronomers eagerly mounted two expeditions to prove Einstein's conjecture. On May 29, 1919, from sites in northern Brazil and the tiny island of Príncipe off the coast of western Africa, the researchers photographed stars that were located near the edge of the Sun during a total solar eclipse, a rare occurrence whose shadowy visage was visible from those tropical regions on that day.

Eddington, a member of the Príncipe brigade, called his participation in the verification of general relativity the greatest moment in his life. At the end of 1919, he presented the results of this fabled undertaking in the Great Hall of Cambridge's Trinity College, Newton's old haunt. To the delight of everyone, including Payne, who chanced upon a ticket to the sold-out event, Eddington reported that the gravitational deflection of the stellar rays agreed closely with Einstein's calculations.

In what was almost like a religious conversion, Payne deserted the life sciences virtually overnight and informed school authorities that she would be devoting her studies to the physical sciences. She attended as many astronomy courses as her schedule would allow. She was already aware of the inconveniences. A shy, studious, and awkward girl, she trembled when she had to sit by herself in the front row at Rutherford's lectures, the required seating arrangement for the lone woman in a sea of male students. In a physics laboratory, her stern instructor, who had no patience for the women students, would often shout, "Go and take off your corsets!" because he was sure the steel frameworks disturbed the magnetic equipment. During a public night at the Cambridge Observatory, Payne happened to meet and talk with Eddington personally, blurting out, "I should like to be an astronomer." He replied, "I can see no insuperable objection," and proceeded to widen her opportunities for research at Cambridge, which led to her first published paper on the proper motions of stars.

Faced with the prospect that her only job in England would be teaching science at a girls' school after she completed her degree in 1923, Payne was advised to go to the United States, where women had better opportunities in astronomy. Upon hearing a spellbinding lecture in London by the young, sandy-haired Harlow Shapley, Pickering's successor at the Harvard Observatory and the man who had discovered that the solar system is not situated in the Milky Way's center, she set her sights on Massachusetts, home to the largest storehouse of astronomical data in the world.

Her Cambridge professors and colleagues were highly supportive in their recommendations. Leslie J. Comrie, who had helped Payne put Newnham College's telescope in working order and was then teaching at Swarthmore College in Pennsylvania, wrote Shapley that Payne was "the type of person who, given the opportunity, would devote her whole life to astronomy and that she would not want to run away after a few years training to get married." She got the fellowship.

Harlow Shapley (1885–1972).
*Photograph by Frank Hogg, courtesy of Helen
Sawyer Hogg and Owen Gingerich*

While Shapley hoped that Payne would work on photometry (the
determination of stellar brightnesses) during her stay at Harvard, she was
more interested in the physical interpretation of stellar spectra, a Harvard
specialty. Swift to grasp and apply new ideas, she knew that Saha's work
set the stage. She was excited by the prospect of verifying Saha's theory
with the myriad spectra available in the Harvard plate collection, which
she considered priceless. (When she once inadvertently sat on some plates,
she stayed away from the observatory for days, mistakenly believing
that she had broken them.) Payne compared her research to an archaeo-
logical dig. In her mind the data represented "bones to be assembled and
clothed with the flesh that would present the stars as complete individ-
uals." She had to share the spoils with Donald Menzel, a Princeton doctoral candidate and Henry Norris Russell protégé who was also applying
Saha's ionization theory to the Harvard spectra. It was decided that Menzel would focus on the lines of neutral metals. These features were pri-

marily seen in low-temperature stars, leaving the high-temperature stars wide open to Payne's scrutiny.

"Nothing seemed impossible in those early days," Payne-Gaposchkin recalled years later. "We were going to understand everything tomorrow"—as well as try everything. Even though she had never driven before, she bought her first car in America and at the end of a nighttime observing run could often be seen tearing up the road beside Boston's Charles River. Her early botany training in the systematic classification of plants served her well. She looked at hundreds of spectra (her "celestial flora," as she called them) and selected certain known lines for inspection. She set up a crude system for estimating the intensities of these spectral features, an arduous task. "There followed months, almost a year I remember, of utter bewilderment," she said. Payne's mother once described her daughter as living "largely on her enthusiasms." Payne could work day and night when caught up in a particular problem and would bury herself in papers, her office in total disarray, when concentrating on an assignment. "My office may be disorderly," she responded, "but my mind is not!"

Gradually, answers did arrive. After days and months of grappling with her treasured plates, the intensities of the lines of silicon, in four successive stages of ionization, began to make more sense. With this select key, she was able to determine the temperatures of the hotter stars. (From that day forward, silicon became Payne's favorite element.) Once Menzel completed his degree, Payne broadened her study to include other elements and other spectral classes, confirming that stellar temperatures increased steadily from the reddest stars to the bluer ones.

With that job complete, Payne proceeded to the calculations for which her thesis is most famous: her computations of the relative abundances of eighteen elements commonly found in the atmospheres of various types of stars. With her guides being both Saha's equations and statistical mechanics, especially the seminal work of the English theorists Edward Milne and Ralph Fowler, she was able to estimate the number of atoms needed to generate a particular spectral feature. Looking over her results, she was immediately struck by the fact that the common elements found in the Earth's crust were likewise present in her stars. For elements such as silicon and carbon, for example, she found roughly the same relative proportions that are seen in terra firma. The similarities were marred, however, by two glaring exceptions: "hydrogen and helium are manifestly very abundant in stellar atmospheres," she reported. The differences were startling. Her results suggested that hydrogen alone could be as much as a million times more plentiful in the stars than either on Earth or in meteorites. And the helium in her stars was about a thousand times more abundant than the heavier elements.

At each major step in her analyses, Payne wrote a paper describing her findings. She completed half a dozen articles before receiving her doctorate in 1925. In each, one sees a woman swiftly applying the laws of atomic physics to astrophysics almost as soon as they were formulated. Bohr's detailed classification of the electron orbits responsible for atomic spectra had just been published in 1923, and Saha's theory was practically new. Payne's meticulous discussions reveal a mind that craved to wring every possible insight out of her bits of data. Ultimately, however, she turned conservative and hesitant when publishing the results on stellar abundances. "In the stellar atmosphere and the meteorite the agreement is good for all atoms that are common to the two. . . . ," she wrote. "The outstanding discrepancies between the astrophysical and terrestrial abundances are displayed for hydrogen and helium." She was on the verge of recognizing that these two elements make up the bulk of stellar material and hence the preponderance of the universe's matter. Yet she pulled back.

Why did she hesitate? "She was bullied," contends Greenstein. "All papers at Harvard, unfortunately, had to be approved by the director Harlow Shapley." In December 1924, Shapley sent Payne's manuscript to Russell, his esteemed mentor and former teacher at Princeton University. A whiz at mathematical computations and a lifelong workaholic prone to nervous breakdowns, Russell was in the vanguard of incorporating modern physics into astronomy. Payne-Gaposchkin recalled that she both respected and feared the Princeton Observatory director, who always seemed to speak with the voice of authority. Russell at first concluded that Payne's findings were "a very good thing." But five weeks later, he had second thoughts and wrote the young graduate student that "there remains one very much more serious discrepancy. . . . It is clearly impossible that hydrogen should be a million times more abundant than the metals [elements heavier than helium]." In an article sent to the *Proceedings of the National Academy of Sciences* in February 1925, Payne withheld her original conclusion and instead wrote that the abundance calculated for both hydrogen and helium "is improbably high, and is almost certainly not real," a statement reiterated in her doctoral thesis. She toed the party line that a star's makeup basically resembled the composition of the Earth's crust.

Hydrogen was certainly ubiquitous in all stars; this was observed and noted by astronomers long before Payne. But the common wisdom held that stellar atmospheres were composed predominantly of gaseous mixtures of the heavy elements, particularly iron. Russell and others had some good reasons at the time to believe this was true. A popular theory of the formation of the planets, for instance, was the tidal hypothesis, which stated that the Earth and its sister planets were wrenched from the Sun by a near fatal collision with another star; thus it was inevitable that the planets and the Sun shared the same composition. In 1914, some ten years before Payne's work, Russell had compared the most common materials in the Earth's crust, as determined by geochemists, with the substances commonly found in the Sun. To a large degree the two compositions, solar and terrestrial, matched. Even earlier, in the 1890s, the American physicist Henry Rowland, who had prepared an exquisite map of the solar spectrum, remarked that if the Earth's crust were heated to searing solar temperatures, its spectrum would probably look very much like the Sun's. Moreover, Eddington, the stellar-structure expert, had figured that the average atomic weight of a star's material was far heavier than hydrogen, the lightest gas of all. He was sure his stellar models wouldn't work with high hydrogen abundances. So strong was Eddington's prejudice that when he applied a quantum rule, known as Kramer's law, to the interior of the Sun and came up with terrifically high hydrogen abundances, he assumed the law was wrong! No one was ready, or equipped, to challenge Eddington's theoretical prowess on stellar interiors.

"Cecilia was a tough cookie," says Greenstein, yet she still acquiesced to Russell's counsel. It is difficult for any graduate student to challenge the leaders in their field, especially a giant such as Russell and, most of all, Shapley, on whom she had an innocent crush. Although Payne and Shapley engaged in many long, stimulating scientific discussions, the director always kept his distance personally. Payne, on the other hand, admitted to a slavish, platonic devotion. "In those days I worshipped Dr. Shapley; I would gladly have died for him," she confessed.

Payne-Gaposchkin's autobiography does not elaborate at all on the Russell episode and the controversy over her findings. There is only a vague reference that Russell, whose word could make or break a young scientist, had vetoed some of her cherished ideas. Nevertheless, despite her backing down in print at Russell's recommendation, she still held to her conviction. In *The dyer's hand,* Payne tells of visiting Cambridge University shortly after her thesis was complete and informing Eddington in a burst of youthful zest that she believed there was far more hydrogen in the stars than any other atom. "You don't mean *in* the stars," replied Eddington, "you mean *on* the stars." But astronomers were later convinced that the amounts of elements found in stellar atmospheres would generally represent the star's overall abundances.

It might be argued that Russell, Eddington, and Shapley were not being obstinate so much as cautious. Atomic physics was exploding at the very time Payne wrote her thesis, and several solar features, such as the Sun's opacity, were as yet little understood. Knowledge of the atom's structure had only recently moved from the visions of Democritus and Dalton to that of Rutherford and Bohr. Many more calculations remained to be done to assure certainty; Payne was working with very crude data. Russell warned Payne that hydrogen, because of its simplicity (one proton and one electron), might be exhibiting abnormal behavior that skewed her results. He worried that the hot stars might be superexciting the hydrogen somehow, making it appear that more of the light gas was there. And thoughts of possibly destroying Eddington's magnificent stellar models, which had been working so well up to that point, also loomed large.

Payne's hesitation at officially naming hydrogen the prime element hardly diminishes her accomplishment. Her thesis was the first attempt at combining atomic theory, Saha's new equations, and astronomical observations to obtain good estimates of the elemental abundances in the Sun and other stars, as well as detailed analyses of stellar temperatures and pressures. Published as a 215-page monograph in the summer of 1925, *Stellar Atmospheres* was a bestseller in its day—at least, what qualifies as a bestseller for a technical astronomy book. Within three years, all six hundred copies of the red-covered hardback were sold, despite the hefty $2.50 price tag. A number of astronomers would later describe her work as the most brilliant Ph.D. thesis ever written in astronomy, and honors were showered upon her. In 1926, at the age of twenty-six, she became the youngest astronomer listed as distinguished in *American Men of Science*. Edwin Hubble, whose observations would soon confirm that the universe was steadily expanding, joked that she was "the best man at Harvard." But these many recognitions were shallow triumphs. Mainly because of her gender, a respected professional position worthy of her expertise eluded her. Historian Peggy Aldrich Kidwell, who has written extensively on Payne-Gaposchkin's work and life, points out that women were either ineligible, or simply unwanted, for posts at the colleges boasting the best observatories. Paid for a time as Shapley's technical assistant while conducting research and lecturing, Payne didn't receive an official Harvard appointment until 1938, and the courses she taught at the school were not listed in the university catalogue until 1945.

In the summer of 1933, to recover from unrequited love and the death of two dear friends, Payne took a trip to visit Europe's top observatories, including stops at Leiden, Copenhagen, and Stockholm. She traveled alone in the Soviet Union to see the Pulkovo Observatory (once an eminent institute fallen into ruin under Stalin's brutal regime), with the warning that no government would protect her. Afterward, moving on to the German city of Göttingen to attend an astronomy conference, her life changed dramatically. There she met the Russian astronomer and refugee Sergei Gaposchkin, then stateless and living in Germany under the threat of Nazi persecution. Her concern for his plight was immediate. "Attended scientific sessions all the morning, and met Gaposchkin, who turns out to be the dominant fact of the . . . meeting so far as I am concerned. . . . It does seem as if it is my place to find some way out for him," she wrote in her diary.

Upon returning home, she quickly arranged for Gaposchkin's visa to the United States. By March 1934, just eight months after their first meeting, they were married. Together they had three children, two boys and a girl, and devoted the rest of their professional careers to the study of variable stars. As a scientific team they had hoped to arrange the variables into a coherent pattern. Obtaining observing time on a telescope was difficult for Payne, as it was thought improper for men and women to spend the night together on an isolated mountaintop. And not until 1956 was she made a full professor, the first woman at Harvard to attain this rank and perhaps twenty years after a man of her achievements would have earned the position. During a small celebration of the event, Payne-Gaposchkin, by then portly in figure, had the good humor to remark, "I find myself cast in the unlikely role of a 'thin' wedge." She continued to study her beloved stars until shortly before her death in 1979.

Jesse Greenstein had met Payne when he was a young Harvard student, just a couple of years after Payne had completed her thesis. "The obvious discrimination against her as a woman scientist worthy of normal academic recognition exacerbated the stressful life she led," he says. "She was unhappy, emotional. . . . But with me, she was charming and humorous as we exchanged quotations from T.S. Eliot, Shakespeare, the Bible, Gilbert and Sullivan, and Wordsworth." William Wordsworth, the nineteenth-century English poet, provided Payne-Gaposchkin with one of her favorite quotes, a passage that sustained her through her trials: "Knowing that Nature never did betray / The heart that loved her . . ."

It is ironic that, just four years after Payne's initial foray into stellar compositions, it was Russell himself who principally persuaded astronomers that there was an overwhelming preponderance of hydrogen in the Sun and the stars. After collecting more detailed observations of the Sun, with the help of his steadfast assistant Charlotte Moore, Russell concluded that many difficulties in interpreting the solar spectrum could be overcome if "the solar atmosphere really does consist mainly of hydrogen. . . . If this is true, the outer portions of these stars must be almost pure hydrogen, with hardly more than a smell of metallic vapors in it." Russell compared his findings on the Sun with the hydrogen abundances Payne had earlier calculated for hotter stars, and he specifically mentioned in his landmark 1929 paper that there was "a very gratifying agreement." Russell left much unsaid in that seemingly generous statement. As historian Kidwell notes, "Russell . . . did not mention that Payne had dismissed her data on hydrogen as probably spurious, nor allude to his role in shaping this conclusion."

All doubts concerning the preponderance of hydrogen fully disappeared once the Sun's opacity was better understood and as soon as others successfully applied the most advanced theory of the day, quantum mechanics, to the problem. Today it is known that roughly 98 percent of the Sun's mass is made up of hydrogen and helium, with all the heavier elements making up the remaining 2 percent. In number, hydrogen atoms dominate by far—there are only 63,000,000,000 helium atoms for every 1,000,000,000,000 hydrogen atoms. Oxygen and carbon, the next most abundant elements, can manage only about half a billion atoms for every trillion hydrogen atoms, amounts that are two thousand times less.

Russell's original suspicions about cosmic abundances in 1914 were, in the end, partially correct: Except for hydrogen and helium, the ratio of heavy elements (sparse as they are) in the Sun do roughly match up with the ratios found in the Earth's composition. This is the signature of the

Sun's and planets' common origin out of a swirling cloud of interstellar matter some five billion years ago. Through Payne's pioneering efforts, and the achievements of those who followed up on her suspicions, a new perception of the heavens' composition arose: Hydrogen, the simplest element, became the dominant cosmic ingredient; earthly elements, such as carbon, oxygen, nitrogen, and iron, were but bits of trace "dirt" in the celestial mix. Nature, it seems, did not betray Payne-Gaposchkin after all.

STELLAR ODDBALLS

Jesse Greenstein, who had been studying at Harvard through the late 1920s, essentially missed out on the early excitement over stellar abundances. Soon after obtaining his master's degree at the age of twenty-one, he had to return to New York City. His family's finances devastated by the Great Depression, he worked in the family's manufacturing and real-estate businesses for four years to help reclaim the family fortune. (He credits his later ability to raise money for science to this experience.) But by 1934 Greenstein was able to return to Harvard for his Ph.D. and three years later became a postdoctoral fellow at the Yerkes Observatory in Williams Bay, Wisconsin, then a town of six hundred people, situated on a scenic glacial lake in farming country. It was there that Greenstein was eventually introduced to the universe's "stellar oddballs."

At this time, propelled by the success of Saha's work, astronomers generally assumed that every star shared a similar composition; Greenstein contends that this belief in a uniform composition helped scientists move forward. It served as an initial guide in interpreting the myriad stellar spectra. But astronomers soon began to uncover some interesting exceptions to that rule. In the mid-1930s a young and up-and-coming astronomer at Yerkes named W. W. Morgan began to find strange element anomalies in certain A-type stars. He observed stars more abundantly endowed with rare-earth elements than expected and others well stocked in silicon, manganese, europium, and chromium. In all, he saw half a dozen different oddities in the composition of these stars that temperature, luminosity, or pressure alone couldn't account for. Such special cases were disturbing to the overriding notion that all differences in stellar spectra should arise only from differing stellar environments.

By 1940 Yerkes astronomer Nancy Roman noticed the other extreme—stars with few heavy elements at all, although the stars' colors and temperatures suggested that such elements should have been present. These stars resembled our Sun, except that they displayed hardly a sprinkling of the heavier atoms. Around this time Yerkes Observatory director Otto Struve, a member of a German-Russian family distinguished for its long line of astronomers (Otto was the grandson of Otto Wilhelm von Struve), encouraged Greenstein to look at Upsilon Sagittarii, another curious star. "Good astronomers have an eye—you know, like you smell a Rembrandt behind the dirty wall," Greenstein once commented on Struve's shrewd perception. Indeed, Upsilon Sagittarii, or Upsilon Sag for short, didn't seem to have any hydrogen in it at all! It was a fortuitous find. These early efforts to sort out the true composition of the stars would eventually offer experimental evidence for the new theories then under development on the long-sought source of stellar power—a research arena with its own long history.

Nineteenth-century astronomers, long before the concept of atomic energy was even a glimmer on the theoretical horizon, faced a formidable assignment in explaining why the Sun shines. They already realized that the energies obtained from chemical reactions, such as the burning of fossil fuels, were much too feeble. If the Sun were one huge lump of coal, emitting the same radiations that currently warm the Earth's surface, it would burn up completely in ten thousand years or so, far too short a time to accommodate the long-lasting evolutionary schemes geologists and Darwin were then introducing. To get around this shortcoming, Victorian scientists fashioned a variety of imaginative mechanisms to account for the Sun's continual burning. The English physicist Lord Kelvin proposed that a persistent rain of meteorites, kindled by their plunge into the Sun, served as a source of radiant energy. Later, both Kelvin and Hermann von Helmholtz decided that the Sun could derive all its thermal and radiant heat from gravitational contraction, a formidable force when dealing with celestial-sized masses. They surmised that as gravity pulls the solar gases inward, compressing and heating them up, some of the resultant energy continually flows out into space. The two physicists calculated that the Sun merely has to shrink some seventy feet a year to account for its present luminosity, a rate of collapse that would hardly be noticed over the span of recorded history, since the Sun's diameter is nearly one million miles. From their calculations, they figured that the Sun could shine for a few dozen million years in this manner.

Unfortunately, this seemingly reasonable deduction fell apart once evidence from the fossil and geologic records, such as rates of sedimentation, disclosed that the Earth was more than one billion years old. By carefully measuring the rate at which a piece of pitchblende (a uranium ore) spewed its radioactive particles, Ernest Rutherford established in 1904 that the rock had to be at least seven hundred million years old, more than ten times the estimated age of the Sun. (Today the ages of meteorites, those rocky fragments left over after the solar system coalesced out of a nebulous cloud of interstellar gas, tell us that the Sun and its attendant planets formed about four and a half billion years ago.) Needless to say, having an Earth older than the Sun was a scientific embarrassment. To resolve this troubling paradox, certain foresighted scientists in the first decades of the twentieth century, spurred by the revolutionary new fields of quantum mechanics and particle physics, began to think of "subatomic" energy sources that would allow the Sun to burn for billions of years.

The Frenchman Jean Perrin, whose elegant experiments had so convincingly demonstrated the existence of atoms, suggested as early as 1919 that the condensation of hydrogen atoms into heavier atoms could account for the heat of the Sun. One helium atom, for example, weighs slightly less—roughly 1 percent less—than four hydrogen atoms. That lost mass, transformed into pure energy according to Einstein's famous equation $E = mc^2$ (energy equals mass multiplied by the square of the speed of light), would constitute a "colossally larger reserve than the energy of gravitation to which Helmholtz and Kelvin have thought they could attribute the origin of solar heat," asserted Perrin.

For a while, Eddington toyed with that notion as well. "The view that the energy of a star is derived by the building up of other elements from hydrogen has the great advantage that there is no doubt about the possibility of the process," he noted in his 1927 book, *Stars and Atoms*. "To my mind the *existence* of helium is the best evidence we could desire of the possibility of the *formation* of helium." He called this process "the transmutation of elements," what is now known as fusion or nucleosynthesis. When Eddington's critics responded that the Sun's interior was simply not hot enough to bring about these transmutations, Eddington readily responded that they should "go and find a hotter place." However, Eddington admitted (also in *Stars and Atoms*) that he was more attracted to the idea that the stars were fueled by the direct and full annihilation of matter into energy, rather than element synthesis. By some sort of mechanism (he couldn't offer an explanation), matter turned completely into pure energy. For some, this idea nicely meshed with the view that stars were evolving from giants to dwarfs and consequently losing mass over the eons. On top of that, Eddington's stellar models still incorrectly concluded that stars contained little hydrogen, making the gas less attractive as a prime source of energy.

But these erroneous assumptions about hydrogen soon changed. The concept of hydrogen fusion was made all the more inviting by Russell's announcement in 1929 that hydrogen was indeed the major component of the Sun and the stars. A number of gifted young researchers, such as George Gamow, Robert Atkinson, and Fritz Houtermans, were already approaching the problem, knocking down various theoretical obstacles that had prevented others from figuring out how fusion might take place in a star.

By 1938 Hans Bethe and Charles Critchfield in the United States and Carl von Weizsäcker in Germany at last independently showed, in a series of steps that elegantly moved from one nuclear reaction to another, exactly how the Sun and stars can be powered by the welding of four atoms of hydrogen into helium. Normally, hydrogen nuclei, or protons, strongly repel each other, since they are positively charged. But deep in the core of a star, where temperatures reach over ten million degrees and densities are twelve times that of lead, protons can gain enough energy to collide with a force that sometimes overcomes the electromagnetic repulsion. This enables some of the protons, following an involved chain of reactions as outlined by Bethe and von Weizsäcker, to stick together with a powerful nuclear glue called the "strong" force. In the Sun, about one in every ten thousand billion billion proton collisions gives rise to a nuclear reaction. Long odds, but the firestorm under way in the Sun's heart still enables it to convert approximately half a billion tons of hydrogen into helium with each tick of the clock. In the process, about four million tons of mass are transformed each second into pure energy, which eventually bathes our entire solar system in heat and light. The Sun has been doing this for nearly five billion years and has enough hydrogen fuel in its core to continue for about five billion more.

As these theories on stellar fusion were being published, Upsilon Sagittarii beckoned, a star already known to harbor barely a whisper of hydrogen in its outer envelope yet which displays rather large amounts of helium. It seemed to be related to Bethe's work on the fusion of hydrogen into helium. "Otto Struve encouraged me to work on this object," says Greenstein. " 'You ought to look at it. It's a real oddball,' he told me around 1940." This was Greenstein's first entry into the field of stellar composition, and it would become his life's work.

"Looking at the freaks, the exceptions, makes us look hard at what we consider normal," says Greenstein. For his study of Upsilon Sag, Greenstein traveled to Yerkes's southern outpost in Texas, the McDonald Observatory, which had just dedicated an eighty-two-inch telescope. Using a coudé prism spectrograph, one of the best in its day, Greenstein launched a program to take spectra from across the board of stellar types to discover whether stars were truly the same or exhibited subtle differences in composition. His results came out at the close of World War II.

Upsilon Sag, one of Greenstein's key subjects, was the first clear case of a star displaying in its outer atmosphere much more helium than hydrogen, which supported the idea that helium was being forged out of hydrogen by nuclear burning, just as Bethe and von Weizsäcker had shown on paper. A very large, bluish supergiant star, Upsilon Sag is

Jesse Greenstein.
California Institute of Technology

about fifteen times more massive than our Sun and burns one hundred thousand times brighter. Consequently, it will quickly exhaust its fuel in several million years or so. (By comparison, our Sun will take one thousand times longer to fuse all its hydrogen into helium.) Usually, the bulk of the products of nuclear burning stay inside a star's core, but in Upsilon Sag either the stellar material has been dredged up to the surface or its hydrogen-rich envelope has been stripped away, possibly in the course of gravitationally interacting with a companion star.

Peculiar stars are not fascinating for their quirks alone but for what those oddities can reveal—just as physicians can learn the most from those who are sick. "It was certain that one had in this star evidence for nucleosynthesis, although that word, I guess, didn't yet exist," says Greenstein. By observing the surface of this freak star, Greenstein was able to infer what was going on inside the heart of a star. And what he perceived was a grand evolution. Stars formed, they processed the elements through a complex chain of nuclear reactions, and then they returned some of that material to space. Any star that is now being assembled incorporates the entire history of the universe in its contents. "Space is one big nutrient tank!" points out Greenstein. "We are all a bit of stardust. To get the hemoglobin for our blood you need stars that made carbon, as well as stars that exploded in making iron."

When Greenstein arrived at Caltech in 1948, he wanted to blame all peculiar compositions on nuclear physics. He and others began to talk of "generations" of stars, a term introduced a few years earlier by Mount Wilson astronomer Walter Baade. The first generation is composed solely of pristine hydrogen and helium (like the stars Nancy Roman had examined), but the second and third generations are polluted more and more with heavier elements, substances somehow generated inside the stars themselves and then scattered into space for recycling in infant stars. Given this scenario, astronomers and physicists began to think more seriously about the origin of the elements. In a wonderful interplay between theory and observation during the 1950s, the modern picture of nucleosynthesis at last came into focus. "Whether man should impose his need for rationality on the universe is not obvious, but scientists exist on the hope that nature is not tricky," Greenstein once observed. "Progress depends on the faith that natural law may be difficult to understand, but should not be stupid."

Before the concept of nucleosynthesis was understood, the elements were basically manna from heaven. The ninety-two elements and all their assorted isotopes were viewed as primordial entities, handed down whole at the universe's birth. But stars could now be recognized for what they were—element cookers, the very crucibles sought for so long by the early alchemists. We shall see that it is within their fiery hearts that matter and energy receive form.

5

Celestial Alchemy

Ay, for 'twere absurd
To think that nature in the earth
  bred gold
Perfect i' the instant: something
  went before.
There must be remote matter.

—BEN JONSON, *The Alchemist*

U pon completing a degree in mathematics at Cambridge University in 1936, Fred Hoyle stayed on to pursue graduate work in theoretical physics during the closing stages of the golden age of quantum mechanics. Although he had established himself at Cambridge as an independent researcher, funded by private scholarships, Hoyle still needed a supervisor to qualify for a student income-tax exemption, which is how Paul Dirac, the brilliant and reclusive theorist who first posited the existence of antimatter, came to be Hoyle's adviser.

"One of my friends got hold of Dirac and explained the situation to him," recalls Hoyle. " 'You don't want any students, and Hoyle doesn't want a supervisor. Will you take him?' this friend asked on my behalf. Given Dirac's sense of humor, this amused him and so he agreed, inviting me to tea at least once a term." During the 1938–39 academic year, as war clouds gathered over Europe, Dirac eventually warned Hoyle that theoretical physics was running out of steam. The secrets of particle physics, investigators came to learn in the coming decades, would no longer be revealed at cozy university laboratories, such as the Cavendish, but instead by huge consortia of researchers, who would build immense machines to smash the atomic nucleus into smaller and smaller bits.

Quantum mechanics itself was proving to be a disappointment to Hoyle. Unable to explain the devilish behavior of atoms and nuclear particles with the mechanistic laws of classical physics, scientists had devised, primarily during the 1920s, a radically new means of thinking about the microcosm. In that venue the equations of quantum mechanics replaced surety, a hallmark of Newtonian theory, with uncertainty. Researchers learned that events within the minuscule realm of the atom do not flow smoothly and gradually, the way a planet orbits the Sun; rather, they change abruptly and discontinuously. Energy and motion are served up in discrete bits. Nature at this level turned into a game of probabilities rather than precise outcomes. The words "always" and "never," used so readily in describing the physics of objects in the everyday world, came to be replaced with the terms "usually" and "seldom." Einstein railed against these uncertainties inherent in quantum mechanics and announced that he "shall never believe that God plays dice with the world." Hoyle followed suit. "Instead of accepting open defeat," he has explained, "I followed the military strategy of retreating, hopefully to fight another day."

Elected a Fellow of St. John's College at Cambridge in 1939, Hoyle moved into astronomy almost by happenstance. He came in contact with astronomer Raymond Lyttleton at St. John's and, intrigued by Lyttleton's work, began to collaborate with him on problems of gas-accreting stars and stellar models. The departments of astronomy and physics had formerly been worlds apart on the Cambridge campus, each separately competing for attention in its own way. Astronomy, with its long, rich heritage, was a subject that already held great prestige at the school; physics, on the other hand, was reaping more recent kudos for its spectacular atomic experiments at the Cavendish Laboratory. Cambridge physicists such as Ralph Fowler, though, were beginning to bridge the gap between the two rival disciplines.

In 1926 Fowler applied the laws of quantum mechanics to the structure of aging white dwarf stars and was at last able to explain their curious composition. As Arthur Eddington had pointed out, a ton of white dwarf stuff "would be a little nugget that you could put in a matchbox," which made it the densest material then known in the universe. Having run out of its fusible fuel, a white dwarf contracts and heats up, squeezing a Sun's worth of mass into an Earth-sized space. Fowler figured that temperatures inside the dwarf become so extreme that all its electrons and atomic nuclei, like droves of little marbles, are packed into the smallest volume possible, creating an ultradense material impossible to assemble on Earth.

Hoyle would perform similar feats of creative science when he applied his expertise in nuclear physics to the inner workings of a star, advancing the art of celestial alchemy begun by Bethe and von Weizsäcker. Already labeled an outsider at posh, highbrow Cambridge because of his working-class background and north-country accent, Hoyle was quite practiced in venturing into unfamiliar territories. Indeed, he became a seasoned veteran at academic combat.

Born and raised in the county of Yorkshire in northern England, Hoyle inherited the region's rugged individualism and its passion for the game of cricket. His father was a struggling wool merchant, and Hoyle often walked to school to the resounding hum of the cloth factories that dominated the industrial valley where he lived. His mother, a schoolteacher, taught him the multiplication tables up to 12×12 before he was six. Bored by formal education, and often cutting classes, Hoyle largely taught himself, displaying a particular fancy for encyclopedias, popular science books, and a chemistry set his father owned. In 1932, at the age of seventeen, he won two science scholarships to Cambridge. By 1945, recognized for his ingenuity and original thinking, he became one of Cambridge's youngest lecturers, rising to the coveted Plumian professorship in 1958. All the while, he captivated the public with a seemingly endless stream of science popularizations and science-fiction tales.

Hoyle has since retired to a high-rise apartment in the resort town of Bournemouth on England's southern coast; huge glass windows offer a view in the distance of the region's famous cliffs along the English Channel. The dark, wavy hair of his youth now gray and combed back, Hoyle speaks in a precise, controlled manner, but at unexpected moments he punctuates his discussion with an amusing joke and a sudden smile transforms his serious demeanor. Asked how he came to study the origin of the elements, Hoyle, settling back in a well-stuffed chair, recalls a wartime visit to the West Coast of the United States.

During World War II Hoyle became involved with radar development for the British Navy, as was the case for many bright young physicists in Great Britain. In November 1944, toward the end of the war, this work took Hoyle to the United States and the huge dockyards at San Diego where ships were being outfitted with the latest radar equipment. Eager to take advantage of being so close to Mount Wilson Observatory, the premiere astronomical observatory of its time, Hoyle arranged for a

Fred Hoyle.
California Institute of Technology

lift to journey the 120 miles north. He went by tram, at a cost of 25 cents, on the final leg from Los Angeles to Pasadena, "which in those days was planted the whole way by orange groves," he remembers. "A sandwich purchased at close on midnight at the Huntington Hotel cost 10 shillings, which seemed a mighty lot to pay for a sandwich in those days."

The observatory's headquarters on Santa Barbara Street were largely deserted, as most of its staff had been assigned to war-related projects. An exception was Walter Baade, a German émigré who had been designated an "enemy alien" and restricted to the Pasadena area. For an astronomer, this was more of a bonanza than a hardship; with the Los Angeles area blacked out nightly during the conflict under fear that the Japanese might attack the West Coast, the night sky in southern California was darker than it had been for decades. With almost unlimited time on Mount Wilson's famous one-hundred-inch reflector, the largest telescope in its day, Baade was acquiring superb data.

Spending the weekend in Baade's company, Hoyle came to learn the details of the German's pioneering work on supernovae, done in collaboration with Caltech astronomer Fritz Zwicky. More than an explosion *on* a star, Baade and Zwicky were talking of the very obliteration *of* a star, a phenomenon only then becoming accepted by the astronomical community. It became clear that a star could ferociously blaze for weeks with the intensity of a billion suns. Scientific journals were so scarce in wartime Britain that Hoyle was able to peruse the literature on supernovae for the first time in California. "So it came about that I left Pasadena richer by far more than the 10 shillings I had spent on a sandwich," says Hoyle, "richer in now possessing a handful of much-valued reprints, and in having for the first time an idea of just how exceedingly high stellar temperatures and densities might become during the late stages of stellar evolution." When he returned to England, Hoyle began to ask what elements a star might concoct under such explosive conditions.

The idea of brewing a variety of elements within a star was already in the air. The British astronomer Robert Atkinson, who thought of a star as a giant cooking pot, had written a paper in 1931 that attempted to demonstrate how all the elements could be forged inside a star, but physicists' rudimentary knowledge of the atomic nucleus at that time doomed his effort. Several years later Bethe and von Weizsäcker's success at showing exactly how hydrogen is converted into helium in the fiery bath of a stellar core renewed interest in the question, but the overwhelming problem was finding a place hot enough to carry out the required nuclear reactions. According to initial estimates, the synthesis of elements heavier than helium required much higher, more extreme temperatures than those found in a typical star. Otherwise, the heavier nuclei would never overcome their electrostatic repulsion, thus preventing them from fusing. In supernovae, Hoyle found a possible alternative site.

"It was but a short step from there to seeing that temperatures might well be so high that the abundances of the elements could be calculated from statistical mechanics," explains Hoyle. Lack of information on nuclear "cross sections," the probability that a particular nuclear reaction can take place, thwarted his calculations for a while, until he went to the Cavendish Library one day and unexpectedly bumped into nuclear physicist Otto Frisch, who possessed a volume on this hard-to-find data. Within a year, Hoyle published his first paper on the subject, "The Synthesis of the Elements from Hydrogen," in the *Monthly Notices of the Royal Astronomical Society*. In the paper, Hoyle ventured that as the inner core of an aging star suddenly collapses and its temperature soars, heavier and heavier elements, up through iron, are constructed and then spewed into space in the star's final explosive death throes. Hoyle's statistics even showed that elements huddled around iron on the periodic table would be relatively abundant, just as they are on Earth. Strangely enough, Hoyle's publication was little noticed when it appeared in 1946. "It certainly didn't create a furor," remarks Hoyle.

What was missing was the exact mechanism, the nuclear route, by which elements more massive than helium are forged out of the elements preceding them on the periodic table. Hoyle's statistics appeared to show that it can and does happen in supernovae, but at that stage neither Hoyle nor anyone else could yet explain on the submicroscopic level how an atom as simple as carbon is formed from helium. The seventeenth-century writer Ben Jonson shrewdly observed that gold couldn't have been made on Earth, that "something went before." This was obviously a lucky guess on his part given the state of knowledge in the 1600s, but it was correct nonetheless. Before the atomic age, physicists had generally assumed that the elements always were and would always be. But the revelations emerging from atomic physics laboratories in the first half of the twentieth century made the idea of constructing elements within the hot interiors of stars more and more attractive. As Eddington remarked in 1920 upon seeing Ernest Rutherford and his expert staff transforming elements by bombarding them with atomic particles, "What is possible in the Cavendish Laboratory may not be too difficult in the sun."

But any theoretical scheme to fabricate within stars any elements more massive than helium was stymied by a formidable nuclear roadblock: No one could get past helium-4, the common isotope of helium whose nucleus consists of two protons and two neutrons. Throw a neutron or a proton at a helium nucleus and it may stick—but only for an instant. Any atom with five nuclear particles, known in the trade as having mass 5, decays extremely quickly. After helium-4, the next stable nucleus is an isotope of lithium with mass 6 (three protons and three neutrons). For nuclear physicists the jump from mass 4 to mass 6 was a chasm as yawning and as unbridgeable as the mighty Grand Canyon. Without a sizable supply of mass 5 in a star, it seemed fruitless to consider building atoms with six or more nuclear particles. How could you possibly proceed from helium to lithium, from lithium to beryllium, from beryllium to boron, or from boron to carbon (and so on) up the periodic table? Even Bethe, in the course of his early hydrogen fusion work, had surmised that "under present conditions, no elements heavier than helium can be built up to any appreciable extent" within a star's interior. Other respected astrophysicists tackled this question as well and arrived at the same dismaying conclusion.

Facing what looked like an insurmountable barrier to the creation of elements within stars, others began to attack the problem from a completely different angle, and fields as diverse as cosmology and geology offered some interesting clues. More than a century ago, in the fall of 1889, Frank Wigglesworth Clarke, a chemist with the U.S. Geological Survey, read a paper before the Philosophical Society of Washington outlining a research program that was to become his lifetime pursuit: "The Relative Abundance of the Chemical Elements." Over the next forty years, Clarke and his colleague Henry S. Washington analyzed innumerable terrestrial rocks in hope of finding some periodicity, a regularity, that would help them better understand the periodic table of the elements. No such regularity appeared at first. They were foiled by the simple fact that the most plentiful and volatile elements, hydrogen and helium, had long escaped from the Earth, while other elements had sunk deep into the Earth's core, far from view.

By the 1920s and 1930s other researchers, especially Victor Goldschmidt, the Swiss-Norwegian father of modern geochemistry, recognized that meteorites were far better objects of study because, unlike weathered and reprocessed terrestrial rocks, they remain pristine and untouched in the vacuum of space. Eventually, by combining data from meteoritic, terrestrial, and astronomical sources—the spectral messages emanating from the stars—scientists were able to construct a cosmic abundance graph that displays the relative amounts of each element found throughout the universe. The very shape of this abundance curve has been fashioned by cosmic events that have occurred in both the distant past and more recent epochs. The graph is a wild roller coaster ride that begins on an extremely high hill of plenty at hydrogen and helium, takes a striking dip for the next few elements along the periodic table, then rises back up a bit at carbon and oxygen, and dwindles from there, except for one more majestic peak of abundance at iron. It is a landscape carved by the very forces that gave birth to the elements. Within its peaks and valleys are powerful clues to the history of the stars and galaxies.

Hydrogen accounts for some 93 percent of the total number of atoms in the universe and roughly three-quarters of its mass. Helium has cornered about 6 percent of the atoms, which provide about a quarter of the universe's mass. It is a striking fact that the remaining elements beyond helium—all the "stuff" that predominantly makes up both people and planets—constitute a mere 1 percent of the universe's matter, and these elements generally become increasingly rare as the weight of the

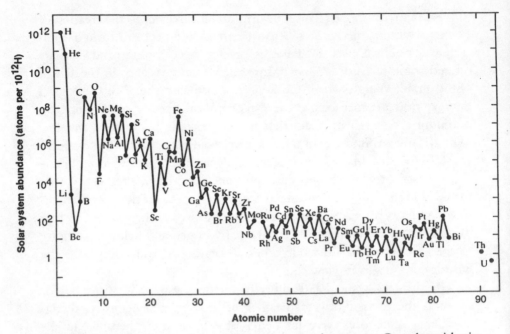

The relative abundances of the elements in our solar system. On a logarithmic scale, the graph displays the number of atoms of each element for every trillion atoms of hydrogen.
Reproduced by permission of Oxford University Press from The Elements *(1989) by P. A. Cox*

atom increases. For every trillion atoms of hydrogen, for instance, there is roughly one atom of uranium. This is the great cosmic stew, and one of astronomy's chief jobs has been to determine the exact ingredients of the stew and figure out how nature arrived at that particular recipe.

William Huggins, as he pursued his pioneering spectroscopic work in the late 1800s, early on suspected that the universe displayed a uniform chemistry. And the successful application of atomic physics to deciphering the varied stellar spectra initially appeared to support Huggins's opinion. By 1948, at a meeting in Zurich, astronomer Otto Struve confidently reported that "the most striking result of [their] discussions is the remarkable degree of uniformity that has been observed in the most widely different astronomical sources. . . . The first conclusion of this symposium is the establishment of a list of what we might call the normal abundances of the elements in the universe. These abundances seem to have the character of a universal law of nature." And if there were a universal law, it seemed to imply that a universal mechanism was at work. With some theorists still unable to show how the heavier elements might be made in stars, others became encouraged to seek an explanation for the cosmos's chemical uniformity in the behavior of the universe at large. The leader in this effort was a jocular Russian émigré named George Gamow.

ELEMENTARY COOKING

George Gamow was an eclectic scientist whose curious mind, like that of a child, constantly flitted from question to question. He was once described as the "swashbuckling physicist," and his curiosity roamed the entire breadth of the physical world, from the workings of the atomic nucleus to the origins of the universe. He was a pioneer in merging the microworld to the macroworld. A lively man with an original (some might say impish) sense of humor, Gamow was often described by his peers as exuding a joy as he talked about science—so much so that colleagues have wondered whether Gamow's fun-loving approach led some scientists to not take his work seriously.

Grandson of a czarist general, Gamow was born in Odessa in 1904 and received his Ph.D. in physics from the University at Leningrad in 1928. Afterward he spent time in Göttingen, Copenhagen, and Cambridge, all world centers in the development of quantum mechanics. Max Delbrück, a quantum physicist who was instrumental in founding the field of molecular biology, once recalled the moment when he first sighted his friend Gamow in Germany:

> In the Cafe Kron & Lanz, in the heart of the town, you could sit by the window on the second floor and watch life go by. Somebody pointed out to me a slightly sensational figure: a Russian student of theoretical physics, fresh from Leningrad. . . . And quite a figure he was too: very tall and thin, and a grating high-pitched voice . . . playful, irreverent, and thoroughly unconventional.

A fair-haired and nearsighted giant known as Geo (pronounced "Joe") to his friends, Gamow had made his first major contribution to physics at the age of twenty-four when he used the equations of quantum mechanics to explain how radioactive elements, such as uranium, could eject entire helium nuclei, historically known as alpha particles, when they decay. By all the laws of nineteenth-century classical physics, there was never enough energy within an atom for a proton or a neutron to break free from a nucleus's steely grip. Yet the incessant clicking of a Geiger counter stationed near a piece of radioactive material obviously indicates that particles still manage to escape from time to time. For a while even modern physicists couldn't explain this amazing feat; it was as difficult to fathom as if someone standing in a windowless and locked room had suddenly popped up outside without opening the room's door.

But Gamow keenly grasped that, in the probabilistic world of the atom, there were small but real odds that a proton or a neutron could acquire enough energy every once in a while to "tunnel" through its nuclear barriers and fly out of the atom—a solution that, to some, appeared more magical than scientific. Yet Gamow's calculations on radioactive alpha decay matched the data perfectly, an achievement that made such world-class figures as Bohr and Rutherford sit up and take notice. Gamow's effort was the first important application of quantum wave mechanics to the field of nuclear physics. Furthermore, his work helped reveal that atomic particles such as protons have the exact same chance to tunnel into a nucleus and stick to it, a theoretical breakthrough that allowed subsequent investigators to solve the problem of fusing hydrogen in a star.

In the early 1930s Gamow moved from Europe to the United States and eventually settled at George Washington University in Washington, D.C. His interest in the problem of nucleosynthesis, the creation of atomic nuclei, began a few years later when he noted that the rate at which various thermonuclear reactions take place must have played a role in setting the relative abundances of the various elements. By 1942, he was imagining the bulk of this process occurring in the earliest stages of the expanding universe, a cosmological fact established less than two decades earlier.

In the 1920s the scientific view of the world was being drastically revised on both ends of the distance scale. Science was facing more than a revolution—it was undergoing a complete reconstruction. At the same time that the Austrian physicist Erwin Schrödinger was introducing atomic physicists to the radical notions of quantum wave mechanics—particles as waves, waves as particles—our home galaxy, the Milky Way, was discovered to be but one among billions of other galaxies spread throughout the vast gulfs of space. Aided by astronomy's newfound comprehension of the chemistry of the stars, the imperious American astronomer Edwin Hubble recognized that the Andromeda Nebula and other misty, spiraling objects in the nighttime sky were separate "island universes," a concept contemplated by the great German philosopher Immanuel Kant as early as the 1700s. The cosmos, cozily centered on us for so long, opened up a millionfold. More startling, Hubble and his crackerjack assistant Milton Humason confirmed in 1929 that these myriad galaxies were racing away from one another in a marathon of cosmic proportions. The entire universe was expanding.

A few years before Hubble directly observed that the universe was ballooning outward, certain theorists who were delving into Einstein's new and startling theory of general relativity had already anticipated that space-time might be dynamic instead of static. A young Russian mathematician and hot-air balloonist named Aleksandr Friedmann, for example, came up with a solution to Einstein's equations in which the universe forcefully expanded, a result that Einstein himself had earlier considered but rejected (to his later regret); the twentieth century's most revered physicist referred to this decision as the greatest blunder in his life. Given the long-standing prejudice in the pre-Hubble era for a tranquil, unchanging cosmos, where the stars carry out their lives in stationary splendor, Friedmann's finding did not receive much notice, at least at first, and Friedmann had little time to champion the idea. In 1925, just a few years after completing his calculations, the creative Russian researcher died of typhoid fever while still in his thirties.

Unaware of Friedmann's work, Belgian priest and astronomer Georges Lemaître independently reached the same conclusion in 1927, but he went one step further. By mentally putting the expansion of the universe into reverse, as if he were shifting some giant cosmic transmission, Lemaître imagined the galaxies moving ever closer to one another, until they ultimately merged and formed a compact fireball of dazzling brilliance. Boldly picturing the cosmos at earlier and earlier moments, Lemaître came to suggest that the universe began with the explosion of a "primeval atom," a state of extremely hot and highly compressed matter. Today's galaxies became fragments blasted outward from this original sphere of material, which the Belgian cleric figured was about the size of our solar system. "The evolution of the world can be compared to a display of fireworks that has just ended: some few red wisps, ashes, and smoke," wrote Lemaître. "Standing on a cooled cinder, we see the slow fading of the suns, and we try to recall the vanished brilliance of the origin of the worlds." From this poetic kernel would emerge the vision of the "big bang," a cosmological model that shapes and directs the thoughts of astronomers today as strongly as Ptolemy's crystalline spheres influenced natural philosophers in the Middle Ages.

Gamow latched onto this idea with relish. The vision was not unfamiliar to him because he had trained under Friedmann while in Russia. By the late 1940s Gamow had become the astrophysical community's most enthusiastic supporter of the big bang model and the scientist most closely identified with it. How the universe came to construct its varied assortment of atoms beyond helium, from lithium to uranium, was still a problem that vexed astronomers. With a stellar answer still not assured, Gamow contended that Lemaître's cosmic egg provided a superb locale for conducting a bit of "elementary cooking," as he liked to put it. By Gamow's estimate this fiery miasma, so hot and dense, could have served as a marvelous soup in which the ninety-odd chemical elements were brewed at the universe's birth in one fell swoop. The newborn universe became one giant fusion reactor.

Working as a consultant at the Applied Physics Laboratory of Johns Hopkins University in nearby Maryland, Gamow came to work closely with Ralph Alpher and Robert Herman, two young employees at the lab who eagerly joined Gamow's crusade. Alpher, who was pursuing his doctoral degree at night at George Washington University with Gamow as his adviser, was scooped on his original thesis topic and in search of a new problem. At an American Physical Society meeting held in 1946, such a problem handily arrived. Eagle-eyed Alpher, who was developing an interest in the origin of the elements, spotted an abstract in the conference program, submitted by Argonne Laboratory physicist Donald Hughes, that surveyed neutron-capture cross sections for some thirty elements, from light to heavy. The cross sections were a measure of the ease at which the materials absorbed neutrons. Hughes was simply attempting to determine what materials might be best for nuclear-reactor construction; but for Alpher and Gamow, access to this type of information, which had been scarce and classified during wartime, was a cosmological breakthrough.

Hughes's figures appeared to be related, in a rough fashion, to overall cosmic abundances. The materials on his list that captured neutrons readily were also the most rare in the universe, which made sense since the added particles would quickly convert the nuclei into other elements. Conversely, substances that were slow to capture neutrons (thus avoiding transmuting into something else) tended to be the elements most plentiful in the heavens. Was this the mark of the very process that occurred in the early universe, when neutrons would have been flying about, helter-skelter, in the superhot and superdense embryonic plasma? Alpher had his thesis topic.

To describe the original stew of neutrons at the beginning of time, Alpher introduced the term *ylem* (pronounced I-lem), a derivation of an ancient Greek word meaning the basic substance out of which all matter was supposedly derived.[1] As the temperature of the universal ylem dropped, some of the neutrons decayed into protons, and these protons promptly began to stick to available neutrons, first forming nuclei of deuterium (a form of hydrogen with one proton and one neutron), then tritium (two-neutron hydrogen), and finally helium and the heavier elements. "In the beginning God created radiation and ylem," Gamow would later write in a whimsical takeoff on the biblical Genesis. "And ylem was without shape or number, and the nucleons were rushing madly over the face of the deep. And God said: 'Let there be mass two.' And there was mass two. And God saw deuterium, and it was good. . . ." According to Alpher's first estimates, all the major reactions taking place in the primordial cauldron were essentially complete in less than half an hour, as free neutrons are short lived and decay away, eventually depleting the supply of ylem. More important, he was able to duplicate, fairly roughly, cosmic abundances. Alpher took this initial accomplishment as an encouraging sign.

Alpher and Gamow reported the first results of their atom building in a short, one-page synopsis in the *Physical Review* on April 1, 1948. This paper, entitled "The Origin of Chemical Elements," is now as famous for its byline as for its content. Gamow, ever the prankster, listed the paper's authors as Alpher, Bethe, and Gamow, adding Hans Bethe's name even though Bethe never participated in the work. Gamow couldn't resist the pun on the first three letters of the Greek alphabet: alpha, beta, and gamma ($\alpha\beta\gamma$). That the paper chanced to be published on April Fool's Day only added to the fun. "It seemed unfair to the Greek alphabet to have the article signed by Alpher and Gamow only," remarked Gamow. When Bethe at last found out about the prank, one of the most popular

---

[1] The word *ylem* is widely associated with Gamow, but Alpher was the first to use the term, in a 1948 paper he published in the *Physical Review*.

stories in astronomical folklore, he professed to be amused by the joke and even sat in on Alpher's thesis defense, which drew both a large audience and widespread coverage in the national press because of its dramatic "universe-constructed-in-five-minutes" conclusion.

Alpher and Herman ("who stubbornly refused to change his name to Delter," Gamow once lamented) carried out further primordial-nucleosynthesis calculations on such early computers as IBM's CPC (Card-Programmed Calculator) located in New York City near Columbia University. A far cry from present-day computers, CPC's programs were "written" by weaving masses of cables into plugboards. Later, Alpher and Herman used SEAC (Standards Eastern Automatic Computer), the National Bureau of Standard's first digital computer. In fact, big bang nucleosynthesis was the first large scientific problem tackled by this primitive machine, which was originally designed to analyze 1950 census data. "We

Robert Herman (left) and Ralph Alpher (right) created this photographic montage showing George Gamow as a genie coming out of a bottle of "ylem." Gamow had pasted the joke label on a favored liqueur bottle to celebrate Alpher's thesis defense.
Courtesy of Ralph Alpher and Robert Herman

were on the graveyard shift," recalls Alpher. "We had access from midnight to eight A.M., and the machine was always blowing away vacuum tubes." But not even the computational power of this wondrous new tool, vacuum tubes and all, could overcome innumerable problems with primordial cooking, especially when the universe's expansion was taken into account explicitly. For one, Alpher and Herman could never establish a unique set of conditions that would generate each and every element. The cosmic expansion both dispersed and cooled down the hot primeval ylem before the heavier elements had any real chance to form. As in stars, the absence of a stable nucleus at mass 5, as well as at mass 8, was impossible to bridge. Consequently, their cosmos ended up being composed of mostly hydrogen and helium, and little else.

Moreover, if element production wholly occurred in the first minutes of an explosive creation, all the stars that later formed out of this rich broth of substances would be expected to contain the same proportions of elements—but this wasn't the case. Astronomers were just beginning to notice that old and young stars differed in their compositions—although they contain similar amounts of hydrogen and helium, they drastically differ when the heavy elements are compared. The oldest stars contain less than 1 percent of the heavy-element abundances found in younger stars, such as our Sun. New stars, enriched with heavy elements, apparently inherited the elemental castoffs of previous stellar generations. Matter seemed to be evolving over the eons from simple forms to more complex ones.

More troublesome was the fact that the big bang theory itself, the essential "stove" for any primordial element cooking, was under a cloud in 1948. By turning the measured rate of the universe's expansion in reverse, astronomers at that time estimated that the fateful cosmic explosion occurred less than two billion years ago. New measurements taken in the 1950s would correct that erroneous estimate and add billions of years to the universe's age. But until that correction was made Gamow had to concede that "a universe 1.8 billion years old could not contain five-billion-year-old rocks." Cosmology, as defined by Hubble and his measurements, was giving one answer to the universe's age; geological evidence, however, plainly indicated for a while that the Earth was vastly older. Like some theoretical game of tennis, this momentary paradox flung the ball back into the court of theorists ardently seeking a stellar explanation for the origin of all the elements.

NUCLEAR ASTROPHYSICS

Even as Alpher, Gamow, and Herman were investigating the big bang's proficiency at concocting the elements, the seeds of a new approach were being sown at Caltech's Kellogg Radiation Laboratory. Facing a small picturesque park and pond, the Kellogg Laboratory sits on the edge of the university campus like some massive concrete monolith. In the 1930s, herculean days in nuclear physics, Pasadena was one of the great centers of the nuclear world, along with Cambridge, England; Berkeley, California; and Washington, D.C. "Morale in Kellogg was incredible," recalls Kellogg physicist William Fowler. "We drank too much and caroused too much, but, boy, look at the list of papers." In some experiments, electrons were annihilated with their antimatter mates, the positrons; in others, particles slammed into specified targets, releasing showers of neutrons and gamma rays.

But while other labs switched to high-energy physics or other more fashionable concerns after World War II, the Kellogg Laboratory continued to pursue classical low-energy nuclear physics, in large part because of a decision by laboratory administrators to tackle astrophysical problems, an apt choice with some of the world's top astronomers working nearby at the Mount Wilson and Palomar observatories. This line of research was further stimulated by the arrival of Jesse Greenstein at Caltech. Brought in to establish an astronomy division at the university, Greenstein was particularly concerned with determining cosmic abundances and explaining their origin. He and others were avidly tracing the telltale signs of nucleosynthesis through their spectroscopic studies of various types of stars.

In some ways, the Kellogg researchers were already veterans in nuclear astrophysics, as their specialty would come to be known. When Bethe reported on the stellar routes to making helium, Kellogg workers realized that they had been studying some of the very nuclear processes involved as they bombarded elements such as carbon and nitrogen with protons, just as certain stars do. And in 1939 it was the Kellogg lab that was one of the first to demonstrate that no stable nucleus existed at mass 5. By 1951, when physicist Edwin Salpeter of Cornell University in New York arrived at Caltech for a summertime visit, the laboratory was introduced to the problem of helium burning in stars.

Salpeter was trying to figure out what happens when the helium nuclei, built up over millions and billions of years in the core of a hydrogen-burning star, begin to interact with each other. Physicists already realized that two helium nuclei bumping into one another was a dead end as a source of stellar energy, since any nucleus of beryllium-8 that might result from such a merger is not stable. In less than a trillionth of a second, the beryllium simply disintegrates back into two alpha particles, with the result that energy is neither gained nor lost. Given that obstacle, Salpeter began to explore whether *three* helium nuclei could come together to form carbon-12, a triple play that skips over the beryllium problem altogether. He thought of it as a two-stage process: Two helium nuclei (alpha particles) collide to form an atom of beryllium, but before the beryllium has a chance to fall apart, it hits a third helium nucleus to form an atom of carbon-12, which is stable and so sticks around. This process is particularly likely in a red giant star, whose intensely hot interior can maintain a small but vital supply of unstable beryllium. "It was the first indication," Fowler has noted in evaluating these times, "that . . . hydrogen burning was just the very start of all this nuclear astrophysics."

William A. Fowler, a gregarious and hard-drinking man best known as "Willy" to his friends and colleagues, grew up in Lima, Ohio, where he acquired a lifelong love for railroads by watching the construction of huge locomotives at the Lima Locomotive Works near his boyhood home. By waiting tables and stoking furnaces at fraternity and sorority housing, Fowler worked his way through Ohio State University and obtained a bachelor's degree in engineering physics in 1933. Moving on to Caltech for graduate work in nuclear physics, he fortuitously arrived on campus at a peak of activity.

The Kellogg lab had been constructed in 1931 expressly to test the clinical applications of high-voltage X rays, but the following year was a watershed for nuclear physics. Not only were the positron and the neutron discovered, but in England particles accelerated with man-made devices initiated their first nuclear reaction—a lithium target was bombarded with protons to produce helium. Within days the Kellogg lab converted one of its high-voltage X-ray tubes into a crude ion accelerator and began its own experiments with accelerated particles. The Kellogg researchers were soon producing neutrons artificially by the tens of thousands. Fowler, a newcomer who soon learned to be a shrewd and adept player at the physics game, served a prominent role in designing and building accelerator equipment at the lab for a host of nuclear experiments that studied both the nature of the strong nuclear force and the ways in which neutrons and protons can be captured by an atomic nu-

William A. Fowler.
California Institute of Technology

cleus. After World War II, with the encouragement of Mount Wilson Observatory director Ira Bowen, the Kellogg lab focused its efforts on studying the nuclear reactions responsible for the energy output of the Sun, an endeavor that eventually found Fowler teamed with Fred Hoyle.

In Great Britain Hoyle, too, had suspected that helium burning might involve a direct jump from helium to carbon-12; but, weary of publication battles over his unorthodox theories, he gave the problem to a graduate student, who dropped out of Cambridge with the job unfinished. Losing out to Salpeter in 1952, Hoyle was determined to restake his claim. "To win something back from the wreckage, I decided to work from helium all the way up to iron," recalls Hoyle. A magazine reporter around this time described Hoyle as taking "delight in setting off mathematical firecrackers under his more conservative colleagues." A leading spokesman for the "Cambridge cosmographers," Hoyle was still just one of a handful of physicists who were applying mathematics and physics to the problems of the universe and, by the 1950s, had even more reason to prefer a stellar solution to the origin of the elements. Hoyle's favorite cosmological model of the universe, a rival to the big bang, required stellar nucleosynthesis in order to make any sense of the composition of the heavens. His universe had a cold start—or rather, no starting point at all.

The initial problems with the big bang cosmology in its early years had encouraged a group of young scientists then at Cambridge—astrophysicist Thomas Gold, mathematician Hermann Bondi, and Fred Hoyle—to develop an alternate view of the universe: the "steady state" model. According to Hoyle, they were inspired one evening in 1946 after seeing a movie, a ghost story, entitled *Dead of Night*. Hoyle recalls that the film "had four separate parts linked ingeniously together in such a way that the film became circular, its end the same as the beginning." Gold asked his friends that night whether the universe might be constructed in a similar fashion. During the spirited discussion that followed, they worked out the details: The steady-state universe was still an expanding one (Hubble's data couldn't be denied), but it was a cosmos with no distinct beginning and no preordained end. From wherever one viewed the universe—and from every point in time—it always looked the same, because matter was continually and spontaneously being created to fill in the gaps opened up by cosmic expansion. Galaxies were endlessly forming out of the new material to replace those that receded beyond our view. The Cambridge group estimated that, to keep this process going at a constant rate, only one atom of hydrogen needed to be created each hour in roughly every cubic mile of intergalactic space. Perpetually creating a bit of something out of nothing over the years was easier for steady-state supporters to swallow than imagining a dense and monstrous fireball originating all at once. "It seemed absurd to have all the matter created as if by magic . . . without a blush of embarrassment," declared Hoyle. A steady-state universe provided a safe haven for those who were squeamish at contemplating an honest-to-goodness moment of creation.[2] Many were attracted to the eternal elegance of a cosmos with neither beginning nor end.

---

[2] It is ironic that Hoyle, the tenacious steady stater, gave his rivals a name for their cosmological model. In the late 1940s, during a popular British radio series on cosmology, Hoyle offhandedly described the explosive version of creation as a "big bang cosmology." The adjective stuck and turned into a noun. Gamow, Alpher, and Herman, however, never cared for the term.

It should be noted that, as early as 1932, Arthur Eddington foreshadowed the expression. He was disturbed by the idea that an expanding universe might imply a "peculiar beginning of things," and he wrote in his book *The Nature of the Physical World,* "As a scientist I simply do not believe that the present order of things started off with a bang; unscientifically I feel equally unwilling to accept the implied discontinuity in the divine nature."

While Hoyle's quest for the origin of the elements in stars certainly originated a few years before his association with the steady-state theory, the astronomical community inevitably linked the two, for the theory assuredly needed the heavier elements to be cooked up in stars. Deeming it improbable that a continuous creation would generate anything heavier than hydrogen, and prodded by their desire to avoid a primeval fireball, steady staters recognized that stellar interiors and supernovae were marvelous environments in which to construct the weightier elements. Continuous creation would generate the raw material—hydrogen atoms—and the stars could then process it into more complex elements.

Almost immediately after Salpeter devised his scheme to burn helium into carbon, Hoyle noticed a snag. "The carbon kept slipping away into oxygen as it was produced," explains Hoyle. The carbon tended to capture another helium nucleus fairly quickly, to form oxygen. So why is there any carbon left in the universe at all, which so obviously serves as the cornerstone of Earth's biosphere? Hoyle figured that the synthesis of carbon in a star would be enhanced, building up a reservoir, *if* the carbon could exist in a specific and precisely tuned energetic state. Normally when atomic nuclei are pushed together, they want to separate immediately, as a result of electromagnetic repulsion. But fusion can be favored when the nuclei are at certain energies, what physicists call resonances. At resonant energies, particles can more readily slip past those electromagnetic barriers and interact. In this way, a sparse production of nuclear reactions at some energies can turn into big yields at other energies.

All the while, new astronomical observations were encouraging Hoyle and others in their efforts to deduce how elements are made in stars. In 1952 Paul Merrill, observing from Mount Wilson, reported that he had found some stars whose spectra revealed the presence of technetium, a rare element whose most stable isotope has a lifetime of less than a million years. That meant the technetium had to have been generated in the star itself; if made during the big bang billions of years in the past, the technetium atoms would have disappeared over the eons through radioactive decay, with no chance of regenerating. Technetium is seen on Earth only when made artificially.

The same year that Merrill announced his discovery, Hoyle arrived at Caltech as a visiting professor of astrophysics. Fortuitously, he had come to one of the few places in the world that had the equipment to test his radical idea on the carbon resonance.

During his stay at Caltech, Hoyle dropped by the Kellogg Laboratory and began to ask Fowler and others about the energy levels measured for the carbon-12 nucleus. After assessing the amount of carbon in the universe, Hoyle, brash and confident of his calculations, was boldly insisting that carbon had to have an excited state, a resonance, at an energy near 7.7 million electron volts (MeV).[3] At that energy the helium nuclei would merge into carbon at a rate millions of times faster than Salpeter had calculated. A research group at Cornell many years earlier had reported a resonant energy level for carbon near 7.6 MeV, but competing labs at the Massachusetts Institute of Technology and elsewhere failed to confirm it. Though listed in some reference works, the resonance was highly questionable. Ward Whaling, a young postdoctoral researcher at Kellogg in the fifties, today does not recall ever seeing a 7.6-MeV resonance for carbon listed on the huge energy-level diagrams that papered the hallways of the Kellogg lab. If it was, he adds, the resonance must have been tagged as doubtful.

With that in mind, Fowler was distinctly skeptical that a theorist, a steady-state cosmologist at that, could be making pronouncements about carbon-12, telling experimentalists that the resonance must exist based on astrophysical concerns. "Remember," Fowler once related, "we didn't know [Hoyle] all that well. Here was this funny little man who thought that we should stop all this important work that we were doing . . . and look for this state. . . . We kind of gave him the brushoff."

But others in Fowler's group were not so quick to dismiss Hoyle's hunch. During a well-attended meeting in Fowler's office, with Hoyle and a mob of Kellogg staff scientists crowded into the small room, Whaling took up the challenge. "When the opportunity came to look for this excited state of carbon," says Whaling, "we thought it would be fun to try. Heck, postdocs are always looking for something interesting to work on. We probably do more of that when we're young—trying out wild ideas." Whaling was joined by two graduate students, Ralph Pixley and William Wenzel, as well as a visiting physicist from Australia, D. Noel F. Dunbar.

"The part I best remember is getting the magnet moved," recalls Whaling. The magnet, a huge piece of iron crucial to the measurement, was initially housed in a small, thick-walled room where experimental

---

[3] The energies of elementary particles and atoms are traditionally given in terms of electron volts. One electron volt (eV) is the energy an electron picks up as it crosses a one-volt electric field, the voltage of a penlight battery.

radiation treatments had been given to cancer patients. But a test of Hoyle's hypothesis required a higher-energy particle accelerator and so Whaling needed to move the magnet to a room situated a couple dozen yards around the corner and down the hall. His cheap and imaginative solution was to place the magnet, which weighed several tons, on top of a big sheet of steel and move the entire assembly over a herd of tennis balls. "Well, it worked, but it wasn't very graceful," says Whaling. "The tennis balls kept getting squashed."

The particle accelerator, located on the floor above, generated a beam of deuterons (hydrogen nuclei comprising a proton and a neutron) that was directed down to the room below. Bombarding a target of frozen ammonia, these deuterons transformed the ammonia's nitrogen atoms into oxygen. Each oxygen atom in turn immediately decayed into a carbon-12, releasing an alpha particle that went flying off. Directing these alpha particles through the massive magnet, Whaling and his team were able to measure the particles' energies very precisely. In Whaling's laboratory notebook, on a page dated January 15, 1953, a tiny blip is at last seen among a host of other, much bigger peaks on the graph. It was the first indication that some of the alpha particles were speeding away from carbon atoms that were energized to 7.68 MeV.

"This was the first time that anyone, before or since, predicted a level in a nucleus before it was firmly seen," says Whaling from his present-day office near the Kellogg lab. A chart of the nuclides, the Bible of his field, covers an entire bulletin board. "We can't predict the energy levels of nuclei even today, because the computations are still too complicated," he adds. It's not that Hoyle understood the nucleus better, but he did know what was needed to make carbon in a star." Hoyle had predicted that the energy state would be found at 7.68 MeV. More precise measurements now fix it at 7.654 MeV, a "tour de force," Fowler has said. "No nuclear theorist starting from basic nuclear theory could do that then, nor can they really do it now. So Hoyle's prediction was a very striking one." The finding was further confirmed when the Kellogg lab observed the reverse reaction—an atom of carbon-12 breaking up into three alpha particles.

Hoyle describes the entire episode as "a minor detail." But, he goes on to say, "because it was seen by physicists as an unusual and successful prediction, it had a disproportionate effect in converting them from the currently held view that the elements were all synthesized in the early moments of a hot universe to the more mundane view that the elements are synthesized in stars." During the remainder of his visit to Caltech,

Hoyle went on to describe carbon burning and oxygen burning in stars.

Fowler considered it a "triumph" for Hoyle to predict a nuclear state from astrophysical arguments. His earlier skepticism disappeared. He was so elated by this turn of events that he took his first sabbatical at Hoyle's home grounds in Cambridge, England, where he also came to meet and work on problems of stellar nucleosynthesis with Geoffrey and E. Margaret Burbidge, a young husband-and-wife team who had begun to ask why certain stars had extra dollops of heavy elements. "When Geoff [first] walked into my office I thought he was Charles Laughton, same girth, same double chin," Fowler has recalled. "And then he said, 'Well, I want you to meet my wife.' So we arranged to meet and, my God, . . . she was so incredibly beautiful. . . . I could hardly believe that this beautiful girl had married this character with a double chin and a waist folded over his belt, but they were the perfect team—she the observationist and he the theorist."

The following year, 1955, Hoyle again visited Caltech, with the Burbidges arriving in Pasadena as well on research fellowships at Fowler's invitation. Margaret, a skilled astronomical observer, had attempted to get a post at the Mount Wilson Observatory, but its door was then firmly closed to women. The observatory's director lamely pointed out that there were no toilet facilities for women on the mountain. (Margaret, with great aplomb, simply said she'd use the bushes.) Geoffrey, the theorist, got the observing position instead, while Margaret was assigned to the Kellogg lab. Sympathetic astronomers on Mount Wilson, though, looked the other way when, during Geoffrey's allotted viewing time, Margaret manned the telescope controls.

The teaming of Fowler, Hoyle, and the Burbidges turned out to be one of the most successful collaborations in astronomical history. New observations were spurring them on, lending further confidence that many elements were manufactured inside stars. Some nearby stars, for instance, were found to differ from one another in metal content by factors of three, which strongly suggested that the stars were altering their ingredients over time and not just coalescing out of a ready-made blend spewed from the big bang.

Two other occurrences proved timely for the Caltech team. As a goodwill gesture at an atoms-for-peace meeting in Geneva, the United States released a formerly classified list of neutron-capture rates, which proved invaluable in nucleosynthesis calculations. Around the same time, chemists Hans Suess and Harold Urey published the most complete table of cosmic abundances ever gathered from geochemical and astronomical data. As Suess and Urey reported in their seminal 1956 paper, it was now evident "that the abundances of the elements and their isotopes reflected nuclear properties and that matter surrounding us bore signs of representing the ash of a cosmic nuclear fire in which it was created." The origin of the elements was at last within reach, and the Suess-Urey results served as a superb road map for tracing many of the nuclear processes involved.

In 1957 Margaret Burbidge, Geoffrey Burbidge, William Fowler, and Fred Hoyle jointly published their findings in *Reviews of Modern Physics*. Their formidable paper, "Synthesis of the Elements in Stars," more than one hundred pages in length, opens with an appropriate quotation from Shakespeare's *King Lear:* "It is the stars, / The stars above us, govern our conditions." And so the American and three Britishers came to prove it. By laying out a comprehensive theory of nucleosynthesis in stars, their scientific paper attained a stature that transcends ordinary citations. In astronomy circles the paper is simply referred to as B^2FH (pronounced B-squared F H, from the initials of the authors' surnames), like some chemical formula. In this seminal paper are clearly elucidated a variety of routes to chemical synthesis, including the direct fusing of atoms, the addition of protons and helium nuclei to existing elements, or a nucleus's capture, either slowly or rapidly, of additional neutrons. B^2FH outlines how each route occurs at a specified time and stellar condition. "It was the only time in my life when the world suddenly believed what I had to say. Normally, they don't," says Hoyle wryly. The time was obviously ripe for a solution. Astrophysicist Alastair G. W. Cameron, then working in Canada, independently reached similar conclusions, although he received little notice at the time, having published in a less prestigious journal.

Stellar nucleosynthesis might be imagined as a cosmic game of billiards around the periodic table. The balls are neutrons and protons, and the resulting elements serve as markers for the steplike evolution of a star. Consider the case of our Sun, the closest star at a distance of ninety-three million miles. When the bulk of the hydrogen in the Sun's core is converted to helium some five billion years from now, its central furnace will flame out, and nuclear burning will then take place in a shell of hydrogen surrounding the inert helium core. Its fire extinguished, the dormant core will start to contract and heat up greatly. But in doing so, the core gives up gravitational energy that will push the outer envelope of the Sun farther and farther outward. It is one of the most dramatic transformations that can occur in a star, a grand celestial metamorphosis. The Sun, a rather ordinary G-type star, will swell to gigantic proportions, nearly swallowing the inner planets and changing its predominant hue from yellow to red as temperatures decrease in the greatly expanded surface layers. As a red giant star, the Sun will outshine all the nearest celestial bodies for tens of millions of years.

Over time the Sun's shell of hydrogen, burning at a furious rate, will heap more and more helium upon the inactive core. Once it is compressed and heated to one hundred million degrees, the helium finally ignites and fuses into carbon and oxygen, the two most common elements in the universe after hydrogen and helium. Our Sun, a rather small star, will stop fabricating elements at this stage. Shedding its glowing red outer envelope over time, the Sun will eventually shrink and become a white dwarf star, what is essentially the luminous remains of the blazing stellar core.

But in stars more massive, the fusion process goes on and on. The carbon core gets surrounded by a helium-burning shell, with a hydrogen-burning shell farther out. The center of the massive red giant starts developing a series of layers, akin to the structure of an onion. The carbon and oxygen atoms, heated to a billion degrees, go on to fuse into neon and magnesium. These, in turn, can serve as the raw materials in the construction of even heavier elements, such as silicon, sulfur, argon, and calcium, each chemical group burning (i.e., fusing) in successive concentric shells.

An interesting sideshow also takes place during all this stellar cooking. Free neutrons, produced in certain stellar-fusion processes, can be slowly captured by various elements in the envelope of the star, thus seeding the star with heavier and heavier elements, like added spice. Since neutrons have no electric charge and so are not subject to electromagnetic forces, they can more easily slip into a charged nucleus and fuse. This was the very process that produced the technetium that Merrill discovered in certain red giants. Indeed, elements up to bismuth on the periodic table can gradually get made in this way during a star's lifetime.

If a star is massive enough, the equivalent of eight or more Suns, its core will continue fusing elements until iron is formed, which is the end of the line. The fusion of elements heavier than iron requires more energy than it releases. All this celestial brewing has been simulated on powerful computers, but it is not just a theoretical game. Astronomers see the evidence directly with their telescopes as they sift through the debris of ancient supernovae. It is an interesting interplay between physics and astronomy. Nearly every nucleosynthesis process can be observed in some freak star or supernova remnant.

Once a red giant begins to accumulate iron within its core, death is inevitable. The star faces its waterloo. Bereft of fusion-generated energy to withstand the force of its own gravitation, the core collapses in less than a second! It is a process hard to imagine. Formerly encompassing a volume about the size of the Moon, the star's center is suddenly squeezed into a sphere about a dozen miles in diameter, the size of a thriving metropolis. Under such tremendous pressure, all the protons and electrons merge to form an ultradense ball of neutrons. In the blink of an eye, a neutron star is formed. Like a compressed coil, the newly squashed neutron core, which might be thought of as one giant atomic nucleus, rebounds a bit, generating a powerful shock wave that spends a couple of hours working its way through the star's remaining outer envelope. There light elements rapidly absorb neutrons and convert into heavier nuclei— even the dozens of elements beyond iron, such as gold, silver, iodine, arsenic, tin, and uranium. This wave of element transformation continues until the star's outer envelope is completely blown off, scattering the stuff of future stars and planets. For a while that corner of the universe lights up with the brilliance of millions of suns. Spreading its elemental ashes through space—its tons of newly formed iron, nickel, tin, and copper, to name a few—a supernova is one of the driving forces behind the material evolution of the universe. Its shock wave, reverberating through space, will sweep up and nudge clumps of interstellar gas to condense into new stars. From death comes life.

THE BIG BANG TRIUMPHS

The theory of stellar nucleosynthesis was clinched when abundances for the elements found throughout the universe actually matched those calculated by B^2FH and Cameron. The celestial cycle begins in such clouds as the Orion Nebula, where newborn stars condense out of the gaseous mist, and reaches a grand finale when matter is scattered through space in such supernova remnants as the Crab Nebula. Our bones, our blood, our clothes, the air, and the ground beneath our feet are all the ashes of a previous generation of stars. Stellar winds, powerful supernova explosions, and intermittent blasts off the surfaces of white dwarf stars seed interstellar space with this vital elemental dirt. Within an ancient super-

THE LIFE OF A 25-SOLAR-MASS STAR

Stage	Duration
Hydrogen burning	7,000,000 years
Helium burning	500,000 years
Carbon burning	600 years
Neon burning	1 year
Oxygen burning	6 months
Silicon burning	1 day
Core collapse	less than 1 second

nova remnant located in the prominent northern constellation Cassiopeia, for instance, are seen filamentary, fast-moving knots of heated gas enriched with oxygen, sulfur, magnesium, and silicon. Within a billion years or so, these atoms may serve as the building blocks of new suns and new planetary systems.

There was only one problem with this magnificent picture of the evolution of the elements. A glaring puzzle remained: There was too

The Great Nebula in Orion, birthplace of new stars.
National Optical Astronomy Observatories

much helium in the heavens. Astronomers were hard-pressed to explain where all the helium in the universe came from and why it was so uniformly distributed. It is indisputable that a lot of helium is made in stars, but it didn't look as if the bulk of the helium seen throughout the cosmos could possibly have been made in stellar interiors. The amount of helium observed, nearly a quarter of the universe's mass, far exceeds the stars' collective capability to make it. Hoyle turned his attentions to this problem in 1963 while preparing a course on relativity and cosmology at Cambridge. Collaborating with British astronomer Roger J. Tayler, Hoyle concluded that "mild cooking [in stars] is not enough and that most, if not all, of the material of our everyday world, of the Sun, of the stars in our Galaxy and probably of the whole local group of galaxies, if not the whole Universe, has been 'cooked' to a temperature in excess of 10 billion degrees Kelvin"—in other words, baked in an early primordial fire. The gadfly of astrophysics, Hoyle enjoys playing devil's advocate in science; here was a founder (and still very vocal advocate) of the steady-state theory considering a big bang cosmology to make helium. "When a line of research has turned out profitably," he has said, "the urge is to claim everything one can think of for it. I have always tried to resist this temptation, however, preferring rather to look for exceptions to the general rule, rather as mathematicians look for exceptions to a theorem." (It is purported that this tendency of Hoyle's to challenge conventional wisdom, as well as his later interest in such radical ideas as panspermia—extraterrestrial microorganisms seeding Earth with life—cost him the Nobel Prize.)

A year later, Hoyle's reevaluation of helium's origins received powerful support in one of the most important discoveries in cosmology, the anchor upon which the entire big bang theory hangs. The notion of a primordial explosion originally had many strikes against it: It couldn't make all the elements, and it failed for a while to match the measured age of the universe. But astronomical evidence at last shifted in favor of the big bang. During the 1950s astronomers detected many faint radio sources in the distant universe, which implied that the universe was more active in past eons. The 1963 discovery of quasars, what are thought to be the violent cores of newborn galaxies residing in the universe's distant past, further suggested that galaxies had evolved from some turbulent primordial state. The clinching evidence arrived when two industrious Bell Laboratory researchers, Arno Penzias and Robert Wilson, spotted a uniform wash of microwave radiation, radio waves nearly three inches in length, spread across the celestial sky. While upgrading a three-story-high microwave horn in the suburbs of New Jersey in preparation for a radio astronomy survey, they had stumbled upon the faint, reverberating thunder of the big bang.

Alpher and Herman had predicted the existence of such a microwave background in 1948, about six months after publication of the famous αβγ paper. Curiously, their fascinating calculation was largely forgotten, a victim of its time. Cosmology in the 1940s, Alpher and Herman contend, was "a skeptically regarded discipline not worked in by 'sensible' scientists." They also wonder whether there were sociological reasons for the sparse attention to their work. In the mid-1950s the two collaborators went on to establish distinguished scientific careers in industry, Alpher at General Electric's Corporate Research and Development and Herman at General Motors Research Laboratories. Working in that arena, they were not readily identified as part of the astrophysical community.

Meanwhile, radio astronomy, still in its infancy in 1948, had other pressing concerns, and with the big bang model then on the outs, no one pushed to make the observation. Penzias and Wilson's serendipitous detection sixteen years later swiftly reversed these attitudes. Here was definitive evidence of the universe's changing "weather." One minute after the primordial explosion, the universe's temperature was a blistering one billion degrees. One day later the universe's swift expansion dropped the temperature down to about forty million degrees. At an age of ten million years, the lingering warmth of yesteryear's cosmic fire was room temperature. Today, some fifteen billion years later, with all the mass and energy spread so thin—all the highly energetic light waves born in the primordial explosion stretched to microwaves with the universe's expansion—the overall temperature of the cosmos now stands at a frigid three degrees above absolute zero, the theoretical temperature at which all molecular motions cease ($-273.15°$ Celsius). "This discovery," British cosmologist Martin Rees has commented, "quickly led to a general acceptance of the so-called 'hot big bang' cosmology—a shift in the consensus among cosmologists as sudden and drastic as the shift of geophysical opinion in favour of continental drift that took place contemporaneously. . . . It was a relic of an epoch when the entire universe was hot, dense, and opaque."

The discovery of the microwave background spurred a whole new generation of researchers to reconsider and advance the groundbreaking investigations of Alpher, Herman, and Gamow in computing the amounts and types of elements concocted during the first few minutes of a blazing genesis. The scenario that these new researchers weave from their theoretical and computer-generated musings begins a few seconds after the fateful explosion, a time when the protons, neutrons, and electrons in existence were dashing madly through a dense ocean of neutrinos and photons—"a thick, viscous fluid of light," as one theorist put it. A significant change in the fireball, however, occurred one hundred seconds after the universe's birth. As soon as the expanding universe had cooled to about a billion degrees, the neutrons and protons were able to start sticking together, building up a pool of deuterium. The very instant that that happened, the dam broke, and a host of other nuclear reactions began to take place. Deuterium, a fragile thing, immediately combined with available protons and neutrons to form helium. A small fraction of this helium, in turn, joined with other nuclei flying about to forge lithium. Within minutes it was over. Nearly one-quarter of all the mass in the universe was converted into helium; three-quarters remained as hydrogen nuclei (single protons); a tiny smattering of lithium, helium-3, and leftover deuterium accounted for the rest.

At this stage, the universe had expanded and cooled to the point that its thermonuclear reactor shut down completely. Nucleosynthesis did not begin again in earnest until millions and millions of years later. With the emergence of the first stars out of the primordial gas—and the ignition of their thermonuclear engines—the light elements could at last begin their long and torturous journey up the periodic table.

Describing the conditions of a minutes-old universe is more than a brazen theoretical exercise. Over the years astronomers have been measuring the relative amounts of deuterium, helium, and lithium currently scattered throughout the cosmos. In laboratories, they analyze the chemical composition of meteorites, the pristine leftovers of our solar system's birth. With telescopes, observers search for signs of the primordial elements both in the spectra of stars and in the gases that drift through interstellar space. Even an aluminum foil "window shade," pulled down for a while on the Moon's surface by *Apollo 11* astronauts in 1969 and then brought back to Earth, enabled scientists to determine element abundances from the solar-wind particles that collected on the shade. So far, each and every measurement of a key light element has turned out to be close—remarkably close—to the chemical abundances predicted from big bang nucleosynthesis calculations. This achievement is even more astounding when one considers the vast range encompassed by the predictions: Theory concludes that lithium should constitute less than one-billionth of the universe's mass, while helium makes up 25 percent. Yet, such a broad sweep in magnitude is exactly what observers measure.

The existence of deuterium is a very strong argument in itself for a hot big bang having occurred in the distant past. Nuclear processing invariably causes deuterium to be destroyed in a star—never created. Yet deuterium is seen throughout the universe: in terrestrial and meteoritic water; in the atmosphere of Jupiter; in gaseous nebulae; and in intergalactic space. For now, only a big bang can adequately explain its presence.

Such an accurate match between the theory and measurement of primordial abundances has lent great strength to the big bang theory, perhaps as powerful an argument as the microwave background itself. If anyone still had any doubts in the 1970s, astronomers Leonard Searle at Mount Wilson and Wallace Sargent at Caltech provided some strong observational evidence. At that time these scientists looked at small, blue, compact galaxies in the distant universe and found that the heavy elements in these tiny young galaxies were clearly more scarce than the abundances found in the much older galaxy in which we reside, the Milky Way. That made sense; the Milky Way's stars had more time to cook up the heavy elements. Yet the amounts of helium were just about the same in both types of galaxies, suggesting that helium abundances were high before the first stars were even born. All galaxies, both young and old, were likely supplied with most of their helium early on from the big bang.

Cosmologist Rees provides a small note of caution to all these figurings. "The hot big bang is not yet firm dogma," he asserts. "Conceivably, our satisfaction will prove as transitory as that of a Ptolemaic astronomer who successfully fits a new epicycle. But the hot big bang model certainly seems more plausible than any equally specific alternative—most cosmologists would make the stronger claim that it has a more than 50 percent chance of being essentially correct."

There is more certainty about those epochs in the universe's life where the physics is well known. That period extends from about one ten-thousandth of a second after the "moment of creation" to today, some fifteen billion years later. Uncertainty arrives when scientists attempt to extrapolate farther back in time, where the physics becomes more and more shaky. It is here that additional "stuff" might have emerged from the big bang, flying off and shaping the universe's evolution in a manner yet invisible to our eyes. What else might have been forged in those fateful moments?

The steady-state model of the universe speedily went into eclipse after the discovery of the microwave background, and the big bang theory rose triumphant. But neither cosmological camp could claim complete victory in the story of nucleosynthesis. Researchers seeking the origin of the elements have now fashioned a scenario that incorporates features of both rival cosmologies. Gamow's original idea—a burst of elemental cooking that took but minutes—holds up quite well when considering the creation of the lighter elements; stellar nucleosynthesis, as championed by B^2FH and Cameron, powders the universe with the remaining elements. For his experimental contributions in wresting these secrets from the heavens, William Fowler was awarded the Nobel Prize in 1984. (Appropriately enough, he first heard the news of the prize while attending a conference on nucleosynthesis in the fall of 1983 at the Yerkes Observatory in Wisconsin. As luck would have it, he was in the shower when the phone call came. At six in the morning, three hours before he was to give the first talk at the meeting, word spread like wildfire among the participants. The hotel operator was bewildered by the barrage of telephone calls coming in from around the world. Walking into the hotel breakfast room, Fowler was greeted with a standing ovation.) Practical application of his experimental work was never Fowler's goal. "What we're doing is mainly a cultural and intellectual contribution to the sum total of human knowledge, and that's why we do it," the convivial midwesterner said upon receiving the coveted prize. "If there happen to turn out to be practical applications, that's fine and dandy. But we think it's important that the human race understands where sunlight comes from."

· 6 ·

It's Raining in Orion

In investigating the nature and history of the universe we can hardly do better than to begin by examining what it is made of.

—William A. Fowler

*A bit of talcum
Is always walcum.*

—Ogden Nash, *The Baby*

Astronomer Edward Emerson Barnard was born in 1857 in Nashville, Tennessee, then a thriving cotton center along the Cumberland River. Barnard's father died before he was born. It was left to his mother, an impoverished but cultured woman who earned a little money making wax flowers, to teach her young son to read and write. A formal education was out of the question. Struggling in poverty through the Civil War years, Barnard was forced to leave public school after attending only two months. He went to work when less than nine years old to help support his widowed mother and older brother. But, much like the great German optician Joseph Fraunhofer, Barnard's Dickensian beginnings set the stage for a lifetime of achievement. His stunning and innovative astronomical photographs—he took thousands over half a century at the telescope—were key testimony in encouraging astronomers to overturn their long-held notions about the contents of interstellar space. At the same time that spectroscopists strove to unravel the chemistry of the stars, others puzzled over numerous starless regions sighted throughout the disk of our galaxy. Were these voids truly black and empty, or were they in reality the mark of dark obscuring matter? Could the space between the stars not be so bleak and barren after all?

With the insights provided by the pioneering nuclear astrophysicists in the 1950s, astronomers could think of space as a vast "ecological" system. Elements born in fiery stellar interiors spewed outward, through the action of either a gentle stellar wind or a violent explosion, and were then recycled into new stars. Matter—individual atoms and molecules as well as dust grains finer than talcum—drifted through the disk of our galaxy like flotsam in some celestial river. Today satellites high above the Earth record the continuous stream of particles, the solar wind, that emanates from the Sun. And infrared space telescopes show us wispy streaks, resembling high cirrus clouds, strewn across the celestial sky. With all this evidence about us it is difficult to imagine the time, not much more than a century ago, when astronomers thought of the space between the stars as an unfathomed emptiness. That space should be murky, that space would be "dirty," was difficult for researchers to comprehend; such a concept went against an image of space forged over centuries of observation. Only the infamous, transparent ether was thought to inhabit this vast cosmic realm.

Recognition that interstellar space harbored more tangible substances was not a sudden revelation but a process that extended over many decades. Unveiling this last galactic frontier, the cosmic landscape caught between those shimmering points of light in the nighttime sky, had to await several developments: spectroscopy, the introduction of photography to astronomy, and the persistent, some might even say obsessive, observations of such astronomers as E. E. Barnard.

HOLES IN THE HEAVENS

Barnard learned both persistence and patience at his first job. He was hired to make sure that a gigantic enlarging camera at a Nashville photographic studio, Van Stavoren's Photographic Gallery, was continually pointed at the Sun. The bright sunlight was needed in that pre-electrified era to enlarge small negatives. Previous employees, young boys like Barnard, had fallen asleep at the task; Barnard never did. A picture of Barnard from that time shows a handsome youth with soulful eyes and a determined mouth that speaks of a boy wise beyond his years, despite his Huckleberry Finn–style clothing.

By his teens, Barnard was promoted to assistant at the studio and became intimately acquainted not only with photography but also with the properties of various lenses. The archetypal self-made man, he began to build small telescopes to observe the Moon, stars, and planets. In 1876 he bought a five-inch telescope for the imposing sum of $380, two-thirds of his annual wages. A reading of *The Sidereal Heavens,* a popular astronomy book written in 1840 by a Scottish cleric named Thomas Dick, left a deep imprint on Barnard and forged many of his early ideas on astronomy. From this book's pages, Barnard first learned of great spaces in the heavens that appeared to be deprived of stars.

When the American Association for the Advancement of Science held its annual meeting in Nashville in 1877, Barnard got an opportunity to meet Simon Newcomb, the noted director of the U.S. Naval Observatory. Consumed by a desire to become an astronomer, the young Barnard was anxious to receive some encouragement from the man distinguished for his work on celestial mechanics. Hearing of Barnard's limited schooling, though, Newcomb could only offer the feeble suggestion that Barnard look for comets, an off-the-cuff remark that proved a turning point in Barnard's career. In an era when comet sightings gave the discoverer worldwide celebrity, Barnard officially discovered nine of the fleeting objects between 1881 and 1887, seventeen over his lifetime. This endeavor provided an interesting fringe benefit as well: A patent medicine manufacturer in New York was then offering $200 for each detection of an unknown comet, and Barnard snared the award five times before the prize was discontinued. The money helped him buy his first home in Nashville, which came to be known, appropriately enough, as the Comet House. Barnard's formidable comet-hunting skills led to his appointment in 1883 as assistant astronomer of the Vanderbilt University Observatory in Nashville, where he was placed in charge of the six-inch telescope. There this shy and awkward instructor also acquired his first formal education; although nearly twenty-six years old, married, and far less prepared than his younger, more well-to-do classmates, Barnard became a special student and took courses in mathematics, physics, chemistry, and the modern languages.

In 1887, shortly before turning thirty, the renowned Tennessean comet hunter ventured west to join a group of distinguished astronomers in staffing the newly constructed Lick Observatory atop Mount Hamilton south of San Francisco in California. From San Jose, it took six hours by horse-drawn stage to complete the 366 hairpin turns up to the 4,200-foot-high summit. Living on the isolated mountain for seven years with his wife, Rhoda (the sister of two English artists who had also been employed at the Nashville portrait studio), Barnard began applying his considerable photographic skills to his astronomical pursuits. The recent introduction of fast-drying photographic plates, which replaced the cumbersome wet colloidal process in astrophotography, at last made such efforts more practical.

Terribly self-centered and hungry for attention, Barnard was always plagued by the insecurities born from his indigent past. He protected his discoveries and photographic work with a fierce intensity and wrote wild,

Astronomer Edward Emerson Barnard (1857–1923), standing next to Lick Observatory's thirty-six-inch refracting telescope.
Mary Lea Shane Archives of Lick Observatory

hysterical letters in response to the smallest slight. Radio astronomer and author Gerrit Verschuur, in his book *Interstellar Matters,* aptly described Barnard as a "highly neurotic individual." Competing with his more educated and urbane colleagues, Barnard constantly put off vacations in fear of missing a new discovery at the telescope that he felt would compensate for his poorer astronomical credentials. He could find a comet but, unable to handle advanced mathematics, he could not compute its orbit, a skill far more revered by professional astronomers at the time. Although prone to innumerable psychosomatic illnesses, often related to frequent battles with Lick's dictatorial director, Edward Holden, Barnard always managed to rise out of his sickbed to attend the telescope if the weather was clear. When later working at the University of Chicago's Yerkes Observatory in Wisconsin, he was known to observe when temperatures inside the telescope dome dropped to twenty-five degrees below zero; he stopped only when he feared the telescope might get damaged.

It was a magnificent obsession, and one that paid off handsomely. Barnard's keen eyesight at the telescope was legendary. He suspected that he saw craters on Mars but never published this finding, fearing it was an illusion; cratering on Mars was not confirmed until seven decades later in 1965 when the U.S. space probe *Mariner 4* flew by the red planet. In 1892, after repeated nights of searching with Lick's thirty-six-inch refractor, the most powerful telescope in its day, Barnard spotted a fifth moon around Jupiter. Until that moment no new companion had been seen orbiting the giant planet since Galileo first sighted Jupiter's four largest moons nearly three centuries earlier. Barnard's satellite, closer in to Jupiter and far smaller than the first four, was the last moon in the solar system to be discovered by eye and telescope alone. (Subsequent discoveries have been made either from photographs or by spacecraft.) News of Barnard's achievement was telegraphed around the world, and the acclaim was immediate—a humbling experience for Simon Newcomb. When Barnard was awarded the prestigious Gold Medal of the Royal Astronomical Society in 1897, Newcomb recalled his first meeting with the unassuming amateur astronomer from Nashville: "I did not for a moment suppose that there was a reasonable probability of the young man's doing anything better than amusing himself. . . . It is now rather humiliating that I did not inquire more thoroughly into the case." (Newcomb's foresight was often quite shaky; he also once asserted that no man-made heavier-than-air machine would ever fly.)

Even before his discovery of Jupiter V (later named Amalthea, after

The Pleiades star cluster.
National Optical Astronomy Observatories

the goat that served as wet nurse for Zeus, Jupiter's Greek equivalent), Barnard had begun to take a series of portraits of the Milky Way galaxy that would lead to a complete reevaluation of the nature of interstellar space. Being a junior member of the Lick staff, and in constant struggle with the director over use of the best telescopes and equipment, Barnard was obliged to use a small telescopic camera, contrived from a two-and-a-half-inch portrait lens, strapped to the side of a six-and-a-half-inch telescope, which served as a guiding instrument. The camera required long exposures (up to six hours) because of its small lens. Nevertheless, Barnard was infinitely patient at the most tedious observational chore, and his pictures revealed complicated and detailed structures that were totally unexpected.

After moving to the Yerkes Observatory in 1895, and throughout the rest of his career, Barnard continued adding to this photographic atlas of the sky.[1] Upon photographing the Pleiades, the famous cluster known

---

[1] Barnard's last series of photographs was published in 1927, four years after his death. The prints had to be made in Chicago and then shipped back by truck to Yerkes, and during one of Chicago's infamous mob wars, a stray gangster's bullet pierced a shipment of photographs. For many years the wounded pictures were a popular display at Yerkes.

since antiquity as the Seven Sisters in the Taurus constellation, he remarked that

> the entire group of stars is filled with an entangling system of nebulous matter which seems to bind together the different stars with misty wreaths and streams of filmy light all of which is beyond the keenest vision and the most powerful telescopes.

This was a new and startling image of the heavens, formerly considered so pristine. Dust clouds within the Pleiades were shining by reflected starlight, much the way a fog or mist softly glows around a street lamp. A photograph, unlike the human eye, can continually accumulate light, unveiling sights far too faint to be seen with the unaided eye. Photography turned out to be a technological advance as revolutionary to astronomy as the development of the telescope itself.

Barnard was particularly captivated by the regions of total blackness in his photographs, intervals of starless space interspersed along the Milky Way's river of white. They appeared in many sizes, from small to large, and in varied shapes, such as patches and furrows, that were interposed between bright masses of stars. In 1894 Barnard published these striking images in a British popular-science magazine called *Knowledge*. Seeking an interpretation of these coal-black patches, Barnard echoed the sentiments already voiced by his idol, the great eighteenth-century astronomer William Herschel.

Herschel had lived in an era when a passion for astronomy, despite a lack of formal training, still allowed a diligent observer to make meaningful contributions. Born in Hanover, a province of Prussia, in 1738, Herschel had trained as a musician. Deserting the Hanoverian Guards band and fleeing to England at the age of nineteen, he eventually settled in Bath as a chapel organist. His musical training led him to explore mathematics and later astronomy, which rapidly became his principal interest and increasingly encroached on his musical duties. A skilled craftsman, Herschel began to construct his own telescopes (the most powerful reflectors in their day for the study of faint objects) and in 1781, while searching for double-star systems, encountered a pale green dot that turned out to be the planet Uranus. He was the first person in recorded history to discover a new planet, and the rewards were appropriate: Within a year he acquired a fellowship in the Royal Society, an annual pension of £200, and an appointment as royal astronomer to King

George III. Moving to the town of Slough near Windsor Castle, Herschel continued his nightly vigils until he died at the age of eighty-three.

Two years after his discovery of Uranus, Herschel embarked on an extensive survey of the heavens, a twenty-year effort, to discover new nebulae and clusters, frequently stopping to take star counts in selected fields to trace the structure of the Milky Way. Spending many hours, over many nights, at the eyepiece of his handcrafted twenty-foot-long telescope with its eighteen-inch mirror, Herschel counted the stars that were visible in more than six hundred distinct regions of the sky. From these star counts, an approach that introduced statistical analysis into astronomy, he concluded that the galaxy looked very much like a giant convex-shaped disk, filled with millions of stars.

In the course of his dramatic sweeps across the nighttime sky, Herschel could not help but notice dark regions that appeared to be devoid of stars. He was immediately fascinated. His younger sister Caroline, his tireless assistant, heard him one night exclaim in his native German, *"Hier ist wahrhaftig ein Loch im Himmel!* [Here is truly a hole in the heavens!]," at the sight of a void in the Ophiuchus constellation. He saw a swath of inky blackness snaking through the Milky Way's vast array of stars. It truly did look like a yawning gap in space. Herschel even ventured a guess that these holes in the heavens were formed as nebulae condensed into stars. The stars' great densities, he mistakenly surmised, would attract more matter to them, thus sweeping out these great cavities in space. Barnard, who had come to revere Herschel from his childhood reading of Dick's *Sidereal Heavens,* could only concur. To him the vacancies were actual holes in the star fields, which revealed "deeper depths" beyond.

Thinking of these black regions as vacancies was the popular and traditional view, but murmurs of dissent were arising. Giovanni Schiaparelli, famous for his talk of Martian canals, had already suggested the existence of dark nebulae, which wandered around unseen through the depths of space. And, as early as 1853, spectroscopist Father Angelo Secchi at the Collegio Romano had called Herschel's dark-hole hypothesis "very improbable. . . . It is more likely that the darkness is the result of a dark nebulosity, which seen against a lighter background, absorbs the light." But few listened to this priest caught at the edge of mainstream astronomy. Four decades later, Barnard's editor at *Knowledge,* A. C. Ranyard, secretary of the Royal Astronomical Society, questioned the pre-

A photograph taken by E. E. Barnard in 1907 of a dark "hole in the heavens" in the Taurus constellation.
Photograph by E. E. Barnard, courtesy of Philip Myers

vailing wisdom as well. In a dissenting editorial accompanying Barnard's pictures, Ranyard commented that "the dark vacant spaces referred to by Prof. Barnard seem to me to be undoubtedly dark structures, or absorbing masses in space, which cut out light from a nebulous or stellar region beyond them." But Ranyard's brilliant insight, published as it was in a nonprofessional journal, was totally ignored by the astronomical establishment. The sheer immensity of such dark structures, far bigger than stars or small glowing nebulae, was difficult to accept.

Near the turn of the century, a generous $7,000 donation to the

University of Chicago by philanthropist and astronomy lover Catherine Bruce (she donated a total of $175,000 to American and European observatories during her lifetime) enabled the Yerkes Observatory to build a telescope specifically for astronomical photography. With Barnard's sure hands at the controls, the Bruce Telescope delineated the dark regions, so enigmatic and haunting, as never before. With the increased clarity in his pictures, Barnard was almost ready to make a break with the honored Herschel. Pitch-black lanes meandering through the Taurus constellation led him to wonder whether there might be dark nebulae after all. "If these dark spaces of the sky are due to absorbing matter between the stars—and I must confess that their look tempts one to this belief—such matter must, in many cases, be perfectly opaque," he reported in 1910. But such a conceptual leap was still too great for him. "It is hard to believe in the existence of such matter on such a tremendous scale as is implied by the photographs," he cautiously concluded.

Yet picture after picture only strengthened the case for interstellar matter. Photographing the magnificent Horsehead Nebula, so named for its shadowy profile of a horse, Barnard noted that "one would not question for a moment that a real object—darker looking, but very feebly brighter than the sky—occupies the place of the spot. It would appear, therefore, that the object may not be a vacancy among the stars, but a more or less opaque body."

Years earlier, while conducting a photographic session atop Mount Wilson in southern California, Barnard was struck by the presence of a group of tiny cumulus clouds scattered over the rich star fields of Sagittarius. "Against the bright background they appeared as conspicuous and black as drops of ink," he said. If simple terrestrial clouds can obscure starlight, why not celestial clouds? Astronomers in Europe were reaching the same conclusion. At the Baden Observatory in Germany, Maximilian Wolf was also photographing the Milky Way and its mysterious dark regions, but he approached the problem more quantitatively than did his American acquaintance Barnard. Wolf conducted comprehensive star counts in both bright and dark regions. In an unobstructed sky, the cumulative number of stars generally increases as one goes to fainter and fainter magnitudes. But Wolf saw that the discontinuous changes in the number of stars in the direction of the dark markings, with the faintest stars dropping off most sharply, matched the decreases one would expect if the darkness was due to intervening clouds of interstellar matter blocking out the starlight in those regions.

The Horsehead Nebula.
National Optical Astronomy Observatories

For that matter, there were good scientific reasons for doubting the existence of "holes" in the curtain of stars. Stars were known to move. Over time, any holes that did chance to form would be obliterated; the stars would gradually move in and fill up the cavities. At the very least, the sharp, crisp edges of the holes would be smeared out. And why should all these holes—tunnels, really—be conveniently pointed at the Earth, cutting through the full depth of stars to a vacant space beyond? That was a highly unlikely prospect, unless you contended that the Earth somehow occupied a special location in the heavens.

Despite such compelling arguments, and after more than thirty years of studying these starless patches, Barnard never fully relinquished his belief in holes in the heavens. In 1919, just four years before his death, he published a monumental paper cataloguing 182 dark markings in the sky. (Not until 1960 would a comparable catalogue of dark interstellar clouds be published.) In this impressive review, Barnard conceded that some of the dark zones were undoubtedly obscuring bodies, blocking out the light of more distant stars. "There seems to be no question," he wrote, "that some of them are real objects which are either entirely devoid of light or so feebly luminous when seen against the Milky Way as to appear black." But others, he was careful to add, were "doubtless only vacancies." He remained cautious and conservative to the end. But perhaps Barnard can be forgiven his vacillation. His beautiful photographs still set the stage for a radical reassessment of the heavens' composition. Barnard never realized that the material he saw floating in wispy clouds amidst the stars serves as the building blocks for planets such as Earth and for life itself.

Even as Barnard agonized over an interpretation of the dark, unilluminated regions in his pictures, further evidence in support of interstellar matter was arriving from spectroscopy. In 1904 at the Potsdam Astrophysical Observatory in Germany, Johannes Franz Hartmann was observing the double star Delta Orionis, one of the glittering jewels in Orion's belt, when he noticed certain spectral absorption lines that were produced by calcium atoms caught by chance in front of the star system. Here was evidence that clouds of material, including atoms of calcium vapor, were situated somewhere over the vast distance between Earth and Delta Orionis. Instead of an ethereal void between the stars, Hartmann had detected the presence of gas. Over the next two decades, other astronomers would detect similar effects elsewhere in the sky.

As these observations were being made, there was much talk of widespread interstellar matter but little enthusiasm for recognizing its existence. Except for notable and obvious clouds such as the Horsehead Nebula and the inky Coalsack near the Southern Cross, interstellar space still seemed perfectly transparent. Arthur Eddington, the most eminent astrophysicist of his day, compared his colleagues to guests who, when asked whether they believe in ghosts, reply, "I do not believe in ghosts, but I am afraid of them." Eddington decided it was time for the celestial specters to materialize. By 1926, given Barnard's superb photographs, Wolf's star counts, and the increasing spectroscopic evidence, he took a firm stand. In a Royal Society lecture entitled "Diffuse Matter in Space," Eddington announced that interstellar matter was assuredly spread throughout the galaxy; astronomers must presume it, he asserted. Ironically, it was an incorrect theory of stellar evolution that helped convince him. In the 1920s certain calculations mistakenly suggested that stars shed mass at the same rate as their radiations. For Eddington, interstellar matter had to exist if only to keep the star from evaporating away. The matter would fall back onto the star to keep it fueled. Eddington imagined this gas, like some thin haze, filling all of space but being particularly dense in the dark nebulae. Space, in other words, could be thought of as overcast, exhibiting a variety of clouds both thick and thin.

Eddington concluded that, to attain the level of obscuration seen in the photographs, the dark clouds had to be composed partially of, along with the gas, very fine, solid particles. Henry Norris Russell at Princeton had already expressed a similar idea several years earlier; he had even calculated the amount and type of mass needed to do the job. To account for the observed dimming, the Princeton theorist figured that each grain was less than a tenth of a millimeter long. Yet there were so many of these grains in any one cloud that their collective weight could outweigh the mass of many stars. Eddington was hesitant at first to accept the idea of particles in space. "I have great reluctance (which is perhaps a prejudice) to admit meteoric particles of this kind . . . ," he confessed, "but I cannot suggest an alternative." He toyed with the idea that molecules might be responsible for the dimming, but ultimately he figured that molecules, combinations of atoms, had little chance of surviving the rigors of space. So, dust it was. Once championed by such an august authority as Eddington, the notion of interstellar matter—gas and dust—became far more acceptable. As Verschuur points out, "Eddington's talk was clearly a watershed. It suddenly raised the study of interstellar matter to a respectable level, because of the sheer weight of his reputation."

Final confirmation arrived in 1930 when Robert Trumpler at the Lick Observatory beautifully demonstrated how the light from distant stars is absorbed by dust in the disk of the Milky Way. After a decade of work on galactic star clusters—so named because they are located in the disk of our galaxy   the Swiss born astronomer had become quite familiar with the typical size, color, and brightness of these rich groupings of stars. Indeed, he had studied more than three hundred of them. In the process, he could estimate the distance of a far-off star cluster by judging how much smaller the distant cluster appeared when compared with a nearby cluster. But in doing so he noticed that the stars in the far-off cluster were fainter than distance alone would warrant. Moreover, the distant clusters were also noticeably redder than their counterparts closer to Earth. It all made sense if the disk of the Milky Way were suffused with a subtle fogginess or dustiness, which dimmed and reddened the far-off starlight much the way the Earth's dust-filled atmosphere turns the Sun a deep red-orange at sunset. (The dust preferentially absorbs and scatters the bluer wavelengths, leaving the redder wavelengths to reach our eyes.) Trumpler figured that a star's brightness is reduced by one-half for each one thousand light-years the starlight travels through the dusty plane of the Milky Way.

Trumpler's findings forced galactic mapmakers back to the drawing board. The dustiness of space significantly affected estimates of the Milky Way's size. In 1918, at the age of thirty-two, Harlow Shapley, the former Missouri farm boy and newspaperman who would later head the Harvard Observatory, had banished the solar system from its time-honored position as center of the known universe and placed it in a more provincial position. The Sun was not located at the center of the Milky Way after all. By measuring the distances to a number of globular clusters in the galaxy's halo, Shapley determined that the solar system is actually situated in the galactic suburbs, about two-thirds of the way to the outer edge of the galactic disk. "The solar system is off-center," he remarked many years later, "and consequently man is too."

Shapley's calculations also suggested that the Milky Way extended about 300,000 light-years from end to end, a hefty diameter but a more realistic assessment than the previous estimate of 10,000 light-years. Once the dimming of starlight as it travels through a thin haze of dust and gas was taken into account, though, the dimensions of the Milky Way's spiraling disk had to be reduced back down a bit. Because of intervening interstellar matter, faraway stars appear fainter and consequently more distant than they really are. The one hundred billion or more luminous stars in our galaxy are now believed to occupy a region of space that measures about 100,000 light-years across. That means a ray of light, traveling at some 186,000 miles per second, needs 100,000 years to journey the 600,000,000,000,000,000 miles from one end of the disk to the other (that is, if the ray is lucky enough not to get absorbed by a dust grain along the way).

That interstellar dust and gas are concentrated in the disk of a spiraling galaxy is made quite apparent when looking at photographs of far-off galaxies that are oriented edge-on in the celestial sky. When seen from that perspective, the spiral galaxy comes to resemble a thin phonograph record with a tennis ball stuck in its center. Every spiral galaxy is essentially a gigantic stellar pinwheel: At the center is a huge, round, yet somewhat flattened bulge, containing a dense concentration of stars; surrounding this bright bulbous nucleus is a much thinner disk, a couple of thousand light-years thick, composed of both stars and interstellar matter. When such a galaxy is observed from its side, dark lanes of obscuring dust and gas can often be seen running across the galaxy's luminous center.

Interstellar gases constitute 5–10 percent of the matter in the Milky Way; microscopic dust grains contribute roughly another 1 percent. All total, that is enough matter to construct about ten billion stars like our Sun. Such immense reservoirs of dust and gas in our galaxy might give the impression that the space between the stars is brimming over with matter, that there are atoms everywhere. But such an image is illusory. A cup of air here on Earth contains more than a billion trillion molecules. That same cup out in space would only manage to scoop up a few handfuls of hydrogen atoms. And, as Verschuur points out, "One would need to search a cube whose size is the length of a football field, that is, a volume equal to the interior of the Houston Astrodome, to find one [interstellar] grain."

But space is vast. The very fact that the light of distant stars is still dimmed by these weak concentrations of dust and gas points out the tremendous breadth of interstellar space. A ray of light can circle the Earth nearly eight times in one second; it takes eight minutes for a photon to travel from the Sun to the Earth; but four whole years are required for a beam of sunlight to reach just the nearest star. By adding up all the dust drifting in the long celestial stretches between the Earth and stars even farther off, space can start to resemble a hazy fog. The layer upon layer of dust and gas that floats between us and the Milky Way's center, situated some 30,000 light-years away in the direction of the constellation Sagittarius, reduces the visible light emanating from that region a trillion times over. That means that for every trillion photons of visible light being emitted by the galactic center, only one manages to escape the clutches of an absorbing bit of dusty flotsam on its way to Earth. That's why the Milky Way's rich center remains totally hidden to optical telescopes.

In certain regions the tenuous sea of interstellar dust and gas becomes even more dense, collecting into those intensely dark clouds that Herschel and Barnard viewed as shadowy silhouettes against a bright array of distant stars. There each thimbleful of space can contain hundreds of atoms of hydrogen, as well as a smattering of dust, helium, and traces of other elements. To earthlings, that is still an extraordinary void, a vacuum thousands of times finer than the artificial "vacuums" produced in terrestrial laboratories. Yet, if the solar system were embedded in one of these dark clouds, we'd see hundreds rather than billions of stars. Other galaxies—indeed, the entire splendor of the universe—would be hidden from our eyes.

Many interstellar dust grains are born in red giant stars; such elements as carbon and silicon, which are brewed deep inside these old stars, condense into grains in the star's cooler outer envelope. Billowing like smoke from a celestial bonfire, these bits of graphite and silicate, the stuff of beach sand, are blown off the star into supercold space, where, over time, each grain can eventually become coated with a thin mantle of various ices. Astronomers know the typical size of a grain from the way in which starlight is diminished by the dust motes. If visible light waves are appreciably extinguished, the grains must be a few millionths of an inch across, the size of cigarette-smoke particles. Ultraviolet rays are stopped by grains that are one-tenth smaller than that, the size of viruses. Over the eons these grains can collect and merge to construct ever bigger aggregates. A vast reservoir of such material, leftovers from our solar system's birth some five billion years ago, is believed to reside in a thick halo that surrounds our Sun starting at a distance of about ten billion miles, twice the distance of Pluto from the Sun. Perturbed by the gravity of an occasional passing star or remote planetary body, pieces are periodically nudged toward the Sun. In the warmth of the solar system, these celestial chunks release clouds of vapor and dust that form the glowing heads and tails that we call comets. Comets, no less than "dirty snowballs," may well be clumps of clumps of clumps of interstellar grains.

During the 1930s, Eddington continued to be eerily prescient in his descriptions of interstellar matter. His predictions of its composition at that time come remarkably close to the modern view. Hydrogen, he said, should be the major constituent of these clouds, a fact that was not directly proven until much later. More insightfully, he returned to his innovative idea that the clouds might harbor molecules comprising hydrogen, nitrogen, and oxygen, among other atoms. Only decades later would astronomers come to realize that these molecules, rare as they are, would allow observers to map interstellar space with a clarity far surpassing Barnard's photographs. During their tumbles and collisions within the Milky Way, the molecules emit distinctive radio or infrared waves that can freely pass through the dusty gloom of intervening gas clouds to reveal the temperature, composition, and structure of the interstellar medium.

Thoughts similar to Eddington's later occurred to a young American scientist, but Charles Townes took a detour into Nobel Prize–winning research in physics before coming back to the question of molecules in space.

THE MOLECULE HUNTERS

Charles Townes, best known for both his invention of the maser and his proposal (with brother-in-law Arthur Schawlow) of the laser, ushers a visitor into his comfortable corner office on the top floor of Birge Hall on the campus of the University of California at Berkeley. Through the window, a brilliant fall day provides a spellbinding view of San Francisco Bay sparkling in the distance. In the course of a discussion on his research, Townes, tall and portly, with a high forehead, ruddy complexion, and warm blue eyes behind wide, steel-rim glasses, recalls a pivotal crossroads he faced early in his career.

After obtaining a Ph.D. in physics at Caltech in 1939, Townes joined Bell Telephone Laboratories and was immediately thrust into war work at the company's research facilities then located in lower Manhattan. Like Fred Hoyle in Great Britain, Townes became involved in the design and development of radar systems. In the course of this assignment, he acquired an expertise in the physics of microwaves, short radio waves ranging in length from a millimeter to a meter, and came to see their strengths and weaknesses when used in radar detection. "I recognized that the shorter-wavelength radar being developed was going to get into trouble by being absorbed by water vapor in the atmosphere," he notes. Although unsuccessful in persuading his superiors of the watery complication (a one-and-a-quarter-centimeter-wavelength radar system used in the Pacific at the end of the war turned out to be a failure), Townes and others perceived that this defeat for radar could be transformed into a boon for laboratory science. By shining microwaves on molecules, and then observing how the various atoms absorbed this radiation, scientists obtained a powerful probe of a molecule's structure. Such a technique allowed for measurements far more precise than previously available.

Although intrigued and excited by the application of radar technology to molecular physics, Townes was torn. After the war, he was also attracted to the infant field of radio astronomy. Townes had a talent for spotting the scientific specialty that was off the beaten path yet held great promise. "I like to look at those things that are being neglected," he points out. "If there are a lot of other people in the field, what difference will one more person make? I'd rather do something that people are overlooking."

In the early 1930s Townes's wartime employer had given birth to radio astronomy. Bell Labs physicist Karl Jansky had built a crude antenna amid central New Jersey's potato fields, near Bell's Holmdel station, to investigate strange hissing noises that were disrupting transatlantic radio-telephone communications. After a year of detective work with his spindly network of brass pipes hung over a wooden frame that rolled around on Model-T Ford wheels, Jansky established that the source of the signal—twenty megahertz (MHz), a frequency between the AM and FM bands in the United States—was neither in the Earth's atmosphere nor in the solar system but came instead from the center of our home galaxy, the Milky Way. Here were celestial waves of electromagnetic energy millions of times longer than the waves our eyes perceive as the color red. Jansky affectionately dubbed it his "star noise," and it hinted at processes going on in the galactic nucleus that were not revealed by visible light rays emanating from that dusty region of the sky; the longer radio waves are able to cut right through the intervening dust and gas, in the manner of radar passing through a fog. Years later astronomers would come to learn that the signals Jansky picked up were being emitted by violent streams of charged particles spiraling about in the magnetic fields of space. Just as an electric current, oscillating back and forth within a broadcast antenna, releases waves of radio energy into the air, these energetic, fast-moving particles broadcast radio waves into space. Jansky, who certainly didn't start out to make an astronomical observation, was the first to detect them. He was Earth's first eavesdropper on the universe.[2]

Jansky's unexpected discovery made front-page headlines in the *New York Times* in 1933, but astronomers were slow to appreciate its significance. Their theoretical calculations at the time were suggesting that radio emissions within the galaxy would be quite feeble. Grote Reber was one of the few to ignore the academicians. Upon hearing of Jansky's work, the radio engineer and avid ham-radio operator erected a massive steel saucer, thirty-one feet wide, in his Wheaton, Illinois, backyard to detect Jansky's cosmic static for himself. (Reber's neighbors worried that the three-story

---

[2] In the 1890s, just a few years after Hertz's discovery of radio waves, both Thomas Edison in the United States and Sir Oliver Lodge in Great Britain conceived of apparatuses to record solar radio waves. Nothing, however, became of their schemes.

structure was going to be used to either collect rain water or control the weather.) With this dishlike antenna, a design that has since become radio astronomy's trademark, Reber produced the first crude maps of the "radio" sky. Dozens of young physicists and engineers in both Europe and the United States were introduced to the esoteric art of radio science while working on the development of radar during World War II, and once the conflict ended, they were eager to apply their newfound skills to deciphering the radio signals detected by Reber. Townes was part of that vanguard.

Excited by radio astronomy's potential, Townes consulted Ira Bowen, then head of the Mount Wilson and Palomar observatories, about its future. Townes asked his former Caltech professor, a scientist he greatly respected, what interesting astronomical problems might be explored with radio telescopes. But Bowen, like so many astronomers of that day, expected little to result from radio probes of the universe. "I'm sorry to disappoint you," Bowen told Townes, "but there's nothing that one can do with long waves that would be useful." Since optical astronomers were still carrying on the work initiated by Galileo's scrutiny of the heavens, it was difficult for all but a few visionaries to understand that the cosmos could display a very different picture of itself in waves of electromagnetic energy other than visible light. Tradition was difficult to repress: Lenses, mirrors, and photographic plates—not gangling wires and electronic amplifiers—were the province of astronomy. "Bowen's response was certainly not encouraging," says Townes.

Partly because of Bowen's doubts concerning radio astronomy's merits, Townes instead accepted an invitation to pursue his research in microwave spectroscopy at Columbia University in New York City. After World War II, scientists began to measure the spectra of molecules very systematically. Rotation is one way that molecules absorb and reemit radiation, producing distinctive spectral lines. This is because molecules spin and tumble, but they do so only at certain specified speeds, as if your car could run at twenty, thirty, forty miles per hour and so forth but never at twenty-two, thirty-seven, or forty-three miles per hour. A molecule both absorbs and emits rotational energy in a restricted, steplike fashion. To study this process, investigators use klystrons, the same tubes that generate the radiation in a microwave oven, to inject molecules with microwave energy, which propel the molecules up to a higher spin. The excited molecules then emit very specific radio signals whenever they drop from this high rate of rotation to a lower, less energetic one. By measuring these energy levels, researchers are able to discern the molecular structures of various substances in great detail.

Through this work on molecular excitations, Townes acquired both the knowledge and the techniques that led to his development of the maser, a device that generates an intense, continuous microwave signal. In 1951, as if following the Hollywood script of a young scientist's life, Townes, then thirty-six years old, got the first glimmer of the idea while in Washington, D.C., to chair a conference. Waking up early one morning, he took a walk to nearby Franklin Park and sat down on a park bench. There amid the blooming azaleas, he came to imagine herds of ammonia molecules pumped up to high vibrational energies and then, in response to a trigger, all of these molecules releasing their energy in concert, resulting in a pure and powerful beam of microwaves, ammonia's natural frequency. On the back of an old envelope that spring day in Washington, Townes worked out the first calculations for this *microwave*

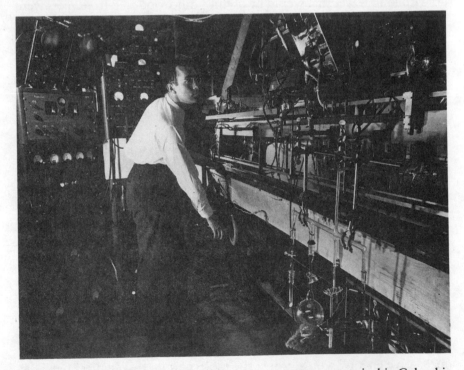

Charles Townes in 1949, using the microwave spectrometer in his Columbia University laboratory.
Photograph courtesy of Charles Townes

*a*mplification by *s*timulated *e*mission of *r*adiation (hence the term *maser*). Within two and a half years, Townes, with the assistance of graduate student James Gordon and postdoc Herb Zeiger, had the first prototype working in his lab. Masers quickly found uses as atomic clocks (still the most accurate timepieces available) and as receivers for radio telescopes and satellite communications. By the 1960s the idea was extended to the visible light range, producing the laser. For his pioneering efforts, Townes was awarded the Nobel Prize for physics in 1964.

During this highly innovative phase of his physics career, Townes never completely abandoned his astronomical interests. As he studied the interaction of microwaves with molecules in his Columbia laboratory, observing and recording the molecules' precise energy levels, he contemplated the detection of those very same spectral lines from interstellar space. He dared to think that the Milky Way might harbor a wide variety of molecules, all broadcasting their unique spectral cries. For Townes, radio telescopes were the perfect means of hearing them.

As early as the 1930s a few theorists had published articles on the possibility that molecules exist in space. Between 1937 and 1941 optical astronomers detected a few species, but most people in the field considered these molecules as nothing more than rare, inconsequential curiosities. Minute traces of such chemical radicals as carbon-hydrogen (abbreviated as CH in chemical notation) and carbon-nitrogen (the cyanogen radical CN), combinations normally unstable on Earth, had been spotted when wisps of gas containing these molecules happened to be caught in front of bright stars. Astronomers even noticed that the CN molecules were heated to three degrees above absolute zero. But this was an oddity that secured hardly a footnote in the textbooks. Only in hindsight, more than three decades later when Arno Penzias and Robert Wilson detected the three-degree microwave background in every nook and cranny of the celestial sky, did astronomers come to realize that the CN molecules were being faintly energized by the fossil echo of the big bang.

By 1950, atomic potassium, iron, and titanium—along with calcium, sodium, CN, CH, and CH^+ (an ionized CH stripped of an electron)— were also seen in space. Yet, even as the inventory of interstellar atoms expanded, few thought that other types of molecules would ever be found in space. The few molecules that were glimpsed were assumed to be merely residue left over from the destruction of dust grains released by stars. Townes's interest in interstellar molecules went against the mainstream. Theorists were convinced that molecules could not long survive the hazards of interstellar space; the molecules would be torn apart by energetic ultraviolet or cosmic rays, it was firmly believed, even as they formed.

For that matter the early radio astronomers didn't have much time to worry about molecules; simple hydrogen was keeping them busy enough. After World War II, spurred by the military development of radar, radio astronomy blossomed. Radio telescope dishes sprouted like mushrooms around the globe, particularly in Great Britain, Australia, and the Netherlands (the clouds that long impaired optical astronomy in those coastal countries posed no obstacle to celestial radio waves). It was not too many years after Townes received his faulty advice that radio astronomy "would not be useful" that the novice field proved its critics wrong. The groundwork was laid during the war. In 1944 the keen insight of a young Dutch graduate student, Hendrik van de Hulst, served as a turning point.

It was a bleak time for students in the Netherlands. The Nazi forces occupying Holland had shut down all Dutch universities. His adviser at the University of Utrecht taken away to detention camp, van de Hulst continued work on his own at the Leiden Observatory, where he began an ambitious thesis on interstellar matter. The noted Dutch astronomer Jan Oort, who was then in hiding because of his vigorous protest of the dismissal of Jewish professors, which led to the university closures, occasionally dropped by undercover to advise van de Hulst. On one such clandestine visit, Oort persuaded van de Hulst to consider how interstellar matter might be traced through its radio emissions. At the time this was still a radical idea: The field of radio astronomy was far from established—only a few isolated researchers, such as the pioneering Grote Reber, were as yet measuring the Milky Way's radio emissions. But Oort had recently read a copy of the *Astrophysical Journal,* which had somehow been smuggled into his country, and was galvanized by a report of Reber's work; he suspected that radio waves would be a superb means of probing the interstellar medium.

Oort's recommendation to the young graduate student was a profitable one. In the course of his calculations, van de Hulst came to see that single atoms of hydrogen floating in space would be emitting a specific type of noise, an unvarying radio hum. This would happen, he reasoned from atomic theory, when the lone spinning electron in a hydrogen atom occasionally "flipped over," like a top, to a lower energy state, generating an electromagnetic wave twenty-one centimeters (8.3 in.) in length (in terms of a radio frequency, 1,420 MHz). Any one hydrogen atom performs this flip, on average, once every eleven million years or so, but the supply of hydrogen atoms in interstellar space is enormous. Van de Hulst figured that there are more than enough atoms, collectively flipping and beeping, to produce a continuous, detectable drone.

By 1951, when equipment became available to detect the weak signal, celestial hydrogen's monotonic hum was at last recorded. At Harvard University, graduate student Harold Ewen and his adviser Edward Purcell picked up the signal with a home-built receiver that jutted out from their physics laboratory window (that is, when the hornlike antenna wasn't serving as a convenient target for undergraduates lobbing snowballs). Soon afterward, researchers in the Netherlands and Australia spotted the hydrogen noise as well.

The twenty-one-centimeter line quickly became astronomy's most proficient surveyor of the galaxy's starscape. Many other disk galaxies in the universe displayed beautiful spiral structures; it was assumed that the Milky Way, too, had spiral arms. But optical astronomers had never been able to see much farther than 20,000 light-years directly through the dust- and gas-filled plane of our galaxy. Only a few spiral-arm segments had ever been mapped. Radio astronomers, tuned to the 1,420 MHz voice of atomic hydrogen, had much better luck. Slicing through our galaxy's dusty byways with ease, the hydrogen signal enables astronomers to map the full structure of the Milky Way's disk. Multiple streaks have been traced nearly all the way around the galaxy, confirming that the Milky Way has several spiraling arms, perhaps four in all, that wrap themselves around the galactic hub like coiled streamers. Moreover, radio astronomers see that the disk is warped. Like the tilt of a fedora, the disk of the Milky Way flips up on one side by about 6,000 light-years and down by a similar amount on the opposite side. All around its edge the disk also exhibits a very subtle scalloping, like the undulating folds of a seashell; there are about ten folds in all. Some astronomers speculate that the scalloping is formed by the gravitational pull of two small galaxies—the Large Magellanic Cloud and the Small Magellanic Cloud—caught in orbit around the Milky Way.

While on sabbatical in Europe in 1955, just a few years after the detection of hydrogen's celestial "song," Townes was invited to an international symposium on radio astronomy convening in England and was asked to speak on the possibility of detecting other cosmic substances via their radio wave emissions. Well known for his molecular-line work,

Townes named several promising prospects, including such molecules as carbon monoxide (CO, the stuff of car exhaust), ammonia (NH_3), water (H_2O), and the hydroxyl radical OH, the oxygen-hydrogen combination that distinguishes all alcohols. "These are very stable molecules that display simple and very intense microwave spectra in the laboratory and hence were the most likely to be detected," explains Townes. "I thought of OH, in part, because of its analogy to CH, which had already been found. If the CH were there, OH surely had to be there, too."

Molecule searches, though, were scarcely a top priority for astronomers in those days. "Van de Hulst, who was running the meeting, politely remarked that my suggestions looked interesting, but the subject was soon dropped," recalls Townes. "I was busy with other things, and no radio astronomer wanted to bother." Only one other researcher, Soviet physicist Iosif Shklovskii, had even published on the subject. Why devote precious radio telescope time tracking rare specimens in space that, according to conventional wisdom, served little purpose and would provide meager information?

But at least one scientist's interest was piqued. Alan Barrett, a student of Townes at Columbia in the 1950s, was determined to find OH after he completed his doctorate in molecular spectroscopy. Moving to the Naval Research Laboratory in Washington, D.C., Barrett, along with Harvard astronomer Edward Lilley, began to search the sky for OH molecules using a fifty-foot paraboloid antenna installed on the roof of the laboratory. Despite their access to one of the best radio telescopes in its day, the two investigators heard nary a peep from OH. But Barrett persisted in his quest, trying again a few years later when he moved to the Massachusetts Institute of Technology. In 1963 he and several colleagues from MIT's Lincoln Laboratory finally snared the elusive molecule. By then measurements in Townes's Columbia laboratory had better pinpointed OH's most prominent frequency—1.667 gigahertz, a wavelength of eighteen centimeters—which expedited their search. The MIT observers saw OH absorbing that exact energy in dust clouds caught between the galactic center and Earth.

The finding did not set the astronomical community on fire, however; except for a handful of interested research groups, it was generally thought that OH was just another oddball species to add to the list of interstellar inhabitants, along with CH, CH^+, and CN. All of them, said many astronomers, were probably short lived. But within two years of Barrett's find, there were surprising and unexpected repercussions. With

OH serving as their probe, astronomers discovered that nature had preceded Townes by billions of years in the construction of a maser. Harold Weaver was one of the few astronomers to follow up on Barrett's discovery of cosmic OH. In 1965 he and his colleagues at the University of California at Berkeley tuned their radio telescope receiver to the hydroxyl molecule's distinctive frequency in order to survey the vast clouds of gas and dust concentrated in the Milky Way's spiral arms. But in the course of their scan, they picked up one of the most pure and intense radio signals ever recorded from space. It was as if some advanced civilization were pointing a powerful beacon straight at the Earth. Soon they discovered similar beams emanating from all over the galaxy—in the Orion Nebula, in a dusty cloud near the constellation Cassiopeia, and in diffuse gaseous regions near Aquila and Cygnus.

They had no idea what process or material could cause such powerful outbursts. In a report in the journal *Nature,* the Berkeley researchers wrote, "To emphasize the surprising nature of the observation . . . we shall speak of this unidentified line [of radio energy] as arising from 'mysterium,' " an unknown substance (reminiscent of Huggins's nebulium).

Within a year of the discovery, though, astronomers had figured out that mysterium was nothing more mysterious than a cloud of hydroxyl molecules—but a cloud that had coalesced to form a gigantic natural maser, the microwave equivalent of a laser, as big as the Earth's orbit around the Sun. The OH molecules absorb energy from nearby stars or the surrounding dust cloud in such a way that many of them eventually wind up at the same energy level, like a row of birds sitting on a telephone wire. There they sit until a chance event—a stray photon or the sudden decay of one of the pumped-up molecules—triggers an avalanche. The molecules dump their energy simultaneously, producing the intense beam of single-frequency radio waves, all precisely in phase and reinforcing each other.

At any one time, dozens of these giant masers can surround a newly born star, like fireworks heralding its birth. The masing clumps form in the violent flows of gas that speed outward from the star as it fires up its thermonuclear engine for the first time. "I frequently point out in public talks on science and technology," says Townes, "that if we had been doing more radio astronomy earlier, we would have discovered masers in the sky long before they were discovered in the laboratory. Some of these celestial masers are so intense that if anyone had taken a look at the sky with a four-centimeter radar set, the kind used during World War II, they would have easily spotted them." It wasn't too long after cosmic masers were discovered that molecule hunting shifted from a snail's pace to a grand prix race.

Townes had transferred from Columbia to MIT in 1961 to serve as an academic administrator, but within six years he was eager to get back into scientific research. He moved to Berkeley specifically to initiate the work in microwave astronomy that he had reluctantly put on hold right after the war. "I was determined to look for molecules," he says. "Nobody was taking it seriously."

Radio astronomers in the 1950s and early 1960s primarily looked at thirty-, ten-, and five-centimeter waves. Conventional wisdom held that the intensity of any radio source in the sky would decrease drastically if you went to wavelengths any smaller. But from his work at Columbia, Townes was certain that the richest regions to mine were likely the short radio waves. Townes set out to build a special receiver that would search for waves only one centimeter long. In the laboratory, he had observed a particular substance veritably scream out at a wavelength of 1.25 centimeters. It was the very molecule that led him to the invention of the maser: ammonia.

Molecules generally broadcast their radio radiation whenever they are stretched, bent, or rotated. For example, kicked up to a higher spin through collisions with other atoms, a celestial molecule will send out a radio wave when it suddenly switches from the high rate of rotation to a lower one. Ammonia, on the other hand, acts a bit differently. The one nitrogen atom and three hydrogen atoms in an ammonia molecule join to form a tetrahedron—a pyramid with four sides. In this configuration, the lone nitrogen atom, perched at the pyramid's apex, can pass back and forth through the plane formed by the three hydrogen atoms located at the base. "The ammonia molecule turns inside out, like an umbrella that suddenly inverts in a strong wind," explains Townes. When it performs this oscillation, along with rotating, the ammonia molecule releases a particularly strong signal.

Ammonia was Townes's prime target. Joining him in the hunt were Al Cheung, a graduate student from Hong Kong; David Rank, a young postdoc specializing in spectroscopy (Townes knew his father, who was also a spectroscopist); Douglas Thornton, an engineer who helped design the new centimeter-wave receiver; and William ("Jack") Welch, then the head of Berkeley's Hat Creek Radio Observatory in northern California, where the search took place.

In the fall of 1968, the Berkeley investigators attached their new receiver to a twenty-foot-wide radio dish at Hat Creek and fairly quickly "heard" the radio cry of ammonia arriving from the galactic center. More accurately, a noticeable "bump" appeared on their graphic record, indicating that a signal was arriving right at ammonia's natural frequency of twenty-four gigahertz. To increase their chances of finding some ammonia molecules, the Berkeley team had aimed the radio telescope at the thickest, cloudiest pathway through the galaxy.

Just as exciting as the discovery was what the signal itself was telling the scientists about the galactic center. Both the height and the width of ammonia's spectral line indicated that the temperature in the Milky Way's center ranged from seventeen to thirty degrees above absolute zero and that some of the clouds in that direction contained as many as one thousand atoms, nearly all of them hydrogen, in each cubic centimeter. On Earth, that would be considered the purest vacuum; for space it was a downright traffic jam of particles. Astronomers had long figured that interstellar space would have no more than ten atoms in each cubic centimeter; finding one hundred times more than that was shocking. Only the presence of the ammonia itself was more surprising.

Astronomers had been so sure that a search for molecules in space would prove fruitless that earlier attempts had been aborted. Harvard physicist and Nobel laureate Norman Ramsey had planned to look for ammonia a few years before Townes had, but the graduate student assigned to the project soon abandoned the effort. The young man was convinced by another Harvard scientist that he was wasting his time; the molecular densities, he was told, would be far too low to detect anything. Meanwhile, in 1967 physicist Lewis Snyder, fresh out of Michigan State University with a Ph.D. in molecular spectroscopy, signed on as a postdoc at the National Radio Astronomy Observatory (NRAO) in Green Bank, West Virginia, specifically to look for interstellar molecules. Teamed with astronomer David Buhl, Snyder applied a couple of times for telescope time, but very skeptical review committees kept putting his proposed searches on hold. Even George Field, then the head of Berkeley's astronomy department and an expert on the interstellar medium, had checked out a few equations and counseled Townes that a search for ammonia "would be hopeless."

"Fortunately Townes ignored my advice," said Field many years later. "The theory for the formation of NH_3 is much more complex than I contemplated in those early days. Theoretical arguments can't always be trusted in astronomy. The universe is far more complex than we can imagine in a lifetime." The molecules were forming within clouds of gas much denser than most theorists had expected, and it is these high densities that shield the molecules from the stray ultraviolet rays that could break them up.

The Berkeley team revealed that ammonia barely qualifies as a pollutant in our galaxy. Only one molecule of ammonia forms for every thirty million molecules of hydrogen. Yet, the detection of this poisonous gas in the heavens, scarce as it is, eventually led to vast improvements in the ability of astronomers to scan the Milky Way.

Within weeks of finding celestial ammonia, the Berkeley group decided to search for water. "Frankly," admits Townes, "I would not have looked for water initially. You have to have fantastic densities and the water has to be highly excited." Expectations were not high. But water's most prominent radio emission at a wavelength of 1.35 centimeters was practically next door to ammonia, as spectra go, so it was relatively easy to retune the receiver a bit and have a look. Water, that ubiquitous earthly compound, did not let them down; it, too, dwelled in the galactic center. On the wall of his office, right by his desk, Townes displays the work of Viennese artist Friedensreich Hundertwasser (which means "one hundred water" in German). The painting was a gift from his wife. It depicts what appears to be huge raindrops overlaid on a giant spiral composed of stripes of red, blue, and green—an appropriate picture for the man who helped discover water in the dusty and gaseous arms of the spiraling Milky Way.

After striking water in the galactic center, Cheung began looking for H_2O in other regions of the sky, particularly in the galaxy's most prominent gas clouds, such as the famous Orion Nebula situated in the starry sword of the mythological hunter. It wasn't too long before Cheung had good news to report. "I remember it was Christmastime in 1968," says Townes. "I was having a party at my home for all my students, while Al was up in northern California working away at the telescope. During the party he called up, and I asked him how things were going. 'Well,' replied Al, 'it's really raining in Orion.'" In fact, the signal was unexpectedly intense—a virtual celestial hurricane. Cheung later realized that he had stumbled upon a water maser, the strongest type of cosmic maser that forms in the galaxy. The power of a water maser is awesome, as if the total luminosity of the Sun over the entire electromagnetic spectrum were pouring out in a small band of frequencies the width of a television channel.

With two finds speedily coming out of Hat Creek—first ammonia, then water—the NRAO (feeling the heat of the competition) at last arranged to give Snyder and Buhl the opportunity they had sought for so long. Using the 140-foot radio telescope at Green Bank, the two investigators were part of a team that clinched the next new cosmic molecule— the embalming fluid formaldehyde (H_2CO). Over the next decade, Snyder and Buhl became one of the hottest molecule-hunting teams around; they were the first to see dimethyl ether, sulfur dioxide, hydrogen cyanide, and a silicon monoxide maser, to name a few. "Pretty soon, astronomers began looking for almost anything—and almost anything turned out to be there," says Townes. Handbooks listing molecular frequencies became dog-eared as astronomers pored over the listings hoping to snare the next new molecule in space. Radio telescope time allocation committees, once so conservative and hidebound, were suddenly amenable to just about any suggestion. "At the time, I think they would have approved a proposal to look for flu germs," says Snyder today with some humor. A great race ensued, giving birth to the field of astrochemistry.

By 1973, after some five years of searching, the new molecule hunters clearly detected a total of twenty-seven cosmic molecules. To date, astronomers have identified about one hundred species of molecules, which dwell in either dense interstellar clouds or the gaseous outer envelopes of cool stars. The selection ranges from molecules composed of two simple atoms to compounds constructed out of more than a dozen atoms. The ever-growing list of cosmic chemicals includes the welding fuel acetylene (C_2H_2), pungent formic acid (HCOOH), the malodorous (smells like rotten egg) gas hydrogen sulfide (H_2S), and the marsh gas methane (CH_4). Astronomers handed out cases of liquor to settle bets once ethyl alcohol was discovered in 1974. It has been estimated that ten thousand trillion trillion fifths, at 200 proof, reside in the gas clouds where the CH_3CH_2OH molecules were first sighted. Of course, with the alcohol molecules spread so thinly out in space, you'd have to distill a volume as big as the planet Jupiter to obtain a single drink.

Many more spectral lines, possibly the signals of molecules even bigger and more complex, have been recorded but remain to be identified. Some of these unknown lines might simply be indicating the pres-

A SELECTION OF INTERSTELLAR MOLECULES

Name	Chemical Formula
Two-atom molecules	
Molecular hydrogen	H_2
Methylidyne ion	CH^+
Methylidyne radical	CH
Hydroxyl	OH
Diatomic carbon	C_2
Cyanogen radical	CN
Carbon monoxide	CO
Carbon monoxide ion	CO^+
Nitric oxide	NO
Carbon monosulphide	CS
Silicon monoxide	SiO
Sulfur monoxide	SO
Nitrogen sulphide	NS
Silicon monosulphide	SiS
Hydrogen chloride	HCl
Three-atom molecules	
Water	H_2O
Ethynyl radical	C_2H
Hydrogen cyanide	HCN
Hydrogen isocyanide	HNC
Formyl ion	HCO^+
Formyl radical	HCO
Diazenylium	N_2H^+
Hydrogen sulphide	H_2S
Thioformyl ion	HCS^+
Nitroxyl radical	HNO
Carbonyl sulphide	OCS
Sulfur dioxide	SO_2
Sodium hydroxide	$NaOH$
Silacyclopropyne	SiC_2
Four-atom molecules	
Ammonia	NH_3
Acetylene	C_2H_2
Formaldehyde	H_2CO

A SELECTION OF INTERSTELLAR MOLECULES (*cont.*)

Name	Chemical Formula
Isocyanic acid	HNCO
Thioformaldehyde	H_2CS
Cyanoethynyl radical	C_3N
Thioisocyanic acid	HNCS
Propynylidyne radical	C_3H
Tricarbon monoxide	C_3O

Five-atom molecules

Methane	CH_4
Methanimine	CH_2NH
Ketene	CH_2CO
Cyanamide	NH_2CN
Formic acid	HCOOH
Butadiynyl radical	C_4H
Cyanoacetylene	HC_3N

Six-atom molecules

Methanol	CH_3OH
Methyl cyanide	CH_3CN
Ethylene	C_2H_4
Formamide	NH_2CHO
Methyl mercaptan	CH_3SH

Seven-atom molecules

Methylamine	CH_3NH_2
Methylacetylene	CH_3C_2H
Acetaldehyde	CH_3CHO
Vinyl cyanide	CH_2CHCN
Cyanodiacetylene	HC_5N

Eight-atom molecules

Methyl formate	$HCOOCH_3$
Methyl cyanoacetylene	CH_3C_3N

A SELECTION OF INTERSTELLAR MOLECULES (*cont.*)

Name	Chemical Formula
Nine-atom molecules	
Ethanol	C_2H_5OH
Dimethyl ether	CH_3OCH_3
Ethyl cyanide	C_2H_5CN
Cyanotriacetylene	HC_7N
Methyl diacetylene	CH_3C_4H
Eleven-atom molecules	
Cyanooctatetrayne	HC_9N
Thirteen-atom molecules	
Cyanodecapentyne	$HC_{11}N$

ence of familiar elements in unfamiliar forms. In recent years, for instance, chemists have started making a stable molecule composed of sixty carbon atoms that assumes the shape of a geodesic sphere. They've dubbed this new substance *buckminsterfuller*ene in honor of the designer of the geodesic dome. Some wonder if the outer envelopes of carbon-rich red giant stars are generously sooting up the universe with these graphite "buckyballs."

Searches for cosmic molecules continue to this day, and for many the Holy Grail, the most sought-after compound, is an amino acid, the stuff of life, as well as the nitrogen bases that are a key ingredient of DNA, the self-replicating molecule that carries an organism's genetic code. There is hope, in that amino acids, the building blocks of proteins, have already been found in meteorites. Observations of Halley's comet, which swooped by the Earth in 1986, confirmed that comets are abundantly enriched with organic compounds. Able to bond with itself, carbon has by far the richest chemistry of all the elements. Perhaps for that reason, interstellar space seems to favor the production of organic molecules, that is, molecules containing carbon. A few venturesome astrochemists even speculate that comets and carbon-rich meteorites, the remnants of the solar system's birth from a whirling pool of molecular gas, may have seeded the Earth with the simplest carbon compounds necessary for life, either by vaporizing during entry or by plunging into the Earth's mantle, where they later released gases into the primitive air.

"If somebody finds a molecule of DNA in interstellar space, that would be exciting," says Townes, "but the most important thing is to use these molecules as tools. We've found enough types to give us almost any kind of measurement that we need." The bulk of the gas in space consists of hydrogen, but while individual hydrogen atoms emit radio waves profusely, hydrogen molecules—which consist of two atoms joined together—are effectively silent in the radio regime. Hydrogen molecules tend to form in the darkest, dustiest clumps of gas in the galaxy, where densities are high and temperatures cold (around $-440°$ Fahrenheit). Radio astronomers would have been as blind as their optical counterparts in studying these opaque clouds—Barnard's clouds—were it not for the fact that the vast array of other molecular species invariably mix in with the mute hydrogen molecules and make a lot of noise. Molecules that would have been destroyed in open space are protected in these clouds by the relatively heavy concentrations of hydrogen and dust. By tuning to each molecule's distinctive frequency, researchers can map the distribution of this dense interstellar gas, much the way neuroanatomists use chemical stains to map the various tissues of the brain.

The workhorse molecule for these endeavors is carbon monoxide—it is the most stable cosmic molecule and, after hydrogen, the most common molecular gas in space. There is about one molecule of carbon monoxide in space for every ten thousand molecules of hydrogen. Celestial carbon monoxide was first spotted in the spring of 1970, not too long after formaldehyde's detection. Several years after their discovery of the microwave background, Bell Labs physicists Penzias and Wilson, along with Keith Jefferts, turned their attention to interstellar molecules and decided to go beyond the centimeter window and seek out millimeter-wave signals. The three attached a special receiver to a thirty-six-foot radio telescope situated atop Kitt Peak in Arizona. Pointed at the Orion Nebula, the telescope picked up CO's characteristic 2.6-mm radio wave emissions almost immediately. The millimeter range, in fact, turned out to be the richest place of all to find molecules. Once the shorter wavelengths were conquered, a flood of molecules came to be discovered. Originally built to study supernovae and radio galaxies but underused, the Kitt Peak radio telescope was suddenly working overtime, its operators deluged with proposals. Of the first forty molecules found in space, exactly half were discovered from the mile-high Arizona site.

By specifically tracing the signal of carbon monoxide across the celestial sky, radio astronomers discovered a whole new class of objects: the giant molecular clouds. The Great Rift, a dark lane of dust and gas silhouetted against the mistlike Milky Way, is a chain of small, nearby molecular clouds; up to a hundred or so light-years across, these small clouds are Herschel's *Löcher im Himmel* and Barnard's dark markings. They can be found all over the disk of the Milky Way. Other molecular clouds, however, are as much as a thousand light-years across and contain more hydrogen gas than a million Suns. These giant molecular clouds, of which several hundred are known, are the most massive objects in the galaxy, yet only a few decades ago their existence was totally unknown. Observers estimate that within the inner Milky Way, the part within the solar system's orbit about the galaxy, about half of the interstellar gas is contained in molecular clouds. Unlike the smaller clouds, the giant clouds tend to line up, like cosmic streetlamps, along the galaxy's spiral arms. Exactly why the clouds should do that is not fully clear, because astronomers are not yet certain what accounts for the persistence of the spiral arms themselves. The most popular theory suggests that the arms are essentially cosmic traffic jams, the luminous result of a spiral-shaped compression wave moving through the Milky Way's smooth disk of matter. According to this idea, gas gets squeezed by the density wave, huge molecular clouds form, and, eventually, big new stars turn on within them, illuminating the spiral.

The giant molecular clouds, in fact, are the galaxy's most prolific stellar incubators. The idea that stars form in interstellar clouds is not new; as long ago as the eighteenth century, William Herschel suggested that the Orion Nebula and other bright clouds were "the chaotic material of future suns." But as a result of their molecular mapping, astronomers now realize that the bright, visible nebulae, which are spawning clusters of stars, are mere blisters situated on the sides of these huge, invisible molecular clouds. Stars do not solely condense, slowly and quietly, in the center of gas clouds, as once thought. They also form, violently and vigorously, on the edge and throughout the cloud. Each new generation of stars digs ever deeper into the dark cloud, kindling a wave of star formation that surges through the cloud like the successive bursts of a string of firecrackers. What were once considered freaks of nature, simple celestial molecules, have turned out to be some of the most powerful tools afforded astronomers in recent years. "That's why it is so important," stresses Townes, "for scientists to look at those things that have been neglected for either poor or incomplete reasons." To fill in the gaps, research groups around the world have been moving some of their astrochemical investigations into the laboratory.

THE COSMOCHEMISTS

The Seeley W. Mudd Laboratory of the Geological Sciences, situated on the southwestern corner of the Caltech campus, resembles an exotic nautical temple. Along with its beige stucco exterior and series of arches that enclose a walkway at its base, the four-story building showcases trilobites, nautiluses, and shells in relief around the borders of its cast-iron window casings.

At the end of a long hallway on the first floor is Room 111, home of the "card-carrying cosmochemists," as one student jokes. The small laboratory is dominated by a bank of lasers. Geoffrey Blake, the young cosmochemist who established the lab, wants to examine how the universe went from atoms and molecules in the extreme environment of space to meteorites and planets. What is the pattern of chemical evolution, he is asking, as stars and planets assemble themselves? Does the chemistry occurring in space just go along for the ride, or does it somehow help determine the final product? Hydrogen is assuredly the most abundant element in our galaxy, and much of it exists in the molecular form—two hydrogen atoms locked in an embrace. But do other molecules, such as carbon monoxide and ammonia, play a crucial role as well, even though they are no more than contaminants in our galaxy?

To find out the answers to these questions, Blake and his associates have been creating a bit of outer space right in the laboratory. To reproduce the conditions of the interstellar medium and the chemical reactions possibly taking place there, the molecules under study are injected into a huge chamber, a twelve-inch-wide steel pipe that rises to the ceiling. The gaseous material is squirted into the vacuum chamber through an extremely small tube. As the gas suddenly expands upon exiting the tube, it cools to just a few degrees above absolute zero, the temperature most molecules experience in the hostile environment of space. A laser, mounted at the end of the chamber, then selectively excites the molecules so that their spectra can be examined in detail.

Astronomers are fairly sure that the tenuous sea of celestial gas is concocting even more complex molecules than yet sighted. As a test of that idea, Blake and his cohorts also focus an ultraviolet laser onto either a graphite or carbide rod, a bar of solid carbon mounted in an evacuated chamber. Under the ultraviolet ray bombardment, streams of carbon ions are ejected off the rod, and soon these ions join with other atoms in the chamber to form ever bigger and longer molecules. Excited by the ultraviolet light, the new exotic compounds fluoresce, giving off distinct infrared light waves. The challenge is to go to the telescope and look for those infrared signatures. "These big molecules could be a major reservoir of carbon in the galaxy," says Blake.

Other research labs, similar to Blake's, are studying how molecules might form on grains. In some cases the Earthbound journey into an interstellar cloud begins with a small tube of methane, one of the molecular constituents of interstellar space. Energized with a spark coil, the tube starts to glow like a hot-pink neon sign. Some of the methane molecules ionize (that is, become electrically charged); others break apart, just as they do when struck by ultraviolet rays in space. The excited molecules race down the tube, enter a vacuum chamber cooled to near absolute zero, and strike a surface, such as a sapphire disk or tiny block of metal, that mimics the core of an interstellar dust grain. The molecules meet and combine on the pseudodust grain, forming a thin frost. Millennia of chemical interactions are compressed into a few hours' time within this laboratory setting. A lamp shines down on the frosty residue so that the combining molecules can absorb and emit light, creating spectra that identify the products. At first researchers see only simple molecules generated, the kind already detected by radio astronomers. But later they begin to observe larger molecules and solids that no one has yet identified in space—molecules composed of long strings of carbon atoms.

Astronomers will not be surprised if some of these laboratory concoctions are eventually detected in an interstellar dust cloud. The first molecule hunters, after looking up a molecule's spectral signature in a chemistry handbook or calculating the frequency themselves, then searched the celestial sky with their radio telescopes for signs of that particular radio feature. It was a grand game of hide-and-seek. But that changed in 1970 when observers, pointing their telescopes at molecular clouds, began to record spectral features that belonged to no known substance. Researchers had to figure out what simple combination of atoms could generate those particular spectral lines. After years of work in the laboratory, spectroscopists figured out that one unknown celestial molecule, at first labeled X-ogen by Buhl and Snyder when they first discovered it in 1970, was actually HCO^+, a molecule that had never before been seen on Earth, and for good reason: It is extremely reactive.

One of the biggest molecules so far detected is $HC_{11}N$—with thirteen atoms, its long length is unusual. It, too, is found nowhere on our planet; if it were, it would be highly explosive in air. "The exotic conditions in space probably create all kinds of highly unusual and reactive species," says Blake. The rotational spectra of such species as CN, CCH, and HCO^+ were not even known, or sought, until they were first seen in the interstellar medium.

The dark clouds, which Herschel and Barnard brought to our attention, are veritable chemical factories, and dust grains serve as the assembly lines. Without dust grains, there would probably be few molecules in space. It all starts when two hydrogen atoms land on a dust grain and join, forming molecular hydrogen. It takes dozens of years for any one hydrogen atom to bump into a grain and stick, but once it does, it takes only seconds for the hydrogen to mate with another hydrogen. The resulting molecule of H_2 moves off the grain and into space, where a passing cosmic ray might knock an electron off the H_2 or split the molecule back up, creating such ions of hydrogen as H^+, H_2^+, or, eventually, H_3^+. These ions go on to react with other elements in the cloud—chiefly, carbon, nitrogen, and oxygen—to form even more exotic molecules. It is only ten to fifteen degrees above absolute zero in those clouds, yet the chemical reactions inexorably progress onward.

Bearded, with wavy, light-brown hair, Blake maintains an air of exuberance as he talks. His hand dances in the air to show the intricate steps involved in creating a specific molecule in space. For example, an oxygen atom might first meet up with an H_3^+ ion and after four steps, with various intermediate species splitting apart and uniting, one might end up with a water molecule and a lone hydrogen atom or possibly an OH radical and hydrogen molecule.

This is more than an academic exercise. All these varied chemicals, although mere specks in the vast sea of hydrogen, are quite important to the formation of stars. As a gas cloud collapses, condensing into newborn stars, it releases huge amounts of energy. Molecular hydrogen, the bulk of the cloud, is incapable of radiating this energy away. So, the job is handled by the other molecular species, as well as the dust grains, even though these components make up such a small fraction of the cloud's composition. The amount of energy lost as the molecules madly spin determines, in part, the rate at which a gas cloud will collapse and ultimately how many stars will be born.

Blake also thinks of molecules in space as telescopic lenses. Carbon monoxide and formaldehyde, for example, are liberally sprinkled throughout a molecular cloud and, as a result, are some of the best molecules to tune into when you want to observe the full extent of a cloud, as if you were imaging the cloud with a wide-angle lens. Molecules of silicon monoxide, on the other hand, allow astronomers to zoom in, to see what's happening closer in—the SiO molecules tend to concentrate in very hot regions, such as the cocoons of dust around newborn stars. "That's the future of this business," says Blake, "to use different tracers to see different regions of star formation." The matter of the universe becomes the very means to examine its most intimate features.

The Greeks arrived at a rather simple formula, elegant in its day, for the universe's composition. The heavens and the terrestrial domain were fashioned out of earth, air, fire, water, and ether. The ether that was once thought to fill the space between the stars is now gone, interstellar matter serving as a replacement. A remnant of the Greek fire remains, only now it is a cauldron that forges the primary elements. Hydrogen and helium emerge from a fiery big bang and over the eons are further transformed inside the hellish interior of stars.

More than a name on an inventory list, each chemical in space is a means of "hearing" and seeing the universe as it really is. The discovery of carbon monoxide eventually allowed radio astronomers to observe, for the first time, the pangs of stellar birth. Calcium offered optical observers firm evidence of interstellar gas. The echo of atomic hydrogen's celestial song resounds through space to reveal the structure of our home galaxy, the Milky Way. And the very proportions of the universe's composition— hydrogen rich, uranium poor—trace the steplike process of elemental cooking. What constitutes the universe cannot be separated from its history—invaluable clues concerning the universe's nature and destiny are offered by each element.

That is why astronomers are nervous. Hints have been arriving over recent years that more is out there—a dark, unknown matter that floats in and around the luminous galaxies. But no one knows what it is. Is this additional, unseen material ordinary or extraordinary? Finding out the nature of this extra stuff may change only certain details in the story of the universe and its evolution; on the other hand, this dark matter—this missing mass—has the potential to alter the entire tale.

PART II

DARK

For now we see through a glass, darkly . . .

—1 CORINTHIANS 13

· 7 ·

A Ride into Darkness

I soon became convinced . . . that all theorizing would be empty brain exercise and therefore a waste of time unless one first ascertained what the population of the universe really consists of. . . .

—FRITZ ZWICKY

Things are seldom what they seem,
Skim milk masquerades as cream.

—SIR WILLIAM GILBERT,
H.M.S. PINAFORE

Halfway through the twentieth century, astrophysicists were on the brink of forging a complete and compelling history of the origin of the elements. Giorgio Abetti, a noted Italian solar physicist, remarked in 1951 that astronomy was "approaching the conception of a harmony of creation . . . and of a unity of matter in all the visible world." An Earth, constructed out of the ashes of a previous generation of stars, circles a small yellow star, whose death several billion years from now will continue the cycle onward. First hydrogen is fused into helium; later, this helium is transformed into carbon, oxygen, and nitrogen. These are the first rungs up the ladder of the elements. All this handiwork is continually exhibited in the spectral messages emanating from the glowing nebulae, luminous stars, and shining galaxies that fill the cosmos. A network of matter is laid open to our inspection by its myriad radiations. Within a few decades of scientists' comprehension of stellar fusion, a thorough tally of the universe's ingredients seemed on the verge of completion.

Yet even as Abetti with such supreme confidence was making his assertion about a unity of matter, clues were emerging that a dark, hidden universe lurks beside the luminous cosmos so long studied with telescope and spectroscope. No one expected this turn of events. Astronomy had crossed a threshold. As if caught in the inky shadow of a solar eclipse, astronomy's concerns suddenly shifted. Long involved with the universe's light, observers now had to peer into the celestial darkness, bleak and cold.

It is true that caches of material, previously invisible, are often un-covered by astronomers. Infrared telescopes spotted protostars gestating within thick cocoons of dust and gas; radio telescopes revealed those immense reserves of interstellar molecules that were once thought impos-sible to assemble in space. Yet all these concealed inventories turned out to be a type of matter very familiar to us, a part of the universal recipe. The dark, hidden universe may be different. It can't be seen, but it can be felt: Its gravitational tugs affect the spins of galaxies and the motions of galaxies within clusters.

It has not yet been established whether this extra, unknown material shares in the harmony of creation, the world of ordinary matter. Astron-omers only know that it doesn't seem to absorb or emit any kind of radiation (at least not any X-ray, radio, or light waves that can be detected so far). Observers must grapple with the prospect that the radiant stars and galaxies, so long investigated, may constitute only a small percentage of what is actually out there in space. Solving this mystery promises to alter and enhance our picture of the cosmos significantly. We may find that the shimmering sky so familiar to us tells us as little about the precise nature of the universe as a pair of on-coming headlights tell us about the shape of a car.

FRITZ ZWICKY AND THE MISSING MASS

Some of the first hints that something was amiss in astronomy's account-ing of the universe's contents arrived in the 1930s. The realization can be traced in part to an eccentric and erratic genius named Fritz Zwicky, a physicist who was often at odds with the astronomical community because of his dogmatic and volatile personality. (Zwicky's abrasiveness was so legendary that a wartime colleague once suggested to him, in jest, that they define a unit of roughness for airplane wings and call it a zwicky.)

Born in Bulgaria of Swiss parents in 1898, Zwicky was educated in Zurich and remained a Swiss national all his life. He arrived at Caltech in 1925 as a research fellow in the physics department, where he studied the physical properties of crystals and liquids. Despite Caltech's relaxed campus atmosphere, a hallmark of the California life-style, Zwicky always retained the authoritative air of a nineteenth-century European professor. He was an aggressive, original, and stubbornly opinionated man, the supreme scientific individualist.

Zwicky's avid interest in cosmic rays, a popular topic in the 1930s, drew him to astronomy and led him to one of the greatest theoretical insights ever made in the field: the implosive creation of the neutron star. This idea was first presented at a meeting of the American Physical Society at Stanford University in December 1933. A fuller description was written up in the *Proceedings of the National Academy of Sciences* five months later.

Zwicky worked on the concept in collaboration with the accomplished Mount Wilson astronomer Walter Baade, Zwicky's complete opposite. They were astronomy's odd couple: Where Zwicky was cranky and imperious, Baade was soft-spoken and even-tempered. Together they conceived of the notion of the supernova, the powerful destruction of a star. This alone was quite a clever deduction given that astronomers at the time hadn't seen a star go supernova in our galaxy for nearly four hundred years.[1] Telescopic observations of ancient stellar remnants, such as the Crab Nebula, and brilliant stellar flare-ups in other galaxies led Zwicky and Baade to their startling conception. Supernovae are intensely more energetic than are novae, which are merely explosions on the surface of a star. For many days, even weeks, the white-hot debris of a supernova can outshine an entire galaxy's worth of stars. And these supernovae, Zwicky and Baade went on to report, were a likely source of cosmic rays, the subatomic particles and nuclei that constantly bombard the Earth and solar system from all directions. That Zwicky and Baade hit upon one possible source of cosmic rays was not apparent for some time; at that

---

[1] Modern-day astronomers at last had a chance to see a nearby star go supernova when the blue giant star Sanduleak-69, located some 170,000 light-years from Earth in the Large Magellanic Cloud, visibly exploded in February 1987.

1933 APS meeting there were other cosmic-ray theories offered that were considered equally reasonable. (For instance, a Caltech colleague of Zwicky's, R. M. Langer, wondered whether our portion of the universe was slightly negative, causing positively charged particles from more distant realms to come racing in, as if a sort of cosmic battery were at work.)

The idea of the neutron star was intimately linked with that of the supernova. Zwicky and Baade suggested that the supernova itself represented the transition of an ordinary star into a body of much smaller dimensions and an extremely high density. Zwicky surmised that the inner core of the dying star would implode—collapse inward—forming a miles-wide, naked sphere of pure neutrons. The energy resulting from that collapse would then radiate away in a fiery blast. Neutron particles were a hot topic at the time, having been discovered by experimentalists only the year before—the same year that a brilliant young astrophysicist at Cambridge, the India-born Subrahmanyan Chandrasekhar, applied Einstein's theory of special relativity to stellar equations and realized that particularly massive stars must collapse in their old age to something much smaller than a white dwarf star.

Needless to say, Zwicky's colleagues greeted his astounding neutron-star idea with much skepticism, and with good reason: Knowledge of neutron physics was as yet too meager to prove conclusively that neutron stars could exist. Astronomers were still trying to absorb the idea of the white dwarf, a shriveled star the size of a planet. Anything smaller was considered extremely unlikely. Even the great Arthur Eddington, responding to Chandrasekhar's intimation of drastic stellar collapse, declared that "there should be a law of nature to prevent a star from behaving in this absurd way." The public, however, adored the concept of a city-sized star, and Zwicky drew much press coverage, even though the first bona fide neutron star, beeping away as a pulsar, would not be found in our galaxy until 1967, more than three decades later.

Given their disparate natures, Zwicky and Baade did not maintain their productive collaboration for very long; they had a falling out (Zwicky accused Baade, German by birth, of being a Nazi) and remained bitter enemies the rest of their lives. Denied sufficient time on the big telescopes to conduct a systematic search for his new class of novae, Zwicky successfully pressed for the construction of a special eighteen-inch wide-field telescope on Palomar Mountain, which he used with great proficiency. During his long-standing program to seek out supernovae, he and his assistants found dozens popping off in galaxies all over the sky. After his years of effort at this task, Zwicky would characteristically boast that only two people knew how to use a small telescope—Galileo and himself (this was a type of humor that was meant to both irritate and amuse the listener).

With the opening of the colossal 200-inch telescope at Palomar in the late 1940s, Caltech at last established an official department of astronomy. Jesse Greenstein, the department's first chairman, inherited the tenured Zwicky, to the dismay of both men. "There is no doubt that Zwicky had an extraordinary mind," Greenstein admits. "He worked on crazy objects that appealed to him emotionally, and this concentration on the peculiar objects of the universe turned out to be a treasure trove for other astronomers." Greenstein's long association with Zwicky was filled

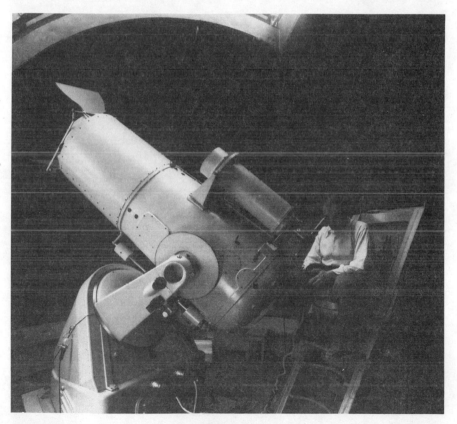

Fritz Zwicky at his telescope on Palomar Mountain.
California Institute of Technology Archives

with conflict, often due to Zwicky's unshakable faith that he could accomplish any endeavor put before him.

One of Greenstein's favorite stories about the tenacious physicist is of Zwicky's supposed foray into military defense. Greenstein recalls:

> I once went into Zwicky's office to reprove him for having raised the salary of the librarian without consulting me, causing an overrun in the budget. I was smoking a cigar, and as I started to yell and scream at him, which was the only way of commanding attention, he began coughing violently and clutching his chest and said at one point, "I was gassed in the war, Jesse." So I dashed out in the hall and got rid of the cigar and came back all apologies for having upset him. About a month or two later, it occurred to me that he was a Swiss national; he had never been in any army, not during World War I nor World War II.

Greenstein learned later that Zwicky had become convinced, shortly after the bombing of Pearl Harbor, that the Japanese would find Pasadena an ideal target for poison gas. He went to the city fathers and offered to design an emergency gas mask, which could be made from odds and ends found around a typical home. Fashioning a prototype, Zwicky arranged for a training truck to come onto the Caltech campus, whereupon he donned his homemade mask, went into the truck, and was gassed. When Zwicky didn't come out after a minute or so, the training personnel pumped out the gas, flung open the truck's doors, and found Zwicky flat on his back, a victim of his own experiment on U.S. soil.

Such stories of Zwicky's eccentricities abound on the Caltech campus, but there was another, very compassionate side to his complex personality. Helen Knudsen, head librarian of the Caltech astrophysics department, recalls a man who was kind and gentle to both students and administrative staff. He chaired a foundation devoted to the support of orphanages. It was perhaps a drive for perfection, suggests Knudsen, that made Zwicky prefer being right rather than friendly. Greenstein was both angered and admiring when Zwicky used departmental funds to ship books to European universities devastated after World War II.

During his professional lifetime, 1921 to 1974, Zwicky published 562 papers. The range of topics was sweeping: cosmic rays, the extragalactic distance scale, the age of galaxy clusters, aerial propulsion, meteors, ionization in gases, quantum theory, elasticity in solids, neutron stars, crystal lattices, electrolytes, gravitational lenses, gravitons, propellants, and quasars. Zwicky was awarded the U.S. Medal of Freedom for his work on jet propulsion during the war and developed some fifty patents, many of them in the field of rocketry. A philosophy of science that he developed and religiously heeded, called the morphological approach, is still revered in Europe. If a possibility exists, this philosophy declares, nature will carry it out and scientists should discover it. For example, if there are galaxies that contain billions of stars, Zwicky had pondered, why not ones that contain only millions? It was an attitude that led Zwicky to conceive of dwarf galaxies, long before they were sighted. An avid space enthusiast, Zwicky once placed an explosive charge on the nose of an Aerobee rocket, then being tested after the war, and triggered the charge at the moment the rocket reached the top of its trajectory. Zwicky always claimed that the fragments of metal, shot into space by the blast, were the first man-made objects to escape Earth's gravitational field.

Wallace Sargent, who arrived at Caltech from England as a postdoctoral fellow in 1959, was quickly captivated by Zwicky, by then an elderly professor. "We Britishers love eccentrics," explains Sargent, now a full professor at the university. A picture of Zwicky currently hangs in Sargent's spacious Caltech office. Zwicky's penetrating pale eyes, set below a wide forehead, look directly at the viewer; his mouth is closed firmly, and his large ears are made more prominent by an old-fashioned, short-clipped haircut.

Sargent shared a common interest with Zwicky, the supernova expert. Trained as a theorist, Sargent wrote his thesis on a supernova's expansion into the interstellar medium. At Caltech, though, he was assigned to work with Greenstein on interpreting the composition of stars from stellar spectra. This meant spending hours in the basement of the Robinson building poring over hundreds of photographic plates. He shared his quarters with Zwicky, who was then actively compiling the famous six-volume Zwicky catalogue, which lists the locations and magnitudes of some 30,000 galaxies in the northern hemisphere. Today this catalogue remains one of astronomers' richest sources on clusters of galaxies.

Although aware of Zwicky's fearsome reputation, Sargent was able to talk with him quite easily, most likely because Sargent, then a lowly postdoc, was not a direct competitor. Astronomers in southern California, particularly the staffs at the Mount Wilson and Palomar observatories, dominated the field of astronomy in the first half of this century. Having the privilege to work with the largest telescopes in the world, they virtually established territorial rights over the universe. Certain astronomers could work only in the light of the moon, which limited them to studying bright stars; observers with the greatest political pull saved the dark, moonless nights for themselves, so that they could tackle astronomy's most prestigious work—the study of far galaxies. "You were not allowed to cross the boundary," says Sargent.

Zwicky annoyed all his associates by breaking these unwritten rules and studying anything he pleased. He was the outsider, a physicist in the midst of classically trained astronomers. Moreover, he was a physicist who continually spouted some pretty wild ideas, as many wrong as right. "Zwicky was one of those people," recalls Sargent, "who was determined to show the other guy was wrong. His favorite phrase was, 'I'll show those bastards,' " which he did to the fullest.

Zwicky's second catalogue, a self-published compilation of bright compact galaxies, was visionary. Since its publication it has served as an invaluable map for pointing out the active galaxies so eagerly studied by today's astronomers. Moreover, two of the galaxies listed allowed Sargent to measure the universal abundance of helium. But in certain circles, this catalogue, known as the Big Red Book for the color and size of its hardbound cover, is more famous for its introduction, in which Zwicky personally lashes out at many of his distinguished colleagues, labeling them "fawners," "apple polishers," and "thieves." He claims they stole his ideas and hid their own errors. "The useless trash in the bulging astronomical journals furnishes vivid testimony," he wrote with a vehemence seen nowhere else in the scientific literature.

Perhaps it is not surprising then, given Zwicky's irascible personality and eclectic scientific style, that he would spy one of the first signs that the universe's ledger books were not quite balancing. Blithely stepping into the celestial territory claimed by others, Zwicky decided to examine all the velocity information then available in the literature on galaxies congregated within the famous Coma cluster, a rich group of hundreds of galaxies some 300 million light-years distant. His statistical analysis revealed that the Coma galaxies were moving around in the cluster at a fairly rapid pace. Adding up all the light being emitted by these galaxies, Zwicky realized that there was not enough visible, or luminous, matter in the cluster to gravitationally bind the speeding galaxies to one another.

Zwicky initially wondered whether galaxies within a cluster were simply more energetic. But that idea wouldn't fly. "It is difficult to understand why under these circumstances there are any great clusters of nebulae remaining in existence at all," he had to conclude. The situation seemed paradoxical. Under the standard laws of celestial mechanics, with the galaxies in the Coma cluster buzzing around so nimbly, the cluster should be breaking apart, but it is very much intact. Consider an analogy: Say that space-shuttle astronauts ignited all the engines and rocket boosters on their spacecraft at full power, yet found themselves unable to lift off from the Earth; shuttle engineers might be forced to conclude that the Earth suddenly and inexplicably had more mass, and consequently a stronger gravitational field to keep such things as shuttles from flying off too easily. Similarly, Zwicky had to assume that some kind of unseen matter pervades the Coma cluster to provide an additional gravitational glue. In his report to the Swiss journal *Helvetica Physica Acta* in 1933, Zwicky referred to this unseen ingredient as *dunkle Materie,* or dark matter. He was demonstrating that matter, although invisible, can still be detected through its gravitational clout.

A year earlier Jan Oort, an up-and-coming Dutch astronomer, noticed a related effect much closer to the Earth. Oort would come to pioneer radio astronomy in his homeland and hypothesize the existence of a vast reservoir of comets, now known as the Oort cloud, encircling our solar system. But Oort's first notable contribution to astronomy was to clearly demonstrate in the 1920s that the Milky Way galaxy rotates about its center—roughly one turn every quarter of a billion years.

Oort went on to measure the speed and direction of many stars moving within our galactic disk. In the course of this work, Oort saw that stars tend to bob up and down, like merry-go-round horses, as they slowly circle our galaxy. A star first moves down toward the galactic disk because it is gravitationally attracted by the disk's immense mass, but then the star overshoots and passes on through the plane of the Milky Way. Yet, like a swinging pendulum, the star eventually slows down and is pulled back up. Such bobbing goes on and on. The speed with which the stars are pulled back and forth, the gravitational force required to do the job, suggested to Oort that there was about twice as much matter in the disk of the Milky Way than could be seen in stars and gas. People began to call it the "missing mass," although what is really missing is the light rather than the mass. Long-held assumptions had to be altered; here was evidence that the light throughout the cosmos might not be a reliable tracer of the matter in the universe. Some believe that as more and more faint stars are revealed to be inhabiting our galactic disk—adding to the disk's inventory of matter—Oort's local missing-mass problem may be diminished somewhat. But Zwicky's dark enigmatic matter, far more ample, cannot be accounted for at all.

When Zwicky first mentioned that clusters of galaxies seemed to be stockpiling vast amounts of dark matter, his colleagues were very doubtful. For one, his analysis of the Coma cluster's internal motions was based on very few data—just seven galaxies. Over time, however, his curious result was only strengthened. By 1936 Sinclair Smith, an astronomer with the Mount Wilson Observatory, proceeded to scrutinize all the available

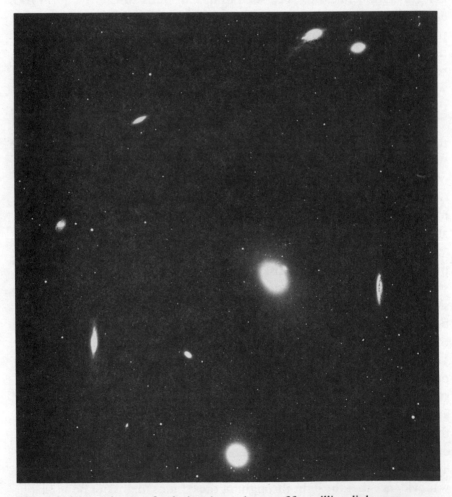

The rich Virgo cluster of galaxies situated some fifty million light-years away. The motions of these galaxies suggest an unseen dark matter inhabits the cluster.
National Optical Astronomy Observatories

data on the Virgo cluster, a rich assemblage of galaxies some 50 million light-years away, and discerned a similar effect. The galaxies were moving around in the cluster relatively swiftly and yet not escaping. "It is possible . . . ," reported Smith, "that the difference represents a great mass of internebular material within the cluster." Variations of Zwicky's and Smith's approaches have since been applied to a variety of clusters, with basically the same result: an indication that "something else" is out there, a dark, nameless matter that outweighs the luminous mass in the cosmos ten to twenty times over.

Faced with a novel problem, Zwicky, in his inimitable way, proposed a novel method to assess the exact amount of dark matter in far-off galaxies. And, just like his theory of neutron stars, it was an idea ahead of its time. In a short, half-page note to the *Physical Review* in 1937, Zwicky suggested that a galaxy could be better "weighed" if it was also found to be a gravitational lens. The roots of this effect lie in Einstein's general theory of relativity, which claimed that a light beam would noticeably bend—get swerved by space-time's curvature—as it passed by a massive celestial body, such as the Sun. The Sun, in this case, becomes the gravitational equivalent of an optical lens. When astronomers monitoring a 1919 solar eclipse confirmed that starlight grazing the darkened Sun did indeed get deflected by essentially the amount predicted by general relativity, Einstein became an international celebrity overnight.

Two decades later Zwicky speculated that nearby galaxies, with masses many billions of times greater than our Sun, could produce an even more intriguing cosmic mirage: Their formidable gravitational fields would be strong enough to split the light of more distant objects into multiple images. In fact, if the distant object is aligned just right—lying precisely behind its gravitational lens—its light can be spread out as a ring (fittingly labeled an "Einstein ring") that completely surrounds the lensing galaxy. Although not the same physical principle, you might think of that light, coursing through the universe, as a stream of water that comes upon a rock and gets diverted to either side of the stone. One stream becomes two or more streams. In space, with light (instead of water) getting bent and split, such an effect becomes an excellent weighing scale: The amount of deflection depends on the total mass of the galaxy doing the bending, no matter whether that mass is brightly shining or darkly hidden.

The farther astronomers venture into intergalactic space with their telescopic probing, the more they realize that this effect is far from rare.

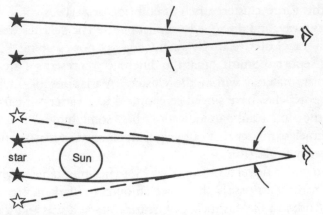

star

Sun

image of star

Two stars are separated by a certain angular distance. When the Sun comes in front of them, however, the stars appear farther apart, as their rays are bent by the Sun's strong gravitational field.
Illustration by John Hamwey

Deep images of the night sky reveal a growing number of luminous arcs, bands, and rings as the light beams of distant quasars and young galaxies streak through the mass-filled universe and get gravitationally deflected and jostled on their journey toward Earth. With gravitational lensing at work, the celestial sky comes to resemble the light of streetlamps reflected in a lake ruffled by the wind.

For many years Zwicky claimed to have proof of a gravitational lens, which would have been a momentous discovery. He continually talked of a spectrogram that he took which displayed two sets of spectral absorption lines, side by side. He boasted many, many times that the pairing could be easily explained as a nearby galaxy amplifying the light of a more distant galaxy located exactly behind it. In effect, the galaxy close in was acting as a gravitational lens, magnifying a galaxy farther off. At a meeting in Armenia in the early 1960s, Caltech professor Guido Münch, weary of Zwicky's incessant bragging about this lensing effect and made bold by many toasts, dared Zwicky to put the infamous spectrogram on his plate, whereupon he would eat it. Zwicky never did produce the evidence. After Zwicky's death, Sargent found the notorious spectrogram among Zwicky's papers. He intended to put it on a plate and carry it to Münch's office but was forced to change his plans. "I decided that the extra set of spectral lines was merely a flaw in the emulsion," says Sargent wistfully.

Astronomers had to wait until 1979 to see their first gravitational lens. While closely perusing a photographic plate to locate the visible counterpart to a newly discovered radio source, British astronomer Dennis Walsh noticed that the radio object's position coincided with two starlike objects instead of just one. Additional observations confirmed that the cozy pair were not the chance alignment of two objects (as often happens). A celestial object's spectrum is as distinctive and exclusive as a fingerprint, but these two spectra were completely identical. They had to be the same object, in this case a quasar, seen in duplicate. (A quasar, starlike in appearance, is the brilliant core of a young, remote galaxy.) The light of Walsh's powerful quasar, eight billion light-years distant, was being split in two by a giant elliptical galaxy located halfway between the quasar and Earth.

Zwicky had expressed the hope of living to the year 2000 and thus having a life that touched three centuries. He died in 1974 at the age of seventy-five, just a few years before the missing-mass problem blossomed into a subject of great importance within the astronomical community. "He probably wouldn't have paid much attention anyway," says Sargent with a smile. "He would surely have had his own ideas, which would have been tangential to everyone else."

Upon examining the Virgo cluster in the 1930s, Sinclair Smith could only conclude that the missing mass would "remain unexplained until further information becomes available." It was a long wait. The problem was largely ignored for more than three decades. Some astronomers thought the missing mass was just an unusual but not too bothersome property of clusters; others believed the dilemma would disappear once theorists could analyze the motions of galaxies in more detail. Observers first had to develop the instrumentation to record galactic redshifts more efficiently and so build up a better sample of data. "Weighing" a cluster, they were confident, had to be much more complicated than either Zwicky or Smith assumed. But a more deep-rooted anxiety may have been at work, and astronomers eventually had to confront it—the uncomfortable thought that much of the universe might be invisible to their eyes and instruments.

Historians of science, poring over the records of scientific discoveries, have often commented that the most revolutionary finds are frequently made by those pursuing backwater fields neglected by others. Astronomy is no exception. While the most famous of her colleagues were tracking down pulsars and quasars, Vera Rubin quietly and determinedly measured the rotation rates of spiral galaxies. The spins she measured were unexpected, and as a result the missing-mass problem suddenly became more provocative than pulsars and quasars.

THE WOMAN WHO SPINS THE GALAXIES

In 1938, when Vera Cooper was ten years old, her family moved from Philadelphia to Washington, D.C. Sharing a tiny bedroom with her sister, Vera slept beneath a window that faced north.

As the sky swiftly darkened from deep indigo to jet black, the little girl with the long brown hair, intensely curious for her age, struggled to stay awake and watch the heavens sparkle above her. It was not the stars themselves that caught Vera's attention. Rather, she was captivated by the way the constellations, over the course of a night, slowly turned around the North Star because of the rotation of the Earth. If a meteor blazed down from the heavens, she memorized its trail. "Don't spend all night hanging out the window," her mother would caution as Vera became mesmerized by the slow procession of the stars.

Vera Cooper has long since added the surname Rubin to her own, and her hair is now gray-white and cut comfortably short. Large glasses frame inquisitive brown eyes. But she still lives in Washington, D.C., and, as an astronomer with the Carnegie Institution of Washington, she is still fascinated by celestial motions. Only now when she ponders them, she travels to mountaintops in Arizona, California, and Chile and utilizes the electronic eyes of the world's largest telescopes.

With this instrumentation, Rubin doggedly pursues an endeavor that has taken up most of her career: measuring how fast spiral galaxies are spinning, from their luminous cores out to the faint wisps of light at their fringes. Such a task sounds tedious and pedestrian—even her colleagues thought so when she started the project two decades and two hundred galaxies ago. But with her painstaking measurements, Rubin helped turn Zwicky's pesky little observation into one of astronomy's most tantalizing mysteries. Her observations, possibly more than any other findings, convinced astronomers that Zwicky's dark-matter concerns were more than a petty aberration. The missing mass was not just a quirky property of clusters; dark matter surrounded individual galaxies as well.

Rubin established that spiraling galaxies are spinning so fast that they have to be embedded in vast spheres of material to keep the stars from zipping completely out of the galaxy, like a discus cast out of the hands of a whirling discus thrower. "The idea was certainly in the air," says Princeton astrophysicist P. James E. Peebles, "but Vera's measurements were very influential in causing people to pay attention to this effect, mainly because her observations were so dramatically clean. Beautiful data."

These data suggest that 90 percent or more of the universe's mass is playing an awfully good game of hide-and-seek with earthly detectors. Astronomers' puzzlement can be measured by the astounding range of objects put forth as candidates for this missing mass—from swarms of hypothetical elementary particles, each mote weighing less than a trillionth of a trillionth of a gram, to a hidden armada of Jupiterlike planets or old, dead stars. Yet Rubin never intended to stir up such ferment, let alone change the way we perceive the universe. When she began her career, she only wanted to keep looking at the stars.

Astronomer Vera Rubin.
Photograph courtesy of Vera Rubin

The stately headquarters of the Department of Terrestrial Magnetism, with its red-tiled roof and three stories of light-beige brick, stands atop a small hill in the northwestern sector of the U.S. capital, right beside the lush greenery of Rock Creek Park. It is one of five research departments scattered over both U.S. coasts that constitute the Carnegie Institution of Washington, a free-spirited research organization established by the business tycoon Andrew Carnegie at the beginning of this century.

The Department of Terrestrial Magnetism was founded in 1904 to map the earth's magnetic field; it retains its awkward name even though seismology, geochemistry, and astronomy have been added to its mission. Its several acres of wide grassy lawns and flowering trees resemble a small college campus, but the bucolic setting is temporarily marred one spring by herds of construction trucks.

Staff members are moving to a newly constructed building next door. The department's old library, with its high ceilings and rows upon rows of rich wooden bookcases, has been closed; the computer system is about to be shut down for a few weeks. Some of the staff have escaped by going on vacation, but Rubin—just back from the Kitt Peak National Observatory in Arizona, where she had four nights of the clearest observations of her life—is staying on. "Each hour is precious right now," she says, "for I won't be able to see my images on the computer for a month."

Rubin sits in her basement office surrounded by cardboard boxes that await the move. Posters mounted on the walls speak of travel to Japan, France, Italy, and Chile. A giant blowup of the Andromeda galaxy on the ceiling and a print of van Gogh's *Starry Night* on the wall by her computer reveal her celestial interests. Warm and cordial, Rubin gives full attention to the chore at hand, whether it is computing, observing, or talking about her multifaceted career. She is a researcher who dislikes controversy—so much so that she often tries to escape it. Yet, somehow, she has always picked scientific problems that have thrown her into the thick of it. This path was certainly not laid out for her; her career has been marked with a series of professional setbacks that might have proved insurmountable to others.

Born in Philadelphia, the youngest of two daughters, Rubin was able to maintain her astronomical interests despite a high school physics teacher who declared, "You'll do all right as long as you stay away from science." Fortunately, her father, an electrical engineer, encouraged her, helping her to build her first telescope when she was fourteen years old and taking her to amateur astronomy meetings in Washington. There she heard talks by such notables as Harlow Shapley, who first discerned Earth's true position in the Milky Way.

At one point Rubin contemplated going to Swarthmore College in Pennsylvania to major in astronomy, until a Swarthmore admissions officer, hearing that Rubin enjoyed painting, suggested she pursue the more ladylike career of painting astronomical subjects. "That became a standard joke in my family for many, many years," says Rubin, laughing. "Whenever anything went wrong for me at work, someone would inevitably say, 'Have you ever thought of a career in which you paint?' "

Turned down by Swarthmore, Rubin entered Vassar College at the age of seventeen and graduated three years later with a bachelor's degree in astronomy. She wanted nothing more than to continue her work at Princeton University, then, as now, a prestigious astrophysics center. Enthusiastic and naive, she wrote away for a catalogue of its graduate school. She never received the catalogue—Princeton did not accept women into its graduate astrophysics program until 1971.

She ended up going to Cornell University, where her new husband, Robert Rubin, was a Ph.D. candidate in physical chemistry. At Cornell, Vera was doubly the outsider: She was a woman and she was in (what was then) an unexceptional astronomy department consisting of only two faculty members. But since her course work was largely in physics, she was in the right place at the right time. Hans Bethe, who would win a Nobel Prize for unraveling the fusion reactions that power the Sun, taught her quantum mechanics; and she learned quantum electrodynamics from the flamboyant Richard Feynman, who would also garner a Nobel.

By the time Rubin arrived at Cornell, astronomers had already known for some twenty years that the cosmos was expanding. They had observed that light waves from distant galaxies are stretched, or shifted toward the red end of the spectrum, and had concluded that a galaxy's redshift is a measure of how fast it is moving away from us as it is swept along by an expanding space-time. The idea that this expansion started with a big bang was just gaining currency.

For her master's thesis, Rubin decided to ask whether the galaxies were swinging around the cosmos as well as ballooning outward. Big bang supporter George Gamow was then speculating that there might be a universal rotation: Stars swirled around a galaxy, like the cream in a newly stirred cup of coffee; maybe galaxies, too, circulated within the universe at large. Gamow was pretty much alone in his view. It was thus a daring question for Rubin to pursue, especially considering the paucity of data she had to work with. Galactic velocities were extremely difficult to measure, and at the time, out of billions of galaxies, astronomers had managed to obtain only 109 redshifts. Nevertheless, upon analyzing these redshifts, Rubin concluded that the galaxies did display some extra, sideways motions apart from the outward movement due to cosmic expansion.

In 1950, just three weeks after the birth of her first child, Rubin announced her findings at the eighty-fourth meeting of the American Astronomical Society, held that year in Haverford, Pennsylvania. The report, her professional debut, was one of fifty papers presented that year. (Around eight hundred would be given at such a meeting today.) No one believed the unknown twenty-two-year-old; her data seemed much too scanty. Her paper had almost been banned from the conference, and it was later rejected by every top journal. "It got an enormous amount of publicity, almost all of it negative," recalls Rubin. "But at least, from then on, astronomers knew who I was."

In hindsight, Rubin suspects her data were too poor to justify her conclusion. But Gérard de Vaucouleurs of the University of Texas in Austin calls it a significant paper. When he first heard about the report, he immediately used Rubin's findings to help him prove that the Milky Way and its nearby neighbors are caught at the edge of and gravitating toward a large collection of galaxies now dubbed the Local Supercluster. It was one of the first hints that the universe has a lumpy texture over fairly large scales. "Vera's results gave me the nerve to publish," says de Vaucouleurs.

Soon after the Haverford conference, Rubin moved back to Washington, where her husband started a new job at the Applied Physics Laboratory (sharing an office with Ralph Alpher, who was then cooking up his elements in the big bang), and she, with her growing family responsibilities, began to feel adrift. In those years before the feminist revolution, she could not clearly see the path from where she was—wife and mother with a master's degree—to where she wanted to be. "I actually cried everytime the *Astrophysical Journal* came into the house," she says. "I knew that getting a degree didn't make me an astronomer, but nothing in my education had taught me that one year after Cornell my husband would be out doing his science and I would be home changing diapers."

The frustrations led her to Georgetown University, the only school in the Washington area with a Ph.D. program in astronomy. Her degree was a family enterprise. For nearly two years, while Rubin's parents watched the children, her husband drove her to the university and ate his supper in the car while she attended her nighttime classes.

Gamow, working at nearby George Washington University, served as her adviser. Possibly influenced by the imaginative Russian, Rubin developed a flair for unconventional research. Her pioneering doctoral thesis tackled the distribution of galaxies. Was there a pattern to their positions in the sky that could be mathematically described? she asked. Or were galaxies and clusters of galaxies arranged more or less randomly? For months she slogged through her calculations on a desktop calculator; today, a computer could complete the same analysis in a few hours. Her result—that there was a noticeable clumpiness in the distribution of galaxies—caused nary a ripple in 1954. In fact, the topic was not seriously studied until fifteen years later. Again she had jumped the gun with too little data, a penchant she attributes as much to her academic isolation as to her eager curiosity. She wasn't constrained by the "party line," as she puts it, that pervaded the more illustrious universities—in this case, the dogma that galaxies ought to be smoothly distributed.

After receiving her Ph.D., Rubin taught and did research at Georgetown. Professionally, her life throughout the 1950s was rather uneventful, but, as evidenced by four short lines in her curriculum vitae, she is enormously proud of the work she was doing then. Ahead of her awards, ahead of her distinguished degrees, she lists these accomplishments: David (born 1950), Ph.D. Geology; Judith (1952), Ph.D. Cosmic Ray Physics; Karl (1956), Ph.D. Mathematics; and Allan (1960), Ph.D. Geology.

Not until 1963 did Rubin's astronomical career finally get the spark it needed. Her husband obtained a National Science Foundation fellowship to study for a year at the University of California in San Diego. There she came to meet and work with Margaret and Geoffrey Burbidge, the husband-and-wife team who had recently helped establish that most chemical elements are made in stars. "That was probably the most influential year in my life," says Rubin. "In my mind, I had at last become an astronomer, for the Burbidges were actually interested in my ideas." They especially shared an interest in her latest concern, galaxy dynamics.

While on the West Coast, Rubin also conducted her first professional observing—at Kitt Peak, which had recently opened. Returning to Washington and fired up by her new pursuits, she eventually quit her post at

Georgetown University and went over to the Department of Terrestrial Magnetism, a place she had visited and secretly fallen in love with years earlier while completing her Ph.D. Rubin asked for a job and got it. She was thirty-six.

The DTM, as it is called, is an unusual organization. Its staff is small, only a couple dozen researchers in all, and the atmosphere is familylike. The daily staff lunches, which each person fixes for the group on a rotating basis, are an occasion for gossip as well as scientific chats. The small dining hall comes complete with blackboard and chalk. The DTM is known for the freedom it grants its researchers—in particular, the freedom from the publish-or-perish edict that reigns in academia. Rubin thrived in this atmosphere.

Once on board, she quickly teamed with W. Kent Ford, a physicist and designer of astronomical instruments. When Rubin arrived at the DTM, Ford had recently helped perfect a special tube that increased photographic efficiencies immensely by intensifying the image. Each photon entering this image tube, which resembled a series of small film cans glued together, generated a cascade of electrons. These particles in turn hit a phosphorescent screen and the resultant glow was photographed, making it much easier to record the spectrum of a far-off galaxy.

The two researchers collaborated for a quarter of a century, until Ford's retirement. They were the perfect complement to each other: Ford, the expert instrumentalist, paired with Rubin, the tenacious analyst. "Vera is a remarkable, wonderful person," says Ford. "However, we do have one intense disagreement: We both think we're more skilled in guiding the telescope. We've bumped heads in the dark trying to get to the eyepiece first to guide the next exposure."

When Rubin and Ford first started working together, they dabbled in quasar research: the study of those mysterious blue specks that dwell at the edge of the visible universe and are thought to be the brilliant cores of young galaxies. Quasars had just been discovered in 1963, and they were the hottest topic around. Rubin, however, came to dislike the field's hurried pace. "People were constantly calling me asking whether I had obtained a certain redshift, before I was sure whether the data were good," she says.

By the early 1970s Rubin and Ford decided to return to the question asked by Rubin's master's thesis: Do galaxies solely go along for the ride as the universe flies outward, or do they move around on their own as well? Again, she found some extra motion, and again her findings were overwhelmingly rejected. The limited tools then at her disposal introduced errors in interpretation, but astronomers still applaud her attempt as groundbreaking. Her basic idea, if not her detailed results, has been vindicated. The cosmic sea is indeed awash with strong, local currents. But years ago, such large-scale streaming, superimposed on the universe's smooth expansion, went against everyone's expectations. Bitter arguments about this "Rubin-Ford effect" broke out at conferences; notable astronomers wrote Rubin to quit the research. "People were very, very . . . outspoken," she says after a diplomatic pause. Distressed by the reception her work was getting, Rubin simply abandoned it. She turned her attention to a problem that seemed far less controversial, even boring: the rotation of spiral galaxies.

Rubin hoped to learn, with little fanfare, why spirals vary. There are dim ones, bright ones, spirals whose starry arms are tightly wrapped, and others with their arms splayed wide open. A galaxy's spin, Rubin guessed, must surely go a long way toward explaining its structure; it might even provide clues on how the galaxy first formed out of a primordial gas cloud. The Burbidges had already looked at some galactic centers, but Rubin was curious about what was happening farther out in the spiral arms.

Rubin had had a head start. Working with Ford, she had already begun to gauge the rotation of the Andromeda galaxy, the closest spiral galaxy to the Milky Way and by far the brightest from our vantage point. Until that work, data on this galactic neighbor had been sparse, which was understandable: In the early part of this century, it took many months to make the first crude estimates of the rotation of Andromeda. One astronomer in 1917 spent night after night, a total of seventy-nine hours, acquiring just one spectrum using the sixty-inch telescope atop California's Mount Wilson. By the 1960s, the rotations of only a couple handfuls of galaxies had been studied in any detail. But the Carnegie image tube that Ford had perfected gave Rubin and Ford a tremendous advantage, especially when attached to their favorite instrument—a telescope at Kitt Peak with a mirror four meters wide. They could record a spectrum in just two or three hours rather than thirty or more.

Andromeda's spiral disk is slightly inclined toward the Earth, so its rotation carries the stars and gas on one side of the disk toward Earth and those on the other side away from it. As a result, the wavelengths of light emitted by material approaching Earth get a bit shorter (that is, become "bluer"); the light waves lengthen (get "redder") for the gas moving away. By measuring these shifts, Rubin and Ford could determine the rotational velocity of the galaxy at various distances from its center, all along the disk. The velocities of the stars and gas are pegged by carefully assessing the extent to which the wavelengths shift.

Individual stars in other galaxies, even a galaxy as close as Andromeda, are generally too faint for their spectra to be recorded easily, so Rubin and Ford focused on clouds of gas lit up by hot stars—but even that operation was tricky. "These galactic knots of gas are so faint that they cannot be seen directly through the telescope," explains Rubin. "We had to set the slit of the spectrograph on a section of the sky where nothing was visible. It was a great act of faith—setting the slit, exposing the photographic plate for two or more hours, and then developing the plate. We went for every photon we could get."

Rubin and Ford, like many other astronomers, later switched to superefficient electronic detectors, called charge-coupled devices (CCDs), that display the final images on computer monitors, making the whole process considerably easier. But when Rubin and Ford initiated their program, photographic plates were the sole means of recording a spectrum. So swift has been the switch to CCDs that preparing an astronomical photographic plate has almost become a lost art form. "In total darkness, I would cut the photographic plates (glass, not film) into two-inch squares, place them in an oven and bake them for hours in an atmosphere of dry nitrogen to increase their sensitivity," says Rubin. One speck of dust that happened to fall on the very spot of interest could ruin a night's work at the telescope. After each observing run, Rubin developed and dried the plates, eventually carrying them home to measure the subtle shifts in the spectral lines under a microscope.

Around 1970, upon analyzing the shifts in Andromeda's spectral lines, Rubin found that the galaxy did not rotate the way she or anyone else would have expected. Most spiral galaxies, including Andromeda, have a luminous central bulge composed of densely packed stars. The spiraling disk that surrounds this bulge, on the other hand, is very thin, and its brightness falls off steadily toward the edge of the galaxy. Astronomers generally assumed that the mass of a galaxy would follow the same pattern as the light: It would be concentrated in the center and slowly decrease toward the rim. Oort, early on, warned astronomers that this might not be the case, but few listened. Nearly everyone presumed that a galaxy harbors less and less mass where its light is diminished.

Given these assumptions, astronomers then took it as a matter of course that stars in a spiral galaxy would revolve around the galaxy's core like planets in a solar system, whose motions adhere to the laws of gravity and motion formulated by Newton. It was Newton who first described the relationship between gravity and the orbital velocity of celestial objects such as stars and planets. Imagine an object (say, Earth) orbiting close to a massive source of gravity (say, the Sun; almost all the mass of our solar system, more than 99 percent, is tied up in the Sun, so it is the gravitational pull of the Sun that determines the speed of the planets). Earth "falls" toward the Sun, pulled by gravity. But the Sun's surface curves away underneath it. Thus, the constant falling, caused by gravity, is transformed into circular motion—an orbit. The stronger the pull of gravity, the faster the orbital speed; and the closer the object, the stronger the pull. According to Newton, that attraction decreases with the square of the distance from the Sun. Thus the inner planets, such as Venus and Earth, practically race around the Sun, while the planets farther out, where the Sun's gravitational influence is much weaker, proceed at a much slower pace. The planet closest to the Sun, Mercury, whips around the Sun at a racy 108,000 miles per hour. Faraway Pluto, on the other hand, orbits at a sedate 10,500 miles per hour; if it went any faster, it would fly out of the solar system. So, like outlying Pluto, stars and gas at the remote edge of a spiral disk were expected to circle the galaxy much slower than stars farther in.

But, to Rubin and Ford's surprise, Andromeda wasn't acting like a gigantic solar system at all. "The rotational velocity of the individual gas clouds remained high at large distances from the center of the galaxy," recalls Rubin. "But we didn't think we were finding a property of the universe—we thought that Andromeda was simply a peculiar galaxy, and that the next one we studied would be more like what we expected."

The importance of the finding became clear only when Rubin embarked on an ambitious project a few years later, in collaboration with Ford and a team of Carnegie postdoctoral fellows, including David Burstein and Bradley Whitmore. Together they examined the spins of a host of spiral galaxies, picking ones that are, like Andromeda, inclined toward the Earth. In spiral galaxy after spiral galaxy, the Carnegie group saw that stars and gas at a disk's edge travel just as fast as matter closer to the center. Like well-matched sprinters racing around a circular track, those in the outer lanes move as fast as those in the inner lanes. If the planets in our solar system adhered to this pattern, the outer ones would have careered off into interstellar space long ago. Since galaxies do not seem to be jettisoning stars the way a sprinkler sheds water, however, something must be holding the stars in. That something has to be gravity, no other known force being powerful enough on a galactic scale. And where there's gravity, there's mass. Rubin realized that a huge reservoir of extra material, invisible to her telescope, must be tucked away somewhere to keep the stars from flying out of the galaxy. It was the Coma cluster problem all over again.

Rubin was not the first astronomer in recent years to suspect that there was more to a galaxy than meets the eye. Before Rubin turned her full attention to galactic spins, radio astronomers had already brought Zwicky's problem of the missing mass closer to home. In the early 1970s they had observed radio-emitting hydrogen gas at the edge of a few dozen nearby galaxies and discovered, as Rubin was to find later for visible matter, that the gas on the edge moves just as fast as the gas located in the inner galactic core. It was a strong hint that the distribution of mass within a galaxy was not at all like the distribution of light. Mass, unlike luminosity, did not seem to be concentrated near the center of a spiral galaxy. There appeared to be lots of mass farther out, beyond the visible disk. At an international symposium on the dark-matter mystery and its history, Canadian astrophysicist Scott Tremaine called these radio observations "the first sign of the crisis," the sudden realization that most of a galaxy's mass is not contained in visible stars. When the radio observations were first made in the 1970s, though, hardly anyone was alarmed. The radio astronomy findings were isolated measurements, and for many years they were either attributed to instrument error or merely ignored.

Rubin's arsenal of measurements—since 1978, the Carnegie group has analyzed more than two hundred galaxies—took the dark-matter issue off the back burner and turned it into one of the most active concerns in astronomy. "I think we learn with our eyes," suggests Rubin, "and the visual impression of seeing the rotation curves was so striking that it was relatively easy for people to accept."

Earth's home galaxy, the Milky Way, participates in the intrigue. From all the light being emitted by the Milky Way, astronomers have estimated that our visible galaxy contains the mass of about 100 billion suns. But gravity, which acts as a kind of cosmic weighing scale, tells another story. The Milky Way is being drawn toward its neighbor Andromeda as though our galaxy had a mass ten times greater than 100 billion solar masses.

Prior to Rubin launching her sweeping survey of galaxy spins, theorists had already stumbled upon one possible hiding place for all this extra matter. In 1973 Princeton astrophysicists Jeremiah Ostriker and P. James E. Peebles, in the midst of studying the structure of the Milky Way, devised a numerical model of the disk and put it into a computer. But in the course of their computer simulation, the disk went wildly unstable. The star's orbits, to their surprise, went from being nearly circular to being very eccentric. Some of the stars even flew off. The two theorists concluded that flat spiral disks could never retain their distinctive shape unless they were embedded in a larger sphere of material. An entirely new picture of a spiral galaxy emerged from their work. Each glowing galactic disk, they conjectured, is but a luminous smudge immersed in a bloated halo of dark, invisible matter. This image was greatly resisted at first, but astronomers latched onto it with much more enthusiasm as soon as radio astronomers and Rubin's group measured those strangely rapid galactic spins.

Over the years, a number of observations have come to support this curious notion that dark halos surround spiral galaxies, including our own Milky Way galaxy. Astronomers have been closely watching how globular star clusters and satellite galaxies, such as the Magellanic Clouds, revolve around the Milky Way, like planets around the Sun. Scattered above and below the disk of the Milky Way, these distant stellar systems are circling our galaxy so rapidly, say astronomers, that they have to be immersed in an extensive sea of material to stay in orbit around the Milky Way. The diameter of this vast sphere, the Milky Way's dark halo, could be five to ten times larger than the visible disk of stars and gas.

Belief in a missing mass is not uncontested. There are a few lone voices in the field of astronomy who find all this talk of dark matter disturbing, arbitrary, and unnecessary. Israeli astrophysicist Mordehai Milgrom, for one, considers the clothing of galaxies in swathes of dark matter to be theoretically unsatisfying. Milgrom suggests that these unexpected motions within galaxies and clusters are actually telling us that Newton's law of gravitation, so reliable in our immediate environs, breaks down in the realm where gravity is so thinned out that its force is barely a whisper. He has written several papers showing how Newton's equations can be altered to account for the curious rotation rates.

The idea that Newton's laws could be wrong is hardly heresy. After all, Einstein showed that Newton's law of gravity is incomplete and fails under special circumstances. "Newton's law fails when objects approach the speed of light," points out Milgrom. "For that we need Einstein's theory of relativity. What I am suggesting is that Newton's law must also be amended when gravitational accelerations are very, very small, as they are in a galaxy's outer fringes." Milgrom's adjustment to Newton's law is, in fact, very successful in reproducing the observed galaxy spins, a point that has been acknowledged by dark-matter specialists. However, his tinkering cannot yet be reconciled with general relativity, a far more detailed theory of gravity that has so far passed every test. Until that happens, Milgrom's radical suggestion remains suspect. When faced with the necessity of accepting the existence of vast amounts of dark matter or fiddling with one of science's theoretical cornerstones, most astronomers will choose the former.

Consequently, a veritable industry of dark-matter searches has been established since Rubin's results were first reported. The telltale footprints of dark matter have now been spotted, not just in spiral galaxies but in other galactic objects as well. Before his untimely death in an observatory accident in 1987, University of Arizona astronomer Marc Aaronson used the Multiple Mirror Telescope (MMT) atop Arizona's Mount Hopkins to study the motions of carbon stars within the Draco dwarf galaxy, at the time one of seven tiny neighbors known to accompany the Milky Way in its journey through the universe. (The endeavor prompted Aaronson, quite impishly, to entitle one of his papers "Carbon Stars and the Seven Dwarfs.")[2] Situated 200,000 light-years from Earth, these carbon stars in Draco appear so faint that Aaronson would sit for hours before the telescope's digital display and actually count the individual photons arriving at the MMT from each star. "We literally rooted for each one," he once joked.

Aaronson needed as many photons as he could get to figure out how fast the giant red stars were moving within the dwarf galaxy. And, as with Zwicky's cluster and Rubin's spiral galaxies, the answer was unforeseen: The stars were much more stirred up than expected, which suggested that a cloud of dark matter permeates the Draco dwarf galaxy to keep its stars in gravitational check. Moreover, without the dwarf galaxies' harboring some extra matter to serve as a protective blanket, these galactic satellites should have been destroyed by tidal forces as they circle the more massive Milky Way.

---

[2] Aaronson's humorous reference to Snow White and the Seven Dwarfs is now out of date; in 1990, astronomers discovered an eighth dwarf galaxy, the Sextans dwarf, circling the Milky Way.

Additional evidence for dark-matter halos comes from elliptical galaxies. An elliptical galaxy, shaped like an egg or football and commonly found in rich clusters of galaxies, resembles the central bulge of a spiral galaxy without the accompanying disk. It, too, can hoard dark matter. X-ray observations made in space have revealed that M87, a supergiant elliptical that dominates the center of the Virgo cluster, is enveloped in a diffuse yet massive cloud of very hot gas. Unseen in visible light, this gas emits its X rays as the individual gas particles speed around at some one million miles per hour. These particles, heated to temperatures of millions of degrees, should have escaped into intergalactic space long ago. The fact that they didn't leads astronomers to conclude that much more matter resides in M87 than previously suspected, providing the gravitational muscle to hold onto all that gas. What is required is a galaxy containing about fifty trillion solar masses—the combined weight of five hundred Milky Ways! The billions of stars packed into M87 can account for 5 percent of that mass; the hot gas takes care of another 5 percent. But the remaining 90 percent remains nonluminous and inscrutable.

Astronomers are developing very clever schemes to unmask this hidden mass. In fact, Zwicky's dream of "seeing" the dark matter through gravitational lensing is now being realized, largely because there are electronic detectors that allow astronomers to probe the distant universe as never before. Using some of the world's largest telescopes in Arizona, Chile, and Hawaii, J. Anthony Tyson of AT&T Bell Laboratories and several colleagues have been deeply imaging particularly dark patches of the nighttime sky with sensitive CCDs. After many hours of cumulative exposure time, a frecklelike array of faint bluish objects emerges in their electronic pictures. It is believed that these dim specks are galaxies situated billions of light-years away and in the first bloom of youth, when hosts of newborn stars gave off tremendous surges of ultraviolet light (their wavelengths now lengthened, because of the universe's expansion, into the blue spectral range). These distant galaxies, some up to two-thirds of the way to the edge of the visible universe, fill the heavens. Some 50,000 of these faint galaxies can be found in each patch of sky the size of the full Moon.

If the light rays from these distant galaxies pass by an intervening cluster of galaxies on their way to Earth, though, they get diverted by the cluster's immense gravitational field. The entire cluster becomes one big gravitational lens; as a result, each far galaxy, originally a dot of blue, comes to look stretched and smeared out by the gravitational lensing. The astronomer then sees an array of faint arcs arranged, like the markings of a dart board, concentrically around the center of the cluster. Writing special computer programs to keep track of the way in which the faint blue galaxies are distorted into arcs, Tyson and his collaborators have been able to trace how dark matter, the major source of the gravitational bending, is spread through a cluster of galaxies. Their computer-generated map of a cluster called Abell 1689, from George Abell's catalogue of rich groupings of galaxies, displays a halo of dark matter that seems to be confined closely to the visible cluster itself. In fact, the bulk of the dark matter appears to be confined to the cluster's center; it then gets thinner and thinner out to the edge of the cluster.

How far do these dark-matter halos ultimately extend? Does the dark matter solely hover in and around galaxies and clusters, or does a portion of it spread out farther still, diffusing into intergalactic space? Could even more dark matter, perhaps another type of matter altogether, be strewn uniformly through the cosmos, marking a return of the ancient Greek ether but recast in a new form? No one knows with certainty. What Tyson's gravitational imaging cannot yet tell us is the exact nature of this dark matter. Yet how much dark matter is truly out there, and how it is distributed, has a great bearing on what it can be. The dark matter might simply be composed of ordinary matter, but in a form that's difficult to detect, such as a host of failed stars, planetlike Jupiters, or black holes. Or it might be exotic matter that requires more cleverness to snare directly. "Nature has played a trick on astronomers, for we thought we were studying the universe," says Rubin. "We now know that we were studying only the small fraction of it that is luminous."

All the extra gravitational tugs pulling at the Milky Way and other galaxies currently support the notion that there is ten to twenty times more dark matter than luminous cosmic material. But the story gets more complicated. The most fashionable cosmological theories contend that the dark matter is actually a hundred times more plentiful than the luminous stars and galaxies. Theorists believe that the universe began not only with a bang but with a sort of cosmic burp known as inflation—a brief instant when space-time did more than expand; it tore outward like a science-fiction spaceship in warp drive. And at the end of this superaccelerated burst of expansion, a flood of bizarre (yet-to-be-discovered) particles was supposedly generated that far outweighs the ordinary, visible stuff that makes up both people and planets.

These conflicting estimates in the amount of dark matter have

A host of distant galaxies (in silhouette) appear as tiny arcs, their light gravitationally bent by a massive cluster of galaxies known as Abell 1689. By measuring the bending, astronomers can map where the dark matter in the cluster is concentrated.
J. Anthony Tyson/AT&T Bell Laboratories

launched a lively debate between two very vocal groups. Many astronomers who are devoted to the observations alone are fond of saying that the "dark matter could be cold planets, dead stars, bricks, or baseball bats," as Rubin amusingly puts its. Cosmologists, on the other hand, more enamored of a universe chock-full of exotic matter, root for the tiny elementary-particle candidates as yet only imagined.

For Rubin, the squabble is an energizing phenomenon. "In a very real sense, astronomy begins anew," she says. "The joy and fun of understanding the universe we bequeath to our grandchildren—and to their grandchildren. With over 90 percent of the matter in the universe still to play with, even the sky will not be the limit."

The debate between the two competing camps—theory versus observation—is hardly subsiding. Meanwhile, the woman who helped start it all, the same woman who could not get her master's thesis published, was elected to the National Academy of Sciences in 1981. Less than one hundred women have ever been elected to this august body, among the more than thirty-five hundred researchers chosen since the academy was chartered in 1863.

But honors are not Rubin's first priority. "Fame is fleeting," asserts Rubin. "My numbers mean more to me than my name. If astronomers are still using my data years from now, that's my greatest compliment."

8

Extraterrestrial Matters

The most clear-cut way to settle the nature of the hidden mass would of course be to detect the objects that make it up.

—MARTIN REES

I t is the fall of 1990. Donald McCarthy has had better weeks. The University of Arizona astronomer has been hard at work at the Multiple Mirror Telescope on Mount Hopkins when his infrared detector up and quits, disrupting a critical observing run. A few days later, he is on his way to work when he is involved in a minor car accident that snaps off the right stem of his glasses and strains his back. By that afternoon, as he and graduate student Todd Henry prepare for the fifty-mile drive from Tucson to the Kitt Peak National Observatory, America's mile-high telescopic mecca, there is the threat of sky-obscuring clouds and rain in the forecast.

"Good luck," a colleague calls as McCarthy wheels a cart full of computer and electronic equipment onto the elevator at the university. "I *used* to have good luck," the beleaguered McCarthy replies.

The drive to Kitt Peak is uneventful. Although the weather is still not cooperating, McCarthy and Henry immediately set to work upon their arrival on the mountain, attaching enough equipment to the university's telescope there to furnish a small laboratory; a river of cables runs directly into the control room just several feet away. The heart of their system—enclosed in a metal container cooled to near absolute zero with liquid helium—is a tiny detector chip, a CCD, just four millimeters wide that acts like an electronic photographic plate. Placed at the focus of the telescope, this ultrathin wafer of silicon gathers not photons of visible light but rather photons of heat—invisible infrared radiation that has journeyed dozens of light-years through space. This detector is so sensitive that the heat of buzzing moths and gnats around the telescope in the summertime can sometimes cause interference. Without the liquid-helium cooling, the detector would get swamped by the heat of its surroundings and thus be unable to distinguish the cosmic infrared rays.

As soon as the hardware is hooked up, McCarthy and Henry wait, hoping for a break in the clouds that will allow them to aim the telescope's ninety-inch-wide mirror and begin their scan of the sky. Even if the weather would oblige, though, there would probably not be any cause for celebration on that night—or for many nights to follow. The researchers here, like investigators in observatories around the world, are looking for one of the last stellar objects (besides black holes) not yet seen with undisputed certainty. They are searching for brown dwarfs, theorized balls of celestial matter that are too small to be stars, too big to be planets, and, so far, too elusive to be detected with assurance by even the most sensitive telescopes.

The planet Jupiter serves as a convenient model for talking about brown dwarfs. Our Sun is roughly one thousand times more massive than Jupiter and about ten times its diameter. A brown dwarf, by comparison, would match Jupiter in size but contain ten to eighty times more mass than the Jovian planet. This would be just short of the enormous density required to sustain a nuclear fire in a stellar core. To do that, a celestial object must weigh more than eighty Jupiters, which is a little under a tenth the mass of our Sun.

Caught in this celestial middle ground, brown dwarfs would be the underachievers of the cosmos—more than a planet but decidedly less than a star. Brown dwarfs may not exist at all or, if they do, may arise in such small numbers as to be no more than an obscure cosmic curiosity. If, however, these odd little bodies are out there in appreciable numbers, then their collective presence might account for a sizable fraction of the missing mass. Both cool and dim, brown dwarfs have long been a favorite choice for the dark matter.

An artist's conception of a brown dwarf situated in the halo of the spiraling Milky Way galaxy.
Kim Poor

THE BARYONIC SUSPECTS

The most conservative dark-matter analysts, the ones who prefer ordinary solutions over extraordinary remedies, like to think that the missing-mass problem will ultimately be shown to be no more than sheer bookkeeping errors: neglecting to count all the very faint stars, extremely dim galaxies, substellar bodies, and gas inhabiting the heavens. Past experience offers them some encouragement in this belief—astronomers uncover new supplies of material almost daily as they improve the efficiencies and sensitivities of their detectors. Space X-ray telescopes, such as the *Einstein* observatory that operated in Earth orbit for two and a half years in the late 1970s, have observed clusters of galaxies immersed in large pools of X-ray-emitting gas, matter that was previously invisible and unknown.

Radio astronomers have detected immense clouds of hydrogen in the seemingly empty gulfs of space between the galaxies. And, with sophisticated photon-gathering devices attached to their telescopes, observers are starting to see more and more stellar material in galaxies. Spiral galaxies that formerly appeared wan and thin when viewed edge-on now seem a bit more lustrous and puffier. Extra layers of faint stars, finally discernible with sensitive detectors, make each galactic disk several times thicker. Such photographic wizardry is also starting to reveal the existence of many dark galaxies—"the dregs of the universe," as one astronomer put it—that are barely visible against the background light of the night sky. These hidden galaxies, unable to form stars as efficiently as the Milky Way, consist largely of gas.

Lastly, infrared astronomers have been finding disks of gas and dust around young and newborn stars, suggestive of material on its way to forming planetary systems. The 1983 flight of the Infrared Astronomical Satellite (IRAS), a joint venture between the United States, the Netherlands, and Great Britain, was especially impressive in providing evidence where before there was only speculation. Sensitive enough to have spotted from London a baseball in New York City's Yankee Stadium, IRAS detected excesses of infrared radiation around such stars as Vega and Beta Pictoris that hint at disklike, dusty structures in the process of evolving into planet-sized objects. Further studies of infant stars in nearby gas clouds suggest that up to half of the newborns are surrounded by dust-shrouded disks, all of them potential solar systems.

Of course, planets alone could not possibly make up the missing mass so sought after by astronomers. The combined weight of all the planets, moons, and asteroids in our solar system is only about one-thousandth the mass of the Sun. Even if a system of planets revolved around each and every star in the Milky Way, all those extra bodies would add just a smidgen to the storehouse of material in our galaxy.

All the newfound X-ray-emitting gas, faint stars, and intergalactic clouds uncovered so far can account for only a small fraction of the dark matter as well. But the same techniques that exposed these additional sources of matter may yet reveal that the missing mass is something quite mundane. Many astronomers are perfectly happy with the idea that more rigorous stalking will unearth each and every cosmic bookkeeping error and balance the books. More advanced X-ray space telescopes, for example, might someday spot diffuse X rays given off by galactic halos generously populated with compact stellar remnants.

Investigators who lean toward this view are bolstered by a fascinating concurrence. As previously pointed out, the fast-paced velocities of galaxies within clusters and the unusual spins of spiral galaxies suggest that there is approximately ten to twenty times more dark stuff in the universe than luminous matter. Taking this dark and luminous matter as a whole, that just about matches the maximum quantity of protons and neutrons, the two major constituents of atomic nuclei, that could have been forged in the first second of the big bang. Collectively known as baryons, these protons and neutrons basically make up everything we visibly see around us and throughout the cosmos, from rocks and trees to comets and nebulae.

Those in favor of the missing mass being some form of humdrum, everyday astronomical object are heavily swayed by this compelling statistic. By conducting primordial cooking on their computers, investigators figure that only a certain amount of ordinary matter, or baryons, could have been concocted during the big bang, and that calculated quantity roughly equals the amount of matter—both luminous and dark—currently estimated to be inhabiting the universe. The agreement is not perfect, but given the various uncertainties in the calculations, it is reasonably close. Is that near agreement between theory and observation sheer coincidence? Or is it an important clue in the missing-mass mystery that should not be ignored?

Some believe that it is a very telling match-up—strong evidence that the missing mass can be made simply out of familiar but not easily detectable astrophysical orbs. Proponents of this viewpoint claim that 10 percent or so of the ordinary matter born in the big bang lit up like Christmas trees, generating the bright celestial panorama so familiar to us, while 90 percent somehow turned dark and hidden. The problem is coming up with a baryonic culprit that can masquerade so effectively as the dark matter, because objects made of baryons are usually rather noisy creatures. They love to advertise their presence by moving about, radiating, and even blowing up, spreading their chemical elements all around. Yet for some reason the dark matter seems to prefer anonymity. Unmasking its identity is turning out to be a formidable assignment. It is as if astronomers must peer into a pitch-black room and attempt to locate ebony marbles scattered about the floor, none of which emit any visible light.

And this dark matter, whatever it is, has to handle a variety of jobs. The enigmatic substance must serve as the extra material surrounding spiraling galaxies; at the same time it must enshroud both ellipticals and entire clusters of galaxies in dark massive halos. "No single candidate can explain all these dark-matter tasks," concludes Bernard Carr, a physicist with Queen Mary and Westfield College of the University of London and one of the many theorists who have been avidly examining all the dark-matter suspects. If the halos of dark matter around galaxies were composed of cold gas, for example, the unenergetic atoms would have fallen into the galactic centers eons ago, and a hot gas would be radiating more X rays than astronomers are presently observing.

It is a frustrating time for astronomers, who would prefer a solution like Occam's Razor—a one-size-fits-all type of astronomical body—to the question of the dark matter. But many dark-matter candidates bear Achilles' heels that prevent them from being seriously considered in this regard. For example, it had been suggested that supermassive black holes, each weighing as much as a million or more of our Suns, might serve as the dark matter around galaxies. But such lumbering goliaths, possible remnants from the first wave of star formation, would eventually wander into the nucleus of the galaxy, making the center more massive than any galactic center yet measured. These roving black holes would also light up occasionally as they passed through the galaxy and gobbled up any mass in their path—a phenomenon that has never been observed.

The dark matter can't be grains of dust. If space were suffused with small particles, in sufficient quantities to make up the missing mass, the heavens would resemble a fog-bound night; only the brightest stars would be visible. And any tiny "snowballs" of hydrogen and helium that might form in a galactic halo would quickly evaporate, like pieces of dry ice transforming into wisps of vapor. One candidate that cannot be dismissed so readily is the brown dwarf, that ball of gas too small to sustain a nuclear fire deep in its core.

No one really knows what the first stars looked like, since they emerged many billions of years ago within an environment vastly different from today's universe. Some theorists imagine the first stars being very big. But others believe that conditions in the early universe, a time when primeval clouds of hydrogen were first coalescing into galaxies or pregalactic objects, may have greatly favored the formation of small stars, brown dwarfs, and Jupiterlike bodies over other types of celestial objects. A more modest version of that process may still be happening today. Astronomers see huge streams of hot gas—enough to fabricate hundreds of suns each year—cooling down and flowing into clusters of galaxies, where the material promptly drops out of sight. To explain that disappearing act, some observers are suggesting that the gas is being converted, quite efficiently, into celestial bodies difficult to see. Since the collective glow of a herd of dim red dwarfs would have been detected by now, that leaves brown dwarfs and Jupiters.

THE HUNT FOR BROWN DWARFS

"I am intrigued by the connection between brown dwarfs and missing mass," says Donald McCarthy. "Astronomers are always looking for discoveries, and here is a potential treasure box."

So far, though, the hunt for brown dwarfs has been burdened by too many maybes and plenty of dashed hopes. In the astronomical journals any hint that a brown dwarf has been found is hedged with a lot of question marks. "It's a volatile subject," says Todd Henry. "First we hear, 'Yes, we've found one,' then shortly afterward, 'No, we didn't.' There are at least ten good candidates so far, and some of them probably do weigh less than eighty Jupiters," the border at which a ball of gas achieves "stardom."

Two interesting brown dwarf contenders are found in the binary star system Wolf 424, located a short fourteen light-years from Earth in the direction of the Virgo constellation. For more than fifty years astronomers have been carefully measuring how the two dim points of light in Wolf 424 orbit about one another. By applying a bit of celestial mechanics, they calculate that the two objects weigh in with masses of about sixty and fifty Jupiters, respectively, certainly low enough to qualify as substellar. Yet there's still room for error in the orbital calculations and, unless they are newly born, the pair burn a bit more brightly than brown dwarfs are expected to shine.

And so it goes. There are other brown dwarf candidates in our galactic neighborhood, but each and every one has a catch, a way to wiggle out of firm identification.

The search for brown dwarfs has its origins in astronomy's enduring interest in extrasolar planetary systems. Contemplation of dark, distant worlds in the heavens goes back to the ancients. Leucippus and Democritus, the Greek atomists, professed belief in other worlds. A few centuries later, the Latin poet Lucretius wrote in his *De rerum natura* of distant planets forming from aggregations of atoms and populated by their own species of animals and people. But a dedicated, methodical search for dark companions around other stars did not start until the late 1930s. At that time astronomers at Swarthmore College's Sproul Observatory, outside Philadelphia, began to photograph nearby stars at regular intervals to observe how these stars shifted their positions against the more distant stellar background as they journeyed around the Milky Way galaxy. These astronomers' specialty is known as astrometry.

Examining data taken over many years, the Sproul observers eventually reported that certain stars deviated ever so slightly from a smooth, straight path in their motions across the sky. These stars traveled through space in a wiggly manner, akin to the wobble of an unbalanced tire. The periodic jiggles suggested that each star might be accompanied by an invisible companion, whose gravitational tugs on the visible star would produce the minute but perceptible wobble.[1] These special double-star systems—with one member visible, the other hidden—are called astrometric binaries, and a few dozen have been found over the years. Rhythmic variations in a star's light can also indicate that a dark companion is circling it. The orbiting companion pulls a star in one direction and then in the opposite direction as it revolves around the star. This periodic tugging provides a spectroscopic means of spotting the hidden body that lurks close to the star: When tugged away from the Earth, the star's spectral lines shift a bit toward the red end of the spectrum; when the star is pulled toward the Earth, its light gets a tad bluer.

Astronomers early on suspected that some hidden companions could simply be balls of gas that just missed being stars. In her 1975 Ph.D. thesis, Jill Tarter, now with the NASA Ames Research Center in California, christened these objects "brown dwarfs" because they were one notch below red dwarf stars, the least massive stars there are, but not completely black. But there was no great rush to the telescopes to try to view these bodies—the technology of the time was not up to unmasking such dim objects. Not until McCarthy stumbled into the field by accident did the situation at last change, and dramatically at that.

The consummate astronomical tinkerer, army veteran McCarthy far prefers hands-on research to theory. He began in the late 1970s to adapt a technique called speckle interferometry to infrared wavelengths, his specialty. (As a graduate student at Arizona, McCarthy had studied under

---

[1] The nineteenth-century German astronomer Friedrich Wilhelm Bessel first used this method to discover that Sirius, the brightest star in the heavens, had an invisible companion. By 1862 this companion was seen to be a white dwarf star.

Frank Low, the father of modern infrared astronomy.) First developed in France, speckle interferometry is a means of filtering out the distortions—the infamous "twinkle"—in a stellar image caused by the turbulence of the atmosphere. A speckle interferometer, mounted on a telescope, essentially takes thousands of snapshots of its target, each snap lasting no longer than a third of a second. A computer then merges all these separate but faint freeze-frames to construct a single, less blurred portrait of the celestial object. There is only one drawback: It takes a hundred times longer to create the final image on a computer than to acquire the data. During one good night at the telescope, McCarthy and Henry can gather up to two billion bits of data, which are stored on eight-millimeter videotape for later analysis. "But it's a price we're willing to pay since telescope time is scarce and laboratory time is cheap," explains McCarthy.

McCarthy first used speckle infrared interferometry to detect young protostars in nearby gas clouds, nascent stars whose visible light is often dimmed or masked by dust in the clouds. But one night in 1982, during an observing run at Kitt Peak's massive four-meter telescope, he and his colleagues chanced upon an entirely new use of the technique. While aiming their infrared interferometer at the double-star system Zeta Aquarii to carry out a routine calibration, they unexpectedly saw not two stars but three. Astrometrists had already noticed a tiny wobble in Zeta Aquarii's motions, the classic sign of a hidden companion, but McCarthy's team was the first to actually see this celestial sibling, a cool star a quarter the mass of our Sun. At the next meeting of the American Astronomical Society, when astrometrists first got wind of the news that a hidden companion had finally been photographed, they were ecstatic.

At 250 Jupiters, the small body that McCarthy had detected in the infrared was much too massive to be a brown dwarf, but it got McCarthy thinking: Since red and brown dwarfs are far more luminous in the infrared portion of the spectrum than in the visible portion, an infrared speckle interferometer might be able to spot these and other faint bodies. "It was fun!" says McCarthy with his characteristic boyish enthusiasm. "You could take the astrometry that people had worked on for decades and at last measure the masses of these previously unseen objects, as well as their brightnesses. I started going on this kick to look at every astrometric binary that I could."

That included a system called Van Biesbroeck 8, or VB 8, one of the faintest stars ever catalogued and a close neighbor of Earth's at a distance of twenty-one light-years in the constellation Ophiuchus. In 1984 Mc-

Carthy and two associates used their speckle interferometer to generate a picture of VB 8 that appeared to show the star accompanied by a smaller, fainter companion. Both the brightness and orbital position of this companion allowed McCarthy to estimate its mass at thirty to sixty times that of Jupiter. That made it the first substellar object visibly detected outside our solar system.

After seeing the dim spot on separate observing runs, using different telescopes, McCarthy's team finally dubbed the modest body VB 8B and released a carefully worded statement to the press, describing VB 8B as a substellar object, possibly a brown dwarf. The media picked up on the story immediately. To the popular press, however, something smaller than a star that orbits around a star could be only one thing: a planet.

"We got the text of our statement exactly right," says McCarthy, "but we couldn't control the headlines that would be attached to it." ASTRONOMERS DISCOVER FIRST PLANET OUTSIDE SOLAR SYSTEM, the papers trumpeted. The cautious "substellar" and "brown dwarf" got lost in the excitement.

McCarthy's announcement was an overnight sensation, but, to his dismay, a very short-lived discovery. Other groups tried to confirm the existence of VB 8B but were never able to spot it. Yet McCarthy's controversial find spurred other astronomers, particularly in the United States, to join the quest to photograph a brown dwarf directly. The electronic infrared instrumentation then being introduced allowed the field to enter a new era. No longer limited to tracking wobbles, hunters of dark stellar companions could now try to snap a picture of their prey. The race to find a brown dwarf was on.

During the initial ballyhoo over VB 8B, McCarthy gave a lecture at Cornell University. Todd Henry, then a senior at the school, was in the audience and was immediately hooked—ever since childhood he'd wanted to look for other planets. Upon graduation, he enrolled at the University of Arizona, dropped in on McCarthy the first day of classes, and straightaway joined in the brown dwarf hunt.

"We know what stars are, and we know what planets are," notes Henry. Planets are generally thought to be bodies, the mass of several Jupiters or less, that emerge from the blending and melding of the disk of material left over after a star's birth. Brown dwarfs, on the other hand, probably condense directly from a cloud of gas, just like stars.

"Searching for brown dwarfs," continues Henry, "is the closest thing to looking for planets that I can do. Maybe someday, in five hundred years, we'll be traveling to some of my finds."

Henry's work—which forms the basis of his Ph.D. thesis—involves conducting a systematic search for brown dwarfs around each and every faint red dwarf within twenty-six light-years of Earth (at least the seventy-seven objects visible from Tucson). Although our Sun is a loner, more than half of all stars come in pairs. And since both members in a pair are usually close in size, a good place to look for brown dwarfs is next to small red dwarfs, which are typically smaller than 250 Jupiters. These stars are so faint that they look like pale smudges with even the largest telescopes. And that is important to Henry's search: A red dwarf is so dim that a brown dwarf companion, fainter and smaller, won't be lost in the glare.

The first stage of Henry's survey, out to seventeen light-years, started out as a simple student project meant to convince his Arizona professors that he could handle research. But after twenty to thirty nights of tele-scope time over two and a half years, the small endeavor ballooned into a fourteen-page paper published in the *Astrophysical Journal*. By 1991 Henry still had not detected a bona fide, undisputed brown dwarf, but he did uncover some prime candidates. Together, he and McCarthy have a few favorites, which go by the unglamorous names of Gleise 623B, G 208-44B, and LHS 1047B. All are paired with red dwarfs located within twenty-five light-years of Earth. Using a variety of observing tech-niques, other groups have added about half a dozen objects to that list. All of these candidates are caught right at the edge of brown dwarfdom. No one is yet sure whether they are true brown dwarfs or merely lightweight red dwarf stars; the uncertainties in the measured masses of these objects are still too great.

And so McCarthy and Henry continue their visits to Kitt Peak, even under threatening skies. "The weather has gotten so bad on my runs that some people have wondered whether I'm looking for brown dwarf clouds," says Henry with a laugh. The clouds never broke the first night of this run, but on the second night conditions improved. The atmo-sphere is jittery, but at least it's clear.

Henry's first target is Wolf 922, an astrometric binary located in the Capricorn constellation. The visible star is a red dwarf, one-quarter the mass of our Sun. "It's awfully faint," says Henry, shaking his head wor-riedly. By meticulously monitoring Wolf 922's motions over a fifteen-year period, from 1963 to 1978, Sproul Observatory astronomers had seen evidence of a wobble; on their photographic plates the movement measured less than a thousandth of an inch. From this they inferred the presence of a dark companion with an estimated mass of one-tenth that of the Sun, or one hundred Jupiters. Henry is gathering further data, hoping that figure might come down to the realm of brown dwarfs.

A herd of white dots jump about on the computer monitor in a random dance. Each flicker represents an individual picture snapped by the infrared speckle interferometer every quarter of a second. It's a herky-jerky movie that, by chance, stays in sync with the beat of a rock tune playing on the control-room radio.

The observing procedure is a tedious one. The telescope is first pointed at a well-known bright star for a few minutes to measure the atmospheric jitter at that moment and is then aimed at the barely discernible target to snap 500 freeze-frames. Afterward, the telescope is moved back to the bright, calibrated star. And so it goes through the night—calibration source, target, calibration source, target—until a total of 3,000 frames of the target are recorded and stored on computer tape. Henry estimates that he spends 5 percent of his research time at the telescope and some 95 percent back at the university analyzing his data. "This is definitely not the type of work that lets you see anything right away," he says. "I may have data already showing a brown dwarf orbiting a nearby star, but I just haven't gotten them through the computer pipeline as yet." (As it turns out, on this night Henry has data showing that Wolf 922's companion is likely a red dwarf after all, but it will be months before he knows that.)

Along with nearby stars, young star clusters and gaseous nebulae in the throes of stellar birth are popular brown dwarf hunting grounds. A newborn brown dwarf, hotter and brighter than an older one, has a better chance to be seen; astronomers can catch them before they cool and drop out of sight. It's a chancy business, though. In 1989 astronomer William Forrest of the University of Rochester in New York thought he saw a bevy of brown dwarfs, "free-floaters" unattached to other stars, in a rich star-forming cloud in Taurus. A year later, it looked as if the suspects were simply background stars made redder by the intervening dust cloud.

More promising is a find by Harvard astronomer John Stauffer and four colleagues. They discovered some brown dwarf candidates in the famous Pleiades star cluster. Infrared images of the Pleiades have resolved half a dozen objects that appear to match the expected color and brightness of brown dwarfs. But isolated candidates like these cannot be weighed and thus labeled brown dwarfs with assurance, which is why finding a brown dwarf paired with another star is essential—their orbital motions can then be studied to determine the mass.

Just one confirmed brown dwarf sighting would be quite a coup. Of course, a close-up image, akin to the Voyager pictures of Jupiter, is presently impossible. "We're detectives, limited to learning about brown dwarfs from only their emissions from afar. This is the very art of astronomy," says University of Arizona astrophysicist Adam Burrows. But theorists like Burrows can still take a calculated stab at describing what a brown dwarf might look like; he and his colleagues have been modeling its properties for several years. Previously involved with neutron star work, Burrows got into the brown dwarf field by getting rid of the neutrons and neutrinos in his stellar equations and substituting hydrogen and helium. "It makes for interesting science," he notes.

At birth an average brown dwarf might have a surface temperature of about 6,000 degrees, largely caused by the gravitational heat that would have built up as the original cloud of dust and gas coalesced into a ball. Ten times smaller than our Sun, it would glow a deep orange-red, as bright as the hot coils on an electric stove. "It might even be mistaken for a red dwarf star," says Burrows, which is why finding a brown dwarf by color and brightness alone is tricky.

After 100 million years, the brown dwarf's surface would cool to nearly 4,000 degrees, the temperature of a blast furnace; by ten billion years it would be down to 1,000 degrees—quite cool for a stellarlike body, though still hot enough to melt lead. "A brown dwarf continues to cool over the eons like the embers of a dying fire," says Burrows. Given enough time, it would cool to complete blackness.

The high densities inside a brown dwarf—a thousand times that of water—would likely compress the predominant elements, hydrogen and helium, into liquid metal. (This does not happen in stars because the greater heat generated by their mammoth nuclear engines keeps the stellar materials gaseous.) This metallic sphere would be surrounded by a thin, outer skin of gas, a few hundred miles thick. The presence of water vapor, carbon monoxide, methane, titanium oxide, and other trace molecules could even produce lots of color in this shallow atmosphere, much like Jupiter's bands and Great Red Spot.

If the brown dwarf's composition includes such heavy elements as silicon, iron, magnesium, and carbon, there might also be grains of dust as fine as cigarette smoke hovering in the atmosphere, which would make it resemble Los Angeles on a smoggy day. Indeed, this light-absorbing "pollution" may be the reason that brown dwarfs are so hard to find; they could be darker than expected, misleading astronomers into thinking they are scarce. But Burrows suggests that a brown dwarf, being the near-star that it is, might also be shooting off solarlike flares and intense bursts of X rays, which might help signal its presence.

While best described as hotter and denser Jupiters, brown dwarfs are not totally incapable of burning like stars. Theory suggests that many dwarfs may be massive enough to ignite and burn first deuterium for ten million years and later hydrogen for a few billion years more. In a body so small, though, the gravitational compression is not strong enough to allow these internal fires to burn very intensely. Ultimately, the heat that radiated away from the dwarf would exceed the heat generated within, and the little substar would sputter out like a choked engine, never to start up again.

Is it theoretically possible to form many brown dwarfs? The experts are simply not sure. Most stars are born in giant clouds of dust and gas that collapse and fragment into stars, but opinion is divided on just how small those pieces can get. Generally, the smaller the stellar species, the more abundant it is in our galaxy. Blue-white supergiants are beautiful but rare; lowly red dwarfs make up most of a galaxy's teeming stellar population. By that measure, brown dwarfs could be the most plentiful of all. But some theories of star formation suggest that star construction dramatically cuts off at masses lower than a red dwarf, vastly limiting the potential pool of near-stars. For that matter, theorists are hard-pressed at the moment to explain how nature could mold large quantities of brown dwarfs or smaller planetlike Jupiters without also making a considerable number of regular stars along the way—stars that would readily be seen with current instrumentation but aren't.

Cosmologists are keen to know whether these theoretical barriers are insurmountable. As pointed out earlier, conditions in the newborn universe may have greatly enhanced the production of brown dwarfs and Jupiterlike objects over larger stars. If it turns out that the universe's dark matter is largely made up of brown dwarfs, observers should find a free-floating brown dwarf in every thirty or so cubic light-years of space. That means several could be residing within a few light-years of us, even closer than Alpha Centauri, the nearest star system after the Sun. Over the entire Milky Way there would be trillions. But so far there has not been much evidence for such an enormous brown dwarf population. The dozen or so candidates found to date are mere drops in the cosmic bucket.

George and Marcia Rieke, a husband-and-wife team at the University of Arizona, have found the brown dwarf pickings equally slim. Long recognized for their infrared studies of galaxies, the two observers were drawn into the brown dwarf hunt by the missing-mass question and began taking pictures of stars in our local celestial neighborhood with their state-of-the-art infrared CCD detector. Infrared interferometers have greater resolution than infrared cameras, but cameras—with their shutters left open—can detect fainter levels of incoming radiation. In this way, infrared detectors can spot more widely separated brown dwarf/red dwarf pairs than speckle interferometers can detect. Yet even with this added sensitivity, the Riekes found no objects they considered good brown dwarf candidates; if brown dwarfs were significantly contributing to the missing mass, the Riekes expected to see half a dozen nearby. This may explain why our solar system doesn't seem perturbed by their presence; a brown dwarf journeying through our vicinity anytime over the last four billion years should have jostled and disturbed the orbits of the planets, the way a heavy truck speeding down a road can set a house rumbling.

The Riekes, along with several colleagues, also took a look at the Rho Ophiuchi cloud, a prolific stellar nursery, and found only three likely substellar sources—"far fewer than expected if brown dwarfs make up a large portion of the missing mass," notes George Rieke. Astronomers using spectroscopic techniques—the monitoring of nearby stars for periodic changes in their spectra—haven't spied too many substellar companions either.

Given these bleak results, McCarthy is not convinced that our galaxy, or universe, is brimming over with brown dwarfs, but Henry and others are more optimistic. "Brown dwarfs could simply be a lot fainter than theorists currently suspect," contends Henry. "It depends on how much dust and molecules are in a brown dwarf's atmosphere."

Astronomers should soon have more opportunities than ever to search. New red dwarfs in our galactic vicinity continue to be found as more sensitive optical and infrared telescopes come on-line. Over the past forty years, the population of known red dwarfs has nearly doubled, and many of these tiny bodies could be paired with brown dwarfs. "I think that if you add up all the small red dwarfs we can't see, throw in brown dwarfs and dead white dwarfs—maybe a couple black holes, dust, and gas—you might be able to make up all the missing mass without neutrinos or other exotic particles," says Henry. "I like the ordinary junk, probably because I don't understand the extraordinary stuff." Deciding whether brown dwarfs are common or rare may have to await new instrumentation, including ever larger ground-based telescopes (such as the giant ten-meter Keck Telescope in Hawaii) and new infrared telescopes scheduled for launch into space over the next decade. It may be that brown dwarfs are better viewed at wavelengths that have not been fully scanned as yet.

Brown dwarfs are Bernard Carr's personal preference, but if it should turn out that the missing mass is not composed of brown dwarfs, Carr would place his baryonic bets on very massive black holes, objects containing the mass of several hundred Suns (less than the million or more solar masses in a supermassive black hole). Such black holes, though, would have to have been created at a special place and time. The death of a star is usually an operatic event whose crescendo scatters lumps of matter far and wide, leftovers that would be readily detectable. But that difficulty diminishes if the explosive deaths occurred far enough in the past that the reverberations died out long ago, possibly before galaxies fully formed. The pregalactic universe may have been inundated with immensely massive stars that formed at a very rapid rate, blazed away with high luminosities, and then quickly expired. The dark matter could then conceivably be the remnants from the universe's first burst of star formation—a host of unseen neutron stars and massive black holes that evolved from that first generation of stars. If that is true, though, these compact stellar bodies had to have ejected little or no mass at their death, otherwise they would have given themselves away by now, which is why Carr is fond of the hefty black holes.

Black holes are "the perfect hiding place," says Carr, who first worked on the physics of black holes for his doctoral degree under the supervision of the noted Cambridge theorist Stephen Hawking. If stars are weighty enough, they should collapse completely into black holes at the end of their lives, instead of exploding and displaying nature's most energetic fireworks array. By swallowing all their matter and turning into black holes, these primeval stars end up hiding their demise from prying telescopic eyes. Only the black holes' gravitational presence would remain to pose as the dark matter.

"I think it's naive, though, to expect the dark-matter problem to have just one solution," cautions Carr. "Just as visible matter takes on many forms, the dark matter likely does too." He can envision a mix of brown dwarfs and old stellar remnants serving as the dark matter. "Finding an answer is the number one problem in cosmology," declares Carr. "We're talking about 90 percent of the universe. Trying to understand the universe by observing only visible matter is like trying to describe a person having only seen their nose."

If the missing mass is truly composed of ordinary matter, gravitational lensing may provide a means of discovering its exact form. Researchers at Great Britain's Cambridge University have provided a start.

IN THE TWINKLING OF A QUASAR

Cambridge University's Institute of Astronomy resides on Madingley Road, about a mile northwest of the town center. Its main entrance, a long tree-lined drive, directs visitors toward what looks like an elegant manor house. The building runs precisely east to west, so that its elaborate portico faces directly south. This historic building was erected in 1823 and is an example of, according to the local historic monuments commission, "the revived Greek style of architecture adapted for special scientific purpose." The building's central dome once housed a telescope; massive slits, formerly needed for other telescopes and instruments and now bricked up, can still be traced in the external masonry.

Today the director of the institute resides in a modern, California-style building of wood and glass, set west of the old observatory. Nearby, almost like an afterthought, is an even smaller structure, originally built to accommodate one of the immense computers used in the early days of digital computing but which now houses the Automatic Plate Measuring facility. There, astronomers routinely scan photographic plates of the night sky.

Many of the plates being scanned are part of a comprehensive sky atlas of the southern celestial hemisphere, a series of photographs that were taken in the early 1980s with the United Kingdom Schmidt telescope, located in Australia. A total of 894 plates, each covering six degrees on the sky (about the size of the bowl in the Big Dipper), map the entire southern heavens. This impressive collection is the southern equivalent of the magisterial National Geographic Society–Palomar Observatory sky survey that earlier mapped the northern celestial hemisphere.

At the Automatic Plate Measuring facility, white gloves are used to handle the plates. A smudge would be disastrous; peering at any one plate through a magnifying glass reveals a plethora of stars and galaxies, as many as a quarter of a million objects, that are barely visible on the plate with the naked eye alone. Since each plate is a photographic negative, the sky appears light, while the celestial objects are black. Through the magnifier, globular clusters look like giant bacteria colonies that have taken over the petri dish.

A team of investigators at Cambridge are currently counting and recording each object on the series of plates, in order to provide a massive data bank that will help astronomers discern the large-scale structure of the universe and allow them to readily pick out particular types of galaxies or objects they might be studying. Painstakingly recording each object on a plate by eye alone can introduce many errors, since people count and assess an object's size in different ways. "The same person can even count differently at different times of the day, such as after tea time," points out Cambridge astronomer Paul Hewett. The Automatic Plate Measuring machine, an instrument funded by the United Kingdom's Science and Engineering Research Council, was designed and built specifically to make the plate scanning a more objective enterprise.

"The APM machine looks somewhat like a World War I tank," notes Hewett. At the start of a scan, the top of the APM rolls back, like the sun roof of a car, and the plate to be read is placed horizontally on an aluminum rack within the machine. Once the top is back in place, a laser fires a narrow and continuous beam of light through the plate, slowly moving in a methodical manner over each inch of the glass. Beneath the plate is a sensor that measures the resulting light variations as the laser beam passes through the successive white and black regions of the plate—the images of the stars and galaxies. In this way, the position, size, and magnitude of every object on the plate is transformed into millions of digital bits that are eventually stored on computer tape. Five hours are required to scan just one plate. The scanner can discern objects as tiny as one arc second in the sky—a span less than a thousandth of an inch on the plate itself.[2] "The machine goes a bit nuts when it encounters a large globular cluster," says Hewett. Rows of empty champagne bottles are lined up along the tops of the file cabinets in the computer-tape-filled laboratory—in the early days, when the machine first came on-line, researchers celebrated each successful scan with a toast.

---

[2] Each degree in the sky, the width of two full Moons, can be further subdivided into sixty arc minutes, and each arc minute into sixty arc seconds. One arc second, therefore, is $1/3,600$ of a degree. Put another way, an arc second is the angle subtended by an American dime when viewed from a distance of nearly three miles away.

Hewett, somewhat of a scanner jock, completed his thesis work at the Royal Observatory in Edinburgh figuring out what could and could not be done with an automatic plate reader. He arrived at the Institute of Astronomy in 1982 and began to use the scanner to search the southern-sky survey plates for good quasar candidates, prospects that his colleagues could then verify at the telescope. This project, now known as the Large Bright Quasar Survey, has so far uncovered more than one thousand quasars. Along the way, Cambridge investigators realized that they could also peruse the plates for quasars whose light has been gravitationally lensed by intervening galaxies or clusters and consequently split into multiple images. Other radio and optical astronomers throughout the world, including researchers at Princeton University and the Massachusetts Institute of Technology, are also sifting through the visible and radio images of thousands of quasars to look for good cases of gravitational lensing. If these various groups come up with enough examples, they might be able to distinguish between various dark-matter candidates.

The idea is to carefully monitor the multiple images to see if they "twinkle." Stars twinkle at night because their light is passing through turbulent masses of air that constantly shift the image about. Similarly, as the visible light or radio radiation from a bright quasar skims past the dark halo of a massive galaxy or cluster on its way to Earth, it too might flicker. Astronomers call this effect "microlensing." If the dark matter in the halo of the lensing galaxy is composed primarily of lightweight stars or brown dwarfs, the quasar's multiple images are expected to dim and brighten as the tiny orbiting bodies pass in front of the quasar's light beam. The extent of the twinkle can peg the type of object: Low-mass stars and Jupiters would cause a shimmer that extends over a shorter length of time than do heftier objects, such as very massive black holes. Verifying this effect, though, requires some patience; just one twinkling can take several months or longer.

Cambridge University astronomers published a report in 1989 on the first possible case of microlensing. They had been closely studying the Huchra lens, named after its discoverer, Harvard astronomer John Huchra. It is quite an unusual gravitational lens: The light from a quasar, which resides billions of light-years away, has been split into four images by the gravitational field of a spiral galaxy situated relatively close by. That wouldn't be so unusual if it weren't for the fact that the four quasar images are positioned smack dab in the middle of the galaxy, making the spiral's galactic center resemble a four-leaf clover or a cross. In fact, the image is sometimes referred to as Einstein's Cross.

Using the Canada-France-Hawaii telescope atop Hawaii's Mauna Kea in August 1988, the Cambridge team found that one of the four quasar components was about 70 percent brighter than it had been the previous year. A month later CCD pictures taken with the William Herschel telescope, situated on the Canary island of La Palma, indicated that the quasar image had faded back down a bit. By November it had returned to its customary brightness. The other three quasar images throughout this time remained unchanged. This suggests that a single body circulating within the spiral galaxy—an object weighing possibly less than eight Jupiters—passed across our line of sight, briefly amplifying the one gravitationally lensed quasar image. One case like this cannot say much, if anything, about the dark matter, but similar evidence, from a host of other galaxies acting as gravitational lenses, could conceivably build up a convincing case that the dark matter consists of swarms of near-stars and planetoids. Several groups are now arranging to monitor known gravitational lenses on a regular basis to track any incidents of microlensing over long periods of time.

Similar strategies can be used to hunt for dark matter closer in, in the halo of our own galaxy. In this venue, stars, rather than quasars, serve as the source of light. A team of American and Australian astronomers as well as a separate group of French observers have launched long-term programs to see if far-off stars in the Large Magellanic Cloud briefly brighten (i.e., gravitationally amplify) should a dark-matter object in the Milky Way's halo pass in front of the distant star.

Decades ago, Einstein had already figured out that a background star would be reshaped and magnified as it passed behind a foreground star, since the gravitational bending of its light rays is similar to the refraction of light by an optical lens, such as a magnifying glass. But since the deflection in such a case is so tiny, Einstein figured that gravitational lensing by stars was, for all practical purposes, unobservable.

Modern instrumentation has changed Einstein's assessment. By automatically monitoring and keeping track of the light curves of several million stars, night after night, astronomers hope to see as many as ten microlensing events a year. Of course, they face the rather sizable task of disregarding variable stars and instrumental glitches before they can confirm or rule out a Milky Way halo populated with brown dwarfs or Jupiters. "There's lots of hay in our haystack before we find our 'needle,' but we're guardedly optimistic," says Kim Griest, a dark-matter hunter from the University of California at Berkeley.

INFLATIONARY MATTERS

Many astrophysicists do not want to leave the final estimate of the dark matter at just ten times more than the glistening stars and galaxies, which is the figure generally supported by current astronomical observations.[3] A number of cosmologists are convinced that the universe harbors far more dark matter—up to a *hundred* times more than the luminous material. Despite the present lack of substantial material or dynamic evidence for such a deluge of dark matter, researchers are irresistibly drawn to the idea by their firm faith that the universe stands poised between open and closed—an assumption that is one part theory, one part hunch, and one part aesthetic wish.

When investigators first discovered that space-time is dynamic, swiftly ballooning outward, it was natural to ask whether that expansion would continue forever. An answer to that question hinges on how much matter truly resides in the universe, for space and matter are irrevocably intertwined. It was Einstein who first taught cosmologists of the intimate relationship between matter and the geometry of space-time with his general theory of relativity. Matter, it has now been shown many times, causes space to warp and bend, as if it were some lumpy mattress. With too little mass in the universe, space curves outward, like some never-ending horn whose gaping mouth goes off into infinity, its surfaces fated never to meet. In this "open," mass-poor universe, the galaxies continue to fly outward, riding the wave of space-time's expansion into an endless void for all eternity. Only a desolate "Big Chill" awaits such a universe and its inhabitants in the far future. The inward pull of gravity is much too weak to quell the ride outward.

But if the universe contains just the right abundance of matter per unit volume—an amount known as critical density—all this mass, taken as a whole, would exert enough gravitational muscle to put the brakes on the universe's expansion and bring the cosmic marathon to a complete halt countless eons from now.

[3] A team of astronomers reported in early 1993 that the space X-ray telescope, ROSAT, spotted a small group of galaxies immersed in hot gas. The gas should have dissipated long ago, unless it is being held in by the gravity of unseen material that outweighs the group's visible matter by 30 to 1. More observations are needed, however, to see if that ratio prevails throughout the universe.

And if the cosmos contains just a dribble of matter beyond the critical level, a sufficient dose to tip the cosmic scales, the universe would reverse its course entirely. As soon as the universal expansion is brought to a stop, space-time would be pulled inward by the combined gravity of all the myriad galaxies. Contracting over the eons, like a deflating balloon, this mass-rich, "closed" universe would get squeezed more and more, until the cosmos curled back up and reformed the dense and terribly brilliant fireball of its youth. The big bang would turn into the big crunch.

In the lingo of cosmology, with its love of the Greek alphabet, theorists often use the letter omega (Ω) to describe the density of the universe—the ratio of the universe's true density to the critical density. Thus, if these two quantities are identical, omega is equal to 1, and the universe stands virtually poised, like a ballerina *en pointe*, between open

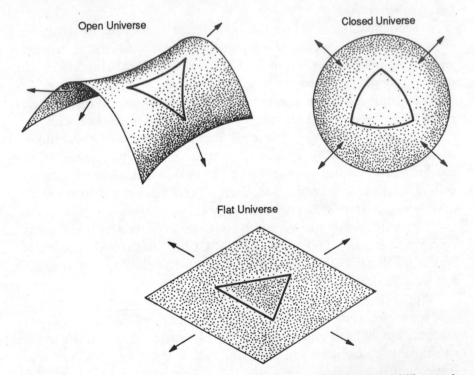

In these two-dimensional representations, an open universe is curved like a saddle, its edges never meeting; a closed universe is curved like a sphere; while a flat universe is an infinite plane. The triangles elucidate the differing space-time curvatures.

Illustration by John Hamwey

and closed. In astronomy department hallways, you can often hear astronomers argue about whether the universe has "an omega of 1"—it's their handy shorthand for a universe brought to critical density.

Although observations alone still seem to suggest that the universe is open, headed for a big chill many, many eons from now, a number of theorists have long suspected that the universe was actually born with a critical density of matter—in other words, an omega equal to 1. That would put the universe right on the dividing line between open and closed. Originally, their reasoning went something like this: If the universe emerged at the dawn of time with even the slightest deviation from critical density, that tiny deficiency would only grow larger and larger over time. Like a small rip made bigger by stretching, the initial shortfall enlarges with the universe's expansion, as matter spreads out thinner and thinner. To be at 10 percent of critical density today (as currently measured by observers) means that the density of the universe at the age of one second had to differ from critical density by less than one-trillionth of a percent.

If the initial deficit had been any greater, the resulting mass-poor universe would have expanded much faster, keeping stars and galaxies (and us) from forming at all. And if the discrepancy had fallen on the other side of the dividing line, providing the extra measure of matter essential for a closed universe, space-time would have collapsed long ago (and no one would be around to read this explanation). The fine-tuning required to make our universe "just right" seemed incredible. What quirk of physics would put us within a hair's breadth of critical density at the beginning of time? More likely, said the theorists, the universe's initial mass was exactly equal to critical density to begin with—we just hadn't detected all this bounty as yet!

Bringing the universe's mass to the point of critical density sounds like a lot, but it really isn't. All that is needed is about 0.000000000000000000000000000005 gram of matter in each cubic centimeter (5×10^{-30} gram/cm^3)—the equivalent mass of a couple of hydrogen atoms in every car-trunk-sized chunk of space. Yet cosmologists know that the big bang couldn't have cooked up even that much ordinary stuff, at least as theorists currently understand the workings of the big bang. The measured abundances of simple hydrogen and helium, as well as all the heavier elements, fall far short of bringing the universe to critical density. At best, baryonic matter can bring the cosmos to within 10 to 20 percent of that enticing boundary point. If the density of protons and neutrons had been any higher when the light elements were assembled in the first minutes of the big bang, astronomers today would be observing completely different amounts of hydrogen, helium, deuterium, and lithium throughout the universe. These limits on ordinary matter, however, do not rule out the existence of extraordinary matter. Just as the Earth's biosphere forms the thinnest of skins over the surface of a globe primarily composed of silicates and iron, so might hydrogen, helium, and all the other elements in the universe serve as the merest pollutants within a celestial sea of dark, unknown particles.

If the suspicions of the theorists are correct, and the universe is indeed poised between open and closed like a perfectly balanced seesaw, one of astronomy's last cosmic assumptions—the supremacy of the elements—must be ripped to shreds. Already removed from the center of the solar system, the galaxy, and the universe by Copernicus, Shapley, and Hubble, respectively, humanity may soon have to deal with the knowledge that it is not made out of the universe's primary ingredients. In a universe brought to the brink of closure, most of the dark matter, at least a good 90 percent of it, would have to be composed of one or more particle species far different from the particles that make up run-of-the-mill, everyday, ordinary matter. Trying to figure out what this special stuff might be transforms the dark-matter mystery, once the sole province of astronomy, into a special challenge for particle physicists.

Physicist Alan Guth, now with the Massachusetts Institute of Technology, gave all these speculations on the universe's density a more rigorous theoretical foundation one winter night in 1979 as he pondered how the tenets of cosmology might be affected by particle physics' most recent conjectures. His mathematical tools were the grand unified theories that attempt to join the forces of nature.

The forces at work in the cosmos are few but varied. Gravity, although the weakest force of all, certainly exercises the greatest influence over very large distances. It controls the motions of planets, stars, and galaxies. Electromagnetism, on the other hand, is the most conspicuous force on the human scale. Its effects are easily displayed in the gentle swing of a dime-store compass or the burning filament of an electric light bulb. Electromagnetism binds electrons and nuclei to form atoms; it controls how atoms link together as molecules. Nature's other two forces, interactions not recognized until the twentieth century, wield their power solely within the realm of the atom. The strong force keeps every atomic nucleus, a packed assembly of protons and neutrons, from flying apart in the face of electromagnetic repulsion, while the weak force controls the way in which certain subatomic particles disintegrate, causing a nucleus to radioactively decay. The weak force also plays a role in nuclear fusion, so vital in powering the stars.

Each of these forces appears to act so differently in our everyday surroundings, yet physicists have come to believe that the four interactions—gravity, electromagnetism, and the strong and weak nuclear forces—are just different manifestations of one ancestral force, analogous to the way that diamond, charcoal, and graphite are different expressions of a single substance. A sparkling gem, a blackish clump, and a greasy lubricant certainly look and feel different to us, but at some level these separate materials are essentially the same: All of them are carbon. At extremely high temperatures their differences disappear. Likewise, it is conjectured that the four forces are fundamentally related and last exhibited their similarities within the fiery kiln of the newborn universe.

The process of unifying the forces actually began in the 1860s when James Clerk Maxwell consolidated electricity with magnetism, but it was another century before a new generation of physicists was able to advance the effort. By the late 1960s, physicists Sheldon Glashow, Steven Weinberg, and Abdus Salam made contributions showing that there is a fundamental and intimate link between electromagnetism and the weak nuclear force; each of the three men would come to receive a Nobel Prize for their notable achievements. Unlike the more familiar forces, this "electroweak" force—the merger of electromagnetism with the weak force—is not perceived at all in our workaday world, only in the brute particle collisions occurring within high-powered accelerators capable of reaching energies of a hundred billion electron volts. Only then does the weak force come to equal the electromagnetic force.

Unequivocal proof of the Weinberg-Salam-Glashow model came in 1982 within the four-miles-long underground accelerator ring at CERN, the European Center for Nuclear Research near Geneva. There, a pencil-thin beam of protons slammed head-on into a focused beam of antiprotons traveling in the opposite direction. In the resultant shower of debris were found some W^+, W, and Z particles, the predicted "carriers" of the electroweak force.

That an atomic particle can be conceived as the conveyor of a force has been one of the revolutionary outcomes of modern physics. When walking about on the Earth, we often get the impression that a force is some kind of invisible entity that pushes or pulls us around. But on the level of atoms, physicists prefer to describe a force as a kind of tennis game: A force between two particles arises from their continually exchanging another, identifiable particle—a sort of subatomic tennis ball. In electromagnetic interactions, for example, the tennis ball is the photon. The Z and W particles, meanwhile, are responsible for transmitting the weak force. And, as an expression of the strong force, something called a gluon constantly bounces back and forth between quarks, what are thought to be the smallest units of matter, to bind them into protons and neutrons. In keeping with this stratagem, a particle called the graviton, not yet detected, is thought to convey the force of gravity.

The universe, in essence, has instituted a division of labor, creating two basic categories of elementary particles. First, there are the particles that give rise to the forces; second, there are other particles, such as quarks and electrons, that serve solely as the building blocks of matter. The force particles are known as bosons, while the building blocks have collectively come to be called fermions. Each category obeys a different set of physical laws as well. Bosons can bunch up and merge, in accordance with Bose-Einstein statistics (hence the name); they flock together. Fermions, on the other hand, are relegated to certain slots within the nucleus or atom, as if they were assigned to specific desks in an elementary school classroom, which allowed Mendeleyev to construct his periodic table of the chemical elements. Fermions are forbidden to pile up (a type of ordering described by Fermi-Dirac statistics). That is why two beams of light, made up of squeezable bosonic photons, can pass right through one another but fermionic people cannot. The quarks and electrons in us just won't budge from their allotted positions, which (fortunately) keeps us from collapsing into a point or radiating away into infinity like a beam of light.

The successful development of the electroweak theory gave physicists the courage to push their unification schemes (at least on paper) to energies as high as a trillion trillion electron volts, a realm where the electroweak force at last merges with the strong force. Altogether, the various mathematical models that describe this particular unification are referred to as grand unified theories, or GUTs for short. Unlike the electroweak merger, though, the GUT unification occurs at such high energies that it is technologically impossible, either now or in any foreseeable future, to duplicate the effect on Earth. But theorists are sure that those searing temperatures were achieved at least once in the universe's history: during the big bang itself. The universe's birth serves as physics' best testing ground, a sort of "poor-man's accelerator," for its grand unifying ideas. It is there, in their studies of the first hellish moments of the universe's creation, that cosmologists and particle physicists join hands in a productive partnership.

These new cosmologists, trained in particle physics, now describe the embryonic universe as swiftly proceeding through a series of physical transitions, each stage altering the early universe's basic properties. The four forces in nature, once united, take on their own identity at specified times in the universe's history. By the rules of this mathematical game, the force of gravity was the first to part company, 10^{-43} second after the initial flash of creation. By the time the universe was 10^{-35} second or so old, the GUT unification was shattered, allowing the strong force to develop its own characteristics. A fleeting moment later, when the primeval fireball was no more than one ten-billionth of a second old, the electroweak force

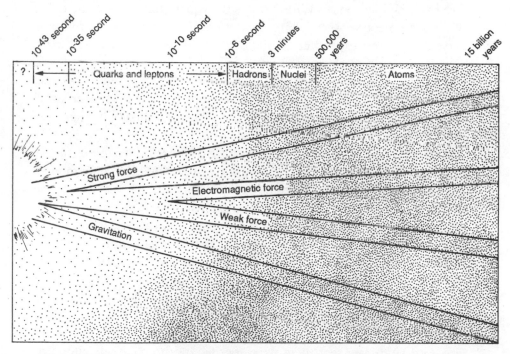

A brief history of the universe. The four forces, once united, become distinguishable in the first microsecond. Afterward, nuclei form, then atoms.
Universities Research Association

divided into its two separate components, the weak force limiting its reach to the dimensions of an atomic nucleus and electromagnetism developing a far, far longer range. All the while, the various particles out of which we are composed congealed, like crystals of ice in a cooling pond of water.

Although primarily trained in the physics of quarks, Guth had been encouraged by a colleague to look into grand unified theories and, while serving a postdoctoral position at the Stanford Linear Accelerator Center in California, he came to apply his newly acquired knowledge to certain cosmological conundrums, even though at the time he was a novice in astrophysics. While at home on the evening of December 6, 1979, he opened up his notebook and proceeded to ask himself how the breakup of a grand unified force might affect the evolution of the universe.

During the 1970s cosmologists were just beginning to view the universe's early physical development as a sort of crystallization, analogous to the way water is physically transformed as it cools from vapor, to liquid, to solid ice. Guth was asking how the universe itself might have fared as it rapidly cooled. Within hours the equations filling up the pages of Guth's notebook were telling the young scientist that a cooling universe did not just expand at its birth, it underwent a tremendous acceleration—a superacceleration that rewrote the script of our cosmic beginnings. And the astrophysical community eagerly listened, because Guth's results were at last offering explanations for why the universe was once so hot, why it keeps expanding, and where it obtained its supply of mass and energy.

The beginning of Guth's theoretical adventure didn't quite start at the beginning, but just a tad later. Guth embarked on his examination of the universe at 10^{-35} second into its birth. By then the observable universe spanned a distance that was only one-trillionth the size of a proton. This unimaginably hot seed was expanding and starting to cool. It was at the stage at which the grand unification was ready to fragment into separate and distinct forces. But that didn't happen right away, if Guth's analyses were correct. Instead, as the temperature of the universe plunged, the little knot of space-time became in some sense supercooled—just as water can sometimes remain liquid below thirty-two degrees Fahrenheit before hardening into ice.

And Guth saw that there were specific and peculiar side effects to this supercooling. The delay in its "crystallization" endowed the universe with tremendous potential energy, like a rock perched on the edge of a steep, high cliff about to fall. While in this odd state, the force of gravity actually became largely repulsive rather than attractive. Space-time, as a consequence, shot outward with an unbelievably explosive speed, but only for a brief moment. Inspired by the heady economic conditions of the times, Guth labeled this special epoch in the universe's history "inflation."

At the end of an infinitesimal flash, a mere one-hundred-millionth of a trillionth of a trillionth of a second, when the observable universe had abruptly swelled from that microscopic speck to the size of a softball (or even larger), the immense latent energy pent up in the space-time vacuum was at last released in an awesome cascade of matter and energy. In fact, it was inflation's demise that put the bang into the big bang and generated all the particles and radiation that surround us today. According to Guth's scheme, every galaxy, dust cloud, and photon in the universe—some 10^{88} particles in all—can trace its origin to that brief but frenzied inflationary spurt. We are simply the residual afterglow of inflation—"the ultimate free lunch," as Guth likes to put it.

After this titanic release of inflation's storehouse of energy, the superacceleration stopped, gravity went back to being an attractive force, and the expansion of the heavens continued at a more sedate pace as space-time coasted outward on the sheer momentum left over from that hyperexplosive thrust. Other investigators were simultaneously coming to the same realization as Guth's, but Guth's work was the definitive catalyst, and soon his ideas were advanced and amended by such physicists as Andre Linde, Paul Steinhardt, and Andreas Albrecht.

The bizarre behavior of an inflationary universe might seem too strange to be real, but Guth quickly learned that there were several sound, cosmological reasons to take inflation seriously. One of inflation's effects on space-time, for instance, is unavoidable: Its swift and fierce acceleration, if only for that fleeting instant of time, pushes the universe's curvature to the very brink between open and closed. Not curved inward and not curved outward, the universe is ironed flat. And with the geometry of the universe so intimately linked with its density, that meant that there had to be a hundred times more matter wandering through the cosmos than currently viewed through telescopes. The contents of an inflationary universe naturally end up at critical density, just as many theorists had long suspected. Omega reaches its magical level of 1. The theory of inflation gave cosmologists, for the first time, a practical mechanism to explain how the universe could have generated enough matter to bring space-time to that enticing, knife-edge boundary between open and closed.

And then there was the troubling uniformity of the universe. Why is the universe so unvarying, at least over very large scales? Why did the galaxies in the northern part of the sky form and develop in exactly the same way that they evolved in the southern celestial hemisphere? Why is the universe's faint hum of microwaves, that fossil echo of the big bang, generally so smooth and unperturbed? According to standard models of the big bang, there was never enough time in the early stages of the explosion to get all the primordial bits and pieces so well blended before they shot off. Put simply, there was no time for each corner of the nascent universe to get its story straight. But Guth started off within a region of space-time that was a trillion times smaller than a proton; thus it was relatively easy for all corners of this infinitesimal speck to readily mix. Inflation then stepped in to maintain the uniformity of this mixture as the bubble of space-time explosively shot outward.

Although inflation's ability to create a homogeneous universe, the type we see, is of course merely indirect evidence that inflation occurred, it is the only kind of proof now available. A definitive experiment would require a particle accelerator that stretched from here to the star Alpha Centauri to re-create the terrible energies of that fateful transition.

The problem with the inflationary scenario is trying to find all the extra matter that inflation demands. So far, that matter has been terribly good at hiding. Since current theory suggests that this extra material cannot be baryons—particles of ordinary matter—the extra motes or objects would undoubtedly have to be exotic. For many researchers this is not as worrisome a prospect as it might sound at first. The history of

SCOREBOARD ON UNIVERSE'S CONTENTS

Matter	Status	Percentage of Critical Density
Luminous stars and galaxies	Observed directly	$\approx 1\%$
Dark matter in galaxies and clusters of galaxies	Inferred from observed galactic motions	$\approx 10\text{--}20\%$
Inflationary matter	Theoretical (not yet seen)	100%

particle physics is filled with stories of finding unexpected and surprising particles, in both accelerator tests and cosmic-ray experiments. The current list of elementary particles, a roster begun only a century ago, is perhaps far from complete. In fact, theorists have already lined up a number of potential candidates, whose properties range from the enchanting to the incredible.

9

WIMPs, a Laundry Whitener, and Other Ghostly Visitors

He was conscious of particles of dark floating between people, some deep substance in which they all swam. . . .

—ANNE TYLER, *CELESTIAL NAVIGATION*

A plausible impossibility is always preferable to an unconvincing possibility.

—ARISTOTLE, *POETICS*

P aul Adrien Maurice Dirac was the Greta Garbo of physics. A London newspaper once described the British scientist "as shy as a gazelle and modest as a Victorian maid." He was so notorious for the brevity of his comments that his Cambridge University colleagues kiddingly named a unit of talkativeness after him—a dirac—which they defined as one word per year. Ever desirous of solitude, the bitter and crippling legacy of an antisocial father and a childhood devoid of friendships, this monastic scientist preferred to keep company with his equations. "A great deal of my work is just playing with equations," he once said, ". . . just looking for beautiful mathematical relations which maybe don't have any physical meaning at all." But sometimes they did. Through his mathematical reveries, the inscrutable P. A. M. Dirac (as he regularly signed his work, allowing few to know his full name) came to discover whole new worlds, theoretical realms inhabited by particles never before imagined.

Dirac was born in Bristol, England, in 1902. His father, an aloof and domineering man, had immigrated to England from Switzerland and taught French at a Bristol technical college. Dirac's mother, a Bristol native, was a ship captain's daughter. Trained in electrical engineering at Bristol University as an undergraduate but unable to find satisfactory employment upon graduating at the age of eighteen, Dirac went on to study applied mathematics and eventually obtained a Ph.D. from Cambridge in 1926. Dirac's originality and creativity in his newly chosen field were readily apparent and, by the remarkably young age of thirty, he was named to Cambridge's Lucasian Chair of Mathematics, the very position once held by Sir Isaac Newton.

By then, Dirac had already completed his greatest achievement in physics. In the late 1920s he had spent several years figuring out how to combine the equations of quantum mechanics—the revolutionary ideas of Louis de Broglie, Erwin Schrödinger, Werner Heisenberg, and Max Born—with Einstein's special theory of relativity, thus reconciling the era's two greatest theories and laying the foundation for the field of quantum electrodynamics. Until then, quantum theory had been violating Einstein's famous equation, $E = mc^2$, which views mass as a dense lump of energy. In carrying out this inspired work, though, Dirac ended up with two sets of solutions, one positive and one negative (similar to the way the square root of a number can be either positive or negative). One set of equations very obviously described the properties and actions of everyday electrons, but the other set appeared to be utter nonsense; it implied that there were electrons with negative energy. Energy, like one's weight or age, was always conceived as a positive quantity. How could particles have less than no energy?

Rather than simply dismiss this curious result as a mathematical aberration (as others might have done), Dirac convinced himself that the solution corresponded to something real. To Dirac, his strange result was actually describing a particle with an opposite charge and spin to the electron. It would be the electron's mirror image, a sort of photographic negative. For a time Dirac pushed the idea that the extra solution was really referring to the positively charged proton. He longed for his theory to explain the only two elementary particles then known, thus fulfilling the age-old dream of obtaining a unifying theory of matter. But a proton is 1,836 times more massive than an electron, hardly the electron's complete opposite. Nearly all of Dirac's colleagues dismissed the electron/proton connection as utter nonsense. Thus Dirac had to conclude, with some reluctance, that his mystery particle would be an entirely new species altogether, one unknown in experimental physics: "We may call such a particle an anti-electron," stated the reclusive theorist in a 1931 paper to the Royal Society of London. It wasn't ordinary matter, but rather anti-matter. Since no one was seeing such particles rushing about, Dirac despaired that his new quantum theory might have to be abandoned.

Dirac would later remark that his equations were smarter than he was, for they predicted the existence of an elementary particle—an antiparticle, really—before it was even discovered. It was the first time in history that a new kind of matter was officially postulated on solely theoretical grounds. Physicists would come to see that if an electron and one of these baffling particles, the electron's doppelgänger, actually met head-on, they would completely annihilate one another in a burst of pure energy. The electron and antielectron vanish to produce two photons—two flashes of gamma-ray radiation. Conversely, wrote Dirac, "an encounter between two hard gamma rays (of energy at least half a million electron volts) could lead to the creation simultaneously of an electron and anti-electron."

"We are agreed that your idea is crazy," a colleague told Dirac upon hearing of this startling conjecture. "What divides us is whether it is crazy enough to be true." It was.

In the summer of 1932, Carl Anderson, a twenty-six-year-old cosmic-ray scientist at the California Institute of Technology, was photographing the thin white vapor trails left by energetic cosmic rays that were passing through a Caltech cloud chamber he had built—a machine specially designed to leave a telltale wake, akin to a jet contrail, whenever an invisible particle whizzed through the cylindrical box. Over the previous two years, he had occasionally noticed something peculiar in his pictures, tracks that were either light negatively charged particles moving upward or light positively charged particles moving downward. By placing a thin lead plate in the chamber, to slow the particles down, Anderson was at last able to pinpoint the direction of travel. A photograph taken on the night of August 2, 1932, made it clear. Anderson saw a particle that behaved just like an electron, except that its track curled the wrong way, to the left instead of the right, under the guidance of the chamber's powerful magnetic field. At first not connecting his find to Dirac's hypothesis, the young physicist swiftly announced that he had discovered an electron with a positive charge, which he christened the "positron." In actuality, Anderson had snared one of Dirac's antielectrons, the first bona fide bit of antimatter. The discovery of the positron earned the young postdoc the 1936 Nobel Prize. (Dirac had already won his prize, which he almost refused because of fear of all the publicity, three years earlier.)

Physicists now know that every type of elementary particle in the universe has a complementary antiparticle, although it took quite a while

An invisible gamma ray enters a bubble chamber at the top of this picture and creates an electron and a positron that spiral in opposite directions within a magnetic field.
Lawrence Berkeley Laboratory

to confirm these other bits of antimatter. Nearly a quarter of a century had to pass before particle accelerators were powerful enough to produce the antiproton, the proton's antimatter mate. The long wait even made some start to doubt that antimatter really existed. But by the fall of 1955, the negatively charged antiprotons finally made their appearance when protons were accelerated within the newly constructed Bevatron at the University of California at Berkeley and hurtled into a copper target with energies of six billion electron volts (the minimum level necessary to coax an antiproton into appearing from a flash of energy). Heisenberg called the discovery of antimatter "perhaps the biggest of all the big jumps in physics in our century."

WHY MATTER AT ALL?

If theory predicts that every particle in the universe will have an alter ego, a complementary antiparticle, one might think that the big bang would have been impartial and made just as many antiparticles as particles in those first blazing moments of creation when energy congeals into substance. Indeed, whenever energetic photons materialize into particles— energy converting into mass according to the guiding rule $E = mc^2$—they always create pairs of particles, one matter and the other antimatter. Collisions within particle accelerators continually yield equal amounts of matter and antimatter in copious abundances. In his 1933 Nobel Prize lecture, Dirac himself spoke of the possibility of antimatter stars. Instead of hydrogen and helium, these stars would be composed of antihydrogen and antihelium, elements that are made out of antiprotons, antineutrons, and positrons. Dirac's speculation seemed quite plausible, especially since the light emitted by these antistars would be exactly the same as the light emitted from ordinary stars. People began imagining entire galaxies composed of antiparticles, which somehow separated out, like oil from water, at the universe's birth. The universe, in this way, would then be half matter and half antimatter—with Earth, by happenstance, caught in the neighborhood of matter.

Astronomical observations carried out since Dirac's day, however, consistently argue for an all-matter cosmos. We and everything around us—from bicycles to popsicles, planetary nebulae to whirling neutron stars—are, by all appearances, composed of matter, particles that swim within a crowded sea of photons. There is about one particle of matter for every one billion to ten billion photons of radiation. The cosmos seems to have a decided aversion to keeping large quantities of antimatter in tow. Outside of an atom smasher, antimatter is as rare as a tropical bird on an arctic ice floe. The fact that our space probes have never been obliterated upon landing on the Moon or the planets is pretty good evidence that the solar system is safely constructed out of matter. If the Viking landers had set down on an antimatter Mars, for instance, the blinding explosions would have dominated the nighttime sky. Moreover, the gamma rays being emitted within our galaxy, as well as from nearby clusters of galaxies, set limits on how much matter is currently mixing with antimatter and fiercely annihilating. The results tell astronomers that less than one particle in a million out in deep space could be antimatter. And as far as science is concerned, no one has yet seen an entire antinucleus from some distant antistar (the two antiprotons and two antineutrons of an antihelium nucleus, for instance) plummet to Earth as a cosmic ray.

For many years the reason behind the universe's preference for matter was not readily apparent. Why should the universe play favorites? It was only with the introduction of grand unified theories in the 1970s that cosmologists could at last fashion some plausible explanations for the universe's prejudice. In hindsight, it is not too surprising that the universe might exhibit a liking for matter over antimatter; over the years, physicists have come to see that some of nature's physical laws already display a clear-cut bias: Time proceeds in only one direction; radioactive cobalt emits many more left-spinning electrons than right-spinning ones; and exotic particles called K mesons seem to fancy one mode of decay more than another when they disintegrate. In regard to the myriad phenomena on display within its jurisdiction, nature is not always evenhanded. When particle physicists first came to recognize some of these biases in the 1950s and 1960s, the revelation severely rattled their world. It had always been assumed that physical interactions would not single out one path over another equally valid one.

Taking such observations into account, Soviet physicist and famed political dissident Andrei Sakharov suggested that the early universe itself may have become a bit skewed, evolving in such a way that the cosmos ended up with more particles than antiparticles, even though it started out with equal proportions of both. But in 1967, when Sakharov first proposed this strange notion, it didn't fit any established theory and so was promptly forgotten. Only when grand unified theories came onto the scene did physicists realize that a matter/antimatter imbalance, just as Sakharov had suspected, was a natural consequence in many of the GUT models. Matter fights it out with antimatter before the first second of the universal clock has even ticked, with matter coming out the winner in an apocalyptic annihilation.

According to GUTs, this momentous event occurred at a time in the far, far past when temperatures in the newborn cosmos were above a billion billion billion degrees. It was the briefest of instants when the weak, electromagnetic, and strong forces were still united in one all-encompassing force. And just as the electromagnetic force is now transmitted by photons, this grand unified force was mediated by supermassive particles called X bosons, which were present in vast numbers and carrying out an interesting task. It was through the intervention of these X bosons (and their partners the anti-X bosons) that quarks and antiquarks, electrons and antielectrons, neutrinos and antineutrinos were able to rapidly switch from one species to the other. Quarks, for example, could turn into antielectrons and antiquarks; antiquarks could become neutrinos and quarks. No particle's identity was yet fixed and inviolate.

But, like some colossal game of musical chairs, the frenzied switching had to stop as soon as temperatures fell and the grand unification was shattered. It was the moment when the universe chose sides. Think of the fluctuating mixture of particles and antiparticles freezing into place as soon as the cosmic clock reached 10^{-35} second. It is postulated that, as a result of that freeze, for every ten billion or so bits of matter and antimatter that settled out of the teeming cosmic soup, one extra particle of matter was made. The X bosons and anti-X bosons exhibited a discernible preference in the way they decayed. When the GUT "music" stopped, the anti-X bosons decayed into roughly 10,000,000,001 specks of matter for every 10,000,000,000 bits of antimatter generated by the decaying X bosons.

Within the next millionth of a second, the quarks and antiquarks specifically paired off and completely annihilated one another, which released a blizzard of high-energy photons. But, thankfully, that tiny surplus of quarks—that one extra quark for every ten billion quarks and antiquarks—remained unpaired and untouched to create the material in the universe that surrounds us and that we are made of. We are the remnant debris from that fierce battle, the thin sliver left behind as the universe tipped the cosmic balance and turned asymmetric. This can also explain how there came to be about ten billion cosmic photons, each the result of a destructive matter/antimatter pairing, for every particle of matter in the universe. Physicists could only take that ratio on faith before the advent of GUTs.

During the next second of expansion, immediately after the quark/antiquark annihilation, the electrons and positrons (antielectrons) staged their own conflagration, annihilating and leaving behind a counterbalancing residue of electrons. Forming first light nuclei, then later atoms, all these leftovers eventually coalesced during the ensuing eons into the galaxies, stars, and planets we see today. Our very lives are based on imperfection. The universe is flawed; its original sin was to choose matter over antimatter.

What happened regularly in the sweltering early moments of the big bang—feverish switching between matter and antimatter—might also be happening today but at a frightfully slower rate. A proton, seemingly one of the most stable forms of matter, would then be mortal; it could disintegrate as a spray of lighter particles. Matter itself faces the possibility of evaporating away. Massive underground detectors, enormous tanks of water or stacks of metal, have been on the lookout for a proton decaying—but so far there has been no success. Physicists know only that the proton's life span must be longer than 10^{32} years, nearly a trillion trillion times longer than the current age of the universe. (Perhaps we shouldn't worry.)

"This work is not yet on the same footing as the calculations of primordial helium and deuterium," says cosmologist Martin Rees. "It is perhaps at the same level as nucleosynthesis was in the pioneering days of Gamow and Lemaître. But if it could be firmed up it would represent an extraordinary triumph." In fact, other scenarios are still being offered. Some scientists are beginning to wonder whether the excess of matter occurred when the infant universe was undergoing its brief, inflationary spurt, creating the conditions whereby matter switches into antimatter and antimatter into matter by quantum-mechanical "tunneling," much the same way that protons and neutrons can tunnel through their nuclear barriers and fly out of an atom as radioactive particles. According to some, the exotic inflationary environment could have allowed more antimatter to tunnel or transform into matter than vice versa. Others have suggested that the imbalance between matter and antimatter may have occurred a bit later in the universe's development; they envision matter taking over when the universe was around one ten-billionth of a second old, the moment when the electroweak interaction split into two separate forces. What excites physicists the most is that evidence favoring one of these latest conjectures could conceivably show up in experiments planned for the next and most powerful generation of particle accelerators. Obtaining an explanation for the universe's choosing matter over antimatter, whatever the ultimate physical details, has been one of the most successful accomplishments in the marriage of particle physics to cosmology. And, for the moment, it has put to rest Dirac's imaginings of antistars in antigalaxies in some antiregion of our universe.

But Dirac, it seems, did write the script for a play that would be acted out many times in the history of particle physics: Hypothetical particles, at first deemed nonsensical, are quickly accepted as natural and obvious once they are discovered. To be honest, physicists have no other choice; they must always amend their theories (or grudgingly accept a competitor's supposition) in light of the new information that nature provides. Dirac had made it acceptable to contemplate and postulate other forms of matter. Once considered a defiant act, proposing a new particle has almost become routine. "These days," notes physicist Anthony Zee in his book *Fearful Symmetry*, ". . . theorists are predicting new particles with wanton abandon. The situation, indeed, has so degenerated that some theorists of my generation are apt to invent new particles for no good reason other than to explore their consequences were they to exist."

Antiparticles were hardly the last substance (or perhaps antisubstance) to come to life from a set of equations sprawled over theorists' worksheets. Others followed. And some of these particles may very well play a leading role in the missing-mass drama.

LITTLE NEUTRAL ONES

Charles D. Ellis, an officer in the English army during World War I, became acquainted with physics when he shared prisoner-of-war quarters in Germany with physicist James Chadwick. Chadwick, who would later discover the neutron, had been studying radioactivity in Berlin under Fritz Geiger (of Geiger counter fame) and was mistaken for a spy when the war broke out. To while away the hours of confinement at the camp, young Chadwick taught Ellis all he knew. Together they even organized a little research lab, which received generous support from Chadwick's German scientific colleagues.

The lessons obviously took. During the 1920s, Ellis, by then fully committed to a career in physics, came to study a troubling anomaly. Whenever a radioactive nucleus decayed by ejecting an electron (a process called beta decay), something went awry. In carefully controlled experiments conducted at the famous Cavendish Laboratory, Ellis saw that the energy of the nucleus before it radioactively decayed was more than that of the system afterward (that is, the combined energy of the depleted nucleus and the fleeing electron). It looked as if energy were actually disappearing during beta decay, and this violated one of the bulwarks of physics—the law of conservation of energy, which states that energy is neither created nor destroyed. Atoms, it seemed, weren't playing by those rules. Energy was somehow getting lost along the way. So distressing was this finding that the distinguished physicist Niels Bohr openly discussed the possibility that atoms might at times violate some of the standard laws of physics.

Wolfgang Pauli wasn't as pessimistic as his Danish colleague. The rotund Viennese physicist had an abiding faith that atoms were obeying the physical laws of the land. Here was a man who was infamous for his rapier-sharp put-downs. "So young and already so unknown," Pauli once described a new physicist arriving on the scene. Colleagues spoke of the "Pauli effect," whereby Pauli's mere presence in a laboratory would cause all sorts of mischief.

Just as Dirac had braved his doubts to predict a new type of matter, Pauli took the rather radical step in 1930 of suggesting (albeit with some hesitation) that an entirely new particle, invisible to ordinary instruments, had to exist to explain the energy discrepancy seen in Ellis's experiments. Every time a nucleus undergoes beta decay, Pauli proposed to some colleagues by letter, this neutral, phantomlike particle is emitted and vanishes off into the night carrying off that extra bit of energy. Usually full of chutzpah, the young Pauli was actually intimidated by the outrageousness of this idea. "Dear radioactive ladies and gentlemen," he teasingly wrote his friends, who were then attending a meeting in Tübingen, Germany. "For the time being I dare not publish anything about this idea and address myself confidentially first to you, dear radioactive ones, with the question of how it would be with the experimental proof of such a particle." He thought of his solution as a "desperate remedy," and only the discovery of the chargeless neutron in 1932 encouraged him to publish it. The noted physicist Enrico Fermi dubbed Pauli's hypothetical mote the "neutrino," Italian for "little neutral one." The name was apt.

The neutrino had no mass, and it had no charge. Indeed, it was nothing more than a spot of energy that flew from a radioactive atom at the speed of light. Physicists at the time found the idea both perplexing and entertaining. During evening theatricals at physics workshops in the thirties, researchers could be heard singing the refrain:

> My mass is zero,
> My charge is the same.
> You are my hero,
> Neutrino's my name.

Fermi perceptively recognized that Pauli's idea would also require a whole new force, what came to be known as the weak force. The weak force enables a neutron to convert into a proton, releasing the electron and the neutrino (actually, an antineutrino) seen in beta decay. (Interestingly enough, the prestigious journal *Nature* rejected Fermi's idea on the weak force as too speculative and too remote to be of any interest to practicing scientists; a small Italian review, however, did publish the hypothesis. Thus, the weak force entered the world of physics with little fanfare.)

It took so long to prove that the neutrino was more than a figment of Pauli's imagination that some physicists began to call his neutrino "the little one who was not there." In fact, Pauli began to wonder whether he had committed the theorist's ultimate sin: postulating a particle that could not possibly be detected. He had good reason to be fearful. Capturing a neutrino is an extremely difficult task. The neutrino, which interacts only via the weak force, is so oblivious to matter that it would take a stack of lead, thousands of light-years in length, to stop one in its tracks (which is exactly why the weak force is called weak). A neutrino could bolt through the entire Earth and collide with nary a thing, as if the Earth were no more substantial than a cloudy mist.

The odds of catching a neutrino are considerably increased, however, if there is a flood of such particles coming at you—a few out of the hordes would thus have a chance of bumping into an atom close by and triggering a weak interaction. As a result of such an interaction, the atomic nucleus would be altered, sending out a flash of radiation that could be spotted with photomultiplier tubes. The construction of nuclear reactors in the 1950s at last provided the necessary neutrino spigot for carrying out this tricky endeavor.[1] By 1956 Clyde Cowan and Frederick Reines, in a difficult but elegant experiment conducted at a South Carolina nuclear power plant, were finally able to corner the ghostly neutrino, or at least see its telltale footprints of light. The experiment was appropriately named Project Poltergeist.

During each second that the giant Savannah River reactor operated, hundreds of trillions of neutrinos were generated in the reactor's core, whereupon they immediately escaped and raced through Cowan and Reines's ten-ton detector set nearby. Only a few of the slippery particles got stopped each hour. With such a sparse harvest, it took more than three years for the two young researchers to gather enough evidence to declare the neutrino a certified member of the particle zoo—to Pauli's great relief. Receiving news of the verification while attending a conference in Geneva, Pauli, by then in his fifties, held the telegram high and gleefully announced to his fellow physicists, "The neutrino exists!" He had lived to see his "sin" forgiven.

The particle that Cowan and Reines detected is known specifically as the electron neutrino because of its appearance in nuclear reactions involving ordinary electrons. Since the detection of the electron neutrino, physicists have found a second type of neutrino, the muon neutrino, which is associated with interactions involving the muon, a more massive relative of the electron. The muon is about 207 times heavier than the electron. A third neutrino, the tau neutrino, is strongly suspected to exist as well. It would be linked to a still heavier cousin of the electron called the tau that was first seen in particle-accelerator experiments in the mid-1970s. The tau is nearly 3,500 times more massive than the electron. To use the jargon of physics, neutrinos come in three "flavors": electron, muon, and tau.

The neutrino still reigns as the most elusive particle known to prevail in the cosmos. Physicists calculate that herds of them—in all three flavors—were created during the big bang, outnumbering baryons, the particles of ordinary matter, by more than a billion to one. In the time it takes you to read this sentence, trillions of cosmic neutrinos silently slip right through you—and more continue to do so unceasingly. Hence, it is not

---

[1] Atom bombs were briefly considered as a source of neutrinos. But, as Fermi wryly noted, using nuclear reactors was certainly better because it didn't require setting off an A-bomb every time someone wanted to check the experiment's results.

surprising that the neutrino was the first elementary particle seriously considered as a dark-matter candidate. Ghostly, ephemeral, and so indifferent to the rest of the universe, the neutrino seemed to meet every qualification required of a missing-mass contender—if only it would put on a little weight.

Pauli, of course, first conceived of the neutrino as a bit of "nothing," a mote of pure energy that simply helped physicists retain the law of conservation of energy. If it is truly massless, having no more substance than a beam of light, the neutrino couldn't qualify at all as a dark-matter particle. Without a rest mass, it would be deprived of any substantial gravitational punch. Endowing a neutrino with a bit of bulk, on the other hand, could lead to enormous cosmological consequences, and theorists do have room in their latest particle physics models to furnish a neutrino with a tiny but essential essence. Researchers seriously began to discuss this possibility in the scientific literature as early as the 1960s.

The idea grew particularly popular in 1980 when experimentalists announced that they may have actually detected the sign of a "massive" neutrino, a neutrino with mass. Frederick Reines and a Soviet group of experimentalists headed by V. A. Lyubimov independently announced, after the completion of difficult and controversial experiments, that the electron neutrino seemed to have a very slight mass. The Soviet tests indicated a mass of around $1/20,000$ the weight of an electron. Such a tiny mass seems inconsequential, but it isn't. With each particle weighing that much, neutrinos would not only account for the dark matter, but, given the abundant presence of neutrinos in the heavens—there are about fifteen big bang neutrinos in every cubic centimeter of space—their combined mass would provide enough of a gravitational tug to bring our expanding universe to a complete halt uncountable eons from now. Here was a way of achieving cosmological nirvana—an omega of 1.

The Soviet team claimed to have seen the telltale mark of a massive neutrino in the radioactive decay of tritium; Reines, on the other hand, reported that he detected some electron neutrinos transforming themselves into either muon or tau neutrinos—a sure sign of mass—in measurements at his old hunting ground, the Savannah River nuclear reactor. Astronomers and physicists alike were immediately captivated by the notion that the smallest objects in the universe—a cosmic ocean of unseen elementary particles—could be controlling the universe's destiny. The two ends of the universal scale were linking up. But was it true?

Fascinated by the possible effects of a neutrino-filled universe, researchers in the Soviet Union, Europe, and the United States speedily went to their computers and began asking how the universe would evolve, and what it would look like today, given that neutrinos have substance. But these computer simulations, which at first looked quite promising, soon encountered difficulties. In the end, a computer's version of a universe filled with neutrinos didn't seem to resemble anything in the real sky.[2] In the meantime, additional experiments failed to detect a neutrino mass to everyone's satisfaction, at least a mass as "heavy" as the one first proposed. Neutrinos may still have substance, but the question is how much? And if they do have substance, is their mass cosmologically significant? For the moment, the neutrino is no longer a front-runner in the dark-matter game, but this appraisal could quickly change if neutrino "observatories" come up with firm evidence of an ample neutrino mass.

The world's first neutrino observatory was established in America's heartland in 1967 and has been gathering vital clues on the quirky nature of the neutrino ever since. The observatory's "telescope" is a huge tank of chlorine-rich cleaning fluid, 100,000 gallons of perchloroethylene, set in the Homestake gold mine situated nearly a mile beneath the Black Hills of South Dakota. Such a depth is required to keep the measurements free from disruptive cosmic rays. It took twenty railroad tanker cars to fill the tank up, roughly the amount of stain remover that American consumers use up in one day.

With this gargantuan apparatus, University of Pennsylvania radiochemist Raymond Davis, the founding father of neutrino astronomy, has been catching a few electron neutrinos out of the legions that are continually spewed into the solar system as the Sun burns its nuclear fuel. As much as 2 percent of the Sun's energy is emitted as electron neutrinos. Physicists estimate that every second some sixty-five billion of these solar neutrinos rain down upon each square centimeter of the Earth's surface.

For more than two decades now, chlorine atoms in the fluid have been occasionally catching some of the cagey particles. The electron neutrino gives itself away by turning the chlorine into an atom of traceable radioactive argon. But the rate of capture has been unexpectedly low—about one neutrino every couple of days. This is just one-fourth to one-third the number of solar electron neutrinos that physicists expected to be snared, given the rate of nuclear reactions thought to be going on within the Sun. Japan's Kamiokande detector, a huge vat of water originally built

---

[2] See chapter 10 for further discussion of such computer simulations.

A neutrino "telescope," a huge tank of cleaning fluid, situated deep underground in the Homestake gold mine in South Dakota.
Brookhaven National Laboratory

to look for proton decay, later recorded a similar deficit of solar electron neutrinos.

Some wondered whether astrophysicists truly knew how the Sun shined; others suggested that the physics of neutrinos needed to be revised. To help decide the matter, more sensitive neutrino observatories have since been erected around the world. Collaborators from the United States and the former Soviet Union initiated a search deep underground in the heart of the Caucasus Mountains, near the Russian town of Baksan. There, several dozen tons of liquid gallium await the shower of solar neutrinos passing through the Earth to turn some of the gallium atoms into radioactive germanium. A similar gallium experiment, called GALLEX, is under way in Italy's Gran Sasso tunnel.

Preliminary results from these newly activated neutrino detectors suggest that the neutrino deficiency, for so long seen in South Dakota and later in Japan, is real and might be understood if electron neutrinos are "oscillating" on their way out of the Sun. A fraction of them may be transforming themselves into the other two flavors, the muon neutrino and the tau neutrino. Since the perchloroethylene and gallium detectors can "see" only electron neutrinos and not the other two types, this might easily explain the shortfall.

The idea that neutrinos might oscillate was first discussed by a student of Fermi's, Bruno Pontecorvo, in 1957. More recently, the idea has been extended by the Soviet physicists Stanislav Mikheyev and Alexi Smirnov, building on earlier work by Carnegie-Mellon physicist Lincoln Wolfenstein. According to this theory, known by its originators' last initials as the MSW model, neutrino oscillations would rarely occur in the vacuum of space, but the effect would be enhanced as neutrinos speed through more dense collections of celestial matter, such as the Sun.

More important to dark-matter specialists, the oscillations cannot take place unless each type of neutrino has some mass. Physicists already know that the electron neutrino, if massive, would be far too light to affect the dark-matter problem appreciably. When a faint bluish-white star in the Large Magellanic Cloud was seen to explode in the southern sky in 1987, the first nearby supernova visible to terrestrial eyes in nearly four hundred years, underground detectors on Earth (the Kamiokande detector in Japan and a similar facility in the United States) caught a few electron neutrinos out of the deluge that shot out of the supernova. Although an exact mass for the electron neutrino could not be calculated from the data—the explosion itself smeared the signal—an upper limit on a possible mass of the electron neutrino was obtained. It was found to be far too small to bring the universe to the verge of critical density. Laboratory measurements place even stricter restrictions on the electron neutrino's mass; that its value might remain zero has not been ruled out.

Some theorists make the simplifying assumption that, should the electron neutrino display even the tiniest of masses, the muon neutrino will be heavier and the tau neutrino will be the heaviest neutrino of them all. In fact, should that progression in masses prove to be true, the tau neutrino has the potential to be weighty enough to govern the universe's affairs, and it is this potential that keeps the neutrino in the running as a serious dark-matter candidate. Neutrino astronomers might have a better chance at pegging the tau neutrino's mass in the 1990s with the opening of the Sudbury Neutrino Observatory, a collaborative venture sponsored by Canada, Great Britain, and the United States. This ambitious detector is now under construction in a deep nickel mine more than two hundred miles north of Toronto and will consist of one thousand tons of deuterium oxide, or "heavy" water (where the proton in each hydrogen nucleus is accompanied by a neutron), encased in a bubble of clear plastic. This casing in turn will be surrounded by 7,000 tons of ordinary water and a vast array of sensitive photon detectors. Numbering 9,500, these photo-tubes will spot the bursts of light released whenever a neutrino strikes a deuterium nucleus. More important, this water detector will be able to see all three flavors of neutrinos—electron, muon, and tau.

The mass of the muon neutrino or the tau neutrino will best be fixed if a star explodes relatively nearby, within 30,000 light-years of Earth. Chances are slim that such an event will occur any time soon, but if it does, all three types of neutrinos will rush from the explosion. Being more sluggish, the heavier particles would arrive at Earth slightly later than the lighter ones, and it is this tiny difference in timing that would allow physicists to determine the masses, if any, for the various neutrino species.

Particle accelerators offer another route to establishing a mass for the tau neutrino. If experimentalists could generate an intense beam of muon neutrinos with a particle accelerator, a beam ten times more intense than levels now attainable, they could aim it at distant targets (perhaps as far as a few hundred miles away) to see if some of the muon neutrinos transform themselves into tau neutrinos along the way. The amount by which the two species "mix" (as the process is called) could establish the tau neutrino's mass. Even if the tau neutrino is not heavy enough to close the universe, it might still make a considerable contribution to the dark-matter pool.

Should the neutrino completely fail as a dark-matter contender, though, the story is hardly over. Numerous other particles, yet to be discovered, serve as viable possibilities for the missing mass. Each has emerged over the last couple of decades as investigators continually refine their theories concerning the varied inhabitants of our subatomic world. If a fraction, or even all, of the dark matter is found to be particle in nature, theorists stand ready to provide suitable candidates. The roots of these efforts can be traced back several decades, when particle theorists

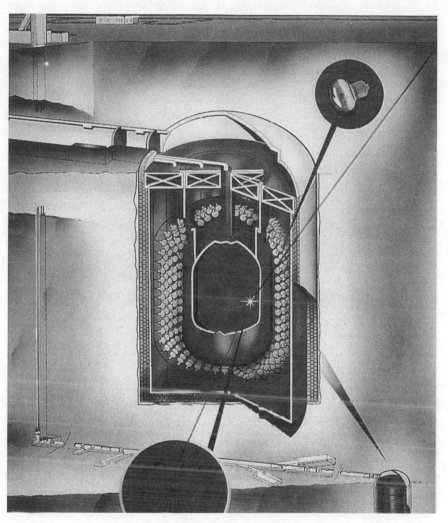

A cross-sectional view of the Sudbury Neutrino Observatory in Canada. Heavy water will be encased in an acrylic vessel and surrounded by photomultiplier tubes.
Atomic Energy of Canada Limited

first began their long trek toward understanding where matter came from and the essential components of its composition.

ORDER OUT OF CHAOS

The discovery of the neutron and the positron in 1932, as well as the theoretical likelihood of a wispy neutrino particle, was just the first trickle in an eventual deluge. Cosmic-ray physicists, taking their instruments up to high mountaintops where they spent weeks in tiny snowbound huts, began catching a bizarre array of new particles as the energetic cosmic rays raced in from space and interacted with atoms in the upper atmosphere. These novel particles, caught on photographic emulsions, were generally highly unstable, with lifetimes lasting less than a millionth of a second. "Who ordered that?" exclaimed the theorist Isidor I. Rabi when the plump muon was first identified in this way.

And as particle accelerators grew over the intervening decades from crude room-sized mechanisms to instruments with miles-long tunnels, achieving energies far higher than those easily studied in cosmic rays, more unexpected particles appeared in the debris. By the 1960s more than one hundred so-called elementary particles had been uncovered, as protons and electrons slammed into stationary targets at speeds near that of light. There were the pion, the sigma, the xi, the kaon, and the omega, among others. It was a veritable Greek alphabet soup. It was extremely difficult to understand how all these varied motes could possibly be related to one another. Such variety was bewildering to the scientists who were seeking simplifying laws, not a puzzling maze, from their energetic probes into the heart of the atomic nucleus. "If I could remember the names of all these particles, I would have been a botanist," Fermi once said in frustration. Theorists began to long for the days, not too far past, when they had to worry only about the electron and the proton.

Confusion reigned until 1963, when Caltech theorists Murray Gell-Mann and George Zweig brought order out of chaos by applying a strategy reminiscent of the ancient philosophers. From the time of Thales and Empedocles, the idea that all matter is derived from fundamental forms has held an irresistible appeal. The Greek atomists went on to think of matter as composed of ultimate bits. Gell-Mann and Zweig independently surmised that many of the particles caught by experimentalists might be composites too, each a different combination of three smaller, fundamental constituents. Zweig called these tiny entities "aces," but, because of a publishing dispute with journal editors at CERN, his idea didn't get circulated. Gell-Mann, in the meantime, always wanted his peculiar bits to have a peculiar name; it was his personal volley against pretentious scientific language. From the start, he had a certain sound in mind, something like "kwork." Serendipitously, right before he published his idea, the widely read Gell-Mann happened to come upon a line— "Three quarks for Muster Mark!"—in a book he often perused, James Joyce's enigmatic *Finnegans Wake*. Here was the perfect spelling for his basic units of matter. For years Joycean scholars have argued whether the term *quark,* as used in that line, pertains to the screech of a gull or to Mr. Mark's children. In German, the word *quark* describes a special runny cheese (but can also mean "nonsense"). Wanting an excuse to pronounce the word as "kwork," Gell-Mann figured the sound might be referring to quarts of ale (although the physics community now seems to prefer rhyming *quark* with the word *mark*).

In the lexicon of physicists, nowadays noted for their quirky terms, these quark types, at first three but now numbering six, are identified as "up," "down," "strange," "charm," "bottom," and "top" (although the poetically minded prefer to call the last two "beauty" and "truth").[3] It is a collection that allowed complexity to be replaced with a wondrous simplicity. Every particle affected by the strong force, the very force that keeps protons and neutrons cozily snug inside an atomic nucleus, could be constructed out of these six essential units. For instance, three strange quarks grouped together produce a short-lived, negatively charged particle called omega-minus. A charm quark paired with an anticharm quark forms the elusive psi particle.

But people don't bump into every type of quark routinely. All of the matter we deal with in our everyday world is essentially made up of the first two quark species, which together form a "family" of quarks. The proton, the very foundation of our material world, turns out to be composed of two up quarks and one down quark. The neutron, the proton's near-twin except for the lack of electric charge, is a composite of two

---

[3] The names *strange* and *charm* are really not as eccentric as they might sound. Certain exotic particles popping up in experiments were found to live a bit longer than anyone expected. These particles were deemed strange. So, the quarks that were later found to be a strange particle's constituents took on the same name. Gell-Mann's scheme first involved three quarks, but other quarks were later hypothesized to take care of certain problems arising in particle physics. The fourth quark was therefore labeled "charm," indicative of its ability to ward off those inherent theoretical ailments.

downs and an up. Together, these two simple quarks form the basis for an astonishing array of structures found all over the Earth and throughout the universe—from shade trees to globular clusters.

The other quark species are far more exotic. Matter composed of strange and charm quarks, a second family, are seen in cosmic rays and are routinely produced in particle accelerators. Astrophysicists are now wondering if tiny neutron stars eventually convert into compact spheres that are largely composed of strange matter. Bottom and top, a third family comprising the heaviest quarks, were more prevalent during the earliest moments of the big bang. Of all these quarks, only the top quark has yet to be seen with absolute assurance in particle-accelerator experiments. (In 1992, physicists at Fermilab near Chicago disclosed that they might have seen evidence of a top quark during particle-smashing experiments conducted with Fermilab's monstrous Tevatron accelerator, but further tests must be carried out to confirm the sighting.)

It is now generally forgotten that this quark scheme was just one of a bewildering variety of theories then being advocated as the most basic form of matter. In the early 1960s, the most fashionable theory was the bootstrap model, which declared that there were no fundamental particles at all, only an ever-percolating stew of mass-energy. Sometimes this stew could taste like a proton, at other times a neutron; it was a nuclear democracy. Within such an egalitarian atmosphere, quarks were not greeted with open arms. Gell-Mann, in fact, first talked of his ordering scheme more as a mathematical bookkeeping device. To ascribe quarks material essence was considered heresy, primarily because each quark had to have a fractional electric charge, a state never before seen or even considered in physics. Only in groups of two or three do quarks produce either a unit of charge or neutrality. The tide eventually shifted, partly because the brilliant American theorist Richard Feynman, a man once described as the Groucho Marx of physics, turned the quest for nuclear substructure into a cause célèbre.

Experimentalists can't hope to fully "see" a quark—it is forever trapped in its subnuclear prison, unable to exist alone. But a number of accelerator experiments do strongly demonstrate that protons, neutrons, and a host of short-lived nuclear particles are indeed made out of pointlike entities. There is proof of this in the way an electron, hurtled down a narrow, miles-long particle accelerator tube at speeds near that of light, slams into a proton and recoils from the fateful collision, like some subatomic billiard ball, as if it had bounced off three smaller particles inside the proton.

The only other structureless and indivisible bits of matter presently known to exist are the electron, the electron's close but heavier relatives the muon and tau particles, and the respective three flavors of neutrinos. Collectively, these six related particles are known as leptons, from a Greek word meaning "small" or "delicate." Leptons stand apart from the quarks in that none of these particles can be manipulated by the strong force. They are controlled largely by either the electromagnetic force or the weak force. But it is curious that leptons, like quarks, do group into three "families," and this situation hints at a significant connection, a more deep-rooted relationship, with the quarks themselves. Indeed, as we saw earlier, grand unified theories suggest that leptons readily turned into quarks, and quarks into leptons, during the first flash of creation.

Are there additional families of particles? This was a question often asked, because the most widely accepted theories of particle physics, collectively known as the standard model, set very loose limits on the number of particle families. The theoretical door was open for thousands of quark and lepton types to pop up in particle accelerator experiments, which could have led to another era of classifying a passel of particles like so many specimens of flora. Theorists had even assigned tentative names to the fourth family of particles; were they to have appeared, they would have been the "high" quark and the "low" quark, coupled with the electronlike sigma and the sigma neutrino.

Some twenty years ago, however, several researchers independently began to suspect that the number of families would be severely restricted. They came to this conclusion by looking over certain astrophysical evidence—in particular, the amount of helium cooked up in the universe's birth. University of Chicago astrophysicist David Schramm; Gary Steigman, now with Ohio State University; and Princeton astrophysicist

	Quarks	Leptons
Family 1:	up, down	electron, electron neutrino
Family 2:	strange, charm	muon, muon neutrino
Family 3:	bottom, top	tau, tau neutrino

James Gunn were among the first to do a detailed analysis and vigorously advocate that the material universe was constructed out of a severely limited variety of building blocks, possibly no more than seven families. "The more species of quarks and leptons there are," points out Schramm, "the more helium the early universe would have made." An excessive number of neutrino species would have speeded up the universe's expansion and overproduced the helium. (If the early universe expanded more quickly, neutrons would have had less time to convert into protons, thus increasing the supply of neutrons for helium production.)

The team's initial paper on the subject, interestingly enough, was rejected by its first journal choice, *Physical Review Letters*. At the time, many physicists saw no sense in making particle physics judgments based on cosmology. The physics community's wariness at turning to the skies for information on particle physics, however, did not curb Schramm's continued interest in the subject. By the 1980s, as the amount of helium in the universe was better assessed, Steigman, Schramm, and several of Schramm's associates from the Chicago cosmology group were able to announce that the number of potential particle families was restricted even more than they originally thought; a fourth family of leptons and quarks was possible, but only barely. More likely, they reported, there were simply three families, which limited nature's basic units to six quarks and six leptons. If there were any additional quark or lepton species, they pointed out, cosmologists couldn't account for the abundances of hydrogen and helium now seen in the cosmos. The physics of the macrocosm, the universe at large, was serving as a powerful probe of the physics of the very small. But some physicists were still highly skeptical. A colleague of Schramm's at Chicago, particle-accelerator experimentalist Bruce Winstein, bet Schramm a case of wine that a fourth family of particles would assuredly be found in the near future.

Nearly a decade passed, however, before the astrophysicists' suspicions could be confirmed on Earth with powerful particle accelerators. The Z particle, that conveyor of the weak force, gave the secret away in the speed with which it decays. The Z decays quite fast (in less than a trillionth of a trillionth of a second), but not too fast. The presence of a fourth family of particles would have allowed the Z to decay even more quickly, by offering an extra route to breaking apart. (Schramm thus won the wager; Winstein settled his bet with a bottle of wine from each of the various countries involved in the Z experiment.)

So physicists are now fairly assured that nature generates its multitude of material forms out of three particle families alone. Particles of matter, it turns out, are either leptons or quark composites, and this simplification was a tremendous boon to further cosmological and theoretical inquiries.

A CHORUS OF WIMPS

At the very same time when astronomers were discerning an added complexity—a dark, invisible richness—in the universe's composition, physicists were making inroads in reducing the apparent intricacy of the microcosm. Matter was separated into quarks and leptons; the forces themselves came to be associated with such entities as photons, gluons, and Z particles, with each transmitting a particular force on the subatomic level. And the engine that drove all this activity was the overwhelming ambition among physicists to unify the forces, to find the very source of their intimate relationship.

Before the first elementary particle, the electron, was even discovered, Maxwell had started physicists on their unifying venture by linking electricity with magnetism. More recently, electromagnetism and the weak force joined hands. And now the grand unified theories, the GUTs, are physicists' attempts to merge the strong with the electroweak.

But it can't stop there. There is one force still left out of all these mergers—gravity. The climb toward a complete unification of the forces continues upward into a mathematical heaven called supersymmetry, where all the forces, including gravity, look and act the same. This uniformity, of course, is no longer in place. Such a state of supersymmetry was maintained only during the first 10^{-43} second of the universe's existence, when cosmic temperatures were monstrously high—high enough to maintain the symmetry. To make a more earthly comparison, warm liquid water is much more symmetrical in structure than cold hard ice, which develops a crystal lattice where atoms must assume definitive positions and directions in space. The molecules in a drop of liquid water are free to point in any direction; the molecules in a crystal of ice, on the other hand, are confined to a precise orientation. Similarly, as the expanding universe cooled, its symmetries broke, causing its former uniformities to be likewise shattered. The forces took on their own identities, and all the particles, once massless, acquired weight.

The first attempts at developing a theory of supersymmetry were made in the 1970s. In more recent times the concept has been incorporated in an extended "theory of everything" called superstrings. At the heart of superstring theory is its redefinition of the fundamental building blocks of nature. At its most basic level, the theory simply states that such entities as quarks, electrons, and neutrinos are not really pointlike particles but rather one-dimensional strings about 10^{-33} centimeter long. Such strings are indeed very tiny: If an atom were blown up to the size of the Milky Way galaxy, one of these strings would be no bigger than a human cell. The forces we experience and the particles we detect would then depend on the manner in which these infinitesimally tiny loops of energy connect, split up, wiggle around, and rotate within a space-time composed of ten dimensions. Four of those dimensions, of course, are the ones so familiar to us—length, width, height, and time. The other six allegedly remain curled up like little submicroscopic balls at each and every point in space and so remain unobservable. With this new picture, all the elementary particles we count, collect, and measure within our expansive four-dimensional space-time continuum are merely oscillations in those still-hidden higher dimensions.

In the past when physicists attempted to join gravity with the other forces, they were faced with a host of infinities in their calculations, a predicament as troublesome as trying to divide a number by zero. It was a sure sign that the methods being used weren't working. But it was discovered that some of these irksome infinities would cancel if, in the long tradition established by Dirac and Pauli, some extra particles were assumed to exist. In theories of supersymmetry (what might be called a super grand unified force), every particle now known in nature actually comes with a partner, a sort of cock-eyed mirror image. Such theories are based on the idea that there should be a balance in the universe between bosons (the force particles) and fermions (the matter particles). In a mathematical sense, the two types of particles are interchangeable.

The equations first conclude that every known fermion is paired with a new boson. Each of these new bosons is distinguished by placing the letter s in front of the name of its companion fermion—every electron comes with a partner dubbed a selectron, while the neutrino has its sneutrino, the muon has its smuon, and the tau has its stau. More generally, every lepton has its slepton, and every quark has its squark.

Perhaps more important for the material world, every known boson is paired with a special fermion, a new matter particle yet to be seen. A different and rather amusing lexicon was established for these hypothetical bits—the suffix -ino is attached to the name of the associated boson.

Thus, the photon comes to have its photino; the W boson, its Wino; the Z particle, its Zino; and the graviton, its gravitino. The use of the suffix is a bit misleading, however, as it means "little" in Italian. If gravitinos, photinos, or Winos exist, they would be far more massive than ordinary particles, possibly the mass of several hundred protons; they might be as heavy as atoms. But akin to neutrinos, they would still be terribly uninterested in interacting with ordinary matter. They would snub it.

At first, some thought that particles already known to exist might be the supersymmetric partners. Similar to the way Dirac had hopes of his positive electron being a proton, it was ventured that perhaps the neutrino was actually a photino. But by the 1980s, theorists were convinced that supersymmetric particles, known in the trade as SUSYs, would be a whole new species of matter.

Supersymmetry is an immensely popular concept among theorists, especially because it continues the tradition in physics of finding unifying links between what were once considered widely diverse entities, such as Maxwell's successful union of electricity with magnetism. Supersymmetry, for one, appears to be an essential ingredient in theories that are attempting to link gravity to the other forces. Experimentalists, too, are excited; the next generation of giant particle accelerators will be attempting to corner evidence of the existence of supersymmetric particles, or at least set limits on what kind of SUSYs can and cannot prevail. Already, with current instrumentation, physicists have discerned that supersymmetric particles, if any truly exist, must weigh more than 8×10^{-24} gram, the collective weight of five protons.

Supersymmetric theories were invented by particle physicists for their own theoretical needs, not to solve the problems of cosmology. But in the early 1980s certain investigators, who were beginning to see that the universe itself offered them a new platform for particle research, realized that some of these supersymmetric particles might serve very well as a dark matter scattered throughout the cosmos. Supersymmetry roughly doubles the number of known particles, as it brings in a "superpartner" for every particle already known to exist. Not all of these particles would be good dark-matter candidates; according to current assumptions, some of the SUSYs would quickly decay into other particles. But the lightest of these hypothetical particles, things like photinos, Zinos, and higgsinos, might be stable enough to hang around in intergalactic space. Hence, it wasn't long before astrophysicists began collectively calling these supersymmetric dark-matter particles (or, for that matter, any similarly acting exotic particle) WIMPs, weakly interacting massive particles. Electrically neutral and virtually invisible, WIMPs would reveal themselves mainly through their collective gravity. Researchers came to recognize that it needn't be just neutrinos that had mass; a host of other particles, as yet undetected and as elusive as the neutrino, could have been produced in the big bang as well. It opened up a whole new avenue in considering the universe darkly.

Cosmologists were drawn into this arena because of an intriguing calculation. If typical masses and expected populations for these WIMPy exotic particles are calculated, the universe ends up with a density near or equal to that height of heights, an omega of 1. "That's either a wonderful coincidence or a very telling clue," notes theorist Joel Primack of the University of California at Santa Cruz. The answer could have been one-millionth the critical density, or it could have been a millionfold. Yet, from particle physics considerations alone, a number arrived that had something very powerful to suggest for cosmologists. Such connections strongly motivate particle physicists to seek answers to some of their puzzles in cosmology. Primack and several colleagues went on to show how WIMPs might play a crucial role in forming galaxies after the big bang. Of course, until a supersymmetric particle is actually caught, all these intriguing suppositions remain sheer theoretical guesswork.

"Do you believe any of this?" Primack had asked his collaborator Martin Rees, shortly after working on the potential WIMP/galaxy connection with the British cosmologist.

"No," replied Rees. "I give it a 20 percent chance." Upon seeing Primack a bit crestfallen at that assessment, Rees was quick to add, "But that's higher than almost anything else I've considered in cosmology."

Yet, theorists still persist in their quest. Kim Griest, a theorist with the University of California at Berkeley, likens it to gambling. "It's high risk, but high benefit as well—to be one of the first people to find out what the universe is mostly made of."

Griest wears two hats. As a particle physicist interested in the dark-matter mystery, he has been industriously calculating the possible properties of WIMPs. As an astrophysicist, he is also participating in the hunt for astrophysical dark-matter candidates, such as brown dwarfs, Jupiters, and black holes, that might be circling within the halo of our galaxy. Searching for a suitable contrast to the WIMP name, Griest decided to call the more sizable, macroscopic dark-matter candidates MACHOs, massive astrophysical compact halo objects. Thus, the dark-matter search has turned into a contest between the MACHOs and the WIMPs.

THE LAUNDRY WHITENER

Is the universe composed largely of invisible neutrinos? Or is it populated with supersymmetric WIMPs? Considering that physicists have been stalking subatomic particles for less than a century, only since the detection of the electron in 1897, it would be quite presumptuous to think that they have cornered them all. But if the dark matter is truly particle in nature, certain astronomical facts give us a peek at some of the particle's properties. For instance, it doesn't give off any type of electromagnetic radiation very well, if at all, and it doesn't bind with ordinary matter, otherwise it would have sunk into the centers of galaxies, along with more ordinary dust and gas. And the lifetime of this mysterious form of matter must be at least greater than the age of the universe, or it would have disappeared long ago.

For some physicists the most elegant solution would involve the axion, a beloved particle that was independently conceived by the American physicists Frank Wilczek and Steven Weinberg to handle certain problems arising in the modeling of the strong force, the force that keeps atomic nuclei from flying apart. And in a fit of whimsy not unusual for those in his esoteric field, Wilczek named it after a laundry additive!

As a graduate student at Princeton in the early 1970s, Wilczek was a central figure in unraveling the mystery as to why we don't get to see lone quarks. Bound in either threes or twos, quarks can never be pulled apart. As two quarks move farther and farther away from one another, the force between them—the strong force—only gets stronger and stronger, unlike the forces of electromagnetism and gravity, whose effects get weaker over long distances. Like slaves on a chain gang, quarks have no means of escaping their confinement.

"This theory of the strong force cleared up many clouds in the world of physics, only to make one previously inconspicuous cloud more obvious," points out Wilczek. By 1976 the brilliant Dutch physicist Gerard 't Hooft had shown physicists that there was an additional and very subtle interaction between quarks that allowed left-handed quarks, their spins turning counterclockwise to the direction of motion, to change sometimes into right-handed quarks, particles with an opposite spin. Physicists were quick to accept the idea, as it explained why a certain particle, the eta-prime meson, a combination of a quark and antiquark, was more massive than first expected.

But there was a cost to this success. 't Hooft's solution also suggested that the neutron, that most neutral of particles, should have an electric dipole moment; its spin should be lining up in an electric field, despite its lack of an electric charge. Many experimentalists have tried to measure such an effect but have always failed to find it. If they did find it, it would be as surprising as if a magnet were able to attract an inert piece of plastic. Keeping the good parts of 't Hooft's interaction (explaining the hefty meson particle), without falling victim to its problems (a neutron dipole moment), required one more subtle fix.

Wilczek, immersed in work on the strong force, had been following the debate on 't Hooft's interaction with great interest. By the summer of 1977, building on a solution introduced by theorists Helen Quinn and Roberto Peccei, he came to realize that the problems with 't Hooft's new interaction would disappear *if* there existed a new lightweight and long-lived particle. His first calculations suggested this particle would weigh about 2×10^{-28} gram, five times lighter than an electron.

"But I couldn't imagine how this particle could have escaped detection," recalls Wilczek. He hoped to save the model by trying to readjust the particle's properties and consequently make it harder to detect, but the model only got uglier.

Steven Weinberg, who was independently coming to the same conclusions as Wilczek, was more optimistic. "Weinberg and I got the same couplings, the same model, the same constraints. But he made one horrific mistake," says Wilczek with a grin. "Weinberg got the name wrong."

Weinberg had wanted to call his new particle the Higglet, but Wilczek suggested that they name it the axion, since the new particle cleaned up problems with something called the axial current. Weinberg agreed, but what Wilczek didn't tell Weinberg was his hidden agenda. Years earlier, during a visit to a supermarket, Wilczek had noticed a new detergent booster on the shelf. It was called Axion, a bleach alternative put out by the Colgate-Palmolive Company. "It sounded like the perfect name for an elementary particle," says Wilczek. "Ever since that day, I carried this secret ambition to use that label." The laundry product's electric blue box, with the name *Axion* in vivid red letters, is now displayed, like a work of pop art, by his office door at the Institute for Advanced Study in Princeton, New Jersey.

By agreement, Weinberg and Wilczek published their idea of the axion at the same time. Wilczek's paper in *Physical Review Letters* had the formidable title, "Problem of Strong P and T Invariance in the Presence of Instantons." Shortly afterward, though, the particle he hypothesized, at least as it was originally constructed, was ruled out. There was a vigorous search at various laboratories, such as the Argonne National Laboratory and the Fermi National Accelerator Laboratory, and at a number of nuclear reactors where the axion should have been copiously produced. No one saw it.

But since the axion was still considered the best solution to those nagging problems with the strong force, other physicists continued to look into the model. With the advent of grand unified theories, in fact, the axion became "new and improved," a fitting evolution given its Madison Avenue beginnings. An axion particle turned up when the grand unification was shattered. Working within this new framework, estimates of the axion's mass plummeted. "They fell through the floor," notes Wilczek.

An axion, as now conceived, makes an electron look decidedly elephantine; each could be billions of times lighter than an electron. And with the strength of its interactions being very, very weak, the axion becomes quite hard to detect. Wilczek soon realized that, if such an axion exists, a billion of them would be poised in every cubic inch of space around us, adding up to some substantial dark matter. "One sign of a good idea is that it has unexpected consequences," says Wilczek. "The fact that axions might have cosmological significance came as a surprise—for free!"

FATAL ATTRACTION

A massive neutrino, the axion, and the most stable of the WIMPs are the leading particle candidates for the missing mass. But the possibilities don't end there. Where there is a new particle physics theory, there is usually some kind of dark-matter contestant that pops out of it, which is duly reported in the scientific literature—just in case. All are an assortment of fossil remnants left over from the big bang. They include quark "nuggets" (boulder-sized lumps of strange-flavored quarks, each nugget weighing as much as a planet), magnetic monopoles (weighty particles of magnetic charge), and things labeled techi-baryons, polonyions, and cryptons. For a while, physicists even considered something called "shadow matter," an odd material that allegedly originated the moment that gravity broke away from its sister forces to evolve independently. In such a universe, there would be shadow electrons and shadow protons flying right through us unnoticed. We couldn't hear it, taste it, or touch it, but we could feel the shadow matter's gravitational tugs: the perfect dark matter—if it had indeed turned out to be real. Plumbing the essence of deep space, astronomers face the twentieth-century equivalent of "Here Be Dragons," that fabled warning that ancient cartographers placed on medieval maps when forced to depict the potential denizens of uncharted waters.

Martin Rees calls himself a genuine "agnostic" when it comes to favoring one dark-matter candidate over another. He gives a 25 percent probability to low-mass stars and Jupiters being the dark matter, 25 percent to black holes, 25 percent to exotic particles, and 25 percent to "things we haven't thought of yet." It might even be a combination of all of the above.

Each generation of astronomers has had to confront a mystery that seems unsolvable at first and then becomes self-evident as soon as an answer is found. E. E. Barnard probed those "holes in the heavens" and came to reveal a component of the galaxy—dark nebulae—that now hold the key to star formation. Enigmatic spots on the sky called quasars were found to be galactic powerhouses, which allowed astronomers to peer to the very edge of the visible universe. Now there is the dark matter. What astronomical tales will it rewrite? "A disappointment has now set in that no answer has jumped out as yet," remarks David Seckel, a theorist with the Bartol Research Institute in Delaware. The great enthusiasm of the 1980s, the overall feeling that answers were within reach, has been replaced with a cautious wait-and-see attitude. The easy answers, such as massive neutrinos, have proved ephemeral. Dark-matter devotees are now at the mercy of technology and theory.

Whispers of evidence emanating from the universe fuel much of the desire to find a dark-matter particle. The cosmic microwave background, the big bang afterglow first detected by Penzias and Wilson in 1964, is almost as smooth as ice; the ripples in its complexion are quite minute. But in an early universe filled with ordinary matter, galaxies collapsing and condensing should have greatly ruffled the sea of microwaves. These irregularities in the microwave background would, in a sense, represent the seeds from which the wide array of galaxies and clusters grew and proliferated. Such disturbances in the microwave background are considerably dampened, though, if there are lots and lots of dark-matter particles around, enough to bring the universe to critical density, which is another important reason why many cosmologists favor an omega of 1. It helps explain why the universe's microwave sea is relatively calm. The Cosmic Background Explorer (COBE) satellite, launched by NASA in November 1989 to map the microwaves with unprecedented precision, confirmed that the radiation is remarkably uniform, varying over the sky by roughly one part in 100,000. (If the surface of the Earth were this smooth, its mountains wouldn't rise much more than 200 feet.)

In his poem "The Two Voices," written in 1832, Alfred Lord Tennyson once mused:

> *This truth within thy mind rehearse,*
> *That in a boundless universe*
> *Is boundless better, boundless worse.*

If a poll were taken among astrophysicists, says Rees, it would reveal that there is a "reasoned prejudice" for a universe filled to the brim with dark matter, enough to bring it to the brink of closure. Many have concluded that a boundless, infinite universe is worse. And Alan Guth's inflation fuels the need (the heartfelt wish, actually) for a universe on the edge. On the other hand, the great Russian author Leo Tolstoy once wrote that beauty is not goodness. Beauty, in the form of a universe poised between open and closed, is thus not necessarily the truth.

The most elegant solution would be to plunk down a particle that we are unaware of, much as neutrinos and antimatter were once unknown. But is that merely a foolish, theoretical desire? "If you're going to make a universe, why not an open, eccentric one suitable for us and not just mathematicians?" poses astronomer Jesse Greenstein.

Greenstein and others wonder if cosmologists are being driven by an almost metaphysical desire for an omega of unity. The spins of galaxies and the jostling of galaxies in clusters still don't indicate such large amounts of dark matter. But then, maybe galaxies are only the tips of the icebergs. Perhaps they are all immersed in a pool of exotic matter, which remains uncounted when galaxies alone are scrutinized.

Evidence will surely arrive as astronomers better examine the intergalactic byways of the universe. Celestial topography, the way in which galaxies mingle and cluster, was undoubtedly controlled by the universe's predominant material. Clues as to the exact nature of this material will arise from the universe itself.

"Like the fifteenth-century navigators, astronomers today are embarked on voyages of exploration, charting unknown regions," Harvard astronomer Robert Kirshner has written. "The aim of this adventure is to bring back not gold or spices or silks but something more valuable: a map of the universe that will tell of its origin, its texture, and its fate."

Just as a macroscopic crystal displays in its regular features the hidden geometry of the atoms within, so too does the universe's structure possess the potential to expose the hidden matter that was assembled at the dawn of space and time. The roots of this quest can be traced to the eighteenth century, when an amateur astronomer on the isle of Great Britain tried, in his own fashion, to explain the essential architecture of the visible universe.

10

The Bubbling Universe

The Eternal Sákí from that Bowl has poured
Millions of Bubbles like us, and will pour.

—EDWARD FITZGERALD, *THE RUBÁIYÁT OF*
OMAR KHAYYÁM

The distribution of galaxies in the redshift survey slice looks
like a slice through the suds in the kitchen sink.

—VALÉRIE DE LAPPARENT, MARGARET
GELLER, AND JOHN HUCHRA, "A SLICE
OF THE UNIVERSE" (*ASTROPHYSICAL
JOURNAL*, MARCH 1, 1986)

In 1750 an Englishman named Thomas Wright published a treatise whose longiloquent title held the promise of lofty cosmological revelations. His opening page, resplendent in black and red type, boldly proclaimed:

An
Original Theory
or
New Hypothesis
of the
Universe

Founded upon the
Laws of Nature,
and solving by
Mathematical Principles
the
General Phaenomena of the Visible Creation;
and particularly
the Via Lactea.
Compris'd in Nine Familiar Letters from the Author to his Friend.
And Illustrated with upwards of Thirty Graven and Mezzotinto Plates,
By the Best Masters.

Via lactea is Latin for "the Milky Way," that celestial river of stars that cuts a cloudy path across the inky nighttime sky and which mystified the many who pondered its breathtaking beauty throughout the centuries. With his novel, homemade telescope, Galileo had perceived that the Milky Way was composed of innumerable stars. But why should the stars arrange themselves in such a streamlike fashion?

Wright announced that his new hypothesis was "an Attempt towards solving the Phaenomena of the *Via Lactea,* and in consequence of that Solution, the framing of a regular and rational Theory of the known Universe, before unattempted by any." He went on to report, perhaps a bit pretentiously, that he had unearthed these ideas from "the Mines of Nature . . . having been flattered into a Belief, that they may probably prove of some Use, or at least Amusement to the World. . . ."

Wright's seemingly boastful declaration that he had devised an "original" theory was not an exaggeration. With his *New Hypothesis of the Universe,* Wright became one of the first persons to consider the position of the Sun—its place in the heavens—in relation to the other stars, which he believed were not randomly distributed at all. He introduced the idea, now viewed as common sense, that our position in space affects how we perceive our celestial environment. He proposed that the Milky Way could be "no other than a certain effect arising from the observer's situation." From Wright would come the first compelling hint that the Milky Way, the known universe in its day, is a flat disk of stars. He dared to impose a particular configuration onto the heavens, an arrangement based more on observation than on fanciful myths. For a self-taught man, this was quite a surprising conception. Geography ruled the destiny of ancient Greece; for the universe, it is topography that heralds its fate. Future astronomers, following Wright's example, would learn to appreciate that an understanding of the universe's overall structure provides significant insights into the history of its birth and ultimately the nature (and amount) of its contents.

Wright was born in 1711 at Byer's Green, a small village six miles southwest of the town of Durham in northern England. The third son of a well-to-do carpenter, he taught himself some mathematics and was particularly keen—in fact, nearly fanatical—in studying astronomy in his leisure hours as a boy. At the age of thirteen, he apprenticed to a clock maker and later made mathematical instruments for a London firm. Wright eventually opened a school teaching mathematics and navigation to seamen, but his favorite pastime was serving as a private instructor for noble English families. He taught geometry to the daughters of Lord Cornwallis, hunted with the Earl of Halifax, and dined regularly for a time with the Duke and Duchess of Kent. His portrait, an engraving in profile, suggests a serious-minded man with double chin, prominent nose, and high forehead, the curls of the requisite peruke caressing his shoulders.

Though limited in formal education, Wright displayed a lively intelligence and was involved in an eclectic mix of endeavors. For one, he was a skilled craftsman and architect. The crenellations on the western towers of the famous Durham cathedral were refurbished based on his design. An accomplished engraver, Wright also published a lavishly illustrated book on Irish antiquities. By hovering on the fringes of high society, he enjoyed the good life, and his tutoring of the landed aristocracy enabled him to partake in their affluent life-style. Indeed, his major works on astronomy, which included tracts on a solar eclipse and a comet, as well as the Milky Way, were funded largely by these aristocratic benefactors.

Modern critics would probably describe Wright's writing style as awkward and ponderous. His scientific discussions are tediously laced with theological lessons and poetic quotations—but then, so were many other works in his day. Yet the elaborate illustrations in *New Hypothesis of the Universe,* thirty-two engravings in all, are a forerunner of the brilliant photographs included in modern-day astronomy books and more clearly convey his seminal ideas than does the text itself.

Hedging his bets, Wright offered a couple of explanations for the Milky Way's appearance. One model pictured the stars moving in a vast ring, much like the rings of Saturn, around a central point. But, strongly guided by religious views, he preferred to think of the Milky Way as a

English astronomer Thomas Wright
(1711–1786).
*Reproduced by permission from the copy in Durham
University Library*

thin spherical shell of stars, with the Earth and Sun off to one side and the
Eye of Providence, the "agent of creation," residing in the center. Wright's
celebrated diagram of the Milky Way—as a flat layer of stars—was actually a first step in imagining this huge shell. "I don't mean to affirm that
[the disk] really is so in Fact," he wrote, "but only state the Question thus,
to help your Imagination to conceive more aptly what I would explain."
Looking along the plane of a big, gently curving shell, in which the solar
system was embedded, earthly inhabitants would readily perceive a disklike structure. The Milky Way appears as a band, Wright mused, because
we observe this thin layer of stars edge-on; the combined light of its
innumerable stars produce the milk-white appearance. This also explains
why, when looking away from the plane, stargazers see fewer stars.

In 1751 Immanuel Kant, an aspiring scientist and private tutor on a
nobleman's estate near Königsberg, Prussia, happened to read a brief

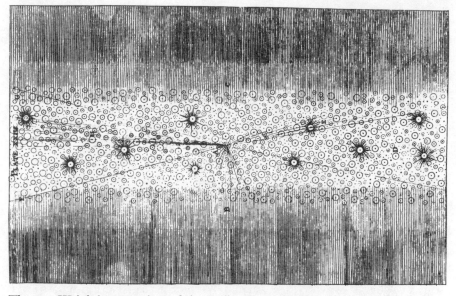

Thomas Wright's engraving of the Milky Way, depicting it as a disk of stars. *Reproduced by permission from the copy in Durham University Library*

summary of Wright's hypothesis in a Hamburg periodical, which selec-tively stressed the concept of the Milky Way as a disk of stars rather than a sphere. This was not surprising since Wright's engraving so wonderfully captured the disklike image. Although he never read Wright's original work, the young Kant was so inspired by the short journal account that he devised his own disklike theory of the Milky Way's structure in a book entitled *Allgemeine Naturgeschichte und Theorie des Himmels* (Universal Natural History and Theory of the Heavens). Published in 1755, this work was virtually ignored until, years later, Kant had achieved consid-erable fame as one of the great Western philosophers. Kant, particularly interested in the dynamics of a disklike Milky Way, had concluded that all the stars must be moving in large orbits around the disk's center; other-wise, according to Newton's law of gravitation, they would all gravitate toward one another, eventually disrupting the disk. Kant generously cred-ited Wright for this inspiration. Without such an acknowledgment, Wright's contributions, completely disregarded by English astronomers at the time, would probably have generated hardly a footnote in astro-nomical history.

A more rigorous, scientific proof of the Milky Way's structure was obtained within decades by William Herschel, eighteenth-century En-gland's Prince of Astronomy. Apparently unaware at first of both Wright's and Kant's speculations, Herschel embarked on a long-term program to investigate the true distribution of the stars, thus founding observational cosmology. By meticulously counting the stars that were visible in over six hundred distinct regions of the sky, and making the simplifying assumption that a high count was evidence of a greater distance to the border of the Milky Way system in that direction, he was able to report to the Royal Society in 1785 that the galaxy looked very much like a gigantic convex lens, filled with millions of stars. Its essential feature was its flatness. He figured that the diameter of this luminous disk was several hundred times the distance between the bright star Sirius and our Sun. Now knowing that Sirius is about nine light-years away, Herschel was estimating the Milky Way's span to be nearly 10,000 light-years from end to end. That is less than a tenth of the current estimate of the Milky Way's extent but a considerable dimension for its day.

The confirming observations undertaken by England's royal astronomer probably provided the amateur Wright no satisfaction whatsoever. More than a decade before Herschel announced his findings, Wright had already repudiated the idea of a universe in the form of a gently curving plane of stars. Always seeking to reconcile his scientific and religious views, he rejected his earlier work for some rather bizarre, medieval-sounding models of the universe, which to him were more theologically pleasing. In the draft of an essay entitled "Second or Singular Thoughts Upon the Theory of the Universe," he even considered the possibility that the cosmos consisted of an infinite sequence of concentric shells; our universe then became a solid sky—the inner surface of one of these shells—with "a vast chain of burning mountains" forming the stars and the material ejected from these volcanoes turning into comets.

Wright, a lifelong bachelor, retired to his birthplace in 1762. He died in 1786 (although he never married, he was survived by a daughter). He had just started constructing a small tower with Gothic windows, which was to be used as his private observatory. The dilapidated stone edifice still stands today on a high hill two miles from his former home, perhaps a fitting testament to the man who was almost famous.

THE COSMIC LANDSCAPE

Despite Wright's eventual misgivings concerning the *New Hypothesis*, his original legacy—the recognition that a deeper understanding of the universe may be revealed in its structure, in the way in which its varied objects are strewn across the celestial sky—lived on through Kant and even led to thoughts of worlds beyond the Milky Way. For countless decades, the misty band of the Milky Way had defined the complete extent of the known universe, which was understandable: The naked eye and, later, crude telescopes were limited to seeing only the near shores of space, not the far horizons. But astronomers in the eighteenth and nineteenth centuries still wondered about the nature of certain wispy patches of light in the nighttime sky that were preferentially located away from the plane of the Milky Way. Herschel sighted thousands of such nebulae during his many telescopic searches. The most prominent of these fuzzy formations, the Great Nebula in the Andromeda constellation, was even noted on star charts centuries before the invention of the telescope. Visible near the "Great Square" of the Pegasus constellation, Andromeda appears as a faint oval patch of light about half the diameter of the full Moon.

The ever-inventive Wright suggested that these cloudy spots, in which no individual star could be distinguished, were evidence for a "plenum of creations. . . . Those in all lykely hood may be external Creations," he wrote, "bordering upon the known one, too remote for even our telescopes to reach." Kant independently arrived at a similar conclusion and introduced to a wide audience the idea of "island universes," far-off cousins of our own galaxy. "Let us imagine a system of stars gathered together in a common plane, like those of the Milky Way, but situated so far away from us that even with the telescope we cannot distinguish the stars composing it . . . ," wrote Kant in 1755. "Such a stellar world will appear to the observer, who contemplates it at so enormous a distance, only as a little spot feebly illumined. . . ." By 1761 the Alsatian philosopher and scientist Johann Heinrich Lambert published his *Cosmological Letters,* which also spoke of a hierarchy of structures throughout the heavens, all controlled by gravitation. This was almost two hundred years before it was widely accepted that other galaxies even existed in the universe.

Yet eighteenth- and nineteenth-century astronomers were at the mercy of their instruments. Given the quality of their observations, it was just as likely that those enigmatic spots were celestial clouds caught at the borders of the Milky Way's disk. By the middle of the nineteenth century, the third Earl of Rosse, William Parsons, aimed his formidable seventy-two-inch reflecting telescope, situated at Birr Castle in Ireland, at the nebulae and noticed that many of the white nebulous patches in question exhibited a distinct spiral structure. With photography not yet introduced to astronomy, Lord Rosse captured the swirling patterns in drawings of splendid detail. He filled his notebooks with them. Many astronomers wondered whether these spirals were simply embryonic globular clusters or planetary systems in the making.

Firm answers finally arrived at the start of the twentieth century with the development of more powerful telescopic instruments, especially in the United States, a rising economic power. "Indeed, because of the success of American astronomers in securing research funds (available largely through newly wealthy entrepreneurs), the placing of expensive and powerful telescopes at good sites and the increasingly sophisticated training of American astronomers, the US emerged as the dominant power in observational cosmology," science historian Robert Smith of the Smithsonian Institution has noted. American astronomers ushered in the age of extragalactic studies—the examination of systems residing outside the borders of the Milky Way—when the massive Hooker telescope, with its immense 100-inch light-gathering mirror, was assembled atop California's Mount Wilson near Los Angeles.

Fresh from a stint in the army during World War I, Edwin Hubble arrived at Mount Wilson in 1919 and proceeded to employ the new telescope (in general use only a few days after his arrival) to follow up on the doctoral thesis he had completed two years earlier at the University of Chicago. An aloof—some would say arrogant—man, Hubble determinedly continued his mission to discern the true nature of those spiraling nebulae. "Suppose them to be extra-sidereal and perhaps we see clusters of galaxies," Hubble had pondered in his thesis. "Suppose them within our system [the Milky Way], their nature becomes a mystery."

Patiently working with the giant reflector over several years, the sparks from his ever-present pipe cutting the dome's darkness, Hubble was finally able to resolve individual Cepheid variable stars on the outskirts of Andromeda and two other spiraling nebulae. The period of the Cepheids' incessant blinking, together with the extreme faintness of their magnitudes, enabled Hubble in 1924 to establish that the nebulae were located far out in space, in a region beyond the shores of the Milky Way. Without a doubt, the spiraling nebulae were independent systems of stars, as many had already suspected. When the venerable Harlow Shapley, one of the last holdouts to the Kantian philosophy, saw the proof before him in a letter from Hubble, he declared, "Here is the letter that has destroyed my universe." The Milky Way, long esteemed as the sole cosmic empire, now turned out to be but one of many galactic kingdoms (what Kant called his "island universes") inhabiting the seemingly endless vacancies of space. Andromeda, the spiral galaxy closest to us, resides some two million light-years away.

Like some extragalactic taxonomist, Hubble, then in his mid-thirties, quickly divided the galaxies he observed into various classes. Along with the spirals, those gigantic stellar pinwheels, he recognized the dense, egg-shaped elliptical galaxies. He also noticed some rather loose aggregations, known as "irregular" galaxies. The Magellanic Clouds, the crown jewels of the southern celestial hemisphere, are examples of this type: chaotic clumps of stars immersed in a rich sea of gas.

With the help of his able assistant Milton Humason, Hubble later confirmed that these far-off galaxies are flying away from one another as the universe expands, a consequence already anticipated by theorists looking into Einstein's new theory of general relativity. Previously trained in law as a Rhodes scholar at Oxford University, Hubble painstakingly (and very cautiously) orchestrated an airtight case to convince the skeptical: Space time was steadily swelling, and galaxies were going along for the ride. Hubble and Humason knew this because the light waves emitted by these galaxies are being stretched and thereby reddened as the universe balloons outward. More specific, Hubble and Humason discovered what has come to be known as the Hubble law, the principle that the farther away a galaxy is situated from us, the faster it recedes, which causes the galaxy's light waves to shift more and more toward the red end of the electromagnetic spectrum. Consequently, a galaxy's redshift became a rough indicator of its distance from our home galaxy, at last providing the means to map the universe, the most extensive unexplored territory of all.[1] "To the cosmologist," says Martin Rees, "entire galaxies are just 'markers' or test particles scattered through space which indicate how the material content of the universe is distributed and how it is moving."

The desire to survey the world, to fix its shape and size and one's own place in it—in short, the desire to make maps—is rooted deep in human nature. Prehistoric humans probably scratched directions to water holes or game trails on bits of bark. One of the oldest surviving maps of the

---

[1] Despite his renown for providing the observational evidence for an expanding universe, Hubble did have his doubts, especially when the farthest galaxies measured in his day were observed to recede from us at velocities of thousands of miles per second, an appreciable fraction of the speed of light. For a time, Hubble wondered whether an unrecognized law of physics, instead of a Doppler shift, was at work.

whole Earth is a clay tablet, carved around 1000 B.C. by a nameless Babylonian who depicted his world as a disk with Babylon at the center. The mapmaker's art reached its ancient zenith when the Alexandrian geographer Ptolemy produced his sketchy outlines of landmasses and oceans; thirteen centuries later (the Dark Ages having intervened), Ptolemy's maps still served as the best guide available to Columbus. Today, with the last traces of terra incognita removed from maps of Earth, and with space probes having poked into nearly every corner of the solar system, astronomers are starting work on the greatest map of all—a map of the universe.

In some ways, this job is more formidable than the one faced by Greek or Roman mapmakers before the age of exploration. Where the ancients could measure, triangulate, and probe their surroundings directly, celestial surveyors must collect and interpret mere photons of light arriving at telescopes in order to map the vast cosmic landscape. Their territory is an expanding space-time that encompasses a volume billions of light-years across.

Discerning the exact way in which galaxies are strewn throughout the universe was a decidedly difficult task when the field of extragalactic astronomy was first established. In Hubble's day, redshifts were a bit tricky to measure. Humason, an accomplished observer who had started out as a mule driver for the Mount Wilson Observatory, had to sit for hours at his telescope to record the spectrum of just one galaxy; sometimes, for the very faintest galaxies, the photographic plate had to be exposed to the sparse dribbles of light over several nights. Even as late as 1960, only several hundred galactic redshifts had been determined, out of the hundreds of thousands of galaxies then visible to astronomers. Given these technical obstacles, astronomers were generally content to just keep track of a galaxy's position on the surface of the sky, noting its celestial longitude and latitude, so to speak, in various catalogues.

Solely noting a galaxy's position on the sky, though, was valuable in its own right. Once galaxies were discovered, the world's leading galactic surveyors—astronomers such as Edwin Hubble, Harlow Shapley, George Abell, and Fritz Zwicky—promptly noticed that many of the galaxies gathered into small groups and even larger clusters. Such mingling is brought about by gravity. Although space-time is continually stretching, moving most galaxies away from one another, gravity is still strong enough to keep close neighbors together and to draw them closer. Our own Milky Way galaxy is part of a small aggregation known as the Local

Group. Its twenty-some members, including the majestic Andromeda spiral, inhabit a region approximately four million light-years wide, but by cosmic standards such a grouping is a veritable pip-squeak. The famous Coma cluster, located 300 million light-years away in the direction of the constellation Coma Berenices, contains thousands of galaxies.

Yet extragalactic astronomers still assumed that over much larger distances this clumpiness would eventually smooth out, the way choppy ocean waves seemingly disappear when viewed from a plane flying high above the sea. In the 1930s, from his lifelong post at the prestigious Mount Wilson Observatory, Hubble declared that the universe was "sensibly uniform," that the galaxies and clusters were distributed fairly evenly throughout the cosmos. And this belief, coming as it did from the world-renowned "emperor" of astronomy, was upheld almost as a law of nature. It became the cosmological principle: The universe was as unvarying and homogeneous as a well-blended daiquiri.

Discussions were certainly held on whether there might be larger lumps—clusters of clusters and so on—in that vast smoothness. The existence of some rather large clouds of galaxies, which appeared to be strung across the heavens, was even noted in the literature. But the phenomenon was never systematically studied until the latter half of this century. A feisty and determined French astronomer named Gérard de Vaucouleurs, now with the University of Texas at Austin, was especially vocal in questioning the cosmological principle, by then firmly entrenched. In the early 1950s, de Vaucouleurs, newly graduated from the Sorbonne, journeyed to the Mount Stromlo Observatory in Australia to revise one of astronomy's Bibles, the Shapley-Ames catalogue of bright galaxies. While updating and correcting the catalogue's listing of southern galaxies, he began to notice that the Milky Way and its neighbors in the Local Group were situated at the edge of a much larger system of galaxies that, together, form a somewhat flattened disk. Viewed edge-on, this disk appears on galaxy maps as a long band that stretches across both the northern and the southern skies. The rich Virgo cluster of galaxies, some fifty million light-years distant, serves as the centerpiece of this enormous system.

This was not a totally new revelation. In the 1920s the Swedish astronomer Knut Lundmark, among others, reported that bright spiral galaxies appeared "to crowd around a belt perpendicular to the Milky Way." But de Vaucouleurs, inspired and encouraged by Vera Rubin's report on galaxy motions at the 1950 American Astronomical Society meeting, was willing to venture that this grouping was a distinct object in the heavens. He dubbed it the "Local Supergalaxy." Overall, this somewhat flattened grouping has a diameter of tens of millions of light-years. Today, astronomers refer to this distinctive collection of galaxies as the Local Supercluster, but when de Vaucouleurs first made his suggestion, he recalls that it "was received with resounding silence." Zwicky, for one, detested the concept of clusters of clusters and refused to believe that the universe displayed such a high level of organization. De Vaucouleurs suspects the idea was also resisted because it made life more complicated for those attempting to measure the universe's rate of expansion, cosmology's Holy Grail; such calculations are made easier when a uniform universe is postulated. In 1961 the American astronomer George Abell compiled a list of other prospective superclusters, lumpy intruders in the universe's supposedly monotonous landscape, but it still took nearly a quarter of a century for the word *supercluster* to enter astronomy's standard vocabulary.

A revolution in technology was instrumental in convincing astronomers that the cosmos exhibited a distinctly irregular texture over very large scales. By the 1970s, as observatories replaced light-squandering photographic plates with more efficient electronic detectors, such as CCDs, it finally became possible to determine a galaxy's redshift in a matter of minutes or half-hours rather than an entire night. Perhaps more important, the redshift measurement of some far galaxy that once required such gargantuan telescopes as the 200-inch instrument on California's Palomar Mountain could now be done on a more modest-sized telescope. Armed with this new equipment, astronomers began surveying other populous regions of the celestial sky, only to affirm the existence of additional superclusters, beyond our Local Supercluster. The Coma cluster, for instance, appears to be just one part of a much larger association of galaxies; a bridgelike connection joins Coma with another cluster. Superclusters were also found to meander through the constellations of Ursa Major and Lynx, through Pavo, Indus, and Telescopium, and through Hydra and Centaurus. One of the most spectacular of these formations is the Perseus-Pisces supercluster, which forms a gently curving sheet that stretches across a long swath of the northern heavens.

With superclusters becoming the rule rather than the exception, extragalactic surveyors began to suggest that all these filamentary chains of galaxies connected up to form a lacy web of superclusters, a crochet of galaxies winding their way through the cosmos. This vision was especially championed in the East, by both Soviet theorists and a group of Estonian astronomers. In 1980 Jaan Einasto, Mihkel Jôeveer, and Enn Saar reported that the "vast majority of galaxies belong to cluster chains. . . . The system of cluster chains resembles a string polyhedron. . . . It seems reasonable to associate superclusters with polyhedron walls. . . . This distribution resembles cells." To the Estonians, the universe displayed a distinct cellular structure.

Redshift surveyors were perhaps more surprised by what they *didn't* find. In between the superclusters, astronomers began discerning huge regions of space—immense voids—that appeared nearly empty of galaxies. An important property of the universe's structure might be where *nothing* is found. The most dramatic of these cosmic abysses was revealed in 1981 in the vicinity of the Boötes constellation. This Boötes void, a monstrous sphere of space with virtually no bright galaxies, spans nearly 300 million light-years from end to end. In the popular press, it became the "hole in space" that defied explanation.

There had been hints of such patterns earlier, even before observers started mapping specific voids and superclusters. With redshifts scarce, theorists who were interested in analyzing the distribution of galaxies had sought out catalogues of galaxies, which simply listed the galaxies' positions on the celestial sky. In the early 1970s, Princeton astrophysicist P. James E. Peebles especially turned to the extensive Shane-Wirtanen survey to help him describe, in mathematical terms, just how clumpy the universe really is. He decided to take a cosmic census. Given the position of one galaxy, he asked, what were the odds of finding another galaxy at some specified distance on the celestial sphere? What were its chances of being a member of a cluster? Other researchers had also attempted the proof before Peebles did (including Vera Rubin for her doctoral thesis), but all had lacked both the data and the computational machinery to establish an unambiguous answer. Through such statistics, theorists hoped to glean important clues on one of astronomy's outstanding mysteries—how galaxies came to be born. "What fascinated me," Peebles has recalled, "was the thought that if we could understand the way that galaxies clumped, we might be able to understand how the universe came to be the way it is." Since the galaxies' positions today are the end products of yesteryear's tumultuous era of galaxy formation, their distribution serves as a map through time, back to the era when galaxies were first condensing. To Harvard astronomer Robert Kirshner, one of the discoverers of the Boötes void, this galactic venture can be compared to the way an archaeologist gleans clues from a culture's past. "Just as the texture of an antique fabric is the result of the vanished loom that made it," Kirshner has noted, "the present texture of the universe is a result of physical processes operating in a distant and inaccessible epoch."

The Shane-Wirtanen survey, a remarkable undertaking by Lick Observatory astronomers C. Donald Shane and Carl Wirtanen in the 1950s, counted all the myriad galaxies in the northern sky down to the nineteenth magnitude, objects as much as one billion light-years distant.[2] Using this immense pool of data, Jim Peebles and a small army of associates, many of them postdocs or graduate students working on dissertations, verified that galaxies are not just randomly scattered over the sky but congregate in ways that can be mathematically defined. More intriguing, the way in which the galaxies assembled themselves seemed to require the presence of extra, dark matter throughout the universe. A universe sparse of matter and constantly expanding, Peebles figured, would not have had the gravitational power to round up such a rich array of galaxy groups and clusters. It was a harbinger of the great dark-matter debates to come.

While trudging through their statistics, the Princeton researchers also plotted the Shane-Wirtanen galaxy counts onto a two-dimensional map of the celestial sky. The eye-catching result was turned into a popular poster entitled "One Million Galaxies." Although this map portrays only galaxy counts, with galaxies both near and far piled up on one another at their specified position on the grid, the picture is alluring nonetheless. Standing back from it, a viewer can perceive the universe as a network of knotlike galaxy clusters, curving filaments, and empty voids. It is a bewitching mosaic of great richness and texture.

But were these fascinating features, crawling all over the famous poster, no more than statistical flukes, the eye picking out patterns in a random assortment of objects? Were they only illusions? asked Peebles and others. Could they be the galactic equivalent of the infamous canals that some nineteenth-century astronomers were so sure traversed the surface of Mars (and were undoubtedly constructed by intelligent beings)? Certainty was elusive, for what was missing in these discussions of a possible cosmic texture was that vital third point of reference—knowl-

---

[2] The higher the magnitude, the dimmer the object. Magnitude 6, for example, is exactly one hundred times fainter than magnitude 1, which is the brightness of a star like Antares. Some of the faintest objects yet photographed are around magnitude 26 and 27.

edge of each and every galaxy's actual distance in space. Astronomy needed to dive into the very depths of the universe.

MAPPING THE UNIVERSE

John Huchra exudes an air of tell-it-like-it-is, his conversation occasionally sprinkled with the colorful expletive for emphasis. To cap this image, the bearded and bespectacled astronomer, stocky in build, is almost never seen without his jaunty brown hat, the same kind worn by moviedom's Indiana Jones. A witty, nonstop storyteller, Huchra majored in physics as an undergraduate at MIT and helped pay his way through college by working as a teamster, unloading trucks every summer in New Jersey. More interested in stars than defense work, he switched to astronomy as a graduate student and journeyed westward to pursue his Ph.D. at MIT's California rival, Caltech.

Huchra often likes to describe himself (with an explicit wink of the eye) as Wal Sargent's "dumbest graduate student." In the early 1970s, while his friends in the Caltech astronomy department were fully funded to conduct their graduate research, Huchra had to supplement his income by manning the eighteen-inch Schmidt telescope on Palomar Mountain in search of supernovae, a continuation of Fritz Zwicky's original endeavor. There were some side benefits, however: Huchra relocated the asteroid Ganymed, which had been "lost" since the 1930s, and his find sparked others to seek out new or lost Apollo asteroids. He also discovered a comet, now known as Comet Huchra, although it will take some time for this comet to become famous—unlike Halley's comet, which periodically flies by the Earth every seventy-six or so years, Huchra's comet won't be returning until the year 2885.

Huchra's doctoral dissertation, completed in 1976, involved starbursting galaxies, but he would soon specialize in charting galaxies when he arrived at the Harvard-Smithsonian Center for Astrophysics (CfA) to launch his professional career. It was at the CfA, the union of the Harvard Observatory with the Smithsonian Astrophysical Observatory, that Huchra met both Margaret Geller and Marc Davis.

Encouraged by Geller, a Peebles' protégée while a graduate student at Princeton, Davis was eager to conduct a comprehensive redshift survey, using a sixty-inch telescope at the center's observing post on Mount Hopkins in Arizona. Davis himself was a Princeton alumnus, and Peebles' statistical work there was beginning to persuade astronomers that a three-dimensional map of the heavens, rich in detail and more sweeping than the mapping of specific superclusters, could shed some much-needed light on cosmology's biggest questions; for instance, from what shadowy origins did the galaxies, those prolific cosmic denizens, arise? But Davis's decision was a chancy one. Young researchers ordinarily avoided such long-term, dedicated projects because they didn't advance careers. In some university departments, such tedious data gathering was considered more akin to butterfly collecting than frontier, tenure-getting research. Yet the raw numbers would be manna to the data-starved field of cosmology.

Unable to raise a quarter of a million dollars to buy the latest commercial electronic instrumentation that was desperately needed for such an ambitious project, Davis and colleague David Latham built their own telescopic detector for $25,000, based on a design by Stephen Shectman. The first leg of the project, just getting the moribund sixty-inch telescope into working order, was a struggle. "We had to completely rebuild the spectrograph, assemble the detector, install a computer system, and write the operating software," notes Davis. They were embarking on no less than the galactic equivalent of Herschel's ambitious scheme to map the distribution of the stars two centuries earlier.

By the spring of 1978, after great Sturm und Drang, the CfA system was finally up and running. Because of his crafty ability to make a telescope "sing," the result of all those nights atop Palomar Mountain with the eighteen-inch telescope, Huchra joined forces with Davis to oversee the redshift measurements. Huchra had already put Davis onto Shectman's detector design and had helped Latham rebuild the spectrograph. Graduate student John Tonry whipped the computer software into shape. For some two hundred nights, over a period of three years, the Harvard-Smithsonian team pegged the redshifts of some 2,400 galaxies over a third of the celestial sphere, out to a distance of nearly 300 million light-years. This was a depth several times farther out than the Local Super-cluster. It was a reconnaissance mission of cosmic dimensions.

Upon finishing their initial scan, the CfA survey team plotted its results and reported that the map's panorama of extragalactic space appeared to display filamentary "patterns of connectedness surrounding empty holes on the sky." In their eyes, the distribution of galaxies could best be described as "frothy." Davis tried to persuade others, particularly Peebles, that there were specific hints of a spongy cosmic architecture in the pioneering CfA map. Peebles wasn't as yet convinced, but, nevertheless, the talk of voids and threadlike superclusters snaking through the universe was getting louder and louder within the astronomical community; in 1981, discovery of the colossal void in Boötes especially was generating headlines. Supporters of a cellular universe—and their numbers were growing—pointed to the CfA survey as proof of the lacy panoply of superclusters. Yet there was another contingent of astronomers, those still skeptical of large-scale structures, such as Peebles, who regarded the Boötes void principally as a freak and, upon viewing the first CfA map, declared that Hubble's edict of a bland, homogeneous universe still appeared quite viable. Hubble had died in 1953, but his gospel of uniformity, over very large scales, hung on tenaciously.

What the new data did offer was an exciting new avenue of exploration. The growing power of computers was enabling researchers to begin simulating the birth of galaxies. And the challenge for these new digital investigators was to match their results with the latest maps of the universe. A reasonable replication, it was assumed, might even help them decide the general composition of the heavens, the predominant material that was at work in erecting the universe's structures. Within those computer-generated charts were the vestiges of the universe's past and an inkling of its future.

THE GANG OF FOUR

In Durham, England, where Thomas Wright made such a bold attempt at formulating a post-Newtonian cosmology more than two centuries ago, Carlos Frenk continues to speculate on the nature and structure of the universe. But whereas Wright played out a variety of cosmic models, both inspired and eccentric, within his fertile imagination, Frenk conducts his more rigorous theoretical musings on a computer at the University of Durham.

Frenk, a convivial Mexican of German-Spanish descent, runs a hand through his straight black hair. His steel-rimmed glasses are unable to hide his warm brown eyes, and a smile or a laugh breaks out across his mustachioed face at least once a minute. He sits in his favorite Durham pub, just a few minutes' walk from the university's physics building. The stuffed chairs, gilded mirrors, and small wooden tables evoke an atmosphere that matches the pub's name—The Victoria.

"This is my local pub. I feel comfortable here," he says with a nod at the room. "I know the streets, I know the houses, and I know the neighbors. This is the local part of my personal universe. The term 'local' is a psychological state. You're familiar—at ease—with things that are local. I wasn't around in the sixteenth century, but I imagine that the scientists then felt that their local universe was the solar system. They were comfortable with it and could understand it to some extent. The next big step was to regard the Milky Way galaxy as a local environment. That took about four hundred years. We know how it's laid out, we know how it works, we know which direction we're going. Then we soon went from the local galaxy to the local collection of galaxies. If you asked astronomers these days, 'What's your local astronomical pub?' they'd probably say the Local Supercluster."

After majoring in physics at the National University in Mexico City, Frenk had no intention of working in astronomy. "I could imagine the size of an atom, if I tried really hard, and I could picture an atomic nucleus. But a galaxy or cluster of galaxies was beyond me; it was too overpowering, too awesome," asserts Frenk. "Certain words often separate a physicist from an astronomer. I was taught physics in terms of centimeters. Megaparsecs were something else!"

But a meeting with Martin Rees, a charismatic figure at Cambridge University's Institute of Astronomy, inspired Frenk and convinced him to pursue a graduate degree in astrophysics, despite Frenk's lack of expertise. "Cosmology was almost an amateur activity back then. It hadn't yet become the mega-enterprise that it is today," he recalls. "With about two weeks of dedicated study, you could catch up on the subject and practically be on par with the experts."

For Frenk, the mid-1970s at Cambridge was a special, invigorating time. Only a decade earlier, the big bang theory of the universe had at last triumphed over the steady-state model when the remnant echo of the primeval explosion was detected with a radio telescope on the East Coast of the United States. At teatime discussions, punctually held at four o'clock in the afternoon, students and faculty at the institute could be heard championing their favorite method for forming galaxies.

Soviet theorist *extraordinaire* Yakov Zel'dovich, the irrepressible and ebullient mentor to an entire generation of Soviet astrophysicists (as well as one of the key designers of the Soviet hydrogen bomb), had recently introduced a theory of galaxy formation that came to be known as the "top-down" model because it envisions galaxies fragmenting from larger, primordial structures. According to this scenario, flat gargantuan clouds of gas were the first entities to emerge right after the big bang. One might ask why the uniform sea of particles, spewed from the big bang, broke up at all; it obviously did, as witnessed by the myriad galaxies dotting the celestial sky. To explain this fragmentation, most theories of galaxy formation start with the premise that the primeval blast somehow sent a series of waves rippling through the newly born sea of particles, both large and small fluctuations in the density of the gas. The theory of inflation now suggests that these waves originated around the era of grand unification, 10^{-35} second after the big bang, when quantum jitters first stirred up the primordial plasma.

It was a triumph for astronomers in 1992 when NASA's COBE satellite at last detected these primeval ripples. They appear as very slight differences in temperature, as little as $\frac{1}{100,000}$ of a degree, in the overall wash of microwave radiation that emanated from the big bang and now fills the universe. These patches on the celestial sky, where temperatures are either slightly higher or slightly lower than surrounding areas, mark off the regions of the early universe that once had slightly greater or slightly lesser concentrations of matter. Here, preserved like fossils, are the first structures to have arisen out of the smooth primordial plasma, the template out of which grew the galaxies, clusters of galaxies, and the great voids in space.

When Zel'dovich first theorized such ripples, decades before they were actually detected, he imagined that fast-moving photons in the early universe might have completely damped the "tiny" galaxy-sized ripples, giving the large-scale undulations free rein. As these monstrous waves moved through the cosmos, they allegedly broke the smooth and ancient ocean of matter into supercluster-sized segments.

Each of these "pancakes," as the Soviet researchers amusingly dubbed the primordial clouds, would have stretched over tens of millions of light-years and contained enough material to form some 1,000 trillion suns. Galaxies came about, argued Zel'dovich and his colleagues, as turbulence and shock waves fragmented each massive sheet into smaller sections, like pieces breaking off a gigantic slab of peanut brittle; and the newly sighted voids and cigarlike filaments would appear quite naturally as the pancakes, initially scattered about randomly, collapsed and intersected over time. It was even suspected that superclusters, each supposedly forged from a separate pancake, might ultimately connect to form a network of cells, weaving a pattern that resembled a lace tablecloth throughout the cosmos. Members of Zel'dovich's group saw such patterns emerge when they carried out computer simulations of the process.

But the top-down theory is a relative newcomer when it comes to explaining galaxy formation. Its major competitor is an older, more conservative hypothesis of "hierarchical clustering," a process that forges galactic structure in the exact opposite direction as in the top-down scheme. Long championed by Princeton's Peebles, hierarchical clustering has galaxies forming first, then gravitationally gathering into clusters and, later, superclusters as the universe expands and evolves. The universe comes to participate in a giant game of building blocks. Not surprisingly, the theory has been loosely tagged the "bottom-up" model, since it claims that smaller knots of matter, pushed and squeezed by those ripples emanating from the big bang, would be the first entities to coalesce.

Such were the options being avidly discussed at Cambridge, where Frenk first met Simon White, then a fellow at Churchill College who was earning kudos for his seminal computer work on the formation of galaxies and clusters. "I would walk from the institute over to the Cavendish Laboratory, which housed a station connected to Cambridge's central IBM computer," recalls White. "There I tried to persuade my rather large box of cards to go through the card reader. And, in those days, before the invention of the laser printer, the pen-and-ink plotter would wear out drawing my hundreds of tiny circles on top of one another."

Working with Rees in 1977, White showed how ordinary matter might condense out of a primeval cloud, which was composed primarily of dark, unknown matter, to form the luminous galaxies so familiar to us today. In the picture painted by White and Rees, the nascent heavens at first look like a regular soup, a hefty broth of dark matter smattered with ordinary gas, mostly hydrogen and helium. Yet soon the two diverse ingredients, light and dark, begin to separate, creating a rather lumpy cosmic stew. At some point, the hydrogen and helium start to radiate away their energy; cooling in the process, the gases sink to the center of the dark clump, forming what we now call a galaxy. In the meantime, the dark particles, whatever they might be and which by definition cannot radiate brightly, remain suspended in and around the nuggets of shining matter. The luminous galaxies thus become embedded in dark halos, like white raisins in a chocolate pudding. It was one of the first times in the scientific literature that luminous matter was relegated to a subsidiary role in an astrophysical process, with the mysterious dark matter taking center stage.

A tall and lanky Britisher from Cornwall, his hair a mass of tousled brown curls, White can often be spotted at astronomy conferences clutching a well-worn leather case bulging with papers. "We had this unwritten rule," says Frenk of his friendship with White. "Outside the confines of the Institute of Astronomy we would not talk about science. And inside, we would not talk about anything *but* science. We'd switch from one to the other as we crossed the road." After a brief pause, Frenk sheepishly confesses that the rule was soon broken, "when we started working in the pubs."

Over pints of dark English beer, Frenk and White avidly debated their pet theories on the origin of structure in the universe. When White moved on to the University of California at Berkeley in 1980, he arranged for Frenk, then finishing his thesis on the origin of globular clusters, to join him a year later. By that time Marc Davis, who had recently transferred from Harvard to a more receptive Berkeley, had an idea.

"Marc taught me a very big lesson," says Frenk. "If you think small, you'll only accomplish small things, but if you think big, you'll get big things done. It's an American way of thinking that is very different from the European. It's the same mentality that led to the construction of America's great telescope projects."

It was a fortuitous convergence of interests. Having just supervised the CfA redshift survey, the first major attempt at obtaining a comprehensive, three-dimensional view of the heavens, Davis was anxious to figure out how the galaxies came to be distributed in such a "frothy" manner. At the same time, White aspired to extend his pioneering computer simulations to the universe at large, to see how newborn galaxies might move outward in an expanding space-time and subsequently interact through the simple force of gravity. Initial attempts by such early computer cosmologists as Cambridge's Sverre Aarseth, from whom White had borrowed the numerical codes for his first simulations, were proving interesting, yet they still remained crude.

The prolific genius Isaac Newton appears to have anticipated, centuries earlier, such simulations of the universe's development. In a letter Newton had remarked:

It seems to me, that if the matter of our sun and planets and all the matter of the universe were evenly scattered throughout all heavens, and every particle had an innate gravity toward all the rest, and . . . if the matter were evenly disposed throughout an infinite space, it could never convene into one mass; but some of it would convene into one mass and some into another, so as to make an infinite number of great masses, scattered at great distances from one another throughout all that infinite space. And thus might the sun and fixed stars be formed. . . .

Newton's law of gravity can be exceedingly simple to apply when dealing with just two bodies or masses. Things get more complicated when three or more masses are involved. The great nineteenth-century French mathematician Jules Henri Poincaré spent a good part of his life trying to solve the "three-body" problem, only to discover that it had no exact solution. A computer, on the other hand, can manage an approximation fairly well by keeping track of a vast number of gravitating particles—as many as its electronic memory can manipulate.

Before the days of digital computers, though, these calculations, known as N-body simulations, were primitive indeed. In the 1940s, at Sweden's Lund Observatory, Erik Holmberg set up an array of seventy-four movable light bulbs (his N-number of bodies) to simulate the close passage and interaction of two disk galaxies. Since light intensity diminishes with distance, in the exact same way that the force of gravity does, Holmberg could assume that each bulb represented a clump of gravitating mass. In this way, the light intensity measured with a photocell at each bulb's position established the total "force" that particular light bulb felt as a result of the presence of all the other bulbs. Once the gravitational force was calculated, Holmberg moved each light bulb (his bit of a galaxy) accordingly. Step by step, a picture of the cosmic collision emerged. The outcome was impressive: Each galactic disk developed spiraling arms as a result of its "enlightening" encounter.

Even after scientists were able to progress from light bulbs to computers, difficulties arose as more and more masses were included in the calculations. A sizable number of particles must be considered to make the simulation of a physical system realistic, but computing all the complex interactions between those multiple bodies requires more and more time as the number of particles increases. Even with the most powerful computer now on the market, it could take the age of the universe to compute anything interesting if you deal with each and every particle individually in your computer program. The trick in the field of computer simulations has been devising mathematical shortcuts to handle these calculations relatively quickly and easily.

By the 1970s, with the mathematical techniques in hand, astrophysicists were replicating the motions of stars within globular clusters and taking their first tentative steps in simulating the evolution of the early universe by adding in the numerical codes necessary to describe an expanding cosmos. Just dealing with a few hundred particles, each representing an individual galaxy, could use up a scientist's allocation of computer time for a year. Peebles accidentally got the game started in the summer of 1969 when he visited the Los Alamos National Laboratory and, looking for something to do during his month's stay, decided to use the lab's state-of-the-art mainframe computer to mimic the development of a cluster of galaxies.

In the spring of 1980, the infant field of computer cosmology was particularly energized when Russian and American experimenters suggested that the elusive neutrino might have a tiny yet discernible mass. From earlier analyses, the Hungarian theorist Alex Szalay already realized that, if the evidence were genuine, neutrinos would have completely controlled the overall structure of the heavens. Neutrinos arc so abundant, far outnumbering the particles of ordinary matter, that if they have the slightest mass, say $\frac{1}{20,000}$ the weight of an electron, then they could provide the critical density of an omega of 1, thus rewriting the entire history of the universe's evolution.

Zel'dovich and his Soviet colleagues found neutrinos especially attractive because they provided the perfect mechanism for their top-down theory of galactic formation—the idea that immense pancakes of matter, spanning millions of light-years, emerged first after our cosmic birth and then later fragmented to form galaxies. Szalay had seen that, with a little mass, neutrinos can accomplish this job with ease. Imagine the infant universe as a sea of particles. This sea, however, is not perfectly smooth. Reverberations from the big bang are, in some sense, "ruffling its surface." Moving at speeds near that of light, massive neutrinos wipe out the small-scale ripples, leaving only the very largest undulations to corral the phantom particles into a multitude of gigantic clouds, the size of today's superclusters. These giant clouds—the pancakes—act like gravitational traps. Ordinary matter, which settles out of the cosmic sea after the neutrinos do, is drawn by gravity into those ready-made neutrino clouds, like water into a whirlpool. The dark matter, if you like, carves a system of gravitational highways through the cosmos that the luminous galaxies must follow. A memory of the universe's initial conditions is thus retained in the pattern of its present-day structures. Neutrinos, it was thought, could be the dark, unseen mass hovering in and around galaxy clusters.

In the Soviet Union, physicists Sergei Shandarin and Anatoli Klypin produced the first computer simulations of a neutrino-dominated universe. Excitement arose when these early computations appeared to match the celestial voids and filamentary superclusters then being spotted in the real sky. It seemed that the evanescent neutrinos couldn't help but fabricate the immense structures, so hard to explain in any other way. Shandarin, a disciple of Zel'dovich and the top-down school, had been generating his cosmic pancakes and filaments on a crude Soviet computer. "It was known as the Large Electronic Computing Machine," recalls Shandarin, a dark and heavyset man who has since moved with his family to the University of Kansas. Constructed out of transistors, according to Shandarin, "instead of integrated circuits, it was very sensitive to heat and often broke down." Limited at first to displaying his results as pages and pages of numbers, Shandarin was finally able to make some graphs (by hand, though, because of a lack of equipment) in 1981, and he showed them off at a conference in Italy. A very interested Simon White was in the audience.

"Although people often used the word 'pancake' in regard to a neutrino universe, I was struck by the fact that Sergei's picture looked filamentary," recalls White. "There was a central blob, surmounted on one side by a bulge. And with two cylindrical 'filaments' sticking out of the bottom, I came to think of his figure as the 'Cosmic Chicken.'"

The dark-matter mystery appeared on the brink of a solution, and several astrophysicists, including White, quickly scrambled to their computers to build on Shandarin's initial foray. Computers have introduced a new instrument into an astronomer's toolbox, allowing a researcher to directly tweak the cosmos, or at least to produce a reasonable facsimile of the cosmos's behavior. Re-creating the birth of galaxies, formerly an inaccessible realm, now requires only a sufficiently powerful computer and the appropriate software. Mathematical "particles" represent the matter that forms galaxies; these galaxies, in turn, then grow and evolve over time, shaped by the dictates of gravity. Eons speed by in minutes. Often an astronomical theory cannot be evaluated for years, until the data are at hand. But, in the meantime, a computer offers a means of both testing the model beforehand and graphically simulating regions or events unreachable by either telescope or space probe.

The Berkeley team of Davis, Frenk, and White joined the effort with their own simulation of a neutrino-filled universe. It involved some one thousand particles and one hundred hours of computer time, a vast amount in its day. They, too, wrote a paper praising the virtues of massive neutrinos, especially their ability to create immense structures. "But we had a sentence at the end of one of our papers pointing out a potential problem," says Frenk. When the neutrino clouds in their simulation did crystallize, the distribution of galaxies was unusually tidy. Eerily tidy. "We discovered that a neutrino universe produced voids and filaments much too cleanly and efficiently," explains White. When galaxies did emerge in the computer runs, they ended up huddling in dense knotty clusters that didn't resemble anything in the real sky. Given these problems, the Berkeley team eventually concluded that it might be wise to look elsewhere for a resolution of the nature of the dark matter.

This finding reverberated through the astrophysical community. As the 1980s wore on, other clues emerged that cast considerable doubt on neutrinos as the missing mass. Astronomer Marc Aaronson, from his perch at the Multiple Mirror Telescope, was finding evidence that dark matter was hovering around tiny dwarf galaxies, a troublesome discovery for neutrino aficionados. Energetic neutrinos can't settle down into a space the size of a dwarf galaxy. It would be like trying to corral a swarm of angry bees—it is hard to stuff the frisky particles in. And, in the laboratory, no one was able to duplicate the neutrino-experiment results and so confirm that the neutrino did indeed have a measurable mass. Without mass, neutrinos are fated to whiz through the universe unabated, oblivious to ordinary matter. The neutrino, for so long the darling of the missing-mass set, was proving problematic, and eventually the ghostly particle fell out of favor as a dark-matter contender.

But that hardly stopped the dark-matter campaign. Very quickly, astrophysicists turned to the host of other elementary particles imagined by physicists in their quest to unify the forces, particles such as gravitinos, photinos, axions, and other assorted WIMP's. Where neutrinos are fast moving, and so considered "hot," the hypothetical WIMPs act differently. By the figurings of WIMP specialists, these particles would move much slower, at least when compared with the neutrinos. Being less energetic, the new contenders were promptly christened "cold dark matter," or simply CDM. Moreover, here was the stuff that could accommodate the bottom-up scenario exquisitely—the dark matter that would nicely coalesce around objects as small as dwarf galaxies. Whereas fast-moving neutrinos can forge only big structures first, cold dark matter, being more sluggish, initially constructs smaller building blocks, which then merge and consolidate into bigger and bigger galactic entities. The question was whether a computer simulation of this process would resemble the real universe, as depicted in Davis's CfA map. Simulating a universe of cold dark matter is easier said than done—by far, an extremely ambitious theoretical enterprise. The small structures that pop up first require much better codes to handle the higher resolution. In regard to computer resources, it is a demanding process that requires state-of-the-art numerical techniques.

To help them handle the complex calculations, the Berkeley researchers added a new British member to their collaboration. George Efstathiou, the son of Cypriot immigrants, had already adapted a plasma-physics numerical code to problems in cosmology. Then at Cambridge, he had stripped the complex program to its bare bones, throwing out any mention of electrical charges and ions and adding in an expanding universe. With its 6,500 lines of programming and its ability to handle tens of thousands of gravitating particles, rather than just several hundred, Efstathiou's program was just the computational tool needed by the Berkeley team.

The four investigators simulated the development of a universe filled with cold dark matter in much the same way that weather forecasts are generated. They established a set of initial conditions and then examined how the clouds of matter in their representative slice of the cosmos evolved over the universe's lifetime. They began as close as possible to the era of galaxy formation, about a few billion years after the universe's creation, and worked their way up to the present day. This mini universe, confined within the frame of a computer, at first appeared as a uniform mist of particles; but then quantum fluctuations (waves enlarged by inflation) rippled through the cold dark matter and began to sculpt their grand design. The universe soon became mottled; very small clumps formed all over the place. Yet, at the same time, the cold-matter lumps started to line up into longer structures, as if a galaxy that is destined to end up in a supercluster gets an inkling of it in the earliest moments of the universe's history.

The many thousands of particles in the computer were not real, of course, but rather ghostly markers that represented clumps of matter, weighing billions of times as much as the Sun, at certain positions and velocities in digital space and time. Tugging at one another in a complex gravitational dance, they began to attract one another and assemble themselves into groups and large clusters. One thousand times this computer universe—a hypothetical cube—evolved and "expanded." Ten million years went by in each step, a mere blip in the life of a galaxy. By the end, about ten billion years had elapsed.

Their first runs consisted of some 30,000 particles. Once they gained access to a supercomputer, the Berkeley collaborators eventually dealt with up to a quarter of a million particles. "In some ways," notes Frenk, "using supercomputers is a step back to those days when computers were demi-gods with their own little temples (air-conditioned rooms) with special priests (computer operators) attending them. Back then the offerings were cardboard cards which had to be punched just the right way. Now, I make my offerings once again."

Thinking at first that they would probably rule out cold dark matter, as they had done neutrinos, the Berkeley team was actually surprised to see that their computer-generated portrait of the universe's structure matched quite nicely with the CfA map, with its hints of voids and supercluster chains. The likeness was especially good when they assumed that the cold dark matter filled the universe to the brink of closure. If the computer simulations were correct, galaxies had to be viewed as merely a bright, luminous foam—a mere 1 percent of the universe's contents—that tops the densest regions of a rather cold and substantial dark-matter sea.

The four collaborators continued this work through the 1980s as a group scattered across the globe. While Davis remained at Berkeley, White moved on, first to the University of Arizona and more recently to Cambridge. Frenk migrated to Durham, and Efstathiou accepted a professorship at Oxford University. For many years, Davis, Efstathiou, Frenk, and White dominated the field when it came to simulating a universe filled with cold dark matter. The considerable influence they wielded led some to nickname them the "Gang of Four" (the term first applied to Mao Tse-Tung's widow and three of her cronies when they tried to seize power in the Republic of China after Mao's death). By the 1990s, though, many other researchers were joined in the effort with even more extensive codes and millions of particles in their simulations of the universe's large-scale structure. Such computer efforts have made cosmology more respectable, for they can offer definitive predictions that can then be compared with the real universe. But a simulation is not a proof, merely a suggestion that ordinary matter immersed in a sea of dark, exotic, sluggish particles *might* explain the topography of the universe. "Not knowing what this dark matter is, yet realizing that it constitutes most of the material universe," says Frenk, "is equivalent to medieval scholars pondering whether the Sun goes around the Earth or the Earth around the Sun. It's a similar crisis." Whatever the outcome, the simulations will never be for naught, for the dark matter—whatever its true nature—must act as observed, much the way Maxwell's equations of electromagnetism continued to work even after the ancient ether disappeared.

Just as the future of the Earth might be determined by the thin skin of organics covering its surface, so too might the universe's rare added spice—the luminous stars and galaxies—be the determining factor in the universe's long-term evolution. With that in mind, simulators of the early universe are beginning to add ordinary matter to their dark-matter ingredients, to see how its varied electromagnetic radiations, pressures, and shock fronts might have affected the universe's evolution. All the while, investigators have had to keep their eye on the long strides taken by the cosmic mapmakers, whose pace has been swift. As the Gang of Four and others were carrying out their cosmic weather forecasts, the universe

Three of the "Gang of Four," leading investigators of the cold dark matter (CDM) model during the 1980s. (Left to right): Simon White, George Efstathiou, and Carlos Frenk.
Photograph courtesy of Carlos Frenk

offered further revelations regarding the shape and extent of the heavens' framework.

"LIKE . . . THE SUDS IN A KITCHEN SINK"

Around 1985, evidence that the universe was filled with distinct structures was still considered inconclusive by some. So inconclusive, in fact, that when John Huchra and Margaret Geller embarked on a more ambitious and systematic redshift survey that year, they had no special interest in determining the distribution of galaxies. They expected it to be more or less regular. The two investigators, with Huchra manning the telescope and Geller handling the theoretical analyses, were much more interested in tackling some of the bread-and-butter issues in extragalactic astronomy, such as finding out how many galaxies there are in a given volume of space—an old and fundamental question in astronomy. Geller, a very vocal critic of reports on extremely large structures in the universe, suspected that the Boötes void was simply an illusion that would go away as more and more redshifts were mined and the cosmic map filled in.

Instead of surveying a very broad swath of sky, as the first CfA redshift team had done, Huchra and Geller decided to take a representative slice of the heavens—a thin pie wedge 6 degrees thick and 117 degrees wide, with Earth at the apex. At the far edge of the slice, 650 million light-years away, were galaxies 6,000 times too faint to be visible to the naked eye. This was taking them some two times farther into space than the original CfA survey. They chose this strategy, a more narrow yet deeper sweep across the sky, to obtain a fair sample of the universe's population, much the way a globe-spanning strip across the surface of the Earth would likely catch both oceans and continents.

Upon finishing their initial observations, Huchra and Geller, almost as an aside, instructed a University of Paris graduate student, Valérie de Lapparent, to construct a map of the survey's redshifts as part of the thesis she was completing at the Harvard-Smithsonian Center for Astrophysics. De Lapparent herself had put in many nights at Mount Hopkins gathering part of the data.

"We held off plotting the results," recalls Huchra, "because we 'knew' they were going to be smooth." More concerned at first with galaxy correlation statistics and luminosity functions, they just presumed that clusters and superclusters would show up as random lumps amid a generally diffuse background of galaxies. They were wrong—dead wrong.

Margaret Geller and John Huchra.
Harvard-Smithsonian Center for Astrophysics

Late that summer, after days of entering the redshift data into the computer and preparing her plot, a puzzled de Lapparent showed the results to her advisers. The galaxies weren't randomly scattered over the chart, as the CfA group had expected. Instead, their assembly exhibited a strange and very conspicuous architecture, as if the ghost of Thomas Wright were hovering about. Huchra, who was in charge of the observations, did a double take. His first thought was, "How did I screw up?"

"I must have spent two weeks going around in circles making sure I hadn't committed some sort of experimental error," says Huchra. "Whenever I go to the telescope and collect data, my view of the world changes and evolves. Sometimes very slowly—three cloudy nights on a mountain and it's not going to change very much—but sometimes, the change can occur very rapidly. My first thought, though, under those circumstances is, 'What did I do wrong?' If you're a good experimentalist, that *must* be your first concern."

Yet the data immediately converted Geller, who was astounded by the picture she beheld. "I knew John couldn't have fouled up," she says.

"The structures were so obvious. I recognized right away that it was something extraordinary, and it changed our lives."

On de Lapparent's map, the galaxies weren't scattered as a uniform mist, featureless and boring. Nor were they linked with one another to form a lacy web of threads, as previous evidence had been suggesting. Instead, the one thousand or so galaxies in that first slice of the redshift survey were congregated along the surfaces of gigantic, nested bubbles, which Geller immediately likened to a "kitchen sink full of soapsuds," an analogy that found its way into their official report. Inside the bubbles were equally huge voids. All the previous observational hints and theoretical discussions of a universal frothiness suddenly, and quite dramatically, came into focus.

Peebles, formerly so concerned that astronomers claiming to see large-scale structures might have been merely picking patterns out of noisy data, was at last convinced; for him a curtain had lifted up. The CfA team had found that galaxies group themselves in surprisingly sharp and coherent structures. Galaxies, already known to assemble into clusters, which collect into superclusters, now appeared as if they were rolling into hollow, bubblelike spheres up to 300 million light-years across. These bubbles, in turn, huddled together in a sort of cosmic foam. Thomas Wright, so enamored of his spherical shells, would probably have been pleased. For a time, some wondered whether all these voids were blown out by a series of early and powerful supernova explosions. The cosmic shock waves were imagined to have swept, like a snowplow, the primordial gases into the thin, spherical shells. But it is now known that stellar explosions fall far short of providing the necessary oomph to clean out a bubble the size of a giant void.

The most noticeable feature of all in the first slice was a curious shape in the center, where a few bubbles interconnected. Many people mistook it for a joke. The shape resembles a wiry figure sometimes dubbed the "Harvard stickman." The prominent Coma cluster makes up the torso of this figure, which is likely to become a classic image in astronomy textbooks for decades to come. "If we had a nickel for every time that picture has been reproduced, we'd be very rich," says Geller with a chuckle.

With these startling results, and with their newfound interest in cosmic cartography, Huchra and Geller added a new title to their résumés. "When people on airplanes asked me what I do, I used to say I was a physicist, which ended the discussion," says Geller. "I once said I was a cosmologist, but they started asking me about makeup, and the title 'astronomer' gets confused with 'astrologer.' Now I say I make maps."

Between 1985 and 1991 the two collaborators stacked four additional slices onto their first slice, opening up the original wedge like a bellows. And in another region of the sky, they scanned half a dozen more slices. Each round of the search begins at the center's modern concrete edifice off Garden Street in Cambridge, the present-day extension of Edward Pickering's and Annie Jump Cannon's former territory. In a third-floor room some forty cardboard boxes are lined up on shelves according to the celestial position of their contents—hundreds of Polaroid shots of galaxies, with vital statistics on each. Huchra and Geller send pictures of the targets they've chosen to southern Arizona, where two weeks out of every month, when the Moon is a sliver and the night sky is darkest, a team of Harvard-Smithsonian astronomers, and sometimes Huchra or the occasional graduate student, repair to a small dome on the side of Mount Hopkins. There they train the center's sixty-inch reflecting telescope on the distant galaxies to gauge their redshifts. Over the course of a clear winter night, they can measure the distances to about thirty-five galaxies. (Huchra's personal record is fifty-two.) All told, they have measured more than 12,000, which leaves only 100 billion or so to go.

The light from each galaxy is broken down into its component wavelengths by a spectrograph, much the way a prism creates a rainbow out of sunlight. The redshift caused by the galaxy's motion is measured from the shift of well-known spectral lines, such as the wavelengths at which hydrogen and oxygen emit and absorb light. The more distant the galaxy, the faster it rushes away from us, and the farther the spectral lines are shoved over to the red end of the spectrum.

The spectroscopic data, collected on computer tape, is then sent back to Massachusetts, where the redshifts are determined and the resulting galactic coordinates are added to the map. Geller often studies the results on a computer-graphics terminal. Manipulating a series of eight knobs, she can examine the bubbly structure from any angle. Each of the thousands of points represents a separate galaxy. These galaxies whiz by as she zooms into the wedge, flying through the voids like a spaceship in hyperdrive.

As the survey expanded, so did the structures it revealed. The most spectacular feature to date is the Great Wall, an unmistakable band that runs completely across the computer screen. This thin sheet of galaxies stretches a half-billion light-years from end to end (at least, that's as far as

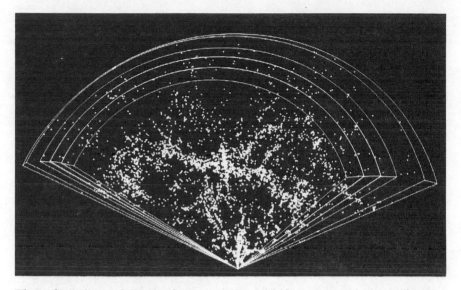

These four slices of the sky from the CfA redshift survey, with the Milky Way situated at the apex, display the universe's foamy texture over a distance of nearly half a billion light-years. Each point represents a galaxy.
Margaret Geller and John Huchra, Smithsonian Astrophysical Observatory

they've been able to measure so far). Intergalactic space, once imagined as a faceless ocean, has come to resemble a tangled archipelago of galactic islands. The immense size of these structures has left astronomers almost as surprised as Columbus surely was when he set out for India and instead bumped into the New World. A related redshift survey, supervised by Brazilian astronomer Luiz de Costa, has been revealing an identical cosmic frothiness in the southern celestial hemisphere.

For Geller, the spherical shells of galaxies and gargantuan voids have become the continents and oceans of the universe. "I find all these patterns artistically pleasing," she says. "It's a pattern you can remember." As a young girl growing up in New Jersey, Geller flirted with the idea of a career in the visual arts; influenced by her father, a noted solid-state chemist, she eventually turned to science. Always fascinated by mathematics, she learned algebra on her own while still in grade school. Yet, ironically, she ultimately came to deal with design, only this time the grandest and largest design of them all. Along the way, Geller, a forthright woman with dark curly hair and a ready smile, became the second woman, after Cecilia Payne-Gaposchkin, to attain the rank of professor in the Harvard astronomy department.

In addition to widening their survey, the Harvard-Smithsonian team is pushing it deeper into space in one selected and very narrow strip, akin to a geologist's taking a core sample. In this way, they will be mapping not only space but time, for the farther astronomers probe distant space, the further they travel back into the universe's history, because of light's finite 186,000-miles-per-second velocity. The light from a galaxy one billion light-years distant shows us what that galaxy looked like one billion years ago. Another team of researchers, from Great Britain and the United States, has already tried this approach, probing the universe along two thin cores in opposite directions from Earth. Each core extends outward some five billion light-years. What they see is evidence for a series of Great Walls, perhaps arranged in a kind of honeycomb structure. "It's as if we pierced an extremely narrow needle through the universe and hit one wall after another," says team member Alex Szalay, who now divides his time between Eötvös University in Budapest and Johns Hopkins University in Baltimore, Maryland. These walls, of which the CfA wall is the nearest, are separated by voids some 400 million light-years across.

Will astronomers continue to find bigger and bigger collections of matter as they expand the breadth of their cosmic mapping? Will there be vaster voids and lengthier walls? Or will the universe's texture eventually smooth out over those immense distances, the creed that Hubble long opined? The same team of astronomers that discovered the famous Boötes void—Harvard's Robert Kirshner, Yale's Augustus Oemler, MIT's Paul Schechter, and Stephen Shectman with the Observatories of the Carnegie Institution of Washington—is beginning to think that the end of large-scale structure is in sight. Using the one-hundred-inch telescope at the Las Campanas Observatory in Chile, these observers (informally known as KOSS, pronounced like the word *chaos,* based on their collective initials) have been probing a slice of space four times deeper than the Geller-Huchra CfA redshift survey. And preliminary results are suggesting that over scales of a couple of billion light-years or so, the universe begins to look fairly homogeneous. When looking at the KOSS map, the bubbly (some prefer to say spongy) distribution of galaxies becomes indistinct and comes to look as unvarying as a large swath of pristine prairieland. "That's what we were taught should happen," says Shectman, "but we weren't seeing it until now."

By pushing such surveys deeper into space—and thus further back in time—redshift surveyors hope to find clues as to how the bubbles and voids came to emerge over scales of hundreds of millions of light-years in the first place. How were they built, especially since the relatively smooth microwave background suggests the universe's contents were initially spread out fairly uniformly? The conventional view is that the walls and bubblelike spheres of galaxies were pulled together by gravity—specifically, by the gravity of lots and lots of cold, slow-moving dark matter spread throughout the universe. All these dark particles, if they truly exist, would have received their initial gravitational nudges from random fluctuations rippling through the primordial ocean of particles, the same ripples detected by NASA's COBE satellite. And, once the first tiny clumps of gas emerged, these clumps attracted more and more matter, leaving the sparse regions even emptier. Galaxies turn out to be the snow-capped mountain peaks, hills of brightly lighted baryons, rising above a featureless plain of dark matter. But could the smooth soup of matter born at the dawn of time have turned into a lumpy stew so quickly? Computer simulations of an evolving universe stuffed with lots and lots of cold dark matter have been able to reproduce some great walls and bubblelike voids, but just barely and only with lots of computational tinkering. Modelers are dancing on the edge of a theoretical abyss.

Astronomers are getting nervous. Models of galaxy formation are straining under the new data that assault them almost daily. As astronomers look out to the most distant reaches of the cosmos, they are finding galaxies and quasars—the highly energetic cores of young galaxies—popping into existence at earlier and earlier times, less than two billion years after the big bang. Gravity alone, triggered by those inflationary fluctuations, has trouble making galaxies so early. This has made some wonder whether, eons ago, gravity got a little help making galaxies; perhaps imperfections in the fabric of space-time, flaws that emerged as the universe and its contents first "crystallized," triggered the early formation of galaxies and the later development of vast structures. Defects labeled "cosmic strings" and "textures," energy-packed remnants of the original primordial fireball, may have stuck around for a while and acted like enormous gravity wells into which the primordial gas and dark matter plummeted and then coalesced. For that matter, maybe the missing mass is not solely "hot" or "cold"; maybe the dark matter's secret formula has several ingredients. Massive neutrinos, for example, could have forged the large voids and superclusters, while an assortment of Jupiters or cold

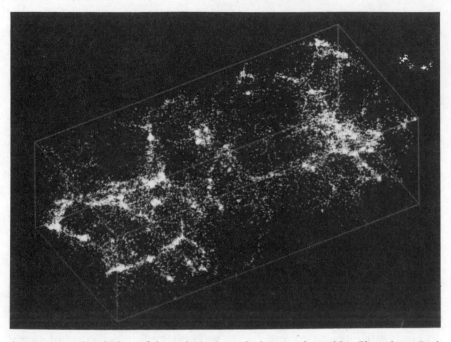

A computer simulation of the universe's evolution conducted by Changbom Park and J. Richard Gott, III, at Princeton University. A spongelike pattern of walls, filaments, and clusters of galaxies arise by the action of gravity.
Changbom Park and J. Richard Gott, III

WIMPs serve as the dark matter around individual galaxies. Such is the range of ideas now being considered by theorists stumped by the mystery of galaxy formation.

Geller suspects something more is going on—something that future maps may reveal. "I often feel we are missing some fundamental element in our attempts to understand this structure," she says. "Nobody could imagine plate tectonics without a good map of the Earth. And no one could figure out the precise role of DNA before scientists mapped its arrangement of atoms. A lot of science is really the same as mapping. You have to make a map before you understand." And within that map will be the key to the universe's true makeup.

By the mid-1990s Geller and Huchra will have completed their interim goal of measuring and plotting nearly 16,000 redshifts—which, considering that there are billions of galaxies in the universe, is a mere drop in the cosmic sea. Their current map covers only 1/100,000 the volume of the visible universe; in terms of a map of our world, that is comparable to the fraction of Earth covered by the diminutive country of Luxembourg or the Caribbean's tiny island of Trinidad. Huchra and Geller, as well as other groups entering the mapping game, are starting to use fiber-optic arrays to conduct the light from the focal plane of the telescope to the spectrograph. Each fiber, one of many such fibers in the array, is able to collect the light from a separate galaxy in the field of view. Such devices are thus making it possible to measure dozens of galactic redshifts at once and hundreds in one night. The Las Campanas redshift survey is being conducted in such a manner. Months before an observing run, a series of large metal plates is fabricated; each plate has holes drilled out where the galaxies can be found in a particular field of view. Mounting a plate at the telescope focus, an observer places the optical fibers into the holes by hand, aims the telescope at the designated field, and collects his spectral data on some one hundred galaxies at once.

A consortium of researchers at the University of Chicago, the Institute for Advanced Study, and Princeton University ambitiously plans to map one million galaxies over half a decade, using a dedicated instrument in New Mexico that will be capable of taking the spectra of several hundred galaxies simultaneously. "If technology continues to advance, astronomers can expect to have a couple of million redshifts within twenty-five years," notes Geller. "That would still be only one-thousandth of the universe's volume, but then it took hundreds of years to map the Earth."

And as Huchra points out, cosmic mapmakers have just now reached the stage where geographers were when the New World was discovered. "Back then there was a lot of theoretical, yet incorrect, knowledge about what the world was like," he says. "Some thought the world might be flat and you could fall off the edge, but the explorers went out and found out what was truly there. Celestial mapmaking is very similar. Our preconceptions of a uniform universe are now shattered—only we never had to worry about falling off the edge."

· 11 ·

To Catch a Ghost

*It seems that the human mind has first to construct forms
independently before we can find them in things.*

—ALBERT EINSTEIN

*I like to find
what's not found
at once, but lies
within something of another nature
in repose, distinct.*

—DENISE LEVERTOV, *PLEASURES*

It is both fitting and prophetic that a portrait of Thomas Wright as a middle-aged man, a stern-looking visage that embellishes his published works, includes the Ouroboros Serpent, an ancient Egyptian symbol that was used by medieval alchemists to represent the unity of matter: Circling completely around, the serpent's head comes to swallow its tail. Today particle physicists use the same circular figure to illustrate the merger of the microcosm with the macrocosm—the marriage of the subatomic world with the vast universe at large—as they strive to construct a unified theory of all the varied particles and forces in nature. Mapping the overall structure of the universe, an endeavor whose first wavering steps were taken by Wright more than two centuries ago, likely reveals the effects of those forces at work in the very early universe.

The resulting cosmic texture, the bubbly array of galaxies and voids, is the indelible imprint of all the tiny particles of matter that were fabricated in the first minutes of creation. But is this material, the part so stubbornly concealed from our eyes and instruments, primarily "hot" and exotic? Is it "cold"? Or is it merely ordinary?

Almost all astronomers agree that the dark matter is real, but so far this elusive substance can be detected only by observing and measuring its gravitational effects on visible matter: Galaxies within a cluster move around unusually fast, and yet stay together as a cluster; stars situated at the outer edges of spiral galaxies orbit faster than theory would predict and yet do not fly off. Reservoirs of unseen matter, with their added gravitational clout, must exist to keep these galaxies and stars in check. Since everything from protons to planets exerts gravity, the dark matter can, in theory, be made of pretty much anything. Many astronomers are perfectly happy with the idea that it consists of more or less ordinary stuff—hosts of faint brown dwarfs, perhaps, or dark, Jupiterlike plane-toids. On the other hand, a number of physicists are convinced that this unseen material is of the particle (rather than the planetary or stellar) variety. "For one thing, our theories of how the visible stars formed have a hard time making all those brown dwarfs and 'Jupiters,' " says particle-physicist-turned-cosmologist David Seckel. "Also, from what we know about galaxy formation, it is hard to create a universe filled with galaxies if dark matter is solely composed of ordinary matter." But until a new elementary particle, with all the requisite properties, is actually cornered, all thoughts of a new type of matter, invisible and relentlessly aloof as it drifts through the cosmos, must be regarded as conjecture.

All skepticism would disappear, of course, if Earthbound scientists could catch one of the hypothetical particles in a terrestrial laboratory. Since the 1930s, when Fritz Zwicky first talked of *dunkle Materie* hov-ering in and around clusters of galaxies, the hunt for this dark matter has been conducted chiefly through telescopes. No one really thought that laboratory experiments could be sensitive enough to detect the amounts of exotic, subatomic motes estimated to be passing through Earth daily, should the dark-matter particles be real. But that situation is now chang-ing. Major advances in both detector technology and low-temperature physics are allowing the researchers to pursue their dream of snaring the elusive matter directly, and at relatively moderate expense. At a time when particle physics experiments have come to involve hundreds of physicists and technicians, at costs of hundreds of millions of dollars, dark-matter experiments can be conducted within a small laboratory setting. More than a dozen groups around the globe either have started looking or are gearing up for the search. They can be found in Great Britain, France, Switzerland, Germany, Italy, Canada, Japan, and the United States. All are panning for celestial gold.

Each research team has staked out a different theoretical territory, betting that its own custom-made detector has the best chance of finding bona fide evidence of the invisible universe. In Building 904 at the Brookhaven National Laboratory on New York's Long Island, a hollow cylinder of copper sixteen inches tall quietly sat in a liquid helium bath for a few years, awaiting the passage of an axion, an elementary particle that may or may not exist. At the same time, deep within the bowels of the Oroville Dam in northern California, a couple of two-pound chunks of germanium, each surrounded by an array of electronics and special shielding, were hunting for other dark-matter contenders. "It's like the long shot in a horse race," says NASA physicist Floyd Stecker. "The chances are small, but the payoff will be big, likely a Nobel Prize."

PARTICLE ASTROPHYSICS

Bernard Sadoulet of the University of California at Berkeley was one of the first particle physicists to move into cosmology and initiate a serious laboratory hunt for the dark matter. An accomplished accelerator physicist, Sadoulet had been a group leader (one of the many "number twos," as he puts it) in Carlo Rubbia's Nobel Prize–winning experiment at CERN that finally cornered the W and Z particles, those elusive conveyors of the electroweak force. Years earlier, while serving as a postdoc at Berkeley, he had played a small role in the discovery of the J/psi particle, which clinched the existence of the fourth quark, charm. Although his career in particle physics was both productive and notable, Sadoulet grew tired of the "big science" atmosphere, with its armies of physicists and its multimillion-dollar projects. "All the easy experiments had been done," he contends. His last undertaking at CERN, the development of a new particle detector, involved around 150 people, all Ph.D. physicists. (A single experiment at the planned Superconducting Super Collider, the next generation of particle accelerator to be built in Texas, will likely require several hundred collaborators.)

More enmeshed in budgets and administrative duties than in physics, Sadoulet longed to switch to a smaller scientific pond, although one still concerned with fundamental questions. The opportunity arrived in the 1980s when theorists, experiencing a veritable Renaissance of ideas yet without the means to test those conjectures on Earth experimentally, began forging links between the fields of particle physics and cosmology. There was talk of supersymmetric particles filling the universe, perhaps even annihilating in the halo of our galaxy. Theorists were pushing their models farther than experimentalists could probe, entering realms of energy far removed from the levels current technologies can attain. Particle accelerators can now reach energies of a trillion electron volts, yet grand unified theories describe physical processes occurring at energies far, far greater—at a trillion trillion electron volts. As a consequence, the big bang, once the sole province of cosmology, became the theorists' ultimate particle accelerator. The remnants from that primeval explosion speak of the energetic processes of yesteryear—many, many yesteryears ago. The traces are detected in the smooth sea of microwaves bathing the universe, in the bubbly distribution of galaxies, and in the flood of X rays and gamma rays emanating from celestial events that took place possibly at the universe's conception.

In 1984 Sadoulet, then with CERN, arrived at Berkeley on a year's sabbatical, but his visit soon turned into a permanent professorship and a new career—particle astrophysics. By 1987 the U.S. National Science Foundation announced that it was going to establish a number of dedicated centers throughout the United States, each to pursue a specific problem in science and technology. Proposals were requested. Sadoulet and others at Berkeley felt that if they pooled their efforts around the issue of the dark matter they might have a distant chance. Researchers on campus were already attacking the problem from different angles, and a center was expected to consolidate these separate efforts: While Sadoulet worked on his detectors, Marc Davis and his associates were mapping the effects of cold dark matter on the large-scale structure of the universe; Carl Pennypacker and Richard Muller had an idea to observe large numbers of supernovae at great distances and then use the far-off explosions as surveyor stakes to decide whether the universe is geometrically open or closed, which would also reveal whether the dark matter is sparse or plentiful. Others at Berkeley were making meticulous measurements of the cosmic microwave background, whose texture incorporates the earliest effects of the dark matter and offers clues as to its origins.

Successful in its bid, the Center for Particle Astrophysics is now established in Berkeley's Le Conte Hall, a massive three-story building, similar in style to the classical structures predominant in Washington, D.C.; a red-tiled roof, however, adds a distinctive California touch. Here Berkeley researchers—working with collaborators from the nearby Lawrence Berkeley Laboratory, the University of California at both Santa Barbara and Irvine, San Francisco State University, Stanford University, and Brown University in Rhode Island—are breaking down the barriers between narrow specialities and carrying out an interdisciplinary approach to solving the dark-matter problem. Le Conte Hall is where cosmology, particle physics, astrophysics, material science, low-temperature physics, and nuclear physics are undergoing a cross-fertilization. It might be called one of the first "legalized" marriages between the science of the very small and the science of the very big. Before this, particle astrophysics was better described as a wary relationship between ambivalent partners who were just getting to know one another.

Investigators at the center expect no immediate answers; their success hinges on developing state-of-the-art low-temperature detectors, which will be pushing the technology to its limits. In this endeavor, they are perpetuating a long-standing tradition in particle physics: First theorists predict a new particle, and then experimentalists, sparked by the challenge, go out to look for it. Sometimes the hypothesized particle is found fairly quickly (the first particle known to incorporate the charm quark, for instance); sometimes it can take decades (as with the slippery neutrino).

Soft-spoken, with brown eyes, full beard, and thick, salt-and-pepper hair, Sadoulet directs the operations of the center from a large office on the third floor of Le Conte Hall, a massive conference table dominating the middle of the room. Whiteboards cover two walls and are filled with schedules, electronics designs, and detector schematics, indicative of the intense activity at the center. Sadoulet is attracted to a particle solution for the dark matter because he finds it difficult to imagine how ordinary baryons could hide so effectively throughout the universe. How could nature have generated so many brown dwarfs or black holes in the first place? he asks quizzically.

As a particle physicist, Sadoulet is also intrigued by a certain calculation. Assuming that there are exotic dark-matter particles, enough to push the universe to the brink between open and closed, "very general arguments relate that density to the strength of the interactions between these dark-matter particles," says Sadoulet. And that interaction strength comes tantalizingly close to the strength of the weak force, a known entity in nature. "This result could be merely a numerical coincidence," continues Sadoulet, "or it could be something very deep, implying that the particle physics we are now studying, things like supersymmetry, may be responsible for dark matter." This significant match could be a giant hint that dark matter is indeed an unseen, exotic material that naturally arises as the universe evolves according to the laws of nature established at the beginning of time.

"I couldn't disagree more with Stephen Hawking, who says in his book *A Brief History of Time* that we are arriving at the end of physics. Maxwell, the father of electromagnetic theory, said essentially the same thing at the end of the nineteenth century," Sadoulet says emphatically in his French-accented English. "We are far from arriving at the end of physics, for there are so many new things to find. If the dark matter is made out of particles, then there are literally billions of them moving through each of us every second. We don't feel them simply because they interact so weakly."

Experts expect it will take time and new technologies to catch a dark-matter particle. But in the meantime they are using the instrumentation now on hand to rule out certain models and get some experience under their belt. They must learn how to run experiments in such a way that the slightest electronic "noise" does not ruin their attempt at seeing a dark-matter particle passing through. Measurements are already in progress deep underground.

UNDERGROUND ASTRONOMY

A drive from Berkeley, California, to the Oroville Dam on the Feather River takes about two hours. Visitors first travel northeast along Interstate 80 to Sacramento, the state capital, then take Route 70 northward through the numerous nut and fruit orchards that stretch along California's lush Central Valley. The dam itself, spanning one and a half miles across its top, was at one time the largest earthen dam in the world. It was built in the late 1950s to curb the devastating floods that often tore through this rich agricultural region.

Situated at the very base of the dam, with six hundred feet of earth overhead, is a manmade cavern, bored out of the rock to house the dam's imposing power station. The cavern can be reached by either driving or walking down a long concrete-walled tunnel, eerie in its dim fluorescent lighting. Water slowly drips down the walls, forming the occasional stalactite. Throughout the tunnel can be heard the echoing hum of the massive turbines, incessantly spinning ahead. "It's almost like a Jules Verne novel, as if we're about to tap into the energy of the Earth," exclaims Alan Smith.

With his casual striped shirt, suede shoes, and long greying hair pulled back in a hippielike ponytail, Smith maintains a relaxed and comfortable air. A physicist with the Lawrence Berkeley Laboratory since 1953, Smith is a specialist in low-level radiation detection. He first became interested in such studies for medical research, analyzing the long-term effects of low-level radiation exposure on the human body. Later, as the Apollo astronauts brought back their many rock samples from the Moon, the lab came to specialize in creating pristine environments for keeping such specimens well protected from stray radioactive contaminants.

Smith is keen to answer questions, and in a melodic voice he recalls myriad facts with ease. "More than one hundred years ago, Lord Kelvin, the word of God at that time, or close to it, declared that the Earth was roughly one hundred million years old. He arrived at that number by determining how long it must have taken for the Earth to have cooled to its present state. But that figure conflicted with the age of some well-known rocks. Are we at a similar impasse?" asks Smith as he briskly walks down the tunnel to the very bowels of the Oroville Dam. "We almost had it all figured out—the contents of the universe. Now, we're discovering that we don't know 90 percent or more of what's out there. It's crazy!"

At the end of the tunnel is a vast hall, as big as a football field. Amidst the six giant turbines, huge orange cranes ploddingly move back and forth overhead. "Here's our little universe," declares Smith with pride, pointing to an elevated platform at one end of the cavernous chamber, a former visitors' gallery transformed into a physics laboratory. The operation taking place on the high-rise deck, reached by a set of stairs, resembles a small construction site. Dominating the scene is a neat, cubelike pile of lead bricks, each side spanning some three and a half feet. A special detector resides inside the lead pile and is cooled by a continual wash of liquid nitrogen that is fed in from large vats set nearby. As if providing life support, dozens of wires and cables stream out of the pile and connect into banks of amplifiers and other assorted instruments that are arranged like rows of books on metal shelves.

No one event will ring any bells in this experiment—only data gathered over weeks, months, and even years. Researchers here are looking for a unique signal that rises above all the extraneous instrumental noise, a signal that broadcasts the presence of a new, exotic particle that is filling the universe and posing as the dark matter.

Smith first came to Oroville, which was a booming gold-mining camp in the nineteenth century, in connection with other work. After a sizable earthquake shook the area in 1975, he went to the dam to measure the levels of radon in selected wells on the site. A popular theory at the time suggested that sudden changes in radon levels near an earthquake's epicenter might serve as a quake predictor. Years later the site came to mind when researchers from the Lawrence Berkeley Laboratory and the University of California at Santa Barbara were looking for a special spot to observe a rare phenomenon, known as double beta decay, deep underground far from interfering radiation such as cosmic rays.

It was an experiment that would hone the skills of future dark-matter hunters, teaching them how to reduce spurious background noises by a factor of a thousand. For the double beta decay experiment, eight large crystals of germanium had been specially grown—each weighing about two pounds and as big as a fist—and cooled with liquid nitrogen to a temperature of seventy-seven degrees above absolute zero. Some of the germanium atoms are radioactive and decay; in doing this, they normally eject two antineutrinos and two electrons, also known as beta particles (hence the nomenclature, double beta decay). But the Oroville investigators were particularly interested in seeing whether any of the radioactive germanium atoms would eject two electrons alone. This would happen only if the two antineutrinos mutually annihilated, an event that couldn't occur unless neutrinos had mass. (Since particles can annihilate only with their antiparticles, this also implies that the neutrino would not be distinct from its antiparticle, the antineutrino; in this particular case, matter and antimatter would be one and the same.)

If this rare event did take place (a double beta decay with no neutrinos materializing), the physicists didn't expect to see more than a few events over an entire year. Thus it was crucial to get all spurious background noises at Oroville as quiet as possible. It was as if they were trying to distinguish the sound of a single drop of water amidst the roar of a pounding surf. The Oroville researchers applied a number of strategies to sharpen their "ears." With the Oroville chamber lodged beneath several hundred feet of rock and earth, disruptive cosmic-ray counts automatically drop a thousandfold. The entire instrument is also surrounded by a bevy of scintillators, which, if struck by a particularly resourceful cosmic ray flying in from above, briefly lights up, with the flash recorded by a photomultiplier tube. Such outside noise can then be ignored. Some particles are stopped in their tracks even beforehand, by the piles of lead stacked up around the detector. To do this effectively, the Oroville team used lead from a unique mine in Missouri with high concentrations of primordial lead, which is little contaminated with the radioactive uranium or thorium that can introduce false detector signals. A similar experiment, run for a while in the Homestake mine in South Dakota, went so far as to have its detectors shielded with 450-year-old lead from a sunken Spanish galleon. The Homestake investigators reasoned that any residual radioactivity in the lead induced by cosmic rays would have disappeared after centuries in deep water and that radioactive fallout from nuclear blasts could not have penetrated that far down into the sea.

The most problematic radioactive interference emanated from the experimental components themselves. A particularly troublesome noise came from the germanium. A germanium crystal can be made extremely pure, limiting impurities in its atomic makeup to less than one part in a trillion, but by the time the germanium ore is mined, grown into crystals, and transported by plane to its user, it is also subjected to a year of cosmic-ray bombardment, which produces such meddlesome contaminants as radioactive tritium. Confronting such challenges is not new for detector builders at the Lawrence Berkeley Laboratory, where they designed a detector to look for the neutron star believed to be lurking within SN 1987A, the dusty remnant of the supernova that first became visible in 1987 in the southern sky; built the instrument that found the telltale signs of ancient iridium that suggests a giant, dinosaur-killing asteroid may have slammed into the Earth some 65 million years ago; and constructed delicate sensors for the Keck Telescope in Hawaii, the largest optical telescope in the world.

The double beta decay experiment at the Oroville Dam ran four years, from 1984 to 1988, under the direction of Lawrence Berkeley Laboratory physicist Fred Goulding and David Caldwell of the University of California at Santa Barbara. But the anomalous, neutrinoless decay process was never seen. Nor was it seen by other research groups at experimental sites in South Dakota and the Swiss Alps. "There was little point in continuing," says Goulding. "Twelve more years of watching would have improved our limits by only a factor of two. One human lifetime is not long enough. We may be nearing the beginning of an era when scientific experiments will have to be conducted over generations."

Dark-matter hunters with their detector deep beneath the Oroville Dam in California. From left to right: Angela Da Silva, Alan Smith, Bernard Sadoulet, Sheldon Taylor, Donna Hurley, and Fred Goulding.
Benjamin Ailes

The effort, though, still had its rewards. During the course of the long measurement, the Berkeley and Santa Barbara scientists came to perceive that their experimental setup could be subtly modified, making it possible to search for some of the dark-matter particles then being hypothesized. In 1985 the noted theorist Edward Witten, now with the Institute for Advanced Study in Princeton, along with his student Mark Goodman, had written a paper outlining the probabilities for directly detecting various dark-matter candidates, a report that inspired many experimentalists to enter the fray. Upon reading this journal article, Sadoulet came to think of the double beta decay experiment as a vital training exercise in the development of the first generation of dark-matter detectors.

A dark-matter particle is expected to whiz through a detector at nearly two hundred miles per second. With each tick of the clock, millions of these tiny motes, by some estimates, could be flying through each square centimeter of space. It is assumed that, as this intense shower of WIMPs rains down upon the detector crystal (at Oroville, both germanium and silicon have been used), one of the particles will occasionally hit a nucleus in the crystal lattice. And like a set of springs, the lattice should start vibrating under the impact, since the WIMP is expected to have a mass in the same range as an atomic nucleus. A small fraction of the energy from that impact would then be transferred to the electrons in the crystal, making them start flowing as a current. Each crystal that is mounted within the lead pile is monitored by putting an electric field on it and measuring this flow of charge, a method of detection known as ionization detection. Since nearly all the WIMPs will simply pass through the array of crystals as if they weren't there, the pickings will be slim. A single two-pound crystal might experience anywhere from one to one thousand WIMP interactions each day, depending on the nature of the WIMP. An ionization detector, the same kind used in the double beta decay experiment, is a relatively crude device for such a dark-matter hunt, "but it had the advantage of existing," points out Sadoulet. "We could start setting limits."

As with the double beta decay experiment, outside interferences can be stopped by taking such precautions as going deep underground and shielding. Trouble comes from the materials themselves—contaminants are ubiquitous and tricky to find. Soon after the Oroville researchers transformed their double beta decay instrument into a dark-matter detector, a mysterious background signal arose that was not anticipated. It took a while to realize that the added "blips" were coming from radioactive indium, a soft, aluminumlike material used to attach the crystals into place. They soon switched to gold fasteners. The potassium in the phototubes also put out a disruptive noise. An entire year was spent just tracking down every other potential culprit. Every screw, wire, capacitor, transistor, insulator, and resistor throughout the entire setup had to be checked for its level of radioactivity.

So delicate is the dark-matter measurement that the researchers' biggest worry is the radioactivity induced in the materials as they are transported to the Oroville site. Learning from its experiences during the double beta decay experiment, the Oroville team arranged for the special mining, processing, and transport of their detector crystals. Upon excavation from a deep mine, the germanium ore, for example, is directly and speedily taken to the processing plant. And as soon as the germanium crystals are fashioned, they are promptly transported to California by car along a low-altitude route that keeps the densest atmosphere between the crystals and any stray cosmic rays. This prevents the crystals from getting anymore radioactive than they have to be.

Carrying out the Oroville experiment is fairly automatic. Data is recorded right on site, and the condition of the equipment is monitored hourly. A status report is routinely sent over the telephone lines twice a day—four in the morning, and four in the afternoon—to a computer in Building 29 at the Lawrence Berkeley Laboratory. Once a week, a lab worker drives out to Oroville to retrieve the data tapes and replenish the liquid nitrogen. In its continual perusal of the data, the Oroville team is

Crystal of germanium used in Oroville Dam experiment.
Benjamin Ailes

looking for a distinctive signal that rises above the noisy background and fits the profile of a dark-matter particle.

After several years of nearly continual data gathering, the Oroville Dam experiment has so far ruled out the existence of a special, heavy neutrino that had been theorized, one that required a fourth "family" of particle types. This possibility was further eliminated with experiments conducted at both CERN and the Stanford Linear Accelerator Center in California. (As pointed out in chapter 9, the manner in which the Z particle decays indicated that a fourth neutrino was highly unlikely.) "And this proves my point concerning the value of these smaller experiments," says Sadoulet. "With an operation that cost less than half a million dollars, we complemented a large accelerator experiment that had several billion dollars of funding." This massive neutrino had been quite popular as a dark-matter candidate in the 1980s, for it was the easiest candidate, theoretically, to consider within the known laws of physics. Hundreds of scientific papers were devoted to the possibility. It is still conceivable that one of the other neutrino types, perhaps either the muon neutrino or the tau neutrino, could serve as the dark matter. But it will likely take the observation of a nearby supernova, spewing its flood of neutrinos, with an advanced underground neutrino detector to verify whether either of those particles is indeed endowed with the proper rest mass. That means building a neutrino observatory and waiting up to one hundred years for a star to blow up. "That's longer than the lifetime of government funding agencies," wryly points out Santa Cruz physicist Joel Primack. More realistically, one would require several sophisticated neutrino detectors to be on-line at just the right time, a vast investment, say some, in capital and patience.

The Oroville experiment is also ruling out certain "cosmions," a special class of weakly interacting particles that would have not only accounted for the dark matter but also explained why underground neutrino detectors, such as the cleaning-fluid-filled tank at the Homestake mine in South Dakota, were catching only a fraction of the solar neutrinos assumed to be flying out of the Sun. Settling into the solar core over time, cosmions would supposedly have tempered the Sun's central fire, causing less neutrinos to be generated; cosmions were one answer to the missing solar neutrino mystery. Silicon detectors installed at Oroville should have seen at least a few cosmion-related events per day, but they saw none. The Oroville measurements have also taken certain forms of shadow matter out of the running.

A SUPERCOOL SOLUTION

Ongoing detection schemes, such as those conducted in the subterranean grotto at the Oroville Dam, have certainly eliminated a number of candidates for the dark matter, but all those possibilities have been mere long shots at best. A perusal of the scientific literature shows that the most sought after dark-matter particles are the supersymmetric particles, with the most likely being the lightest of these WIMPs. Physicists call these particles "well motivated," because they were first invented by particle theorists for reasons totally unrelated to cosmology. And yet astronomers find them quite handy: WIMPs not only explain the dark matter very nicely, they can also generate enough gravity to maintain the universe in an exquisite balance, keeping the cosmos from expanding forever or eventually collapsing—a balance that many cosmologists are attracted to for both scientific and aesthetic reasons. But given current technologies, it is still a dream to think of catching these WIMPs; the sensitivity of the dark-matter detectors must first be improved upon up to a thousand times to register these ephemeral creatures.

The ionization detectors used at Oroville are just the first step in what physicists in this field envision as a developing line of ultrasensitive dark-matter detectors. The next generation of detectors will be cooled to extremely low temperatures—so low, in fact, that whenever a WIMP races through and happens to interact with the detector crystal, the advanced cryogenic instrumentation will be able to discern the resulting heat or vibrations in the wake of the disturbance. A pure-crystalline detector, made of possibly germanium, boron, or silicon, would attempt to spot the heat a WIMP generates when it bangs into an atomic nucleus. After such a collision, a set of phonons, or sound waves, would ripple through the crystal and just slightly raise its temperature. With most of the energy of a WIMP collision going into heating the detector, rather than into ionization, this is a much more efficient means of spotting a WIMP. The difficulty is in developing a sensor sensitive enough to measure the rise in temperature, which could be as small as a millionth of a degree. This should best be accomplished by cooling the instrument to within a few tens of thousandths of a degree above absolute zero, the temperature at which all molecular and atomic motions presumably cease. The different materials (e.g., germanium, boron, and silicon) would be used to target different dark-matter candidates. Germanium-73, for instance, an isotope with thirty-two protons and forty-one neutrons, possesses a nuclear property known as spin, which enables the germanium nucleus to interact more effectively with certain WIMPs, such as photinos. The Center for Particle Astrophysics has entered into an agreement with the former Soviet Union to obtain supplies of germanium especially enriched with this isotope.

Ning Wang, who arrived from the Republic of China in 1984 and worked toward her doctoral degree in physics at Berkeley for six years, was the first student assigned to work specifically on Sadoulet's advanced detector scheme. She began with a small room in the basement of Le Conte Hall, a few tools, and not much else. Since then additional graduate students have been added to the team, with the laboratory space—strewn with the requisite notebooks, computer monitors, workbenches, and electronics—ever growing.

Wang, her waist-long hair tied loosely in the back, enters the lab in traditional graduate-school garb: casual grey sweat shirt, blue tennis shoes, and green slacks. A modest sign posted outside the basement room discreetly announces the lab's purpose: experimental cosmology. The endeavor sounds romantic, but the work itself more often involves some rather mundane tasks. At the moment, lab members are busily constructing and testing a special dilution refrigerator that will ultimately cool the dark-matter detector to horrendously low temperatures. So far, they have pushed it down to within $^{20}/_{1,000}$–$^{30}/_{1,000}$ of a degree (Kelvin) above absolute zero.

A copper screen surrounds an entire corner of the lab where the system is set up, to block out electronic noises from the outside. "Otherwise," says Wang, "we'd be picking up the local TV stations." The vacuum chamber, designed to bathe the detector in streams of liquid nitrogen and liquid helium, is temporarily disassembled. An octopus of cables, feeding down from above, ends at a small copper coil within the open chamber, where the crystal detector will eventually be placed, the site of the lowest temperature. Among other chores, Wang was concerned with how to attach the sensors to the crystal that will be trapping any stray dark-matter particles. Like some delicate house of cards, each technological move to the final instrument builds on the step before it. When a dark-matter particle interacts with the crystal, it should be knocking into the nucleus of a crystal atom. The resulting high-energy phonons propagate to the surface of the crystal at speeds of a few miles per second. But the interface between the crystal and the sensor, constructed to detect

Ning Wang assembles a prototype of a dark-matter cryogenic detector.
Lawrence Berkeley Laboratory

those sound waves, must be perfectly clean and smooth so it does not
destroy the waves at the interface.

The plan is to have sensors situated on all sides of the crystal detector. A signal from inside—a dark-matter particle nudging an atomic nucleus and vibrating the crystal—can then be traced from the geometry of
the phonons arriving at the surface. The energy deposited from the pho-
non will cause the sensors' resistance to drop slightly, generating a tiny
voltage. How small a voltage one can distinguish determines the quantity
of phonons one can detect. And such a detection is ultimately limited by
the electronic noise in the system, which is why maintaining a tempera-

ture near absolute zero is so vital. The lower the temperature, the lower the noise. That phonons can be recognized and measured has been confirmed by Berkeley researcher Thomas Shutt, who constructed and ran a cryogenic detector consisting of a small sixty-gram disk of germanium, one and a half inches in width. A pilot run of the supercooled detector system is taking place at Stanford University in a shallow underground facility built especially for this next stage in the dark-matter hunt.

Research teams elsewhere are working on variations of the phonon-detection scheme, and each variation is advancing the current limits of technology in low-temperature physics. At Stanford University, for instance, Blas Cabrera's group hopes to mount a series of thin superconducting films around a supercooled crystal in order to map the phonons as they strike the crystal's surfaces. The pattern of energy should, in theory, identify the characteristic signature of a WIMP more accurately than a simple temperature jump might. WIMPs might be capable of signaling their presence in other ways as well. British scientists, for example, have designed a dark-matter detector that will spot the telltale flashes of light emitted whenever a WIMP collides into a detector atom. Hit by a WIMP, the atom recoils, causing the emission of a few photons. To isolate the instrument and keep it from being swamped by disruptive background radiation, the British team is placing its detector in a deep salt and potash mine on the northeastern coast of England near the moors of York. Moreover, the detector will be suspended in two hundred tons of high-purity water, which serves as an additional shield.

A number of investigators in France, Japan, Germany, Switzerland, Canada, and the United States have taken a completely different approach. They are considering designing boxes containing billions of microscopic grains of superconducting metal, each no bigger than a bacterium, suspended in a nonconducting material. They expect to sight a WIMP when it hits one of the grains; the resulting heat would flip the metal granule from a superconducting state to a normal state. The enormous challenge in this task will be manufacturing an array of grains that are scrupulously uniform and developing the electronics that can distinguish the change of state in just one grain.

Physicist Robert Lanou at Brown University in Rhode Island envisions a detector that makes use of liquid helium. "Helium is clean, quiet, simple, and inexpensive," he points out. And at temperatures near absolute zero every possible contaminant freezes out, while helium, which has no natural radioactive isotopes that could cause a disruption, remains liquid. Twenty liters of helium could conceivably register some events—that is, if the WIMPs are cooperative and other, spurious signals can be suppressed.

TUNING IN THE AXION

The very first particle candidate for the dark matter, the neutrino, was quite attractive for a number of reasons. For one, unlike all the other particle candidates, the neutrino is already known to exist—the big bang spewed out hordes of them. And their unobtrusive nature fit the profile of a dark-matter contender perfectly: They could pass through people and planets as though they were ghosts. But no one is yet sure that neutrinos have mass. And computer simulations show that a universe dominated by neutrinos would probably not have condensed into galaxies the way the real universe did, a discovery that took neutrinos out of the running. These particles will likely remain on the sidelines unless a signal from a neutrino observatory forces physicists to accept the existence of a massive neutrino.

But neutrinos were just the first in a long line of suspects. The axion, a popular candidate, is still waiting in the wings. Trying to corner an axion, though, is fraught with difficulty. For a while, it was thought that axions might be impossible to snare, a notion that was not unreasonable. An axion, if it exists, could whiz through a series of steel bank vaults lined up from here to Pluto and not bump into one atom. How could one possibly catch such a will-o'-the-wisp?

In 1983 an imaginative Belgian named Pierre Sikivie, a theorist with the University of Florida at Gainesville, arrived at a clever solution for catching axions. While teaching a course on electromagnetism, it occurred to him that if an axion passed through a particularly intense magnetic field (roughly 200,000 times that of Earth's magnetic field), it should decay and emit microwaves at a specific frequency. Inspired by Sikivie's insight, a team of physicists working at the Brookhaven National Laboratory in the United States built an axion detector consisting of a pure copper cylinder surrounded by a superconducting magnet. The cylinder was just the right size—sixteen inches tall and eight inches wide—for resonating at microwave frequencies, much the way an organ pipe resonates at a given frequency when filled with air. According to Sikivie's theory, if an axion passes through such a cylinder, the magnet should make the axion decay. The resulting burst of microwaves would produce hardly more than a trillionth of a trillionth of a watt of power, but that would still be enough to make the cylinder resonate at detectable levels.

After three years of searching, the Brookhaven researchers did not register any axion-related peeps resonating within their cylinder, but they weren't too surprised. Tuning into the exact microwave frequency depends on knowing a very precise mass for the axion, and current theoretical values are not constrained tightly enough. What the researchers do know is that the axion couldn't weigh much more than a billionth the mass of an electron; otherwise, the neutrino signal that emanated from the spectacular Magellanic supernova of 1987 would have been smothered. ("Heavy" axions would have cooled the supernova so much that the burst of neutrinos emanating from the explosion could not have been seen by underground detectors on Earth.) The axion hunters at Brookhaven scanned the frequencies of 1–6 gigahertz, using copper cylinders of different sizes and repositioning a sapphire rod in each to subtly adjust the frequency. "It's as if we were looking for a specific station on a radio that has five million channels," says Bruce Moskowitz, a Brookhaven physicist who had collaborated on the project.

Sikivie and his colleagues are continuing the search at the University of Florida. There they operate a microwave cavity ten times more sensitive than the Brookhaven model, tuning it with two ceramic rods. It is a frustrating business, because not seeing a signal does not necessarily mean the axion doesn't exist—only that it is terribly hard to trap. Sikivie estimates that the sensitivity of their axion detector probably has to be improved a few hundredfold before axions can be sighted with assurance. He hopes to accomplish that in the future with the construction of a three-thousand-liter cavity surrounded by a gargantuan magnet formerly used for fusion research at the U.S. Livermore National Laboratory.

Dark-matter detection in the laboratory is tricky in more than just technical ways—funding is scarce, and researchers may spend years developing an instrument that could become obsolete with a change in theory. Very speculative candidates abound, such as "quark nuggets," "shadow matter," and "boson stars." One perpetual contender is the monopole, a particle conceived as a solitary magnetic pole, either a north or a south, but not both. Theoretical wizard Paul Dirac first predicted the monopole's existence more than half a century ago when he contemplated nature's many symmetries. If the universe provides us with separate units of electric charge—the positively charged proton and the negatively charged electron, for example—then it's likely, Dirac surmised, that it also cooked up separate particles of magnetic charge. Monopoles naturally arise in grand unified theories as well. Much like neutrinos, monopoles are now out of fashion as a dark-matter possibility, but detecting just one could change that. A large collaboration of Italian and American scientists is taking a look with the new Monopole, Astrophysics, and Cosmic-Ray Observatory (MACRO), a series of detectors set in a football-field-sized arena of iron and concrete, located deep inside Italy's Gran Sasso, highest of the Apennine mountain range, sixty miles east of Rome.

Having a variety of instruments is vital to this enterprise, because different materials and techniques favor different types of dark-matter candidates; the greater the assortment, the better the chances that the true dark-matter particle (if that is what the dark matter is truly composed of) will be detected. The trickiest part for dark-matter hunters will be convincing themselves that they have observed a bona fide dark-matter particle with their detector. How can they be absolutely sure the registered event wasn't an instrumental "burp" or a stray cosmic ray? One way would be to look for a small but marked difference in the dark-matter signal over the course of the year. If they are real, dark-matter particles should be hovering around and through our Milky Way galaxy like a tenuous fog. Thus our solar system would be moving through this dark-matter mist as the Sun orbits around the center of our galaxy at some 130 miles per second. When it is summertime in the northern hemisphere, Earth's twenty-mile-per-second motion in its orbit about the Sun parallels the Sun's motion through the Milky Way, consequently, the Earth would pass through the sea of dark-matter particles a bit faster. Like a car speeding through the rain and picking up more raindrops on its windshield, our planet would pick up a few more dark-matter particles. Conversely, in the wintertime, with the Earth moving in the opposite direction, there would be fewer dark-matter particles hitting the Earth. A genuine dark-matter signal in the laboratory should therefore rise and fall by several percentage points over a year's time—a tiny effect but a potentially observable one.

And there are other ways that dark-matter particles, particularly the WIMPs, might give themselves away. If our entire galaxy is truly submerged in a halo of WIMPs—those supersymmetric weakly interacting massive particles—the Sun should have captured a bellyful over the course of its five-billion-year-old life. Earth, too, could be pooling WIMPs in its core. If so, some of these WIMPs could annihilate, emitting neutrinos much more energetic than those being emitted by the Sun. Several underground experiments, designed originally to learn whether protons decay, are already on the lookout for this WIMP-related signal. The lack of a signal so far, at the levels of sensitivity currently available, has ruled out certain supersymmetric particles, such as two types of sneutrinos. A better view will come with the next generation of neutrino detectors now being proposed, such as a vast array of phototubes strung for hundreds of feet under a deep lake or ocean, with the high-energy neutrinos being spotted by the special light they emit as they speed through the water. Some propose putting the phototubes in deep holes drilled into the Antarctic ice.

WIMPs should also be annihilating in the Milky Way's dark-matter halo, sending out gamma rays, antiprotons, and positrons. Such radiation is conceivably detectable, but trying to distinguish that signal from the vast cacophony of radiative noise emanating from our galaxy could prove even more challenging than finding WIMPs in the lab.

Some physicists don't like the idea of passive detectors at all, believing the signal will turn out to be much too faint. They would rather create WIMPs in powerful particle accelerators. For supersymmetric particles, the smoking gun would be a sort of hole in the accelerator debris, a missing energy that cannot be accounted for. It would be an indication that some unknown particle, an undetectable neutral mote, is taking energy away in the collision. Pauli used a similar strategy when he hypothesized the neutrino to explain the lost energy in radioactive beta decay. Finding just one supersymmetric particle would probably mean that all the hypothesized supersymmetric particles are real, with the lightest and most stable of these particles being excellent candidates for the dark matter.

There was great enthusiasm in the 1980s that the dark matter would soon be cornered. Now, there is a retrenchment; the field has entered a wait-and-see period. All the easy answers have slipped away. Both physicists and astronomers declare that identifying the dark matter is a top priority. "Until we identify the source of the observed gravitational effects we cannot be absolutely sure that dark matter exists, let alone that it is nonbaryonic," Primack, Seckel, and Sadoulet reported in a review of ongoing dark-matter-detection projects. "Identification of the dark matter is one of the most important tasks confronting physicists and astronomers today. What if we don't succeed? We are still left wondering what the universe is about. . . ." Success will surely provide a clearer understanding of the origin of the universe. But for now, dark-matter hunters are buried under a plethora of possibilities. Which avenue is most fruitful will be known only in hindsight, when the particle has finally been snared. When it is, a new era will dawn, bringing a new and exciting vision of the universe's essential makeup. Dark-matter detection will complete this story, at last telling us of the stuff that the universe is made of.

"If dark matter is made up of particles that are not ordinary matter, then it will be the ultimate Copernican revolution," Sadoulet has declared. Having already lost our central position in the universe's topography, we must come to terms with the possibility that the very atoms in our bodies are a minor constituent as well. "We are just this small excess, an insignificant phenomenon," suggests Sadoulet, "and the universe is something completely different."

No matter which of the dark-matter detectors proves successful, physicists and astronomers would be overjoyed by just one event. That occasion, if and when it occurs, would be as momentous as the discovery in 1965 of the universe's microwave background, the fossil echo of the big bang itself.

And if such a discovery were to happen tomorrow? "I'd retire," says David Seckel with a laugh. "I'd retire."

· 12 ·

Copernicus Revisited

One of the great charms of the study of Nature lies in the circumstance that no new advance, however small, is ever final. There are no blind alleys in scientific investigation. Every new fact is the opening of a new path.

—WILLIAM HUGGINS, 1880

We can explain, by fudging here and there, many things.

—COMMENT HEARD AT AN ASTRONOMY CONFERENCE

Assembling everyone on the outdoor patio classroom takes time. The morning session is scheduled to start at nine o'clock, but few arrive until half past the hour. Conference participants are finding it hard to break away from the bright Colorado sun, the vivid blue sky, and the spectacular view of the aspen-filled mountainsides. Aspen seeds, cottonlike wisps, continually float through the air like a summertime snowfall. Friendly chat is heard as colleagues, a few dozen in all, greet one another. The young postdocs in the crowd, at the start of their careers, take the opportunity to mingle with the best in their field. It is an eclectic group of astrophysicists, mostly male, from universities across the United States and around the world.

These scientists have gathered at the Aspen Center for Physics, a rustic complex situated on the edge of the posh resort town, to talk about the formation of galaxies, just one of several weeks-long workshops being held in the summer of 1991 at the renowned institute. The conversation is filled predominantly with such technical phrases as "correlation function" and "power law," but the question of the dark matter continually lurks in the background, sometimes coming out in the open.

"WHERE DOES THE DARK MATTER COME FROM?" session leader Simon White writes in big, bold letters on the patio blackboard. Could it be cold dark matter, or might it be neutrinos? Jupiters, faint stars, and black holes must also be considered. Could it be anything smaller? asks someone from the audience. "Well, I know Jupiters exist, but I don't know about stellar footballs," quips White.

Jerry Ostriker, in the sort of back-of-the-envelope analysis for which the Princeton astrophysicist is so famous, comes up with a rather straightforward argument for assessing the dark matter, based upon observational evidence. He points out that over the last five billion years about 3 percent of all galaxies have experienced a merger with another galaxy. It is not common, he notes, but it does occur. And when such a fateful collision takes place and this added matter spirals into a galactic disk, the disk thickens up in response, because of heating. The thickness of our own galactic disk can be accounted for by smaller satellite galaxies spiraling into the Milky Way over the eons.

But if there is lots and lots of dark matter in the cosmos, enough to bring the universe to critical density, spiral galaxies should be gobbling up mass voraciously. Yet, astronomers are not observing such gluttonous cosmic banquets. Could this mean, asks Ostriker, that the dark matter is not really there or just distributed too smoothly and evenly to impart such an effect?

Later in the workshop, cosmochemist James Truran of the University of Illinois reviews the chemical evolution of the universe, trying to pinpoint the momentous epoch when the first stars turned on, beginning the process of transforming the gaseous balls of hydrogen and helium into such heavier elements as carbon, nitrogen, and oxygen. Some of the oldest stars in the Milky Way are located in the galaxy's outer halo and contain $1/10,000$ the amount of heavy elements seen in our Sun, a far younger star. These halo stars were likely created out of the pure clouds of hydrogen and helium that condensed to give birth to the Milky Way; their pristine, unadulterated compositions suggest that there wasn't a previous population of element-producing stars to taint their contents. The possibility, however, still exists that very massive stars, each more than one hundred thousand times the mass of our Sun, formed very early on and then imploded rather than exploded at their death, leaving few traces of their existence but continuing to lurk around as a dark, hidden matter nonetheless. Yet when Ostriker asks Truran, "Can you yet tell whether there was a very early population of stars that now serves as dark baryonic matter?" Truran can only respond, "I simply can't say."

Thirty years ago, as astronomers were coming to terms with the successful development of the model of stellar nucleosynthesis, Caltech astronomer Jesse Greenstein voiced a cautious note that could equally apply to today's debate over the nature of the dark matter and the ultimate composition of the universe. "We still make wild extrapolations, but now within a range limited by some facts. How close are we to the truth?" he asked in 1963. "The history of science gives us little comfort; guesses as to the ultimate are seldom validated, seldom even remembered."

Telescopes and detectors continue their scans of the heavens. More often than not, the additional bits of evidence these instruments gather daily simply confirm and extend currently accepted models of the universe. But at times a finding can generate new challenges, becoming a piece in the cosmic puzzle that never quite fits in. Such crises in astronomy periodically wax and wane over the decades. In the 1930s Edwin Hubble, after measuring how fast the universe was ballooning outward, turned the clock backwards and calculated how long this expansion could have been transpiring. He was forced to conclude that, based on the evidence, the universe was younger than the Earth! This paradox swiftly disappeared once the art of cosmic distance measurements was refined and advanced, correcting Hubble's initial and mistaken finding. "It's foolish to bet when things are just above the threshold," says theorist Joseph Silk of the University of California at Berkeley. "So many errors creep in." But which of the measurements made today are in error and which are the invaluable clues hinting at a new vision that might lead to a reinterpretation of our cosmic heritage? The process of science does not always provide neat and tidy answers.

Evidence can arrive from unexpected arenas. As Alexander Fleming, the noted Scottish bacteriologist and discoverer of penicillin, noted about the scientific enterprise, "One sometimes finds what one is not looking for." In recent years, for example, extragalactic surveyors have come to learn that galaxies may not be flying outward with the universe's expansion in as regular and orderly a fashion as they once thought. The cosmic sea appears to be awash with a number of strong, local currents. For example, the Milky Way and all its neighbors for hundreds of millions of light-years in every direction seem to be rushing toward an immense concentration of matter in distant space that has come to be known as the "Great Attractor." This localized streaming, if it holds up under further scrutiny, sorely tests astronomers' models of the universe's workings. All in all, this great gravitational magnet, situated roughly 200 million light-years away in the direction of the Hydra and Centaurus constellations in the southern sky, is composed of tens of thousands of galaxies. And just as in both Fritz Zwicky's clusters and Vera Rubin's rotating galaxies, 90 percent or more of the gravitating mass in the Great Attractor is unseen and nonluminous. More recent observations suggest that there may be even bigger collections of mass at distances beyond the Great Attractor. Some claim that the gravitational might of these massive concentrations, pulling us and our galactic neighbors toward them, indicates the presence of far more dark matter in the universe than previously observed, perhaps enough to bring the cosmos to critical density. Moreover, the reverberations of the big bang detected by the COBE satellite are particularly faint, also suggesting that the ripples have been relentlessly moving through a dense sea of dark matter for eons.

In some ways we are experiencing a cyclic return to the original musings of Aristotle and his fellow philosophers. The ancient Greeks spoke of a primal matter receiving form, and transforming into earth, air, fire, and water. The largest component, the essence of the heavens itself, stood alone and apart as the ether. Today, scientists speak of a big bang generating mass-energy that later takes on several forms, such as quarks, electrons, and neutrinos. The quarks combine to form protons and neutrons, the stuff of ordinary life and all the glowing celestial objects in the sky. But are there other forms? Are the Mendelevian elements only a minor detail in the ultimate cosmic makeup? Has the dark matter become a sort of post-Aristotelian ether, renewed and reshaped in our modern concern for the missing mass? Or will this new ether eventually disappear as well, just as Maxwell's ether evaporated in the brilliant light cast by the radical theory of relativity?

No ready explanation for the dark matter awaits in the wings, except perhaps further "epicycles" attached to present-day models. Epicycles were those "wheels within wheels" that Ptolemy, building on work by the Greek astronomer Hipparchus, added to his Earth-centered model of the solar system to explain the apparent motions of the planets, which seemed to trace a series of loops against the fixed background of distant stars. He imagined that each planet was anchored to the outer rim of a wheel, which in turn rolled along a larger circle centered on the Earth. Copernicus radically simplified this model by offering a new paradigm—a completely new way of looking at old, familiar facts—to resolve the growing complications in Ptolemy's cumbersome scheme. By moving the Sun to the center of the "universe," Copernicus made epicycles irrelevant. Each planet, including Earth, simply revolved around the Sun at a different speed. As a result, when a planet was viewed from Earth against the fixed background of stars, it appeared to be moving sometimes forward and sometimes backward, depending on the relative speed and position of each planet. When a swifter-moving Earth bypasses a slower-moving Mars, for example, Mars temporarily appears to move backward in the celestial sky.

Kepler experienced a revelation of similar consequence. Wedded at first to the concept of circles as planetary orbits, he trudged through endless calculations to explain the orbit of Mars and was freed from his toils only by recognizing the ellipse as the preferred planetary pathway. Will an equivalent paradigm shift be needed to explain the dark matter? Tremors are all around us. Zwicky discerned that a large component of the mass in a cluster of galaxies is "missing," unseen and undetected. Decades later, the rumbles got louder: Rubin concluded that individual spiraling galaxies must be immersed in some dark, unnamed material. Are these the tremors that foreshadow a bigger quake ahead, a temblor that wrenches the center of our universe once again? Perhaps the dark-matter anomaly, once explained, will lead to the next scientific revolution, a new view of the heavens as momentous as the ones kindled by Copernicus and Kepler. Or will a solution to the dark-matter mystery merely add a few mundane details to current models of the universe? "I'd love to have this problem solved in my scientific lifetime," says Carlos Frenk, "but my greatest fear is that the solution will be boring."

Despite their common goal to reveal how the universe works, astronomers and physicists in some ways have different expectations of nature. A major tenet that drives many theorists in their study of physics is that nature should be simple and elegant. "Experience has shown that nature does share our sense of economy, efficiency, beauty, and mathematical subtlety," writes theorist Paul Davies in his book *The Mind of God*, "and this approach to research can often pay dividends. . . ." For Einstein, a theory was made more impressive by the "simplicity of its premises." Such a principle has long served as a useful guide in science, and the physics community largely brings this expectation to its study of cosmology—that solutions to its problems should be aesthetically pleasing and natural. The mission faced by astronomers, on the other hand, is to explore and describe the universe as it really is, from the nearby shores of our solar system to the distant realm of the quasars. In the process, they must deal with the immense intricacy of the heavens—its chaos, diversity, and many interactions. While a physical law can be simple, its realization or execution is often quite complicated. A modest example is the weather, a physical arena in which straightforward laws of temperature and pressure can lead to multifarious realities. Astronomers, who continually observe and catalogue a vast array of celestial objects, are well aware of this fact.

For now, as they wrestle with the dark-matter problem, cosmologists don't know which perspective will be the most valuable. Should we expect complexity or simplicity in our cosmos? On the very largest scales, we do observe a rather simple universe, and general relativity describes its behavior fairly accurately. But that doesn't mean that other cosmic properties, such as the universe's composition and structure, will likewise be simple. The universe evolved from a homogeneous plasma to an entity filled with intricate structures. It is as if nature took plain water and somehow constructed an elaborate festival of ice, a display of wondrous ice sculptures. And it is likely that such structures were the result of complicated physics. Star formation itself is an immensely intricate affair involving many mechanisms, such as magnetic fields, gravity, and shock waves. It is as "simple" as the weather.

That may be why the various theories on the nature of the dark matter get some things right but miss on others. If the dark matter is ultimately found to consist of exotic particles, then it will be relatively easy to describe the universe's contents. A handful of numbers, the physical properties of this exotic matter, will essentially tell us all about it. But if the solution is found in more ordinary astrophysical objects, say brown dwarfs, then astronomers will have much more work ahead of them. They will have to figure out how so many near-stars came to be formed. In short, it will be a messy business.

Berkeley's Joe Silk and Princeton's Jim Peebles wrote an article in the journal *Nature*, half tongue in cheek, developing what racetrack fans call a "book," covering the odds on whether anyone as yet has correctly explained the nature of the dark matter and the origin of the universe's structure. The two scientists evaluated each theory—from the canonical model of cold dark matter to the idea of exotic cosmic strings swimming through a universal sea of massive neutrinos—and assigned them longer and longer odds depending on the number of hypothetical particles or unproven physical laws each required. According to these cosmic odds-makers, some of the most conventional theories—that we live in an open universe filled solely with ordinary matter, for instance—have perhaps a one in three chance of being right; other scenarios are so speculative that their overall chances are more than thirty million to one.

"I have this dream that there will be a sort of Sherlock Holmes event," says Peebles. "Someone will look at this great pyramid of evidence that is building up and exclaim, 'Yes, Watson, I think I see it. By Jove, that must be it.' It did happen with quantum mechanics. In 1925, quantum mechanics was, quite literally, a tower of Babel. People knew how to compute atomic energy levels and decay rates, but it was a mish-mash of ad-hoc prescriptions and rules. Then suddenly, with the clarifications of Schrödinger and Dirac, a theory emerged that has worked so wonderfully well ever since."

It is still possible that the crisis will subside or be explained in another way altogether. Perhaps the dark matter is but a delusion. Could Einstein have been right all along? In 1917, shortly after introducing his theory of general relativity, Einstein tacked an extra term onto his equations. He made the adjustment out of desperation. Astronomers at the time were observing a universe that appeared static and unchanging. But the theory of general relativity predicted that the universe should be in some kind of motion, all the galaxies moving inward, for example. To bring his theory in line with observations, Einstein came up with the extra term, calling it the "cosmological constant." It did not define a material substance per se but rather an added energy that permeated empty space and exerted a sort of outward "pressure" on it, affecting the universe's evolution and dynamics. The term, as Einstein used it, indicated that there was a repulsive force at work in the cosmos, a kind of antigravity that exactly balanced the inward gravitational attraction of the galaxies, keeping them from moving. The universe stayed put. But once Edwin Hubble revealed that our universe was rapidly ballooning outward, Einstein quickly (and gladly) dropped the cosmological constant, calling it the biggest scientific mistake of his life. Einstein always believed the constant sullied the symmetric beauty of his gravitational equations anyhow. His original theory, without the constant, could already accommodate an expanding motion.

"Physicists often say that Einstein's equations are more aesthetically pleasing without the constant," responds astronomer Gérard de Vaucouleurs, "but that's not a good reason to dismiss it. We like things to be simple in science, but nature usually turns out to be more complicated." A small cosmological constant at work in the universe would have interesting consequences. Since energy and mass are equivalent, according to $E = mc^2$, this added energy could mimic some of the effects of a missing mass, such as inflating a universe with little matter in it to the very edge between open and closed.

For that matter, estimates of the amount of dark matter in the universe assume that clusters and galaxies are "in equilibrium"—in other words, settled and quiescent. But what if the clusters are more active, continually and steadily exchanging matter and energy with their immediate environment? Such clusters might seem stable, but only because they are viewed over such a short span of time, much the way a mountain appears unperturbed during a human lifetime yet is still subtly eroding away. Simple gravitational models cannot be applied to such systems. Zwicky assumed that gravity alone was at work when he estimated the amount of dark matter in the Coma cluster. But if other forces are involved, then the need to have dark matter in these clusters may disappear, or at least be sharply reduced. Gerrit Verschuur, in an essay on this idea, cautions:

> The cosmologically important "missing mass" problem may not be related to mass. It may be a missing-the-point problem. . . . If we wish to describe the properties of galaxies and describe why they exist, we may have to consider the nature of far-from-equilibrium processes and their apparently magical ability to create order out of chaos, an order or structure that gives the illusion of stability, especially when viewed from our instant in cosmic time. . . . If this point of view is considered then the so-called missing mass problem ceases to be an issue.

Nevertheless, such alternatives are not extremely popular among the larger community of astrophysicists, who are not yet eager to include many more unrestrained parameters into their models. For the moment, "Occam's Razor" prevails, the longstanding rule of thumb established by the English philosopher William of Occam in the fourteenth century. He stated it thus: *Pluralitas non est ponenda sine necessitate,* which can be translated as "plurality must not be posited without necessity." Scientists are strongly guided by the essence of Occam's basic advice, that the simplest interpretation is preferred over an unnecessarily complex one—until forced to do otherwise. "More important," adds Simon White, "many of these alternate theories for the dark matter are incomplete and ill defined. They echo Hamlet's comment to Horatio—'there are more things in heaven and earth than are dreamt of in your philosophy'—but without offering a scientific hypothesis for what those things might be."

Physicists and astronomers alike await the ending to this drama, the search for the ultimate cosmic recipe. The current situation, unsettled as it is, is in all likelihood merely an intermission in the proceedings. For those dismayed by the lack of a gratifying denouement to this story, I offer the optimistic words of Cecilia Payne-Gaposchkin, whose faith in the ability of science to solve its mysteries remained steadfast and unshakable over her lifetime:

It is true that we base our work on observed facts. If nothing were observed, there would be nothing to understand. But the facts are not the reality: that is something that lies beneath the facts and gives them

"Incredible! It turns out the four unifying forces in the universe are air, earth, fire, and water!"

coherence. If science, as I know it, can be described in a few words, it might be called a search for the Unseen. . . . The physical world has no actual substance at all; in my simplistic view its primal quality, the basis of its grandeur and majesty, is consistency. Primitive man worshipped Sun and Moon because they were dependable, predictable. All our observations require that we dig deeper into understanding to show that they, too, are consistent with pattern. Nature has always had a trick of surprising us, and she will continue to surprise us. But she has never let us down yet. We can go forward with confidence "knowing that Nature never did betray the heart that loved her."

Acknowledgments

Several years ago a former editor of mine, seeking a potential topic for my next book, asked me, "What is the most outstanding question in astronomy?" Very quickly I replied, "The dark matter."

I was not particularly eager to write a book solely on the dark-matter mystery. By then, several fine books on the topic had already been published for the general audience, but my editor's inquiry caused me to start thinking about the issue in broader terms: How did astronomers come to learn the composition of the universe at all? The dark-matter riddle, I would soon realize, was only the latest chapter in a centuries-long pursuit to discover the material essence of the cosmos.

Many histories of astronomy tend to be written from one overriding perspective; they prefer to show how advances in astronomy, its new instrumentation and its myriad discoveries over the centuries, have expanded the borders of the known universe—our sense of both space and time. What is not usually addressed directly (if at all) is astronomy's ongoing concern with matter, or more precisely cosmic matters. My desire to fill that gap initiated an endeavor that came to dominate my professional life for the next few years.

I would like to thank Barry and Trudy Silverstein of the Adirondack Mountain Foundation, as well as the foundation's former director Burton Raffel, for inviting me to upstate New York, where I spent a splendid week several summers ago finalizing the outline for this book. It was the first step in a venture that eventually encompassed two continents and more that one hundred interviews in the course of my research, both historic and journalistic.

My gratitude is extended to a host of archivists and librarians, who so patiently answered my questions and pointed me in the right direction amidst the stacks. They include Paula Agranat-Hurwitz and Shelly Erwin at Caltech's Millikan Library in Pasadena, California; Sheila Doyle at the Palace Green Library at the University of Durham in England; Marilyn Gisser with the American Institute of Physics in New York City; Martha Hazen at the Harvard-Smithsonian Center for Astrophysics in Cambridge, Massachusetts; Helen Knudsen at Caltech's astrophysics department library; Jean Sanderson at the Institute of Astronomy in Cambridge, England; and the dedicated staff of the Science Library at the Massachusetts Institute of Technology, my virtual home away from home for many months. (I highly recommend the library's tranquilizing view of the Charles River and Boston skyline.) Some of the quotations by Jesse Greenstein and William Fowler were taken from interviews conducted for the American Institute of Physics History of Physics Project by Spencer Weart and Charles Weiner respectively, who kindly allowed them to be used; likewise, other quotations by Fowler and Greenstein were taken from interviews conducted by John Greenberg and Rachel Prud'homme for the California Institute of Technology Oral History Project.

My deep appreciation goes to those scientists interviewed for the book who so graciously agreed to review the sections dealing with their work. They are Ralph Alpher, Geoffrey Blake, Bernard Carr, Angela Da Silva, Carlos Frenk, Margaret Geller, Owen Gingerich, Jesse Greenstein, Kim Griest, Todd Henry, Robert Herman, Paul Hewett, Fred Hoyle, John Huchra, Donald McCarthy, George Rieke, Vera Rubin, Bernard Sadoulet, Wallace Sargent, David Schramm, Sergei Shandarin, Pierre Sikivie, Alan Smith, Lewis Snyder, Charles Townes, J. Anthony Tyson, Gerrit Verschuur, Ward Whaling, Simon White, and Frank Wilczek. Katherine Haramundanis, in reviewing the chapter on Cecilia Payne-Gaposchkin, provided me with many important insights on her mother.

I am equally grateful to those investigators and historians who so generously gave their time in reading over chapters concerning the areas of their expertise and offering some very constructive criticism. They include David DeVorkin, curator of astronomy at the National Air and Space Museum; Peggy Kidwell with the National Museum of American History; David Park of Williams College in Massachusetts; and Faye Ajzenberg-Selove of the University of Pennsylvania, whose remembrances of the early days of Caltech's Kellogg Laboratory were extremely helpful.

Thanks must also be given to those astronomers, physicists, and researchers who provided me with invaluable background material during long, pleasurable talks about their fields of interest: Charles Barnes, George Blumenthal, Adam Burrows, Conard Dahn, Ruth Daly, David Dewhurst, Alan Dressler, Richard Ellis, W. Kent Ford, Alan Guth, Lindsey Hedges, Donna Hurley, Richard Kron, Don Landis, James Liebert, Robert Lanou, Jerry Ostriker, Bernard Pagel, Jim Peebles, Joel Primack, Martin Rees, Ron Ross, Anneila Sargent, Joseph Silk, David Spergel, Thomas Statler, Ian Thompson, James Truran, Edwin Turner, Neil Turok, Ning Wang, and Gerald Wasserburg. For their administrative assistance in either arranging interviews and visits or providing source material, I thank Jane Dietrich, Robert Finn, Jan Haskell, and Kathie Venturelli at Caltech; John Gribbin in England; Sally Mencimer at the Aspen Center for Physics; James Cornell at the Harvard–Smithsonian Center for Astrophysics; and Rose Sargent at the Center for Particle Astrophysics. Randy Bergman at the Colgate-Palmolive Company was helpful in clarifying the history of Axion and pointing out that the laundry product was a bleach alternative and not a detergent, as widely assumed in scientific circles.

All the while friends and colleagues continually bestowed much-needed support (and sympathetic ears) as I struggled to transform hundreds of pages of chaotic notes into readable text. For this I thank Edward Bliss, Andy Chaikin, Dona Cooper, Elizabeth and Goetz Eaton, Sarah and John Gustafson, Eileen and Mike Lemonick, Elizabeth Maggio, Cole Smith, Sarah and Peter Saulson, and Janna and Jon Yamron, as well as my parents, my brother Chet, my sisters Vicki and Jane, and all of their families.

This book could not have been completed without the cooperation and assistance of the wonderful staff at *Discover* magazine, where some of the material in these pages first appeared. For their particular efforts, appreciation is due K. C. Cole, Roseann Henry, Paul Hoffman, Jeff Kluger, Rob Kunzig, Mark Zabludoff, and Carl Zimmer.

A very heartfelt thanks goes to my agent (and friend) Russell Galen, whose enthusiasm never flagged as he deftly shepherded my proposal to its publishing home. I thank Tom Miller, my first editor, for his great energy in championing my project in its initial stages, along with his able assistant Jim Hornfischer. Later, I had the great pleasure of working closely with Cynthia Barrett, who so expertly guided my manuscript through the final editorial thickets (with her ever-helpful assistant Ari Hoogenboom smoothing the way). I am especially grateful to Gladys Carr for her steadfast support behind the scenes throughout these years.

Lastly, and most important, I must acknowledge my husband, Steve Lowe, whose loving encouragement, high spirits, and sage scientific advice enabled me to bring this formidable project to completion. Thank you, Steve, for being there.

Bibliography

Aaronson, Marc. "Accurate Radial Velocities for Carbon Stars in Draco and Ursa Minor: The First Hint of a Dwarf Spheroidal Mass-to-Light Ratio." *Astrophysical Journal* 266 (March 1, 1983): L11–L15.

Abetti, Giorgio. *The History of Astronomy*. New York: Henry Schuman, 1952.

Albrecht, Andreas, and Paul J. Steinhardt. "Cosmology for Grand Unified Theories with Radiatively Induced Symmetry Breaking." *Physical Review Letters* 48 (April 26, 1982): 1220–1223.

Alpher, R. A. "A Neutron-Capture Theory of the Formation and Relative Abundance of the Elements." *Physical Review* 74 (December 1, 1948): 1577.

Alpher, R. A., and Robert Herman. "Reflections on Early Work on 'Big Bang' Cosmology." *Physics Today* (August 1988): 24–34.

Alpher, R. A., H. Bethe, and G. Gamow. "The Origin of Chemical Elements." *Physical Review* 73 (April 1, 1948): 803–804.

Amaldi, Ginestra. *The Nature of Matter: Physical Theory from Thales to Fermi*. Chicago: University of Chicago Press, 1966.

Anderson, Carl D. "The Positive Electron." *Physical Review* 43 (March 15, 1933): 491–494.

Arnett, W. David, and James W. Truran, eds. *Nucleosynthesis: Challenges and New Developments*. Chicago: University of Chicago Press, 1985.

Ashbrook, Joseph. *The Astronomical Scrapbook*. Cambridge: Cambridge University Press, 1984.

Atkinson, R. D'E. "Atomic Synthesis and Stellar Energy. I." *Astrophysical Journal* 73 (May 1931): 250.

Baade, W., and F. Zwicky. "Supernovae and Cosmic Rays." *Physical Review* 45 (January 15, 1934): 138.

———. "On Super-Novae." *Proceedings of the National Academy of Sciences* 20 (May 15, 1934): 254–259.

———. "Cosmic Rays from Super-Novae." *Proceedings of the National Academy of Sciences* 20 (May 15, 1934): 259–263.

———. "Remarks on Super-Novae and Cosmic Rays." *Physical Review* 46 (July 1, 1934): 76–77.

Bahcall, J., T. Piran, and S. Weinberg, eds. *Dark Matter in the Universe.* Singapore: World Scientific, 1987.

Barnard, E. E. "On a Great Nebulous Region and on the Question of Absorbing Matter in Space and the Transparency of the Nebulae." *Astrophysical Journal* 31 (1910): 8.

———. "On the Markings of the Sky with a Catalog of 182 Such Objects." *Astrophysical Journal* 50 (1919): 1.

Barnes, C. A., D. D. Clayton, and D. N. Schramm, eds. *Essays in Nuclear Astrophysics.* Cambridge: Cambridge University Press, 1982.

Bartusiak, Marcia. "Signposts in the Sky." *Discover* (July 1981): 56–58.

———. *Thursday's Universe.* New York: Times Books, 1986.

———. "Coming Home." *Discover* (September 1988): 30–37.

———. "Wanted: Dark Matter." *Discover* (December 1988): 63–69.

———. "Mapping the Universe." *Discover* (August 1990): 60–63.

———. "The Woman Who Spins the Stars." *Discover* (October 1990): 88–94.

———. "The Hunt for Brown Dwarfs." *Discover* (April 1991): 40–53.

Beckwith, Steven, and Anneila Sargent. "HL Tauri: A Site for Planet Formation?" *Mercury* 16 (November/December 1987): 178–181.

Berry, Arthur. *A Short History of Astronomy.* London: John Murray, 1898.

Blumenthal, George R., S. M. Faber, Joel R. Primack, and Martin J. Rees. "Formation of Galaxies and Large Scale Structures with Cold Dark Matter." *Nature* 311 (1984): 517.

Boardman, John, Jasper Griffin, and Oswyn Murray, eds. *Greece and the Hellenistic World.* Oxford: Oxford University Press, 1988.

"The Bold Star Gazer." *Time* (September 26, 1955): 50.

Booth, Gerald. "Dark Matter: The Universe Beyond Our Vision." *L&S at Cal* (Spring 1989): 4–9.

Brewster, David. *Memoirs of the Life, Writings, and Discoveries of Sir Isaac Newton,* vol. 1. New York: Johnson Reprint Corp., 1965.

Brush, Stephen G. "How Cosmology Became a Science." *Scientific American* (August 1992): 62–70.

Burbidge, Geoffrey. "The Cult of the Missing Mass." *Sky and Telescope* (June 1990): 580.

Burbidge, Margaret, and Geoffrey Burbidge. "Formation of Elements in Stars." *Science* 128 (August 22, 1958): 387–399.

Burbidge, E. Margaret, G. R. Burbidge, William A. Fowler, and F. Hoyle. "Synthesis of the Elements in Stars." *Reviews of Modern Physics* 29 (October 1957): 547–650.

Calder, Nigel. *The Key to the Universe: A Report on the New Physics*. New York: Viking Press, 1977.

Carr, B. J. "Baryonic Dark Matter." *Comments on Astrophysics* 14 (February 1990): 257–280.

Carr, B. J., and C. G. Lacey. "Dark Clusters in Galactic Halos?" *Astrophysical Journal* 316 (May 1, 1987): 23–35.

Chaikin, Andrew. "Great Wall of the Cosmos." *Omni* (August 1991): 34–40.

Chandrasekhar, S. *An Introduction to the Study of Stellar Structure*. Chicago: University of Chicago Press, 1939.

———. *Eddington*. Cambridge: Cambridge University Press, 1983.

Cheung, A. C., D. M. Rank, C. H. Townes, D. D. Thornton, and W. J. Welch. "Detection of NH_3 Molecules in the Interstellar Medium by Their Microwave Emission." *Physical Review Letters* 21 (December 16, 1968): 1701–1705.

———. "Detection of Water in Interstellar Regions by Its Microwave Radiation." *Nature* 221 (February 15, 1969): 626–628.

Chincarini, Guido, and Herbert J. Rood. "The Cosmic Tapestry." *Sky and Telescope* (May 1980): 364–371.

Christianson, Gale E. *This Wild Abyss: The Story of the Men Who Made Modern Astronomy*. New York: Free Press, 1978.

Clerke, Agnes M. *A Popular History of Astronomy During the Nineteenth Century*. London: Adam and Charles Black, 1902.

Computers and the Cosmos. Alexandria, Va.: Time-Life Books, 1988.

Cornell, James, ed. *Bubbles, Voids, and Bumps in Time: The New Cosmology*. Cambridge: Cambridge University Press, 1989.

Cornell, James, and Alan P. Lightman. *Revealing the Universe: Prediction and Proof in Astronomy*. Cambridge: MIT Press, 1982.

Cosmology, Fusion, and Other Matters: George Gamow Memorial Volume. London: Adam Hilger Ltd., 1972.

Cowsik, R., and J. McClelland. "Gravity of Neutrinos of Nonzero Mass in Astrophysics." *Astrophysical Journal* 180 (February 15, 1973): 7–10.

Cox, P. A. *The Elements: Their Origin, Abundance, and Distribution*. Oxford: Oxford University Press, 1989.

Crease, Robert P., and Charles C. Mann. *The Second Creation: Makers of the Revolution in 20th-Century Physics*. New York: Macmillan Publishing Co., 1986.

Dar, Arnon. "Astrophysics and Cosmology Closing in on Neutrino Masses." *Science* 250 (December 14, 1990): 1529–1533.

Davies, Paul. *The Mind of God*. New York: Simon and Schuster, 1992.

Davis, Marc, George Efstathiou, Carlos S. Frenk, and Simon D. M. White. "The Evolution of Large-Scale Structure in a Universe Dominated by Cold Dark Matter." *Astrophysical Journal* 292 (May 15, 1985): 371–394.

Dekel, Avishai, and Martin J. Rees. "Physical Mechanisms for Biased Galaxy Formation." *Nature* 326 (April 2, 1987): 455–461.

De Lapparent, Valérie, Margaret J. Geller, and John P. Huchra. "A Slice of the Universe." *Astrophysical Journal* 302 (March 1, 1986): L1–L5.

De Rujula, A., D. V. Nanopoulos, and P. A. Shaver, eds. *A Unified View of the Macro- and the Micro-Cosmos.* Singapore: World Scientific, 1987.

De Vaucouleurs, Gérard. *Discovery of the Universe: An Outline of the History of Astronomy from the Origins to 1956.* New York: Macmillan Co., 1957.

———. "Supergalaxy." *Discovery* 5 (December 1980): 20–23.

DeVorkin, David. Interview with N. D. Conklin, Niels Bohr Library, American Institute of Physics, 1977.

———. "Community and Spectral Classification in Astrophysics: The Acceptance of E. C. Pickering's System in 1910." *Isis* 72 (1981): 29–49.

———. "Henry Norris Russell." *Scientific American* (May 1989): 127–133.

DeVorkin, David H., and Ralph Kenat. "Quantum Physics and the Stars. I. The Establishment of a Stellar Temperature Scale." *Journal for the History of Astronomy* 14 (June 1983): 102–132.

———. "Quantum Physics and the Stars. II. Henry Norris Russell and the Abundances of the Elements in the Atmospheres of the Sun and Stars." *Journal for the History of Astronomy* 14 (October 1983): 180–222.

Dirac, P. A. M. "Quantised Singularities in the Electromagnetic Field." *Proceedings of the Royal Society of London* A131 (September 1931): 60–72.

Dreyer, J. L. E. *A History of Astronomy from Thales to Kepler.* Dover Publications, 1953.

Drukier, Andrzej, Katherine Freese, and David N. Spergel. "Detecting Cold Dark-Matter Candidates." *Physical Review D* 33 (June 15, 1986): 3495–3507.

Dunbar, D. N. F., R. E. Pixley, W. A. Wenzel, and W. Whaling. "The 7.68-Mev State in C^{12}." *Physical Review* 92 (November 1, 1953): 649–650.

Durrell, Lawrence. *Caesar's Vast Ghost: Aspects of Provence.* London: Faber and Faber, 1990.

Eddington, A. S. "Diffuse Matter in Space." *Proceedings of the Royal Society* A111 (1926): 424.

Efstathiou, G., M. Davis, C. S. Frenk, and S. D. M. White. "Numerical Techniques for Large Cosmological N-Body Simulations." *Astrophysical Journal Supplement Series* 57 (February 1985): 241–260.

Eyster, Eugene H. "Note on the Interpretation of Unidentified Interstellar Lines." *Astrophysical Journal* 86 (November 1937): 486–488.

Feldman, Gary J., and Jack Steinberger. "The Number of Families of Matter." *Scientific American* (February 1991): 70–75.

Ferris, Timothy. *The Red Limit: The Search for the Edge of the Universe.* New York: William Morrow and Co., 1977.

———. *Coming of Age in the Milky Way*. New York: William Morrow and Co., 1988.

———, ed. *The World Treasury of Physics, Astronomy, and Mathematics*. Boston: Little, Brown and Co., 1991.

Field, George B., and Eric J. Chaisson. *The Invisible Universe*. Boston: Birkhauser, 1985.

Finkbeiner, Ann K. "Mapmaking on the Cosmic Scale." *Mosaic* 21 (Fall 1990): 12–25.

Fowler, William A. "The Origin of the Elements." *Scientific American* (September 1956): 82–91.

———. "Nuclear Astrophysics—Today and Yesterday." *Engineering and Science* 32 (June 1969): 8–13.

Freedman, David H. "The Ghost Particle Mystery." *Discover* (May 1991): 66–72.

———. "Concocting a Cosmic Recipe for Matter." *Science* 254 (October 18, 1991): 382–383.

Frenk, C. S. "Galaxy Clustering and the Dark-Matter Problem." *Phil. Trans. R. Soc. Lond. A* 330 (1986): 517–541.

Frenk, Carlos S., Simon D. M. White, Marc Davis, and George Efstathiou. "The Formation of Dark Halos in a Universe Dominated by Cold Dark Matter." *Astrophysical Journal* 327 (April 15, 1988): 507–525.

Gamow, George. *The Creation of the Universe*. New York: Viking Press, 1952.

———. *My World Line: An Informal Autobiography*. New York: Viking Press, 1970.

Geller, Margaret J. "Mapping the Universe." *World Book Science Year* (1984): 141–153.

Geller, Margaret J., and John P. Huchra. "Mapping the Universe." *Science* 246 (November 17, 1989): 897–903.

Gingerich, Owen. "Copernicus and Tycho." *Scientific American* 229 (December 1973): 86–101.

———. " 'Crisis' Versus Aesthetic in the Copernican Revolution." In *Vistas in Astronomy,* vol. 17. Oxford: Pergamon Press, 1975.

———. "The Aethereal Sky: Man's Search for a Plenum Universe." In *Great Ideas Today*. Chicago: Encyclopaedia Britannica, 1979.

———. "Unlocking the Chemical Secrets of the Cosmos." *Sky and Telescope* (July 1981): 13–15.

———. "Ptolemy, Copernicus, and Kepler." In *Great Ideas Today*. Chicago: Encyclopaedia Britannica, 1983.

———, ed. *The Nature of Scientific Discovery*. Washington: Smithsonian Institution Press, 1975.

———, ed. *The General History of Astronomy*. Vol. 4, *Astrophysics and Twentieth-Century Astronomy to 1950,* part A. Cambridge: Cambridge University Press, 1984.

Goldberg, Leo. "Atomic Spectroscopy and Astrophysics." *Physics Today* (August 1988): 38–45.

Goldsmith, Donald. *Supernova! The Exploding Star of 1987*. New York: St. Martin's Press, 1989.

———. *The Astronomers*. New York: St. Martin's Press, 1991.

Grant, Michael. *The Rise of the Greeks*. London: Weidenfeld and Nicolson, 1987.

Greenberg, John. Interview with William A. Fowler, California Institute of Technology Oral History Project, Caltech Archives, 1986.

Greenstein, Jesse L. "The History of Stars and Galaxies." *Proceedings of the National Academy of Sciences* 52 (August 1964): 549–565.

———. "Remembering Zwicky: Fritz Zwicky—Scientific Eagle." *Engineering and Science* (March/April 1974): 15–17.

———. "An Astronomical Life." In *Annual Review of Astronomy and Astrophysics*, vol. 22. Palo Alto: Annual Reviews, 1984.

Gregory, Bruce. *Inventing Reality*. New York: John Wiley and Sons, 1988.

Gribbin, John. *The Omega Point: The Search for the Missing Mass and the Ultimate Fate of the Universe*. London: William Heinemann Ltd., 1987.

Griest, Kim. "Cross Sections, Relic Abundance, and Detection Rates for Neutralino Dark Matter." *Physical Review D* 38 (October 15, 1988): 2357–2375.

Gushee, Vera. "Thomas Wright of Durham, Astronomer." *Isis* 33 (1941): 197–218.

Guth, Alan H. "Inflationary Universe: A Possible Solution to the Horizon and Flatness Problems." *Physical Review D* 23 (January 15, 1981): 347–356.

Guth, Alan H., and Paul J. Steinhardt. "The Inflationary Universe." *Scientific American* 250 (May 1984): 116–128.

Hagmann, C., P. Sikivie, N. S. Sullivan, and D. B. Tanner. "Results from a Search for Cosmic Axions." *Physical Review D* 42 (August 15, 1990): 1297–1300.

Hall, Nina, and Peter F. Smith. "The Race to Detect Dark Matter." *New Scientist* (April 25, 1992): 37–41.

Haramundanis, Katherine, ed. *Cecilia Payne-Gaposchkin: An Autobiography and Other Recollections*. Cambridge: Cambridge University Press, 1984.

Hawking, S. W., and W. Israel, eds. *Three Hundred Years of Gravitation*. Cambridge: Cambridge University Press, 1987.

Hearnshaw, J. B. *The Analysis of Starlight: One Hundred and Fifty Years of Astronomical Spectroscopy*. Cambridge: Cambridge University Press, 1986.

———. "The Analysis of Starlight: Some Comments on the Development of Stellar Spectroscopy, 1815–1965." *Vistas in Astronomy* 30 (1987): 319–375.

Hegyi, Dennis J., and Keith A. Olive. "Can Galactic Halos Be Made of Baryons?" *Physics Letters* 126B (1983): 28–32.

Herrmann, Dieter B. *The History of Astronomy from Herschel to Hertzsprung*. Cambridge: Cambridge University Press, 1984.

Hetherington, Norriss S. "Hubble's Cosmology." *American Scientist* 78 (March/April 1990): 142–151.

Hill, R. D. *Tracking Down Particles*. New York: W. A. Benjamin, 1964.

Holmberg, E. "On the Clustering Tendencies Among the Nebulae: II. A Study of Encounters Between Laboratory Models of Stellar Systems by a New Integration Procedure." *Astrophysical Journal* 94 (November 1941): 385–395.

Horgan, John. "Universal Truths." *Scientific American* (October 1990): 108–117.

Hoskin, Michael. "The Cosmology of Thomas Wright of Durham." *Journal for the History of Astronomy* 1 (1970): 44–52.

Hoyle, F. "The Synthesis of the Elements from Hydrogen." *Monthly Notices of the Royal Astronomical Society* 106 (1946): 343.

———. *Astronomy*. London: Rathbone Books Ltd., 1962.

———. *Encounter with the Future*. New York: Trident Press, 1965.

———. "The Universe: Past and Present Reflections." In *Annual Review of Astronomy and Astrophysics*, vol. 20. Palo Alto: Annual Reviews, 1982.

———. "Personal Comments on the History of Nuclear Astrophysics." *Q. Journal R. Astr. Soc.* 27 (1986): 445–453.

Hoyle, F., and R. J. Tayler. "The Mystery of the Cosmic Helium Abundance." *Nature* 203 (September 12, 1964): 1108–1110.

Hoyle, F., William A. Fowler, G. R. Burbidge, and E. M. Burbidge. "Origin of the Elements in Stars." *Science* 124 (October 5, 1956): 611–614.

Huggins, Sir William, and Lady Huggins, eds. *The Scientific Papers of Sir William Huggins, K.C.B., O.M.* London: William Wesley and Son, 1909.

"An Interview with Bernard Sadoulet." *Physics at Berkeley* (Fall 1989): 6–9.

Janos, Leo. "Timekeepers of the Solar System." *Science* 80 (May/June 1980): 44–55.

Jastrow, Robert, and Malcolm H. Thompson. *Astronomy: Fundamentals and Frontiers*. New York: John Wiley and Sons, 1977.

Jeans, Sir James. *The Universe Around Us*. Cambridge: Cambridge University Press, 1933.

Jones, Bessie Zaban, and Lyle Gifford Boyd. *The Harvard College Observatory: The First Four Directorships, 1839–1919*. Cambridge: Belknap Press of Harvard University Press, 1971.

Kavanagh, Ralph W. "Where Does the Sun Get Its Energy?" *Engineering and Science* 32 (June 1969): 25–30.

Kellermann, K., and B. Sheets, eds. *Serendipitous Discoveries in Radio Astron-*

omy. Proceedings of Workshop no. 7 held at the National Radio Astronomy Observatory, Green Bank, West Virginia, May 4–6, 1983.

Kidwell, Peggy A. "An Historical Introduction to 'The Dyer's Hand.' " In *Cecilia Payne-Gaposchkin: An Autobiography and Other Recollections*. Cambridge: Cambridge University Press, 1984.

Kidwell, Peggy A. "Three Women of American Astronomy." *American Scientist* 78 (May/June 1990): 244–251.

Kirshner, Robert P., Augustus Oemler, Jr., Paul L. Schechter, and Stephen A. Shectman. "A Million Cubic Megaparsec Void in Boötes?" *Astrophysical Journal* 248 (September 1, 1981): L57–L60.

Kormendy, J., and G. R. Knapp, eds. *Dark Matter in the Universe*. Dordrecht, Holland: D. Reidel Publishing Co., 1987.

Kragh, Helge. *Dirac: A Scientific Biography*. Cambridge: Cambridge University Press, 1990.

Krauss, Lawrence M. *The Fifth Essence: The Search for Dark Matter in the Universe*. New York: Basic Books, 1989.

Lankford, John, and Rickey L. Slavings. "Gender and Science: Women in American Astronomy, 1859–1940." *Physics Today* (March 1990): 58–65.

Lanou, R. E., H. J. Maris, and G. M. Seidel. "Superfluid Helium as a Dark Matter Detector." Talk presented at Twenty-third Rencontre de Moriond, Workshop on Dark Matter, Les Arcs, France, March 6–13, 1988.

Larson, Richard B. "Dark Matter: Dead Stars?" *Comments on Astrophysics* 11 (1987): 273–282.

Lauritsen, Thomas. "Kellogg Laboratory: The Early Years." *Engineering and Science* 32 (June 1969): 4–7.

Lemaître, G. *The Primeval Atom*. New York: Van Nostrand, 1951.

Lightman, Alan, and Roberta Brawer. *Origins: The Lives and Worlds of Modern Cosmologists*. Cambridge: Harvard University Press, 1990.

Littmann, Mark. *Planets Beyond: Discovering the Outer Solar System*. New York: John Wiley and Sons, 1988.

Livingston, Dorothy Michelson. *The Master of Light: A Biography of Albert A. Michelson*. Chicago: University of Chicago Press, 1973.

Lloyd, G. E. R. *The Revolutions of Wisdom: Studies in the Claims and Practice of Ancient Greek Science*. Berkeley: University of California Press, 1987.

Longair, M. S., and J. Einasto, eds. *The Large Scale Structure of the Universe*, IAU Symposium no. 79. Boston: D. Reidel Publishing Co., 1978.

Lovell, Sir Bernard, ed. *Astronomy*, vol. 1. Essex: Elsevier Publishing Co., 1970.

Macpherson, Hector. *Makers of Astronomy*. Oxford: Clarendon Press, 1933.

Marschall, Laurence A. *The Supernova Story*. New York: Plenum Press, 1988.

Mathews, G. J., ed. *Origin and Distribution of the Elements*. Singapore: World Scientific, 1988.

McNally, D. "Interstellar Molecules." In *Advances in Astronomy and Astrophysics*, vol. 6. New York: Academic Press, 1968.

Merrill, Paul W. "Technetium in the Stars." *Science* 115 (May 2, 1952): 484.

Milgrom, Mordehai. "Alternatives to Dark Matter." *Comments on Astrophysics* 13 (1989): 215–230.

Mills, Charles E., and C. F. Brooke, eds. *A Sketch of the Life of Sir William Huggins*. Cambridge: Library of the Observatories, University of Cambridge, 1936.

Milner, T. *The Gallery of Nature*. London: W. and R. Chambers, 1858.

Moe, Michael K., and Simon Peter Rosen. "Double-Beta Decay." *Scientific American* (November 1989): 48–55.

Moskowitz, Bruce. "The Search for Dark Matter in the Laboratory." *New Scientist* (April 15, 1989): 39–42.

Ne'eman, Yuval, and Yoram Kirsh. *The Particle Hunters*. Cambridge: Cambridge University Press, 1986.

Nye, Mary Jo. *Molecular Reality: A Perspective on the Scientific Work of Jean Perrin*. London: MacDonald, 1972.

Ogilvie, Marilyn Bailey. *Women in Science: Antiquity Through the Nineteenth Century*. Cambridge: MIT Press, 1986.

Oort, J. H. "Superclusters." *Annual Review of Astronomy and Astrophysics* 21 (1983): 373–428.

Osterbrock, Donald E. "The Rise and Fall of Edward S. Holden: Part 1." *Journal for the History of Astronomy* 15 (1984): 81–127.

Osterbrock, Donald E., John R. Gustafson, and W. J. Shiloh Unruh. *Eye on the Sky: Lick Observatory's First Century*. Berkeley: University of California Press, 1988.

Osterbrock, Donald E., Ronald Brashear, and Joel Gwinn. "Young Edwin Hubble." *Mercury* (January/February 1990): 2–14.

Overbye, Dennis. *Lonely Hearts of the Cosmos*. New York: HarperCollins, 1991.

Pagel, B. E. J. "Nucleosynthesis." *Phil. Trans. R. Soc. Lond. A* 320 (1986): 557–564.

———. "Observing the Big Bang." *Nature* 326 (April 23, 1987): 744–745.

Palca, Joseph. "NSF Centers Rise Above the Storm." *Science* 251 (January 4, 1991): 19–22.

Paneth, Friedrich Adolf. *Chemistry and Beyond*. New York: Interscience Publishers, 1964.

Pannekoek, A. *A History of Astronomy*. New York: Interscience Publishers, 1961.

Park, David. *The How and the Why*. Princeton: Princeton University Press, 1988.

Parker, Barry. *Creation: The Story of the Origin and Evolution of the Universe*. New York: Plenum Press, 1988.

Payne, Cecilia H. *Stellar Atmospheres: A Contribution to the Observational Study of High Temperature in the Reversing Layers of Stars*. Cambridge: Harvard Observatory Monographs, 1925.

Payne-Gaposchkin, Cecilia. "The dyer's hand." In *Cecilia Payne-Gaposchkin: An Autobiography and Other Recollections*. Cambridge: Cambridge University Press, 1984.

Peebles, P. J. E. "The Origin of Galaxies and Clusters of Galaxies." *Science* 224 (June 29, 1984): 1385–1391.

Peebles, P. J. E., and Joseph Silk. "A Cosmic Book." *Nature* 335 (October 13, 1988): 601–606.

Preston, Richard. *First Light: The Search for the Edge of the Universe*. New York: Atlantic Monthly Press, 1987.

Price, Derek J. de Solla. *Science Since Babylon*. New Haven: Yale University Press, 1961.

Primack, Joel R., David Seckel, and Bernard Sadoulet. "Detection of Cosmic Dark Matter." *Annual Review of Nuclear Particle Science* 38 (1988): 751–807.

Prud'homme, Rachel. Interview with Jesse Greenstein, California Institute of Technology Oral History Project, Caltech Archives, 1983.

Quigg, Chris. "Elementary Particles and Forces." *Scientific American* (April 1985): 84–95.

Rees, Martin. "What Is the Dark Matter in Galactic Halos and Clusters?" *Phil. Trans. R. Soc. Lond. A* 320 (1986): 573–583.

———. "Galaxy Formation and Dark Matter." *Highlights of Astronomy* 8 (1989): 45–64.

Regis, Ed. *Who Got Einstein's Office?* Reading, Mass.: Addison-Wesley Publishing Co., 1987.

Rhodes, Richard. *The Making of the Atomic Bomb*. New York: Simon and Schuster, 1986.

Rieke, G. H., N. M. Ashok, and R. P. Boyle. "The Initial Mass Function in the Rho Ophiuchi Cluster." *Astrophysical Journal* 339 (April 15, 1989): L71–L74.

Riordan, Michael. *The Hunting of the Quark*. New York: Simon and Schuster, 1987.

Riordan, Michael, and David N. Schramm. *The Shadows of Creation*. New York: W. H. Freeman and Co., 1991.

Rolfs, Claus E., and William S. Rodney. *Cauldrons in the Cosmos*. Chicago: University of Chicago Press, 1988.

Ronan, Colin A. *Changing Views of the Universe*. New York: Macmillan Co., 1961.

———. *Astronomers Royal*. New York: Doubleday and Co., 1969.

———. *Science: Its History and Development Among the World's Cultures*. New York: Facts on File Publications, 1982.

Rossiter, Margaret W. *Women Scientists in America: Struggles and Strategies to 1940*. Baltimore: Johns Hopkins University Press, 1982.

Rubin, Vera Cooper. "Differential Rotation of the Inner Metagalaxy." *Astronomical Journal* 56 (1951): 47–48.

———. "Extended Optical-Rotation Curves of Spiral Galaxies." *Comments on Astrophysics* 8 (1979): 79–88.

———. "Dark Matter in Spiral Galaxies." *Scientific American* (June 1983): 96–108.

———. "The Rotation of Spiral Galaxies." *Science* 220 (June 24, 1983): 1339–1344.

Rubin, Vera C., W. Kent Ford, Jr., and Norbert Thonnard. "Rotational Properties of 21 Sc Galaxies with a Large Range of Luminosities and Radii, From NGC 4605 (R = 4 kpc) to UGC 2885 (R = 122 kpc)." *Astrophysical Journal* 238 (June 1, 1980): 471–487.

Russell, Henry Norris. "The Solar Spectrum and the Earth's Crust." *Science* (May 29, 1914): 791–794.

———. "On the Composition of the Sun's Atmosphere." *Astrophysical Journal* 70 (July 1929): 11–82.

Sadoulet, Bernard, and James W. Cronin. "Particle Astrophysics." *Physics Today* (April 1991): 53–57.

Saha, M. N. "On a Physical Theory of Stellar Spectra." *Proceedings of the Royal Society* 99A (1921): 135–153.

Sambursky, S. *The Physical World of the Greeks*. London: Routledge and Kegan Paul, 1956.

Sargent, Anneila I., and Steven Beckwith. "Kinematics of the Circumstellar Gas of HL Tauri and R Monocerotis." *Astrophysical Journal* 323 (December 1, 1987): 294–305.

Schwarzschild, Bertram. "Gigantic Structures Challenge Standard View of Cosmic Evolution." *Physics Today* (June 1990): 20–23.

———. "Four of Five New Experiments Claim Evidence for 17-keV Neutrinos." *Physics Today* (May 1991): 17–19.

Shane, C. D., and C. A. Wirtanen. "The Distribution of Extragalactic Nebulae." *Lick Observatory Bulletin* 528 (1954): 91–110.

Shapley, Harlow. *Galaxies*. Cambridge: Harvard University Press, 1972.

———, ed. *Source Book in Astronomy 1900–1950*. Cambridge: Harvard University Press, 1960.

Shapley, Harlow, and Helen E. Howarth. *A Source Book in Astronomy*. New York: McGraw-Hill, 1929.

Silbar, Margaret. "The Lightweight Neutrino." *Mosaic* (November/December 1980): 22–27.

———. "Gravity, the Fourth Force." *Mosaic* 15(2) (1984): 22–27.

Silk, Joseph. *The Big Bang: The Creation and Evolution of the Universe*. San Francisco: W. H. Freeman and Co., 1980.

Smith, Robert. "Edwin P. Hubble and the Transformation of Cosmology." *Physics Today* (April 1990): 52–58.

Smith, Sinclair. "The Mass of the Virgo Cluster." *Astrophysical Journal* 83 (January 1936): 23–30.

Snodgrass, Anthony. *Archaic Greece: The Age of Experiment*. London: J. M. Dent and Sons Ltd., 1980.

Sobel, Michael I. *Light*. Chicago: University of Chicago Press, 1987.

Stachel, John. "Einstein and Ether Drift Experiments." *Physics Today* (May 1987): 45–47.

Starr, Chester G. *The Ancient Greeks*. New York: Oxford University Press, 1971.

Stauffer, John, Donald Hamilton, Ronald Probst, George Rieke, and Mario Mateo. "Possible Pleiades Members with M = 0.07 Solar Masses: Identification of Brown Dwarf Candidates of Known Age, Distance, and Metallicity." *Astrophysical Journal* 344 (September 1, 1989): L21–L24.

Stodolsky, Leo. "Neutrino and Dark-Matter Detection at Low Temperature." *Physics Today* (August 1991): 24–32.

Stone, Richard. "A Trap to Snare a Monopole." *Science* 253 (August 9, 1991): 625.

Stratton, F. J. M. "The History of the Cambridge Observatories." In *Annals of the Solar Physics Observatory, Cambridge*, vol. 1. Cambridge: Cambridge University Press, 1949.

Struve, Otto. "The First Determinations of Stellar Parallax. I." *Sky and Telescope* (November 1956): 9–12.

———. "The First Determinations of Stellar Parallax. II." *Sky and Telescope* (December 1956): 69–72.

Struve, Otto, and Velta Zebergs. *Astronomy of the 20th Century*. New York: Macmillan Co., 1962.

Suess, Hans E. *Chemistry of the Solar System*. New York: John Wiley and Sons, 1987.

Suess, Hans E., and Harold C. Urey. "Abundances of the Elements." *Reviews of Modern Physics* 28 (January 1956): 53–74.

Sullivan, W. T., III, ed. *The Early Years of Radio Astronomy*. Cambridge: Cambridge University Press, 1984.

Sullivan, Walter. *We Are Not Alone*. New York: McGraw-Hill, 1964.

Sutton, Christine. *The Particle Connection*. New York: Simon and Schuster, 1984.

Swenson, Loyd S., Jr. "Michelson and Measurement." *Physics Today* (May 1987): 24–30.

Swings, P., and L. Rosenfeld. "Considerations Regarding Interstellar Molecules." *Astrophysical Journal* 86 (November 1937): 483–486.

Trefil, James. *The Dark Side of the Universe*. New York: Charles Scribner's Sons, 1988.

Trumpler, R. J. "Absorption of Light in the Galactic System." *Publ. Astr. Soc. Pac.* 42 (1930): 214.

Tucker, Wallace, and Karen Tucker. *The Dark Matter: Contemporary Science's Quest for the Mass Hidden in Our Universe.* New York: William Morrow and Co., 1988.

Turner, Barry E. "Interstellar Molecules." *Scientific American* 228 (March 1973): 50–69.

Van de Hulst, H. C., ed. *Radio Astronomy.* International Astronomical Union Symposium no. 4. Cambridge: Cambridge University Press, 1957.

Van Woerden, Hugo, Willem N. Brouw, and Henk C. van de Hulst, eds. *Oort and the Universe.* Dordrecht, Holland: D. Reidel Publishing Co., 1980.

Verschuur, Gerrit L. *Interstellar Matters.* New York: Springer-Verlag, 1989.

———. "Dissipative Structures in Astronomy and the Missing Mass Myth." *Comments on Astrophysics* 15 (1991): 189–205.

Von Baeyer, Hans Christian. "Creatures of the Deep." *Sciences* (March/April 1989): 2–4.

Voyage Through the Universe: Stars. Alexandria, Va.: Time-Life Books, 1988.

Wagoner, Robert V., and Donald W. Goldsmith. *Cosmic Horizons: Understanding the Universe.* San Francisco: W. H. Freeman and Co., 1983.

Waldrop, M. Mitchell. "Supersymmetry and Supergravity." *Science* 220 (April 29, 1983): 491–493.

———. "In Search of Dark Matter." *Science* 234 (October 10, 1986): 152–154.

———. "Pruning the Thickets of Cosmic Speculation." *Science* 243 (January 13, 1989): 168–169.

———. "Particle Physicists Look to the Heavens." *Science* 247 (March 16, 1990): 1291–1293.

Weart, Spencer R. Interview with Jesse Greenstein, American Institute of Physics Archives, April 7, 1977.

Weaver, Jefferson Hane. *The World of Physics,* vols. 1, 2, 3. New York: Simon and Schuster, 1987.

Weiner, Charles. Interview with William A. Fowler, American Institute of Physics Archives, February 5, 1973.

Whaling, Ward, and George M. Lawrence. "Atomic Spectroscopy and the Abundance of the Elements." *Engineering and Science* 32 (June 1969): 31–33.

White, Simon D. M., Marc Davis, George Efstathiou, and Carlos S. Frenk. "Galaxy Distribution in Cold Dark Matter Universe." *Nature* 330 (December 3, 1987): 451–453.

White, Simon D. M., Carlos S. Frenk, Marc Davis, and George Efstathiou. "Clusters, Filaments, and Voids in a Universe Dominated by Cold Dark Matter." *Astrophysical Journal* 313 (February 15, 1987): 505–516.

Whittaker, Sir Edmund. *A History of the Theories of Aether and Electricity,* vols. 1, 2. New York: American Institute of Physics, 1987.

Wilczek, Frank. "Problem of Strong P and T Invariance in the Presence of Instantons." *Physical Review Letters* 40 (January 30, 1978): 279–282.

———. "The Cosmic Asymmetry Between Matter and Antimatter." *Scientific American* (December 1980): 82–90.

Wilczek, Frank, and Betsy Devine. *Longing for the Harmonies.* New York: W. W. Norton and Co., 1988.

Wright, John W., ed. *The Universal Almanac 1990.* Kansas City: Andrews and McMeel, 1989.

Wright, Thomas. *An Original Theory or New Hypothesis of the Universe Founded upon the Laws of Nature, and Solving by Mathematical Principles the General Phaenomena of the Visible Creation; and Particularly the Via Lactea.* London, 1750.

Young, T. *Philosophical Transactions of the Royal Society* 94 (1804).

Zee, A. *Fearful Symmetry: The Search for Beauty in Modern Physics.* New York: Macmillan Publishing Co., 1986.

Zel'dovich, Ya. B., J. Einasto, and S. F. Shandarin. "Giant Voids in the Universe." *Nature* 300 (December 2, 1982): 407–413.

Zwicky, F. "Die Rotverschiebung von extragalaktischen Nebeln." *Helvetica Physica Acta* 6 (1933): 110.

———. "Nebulae as Gravitational Lenses." *Physical Review* 51 (February 15, 1937): 290.

———. "On the Masses of Nebulae and of Clusters of Nebulae." *Astrophysical Journal* 86 (October 1937): 217–246.

———. "On Collapsed Neutron Stars." *Astrophysical Journal* 88 (November 1938): 522–525.

———. *Catalogue of Selected Compact Galaxies and of Post-Eruptive Galaxies.* Switzerland: Offsetdruck L. Speich Zuerich, 1971.

Index